A History of Heterodox Economics

Economics is a contested academic discipline between neoclassical economics and a collection of alternative approaches, such as Marxism-radical economics, Institutional economics, Post Keynesian economics, and others, that can collectively be called heterodox economics. Because of the dominance of neoclassical economics, the existence of the alternative approaches is generally not known. This book is concerned with the community history of heterodox economics, seen primarily through the eyes of Marxian-radical economics and Post Keynesian economics.

Throughout the twentieth century neoclassical economists in conjunction with state and university power have attacked heterodox economists and tried to cleanse them from the academy. Professor Lee, in his groundbreaking new title, discusses issues including the contested landscape of American economics in the 1970s, the emergence and establishment of Post Keynesian economics in the US and the development of heterodox economics in Britain from 1970 to 1996.

Professor Lee's fascinating monograph tells a story about a community of economists that mainstream economists and the state wish would not exist. Mainstream economists and the state attempt to restrict intellectual diversity in economics by using state power to deprive heterodox economists of their jobs and ability to teach economics in the classroom. Despite these attacks, heterodox economists have succeeded in building their community and in doing so have maintained intellectual diversity in economics.

This book will be relevant to both undergraduate and postgraduate students with an interest in heterodox economics in the US and UK, as well as researchers with an interest in the history of Post Keynesian and Marxian-radical economics and in the current state of heterodox economics.

Frederic Lee has a Ph.D. in Economics from Rutgers University, New Jersey, was Associate Professor at Roosevelt University, Chicago, from 1984 to 1991, was previously a Reader in Economics at De Montfort University, UK, and is currently Professor of Economics at the University of Missouri-Kansas City.

Routledge Advances in Heterodox Economics

Edited by Frederic S. Lee, University of Missouri-Kansas City

Over the past two decades, the intellectual agendas of heterodox economists have taken a decidedly pluralist turn. Leading thinkers have begun to move beyond the established paradigms of Austrian, feminist, Institutional-evolutionary, Marxian, Post Keynesian, radical, social, and Sraffian economics—opening up new lines of analysis, criticism, and dialogue among dissenting schools of thought. This cross-fertilization of ideas is creating a new generation of scholarship in which novel combinations of heterodox ideas are being brought to bear on important contemporary and historical problems.

Routledge Advances in Heterodox Economics aims to promote this new scholarship by publishing innovative books in heterodox economic theory, policy, philosophy, intellectual history, institutional history, and pedagogy. Syntheses or critical engagement of two or more heterodox traditions are especially encouraged.

This series was previously published by The University of Michigan Press and the following books are available (please contact UMP for more information):

A History of Heterodox Economics

Challenging the mainstream in the twentieth century

Frederic Lee

Routledge
Taylor & Francis Group

LONDON AND NEW YORK

First published 2009
by Routledge
2 Park Square, Milton Park, Abingdon, Oxfordshire OX14 4RN

Simultaneously published in the USA and Canada
by Routledge
711 Third Avenue, New York, NY 10017

Routledge is an imprint of the Taylor & Francis Group, an informa business

First issued in paperback 2010

Typeset in Times New Roman by
Taylor & Francis Books

British Library Cataloguing in Publication Data
A catalogue record for this book is available from the British Library

Library of Congress Cataloging in Publication Data
Lee, Frederic S., 1949–
    A history of heterodox economics : challenging the mainstream in the
    twentieth century / Frederic Lee.
        p. cm.
    Includes bibliographical references and index.
    1. Comparative economics–History–20th century. I. Title.
    HB90.L42 2008
330–dc22

ISBN13: 978-0-415-77714-8 (hbk)
ISBN13: 978-0-415-68197-1 (pbk)
ISBN13: 978-0-203-88305-1 (ebk)

Contents

Tables

Acknowledgments

The essays in this book have been commented on by many, many friends and colleagues—far too many to thank individually. However, there are souls that directly or indirectly help me to sustain this decade-long project. Writing institutional or social histories of economics is not popular with most economists who prefer intellectual histories. But, in the beginning and even before that Warren Samuels supported my unfashionable tendencies to write such histories. On the other hand, Malcolm Rutherford's own quite excellent historical writings on Institutional economics showed me that I was not alone in writing about the history of heterodox economics. While I always used qualitative data in my historical writings, Sandra Harley help me gain a better understanding of how to engage in such data collection, especially when working with questionnaire data. Moreover, her enthusiasm for exploring the impact of the Research Assessment Exercise on economics made those particular research projects possible. When I first met him, Tiago Mata was a doctoral student at the London School of Economics working on the history of radical and Post Keynesian economics. Our common interests greatly benefited my research and I actually had someone who kept me honest so-to-speak about my interpretations of the historical data which is difficult to interpret in any case. In addition, we both have an interest in oral testimony as a form of data collection and I have learned a great deal from his extensive knowledge of collecting and interpreting such evidence. Finally, there is John Henry and John King. I have carried on a discussion with them about heterodox economics for nearly two decades. They were always interested in what I had to say and always had something to contribute. At times they seem to know more than I did about the history of heterodox economics which helped to keep me humble. Without their help and support, this project would have never been completed.

Several of the chapters have previously appeared in economic journals:

- Chapters 2 and 5 include material that originally appeared in "The Organizational History of Post Keynesian Economics in America, 1971–95," *Journal of Post Keynesian Economics*, 23.1 (Fall, 2000: 141–62); "Alfred S. Eichner, Joan Robinson and the Founding of Post Keynesian Economics,"

Research in the History of Economic Thought and Methodology, 18-C, *Twentieth-Century Economics* (2000: 9–40); and "Mutual Aid and the Making of Heterodox Economics in Postwar America: A Post Keynesian View," *History of Economics Review*, 35 (Winter, 2002: 45–62).

- Chapter 3 includes material that originally appeared in "History and Identity: The Case of Radical Economics, 1945–70," *Review of Radical Political Economics*, 36.2 (Spring, 2004: 177–95).
- Chapter 4 includes material that originally appeared in "To Be a Heterodox Economist: The Contested Landscape of American Economics, 1960s and 1970s," *Journal of Economic Issues*, 37.3 (September, 2004: 747–64).
- Chapter 6 includes material that originally appeared in "Conference of Socialist Economists and the Emergence of Heterodox Economics in Post-War Britain," *Capital and Class*, 75 (Autumn, 2001: 15–40).
- Chapter 7 includes material that originally appeared in "Conference of Socialist Economists and the Emergence of Heterodox Economics in Post-War Britain," *Capital and Class*, 75 (Autumn, 2001: 15–40); and "Making History by Making Identity and Institutions: The Emergence of Post Keynesian-Heterodox Economics in Britain, 1974–96," *History of Economics Review*, 46 (Summer, 2007: 62–88).
- Chapter 8 includes material that originally appeared in "Research Selectivity, Managerialism, and the Academic Labor Process: The Future of Nonmainstream Economics in U.K. Universities," *Human Relations* 50.11 (November, 1997: 1427–60); and "Peer Review, the Research Assessment Exercise and the Demise of Non-Mainstream Economics," *Capital and Class*, 66 (Autumn, 1998: 23–52), published by the Conference of Socialist Economists (http://www.cseweb.org.uk/).
- Chapter 9 includes material that originally appeared in "The Research Assessment Exercise, the State and the Dominance of Mainstream Economics in British Universities," *Cambridge Economics Journal* 31.2 (March, 2007: 309–25), published by Oxford University Press.

Frederic S. Lee
Kansas City
July 2008

1   Introduction

Scholars generally view the history of economics in the twentieth century as an intellectual history, that is, in terms of the history of economic thought. However, for the past decade, there has slowly emerged research on the social construction of communal activities that promoted and sustained the economic ideas and theories. This type of research generates what can be called community histories. Clearly the intellectual and the community histories of economics are distinct in their subject matter, but they are symbiotically related in that one presupposes the other and changes in one will affect the other. The essays in this book are primarily concerned with community histories not of mainstream economics, but of a non-comparable, alternative economics, specifically heterodox economics. But in saying this, an immediate problem emerges in that most scholars in the history of economics do not believe that heterodox economics has an intellectual history and hence deny that a heterodox economics community existed of which a history can be written. That is, they adopt the position—the *continuity-pluralism thesis*— that neoclassical economics dominated economics for all of the twentieth century, although there were often periods of internal pluralism. The significance of the thesis to scholars of the history of economics is its suggestion that throughout the last century no theoretical alternatives to neoclassical economic theory existed; only heretical views that enriched the dominant economic discourse and made important theoretical contributions, while the ones that made no contributions deservedly disappeared.[1] Moreover, the thesis dismisses the possibility that heretical ideas could evolve into non-neoclassical ones independently of their heretical originators or that well-developed non-comparable theoretical alternatives take time to emerge. Thus the continuity-pluralism thesis effectively makes the economic landscape of the twentieth century non-contestable, thereby rendering alternative economists invisible, the existence of alternative economics implausible, and the writing of its intellectual and community history impossible.

The continuity-pluralism thesis clearly captures the development of neoclassical economics since 1900 if not before. For example, the tools, models, and discourse that comprise and concretely define neoclassical price theory can be identified from the textbooks assigned in introductory, intermediate, and graduate economic courses. Table 1.1 lists the twenty-nine core tools and models included in American neoclassical price theory textbooks in the last one hundred years. It is divided into four time periods, the first being the base period, while the next two represent the supposed periods of pre-1940 pluralism and the post-war ascendancy of neoclassical economics, and the last period represents neoclassical economics at the end of the twentieth century. The first entry in each column represents the number of textbooks that included the tool or model and the second entry in parentheses gives the percentage of textbooks that included the tool or model. What Table 1.1 establishes is that the core theoretical tools of neoclassical price theory circa 1900–10, such as scarcity, maximization, utility and marginal utility, marginal products and the law of diminishing returns, supply and demand curves, and marginal productivity principle of distribution, and the core model of competition have been retained throughout the century. In addition, it shows that the number of core theory components have increased over time, to include, for example, utility functions and income and substitution effects, production functions, monopolistic competition, oligopoly, game theory, and general equilibrium. These two points imply that while there have been significant theoretical developments in neoclassical economics there has been no break—that is a period when neoclassical economics did not exist and a period in which it did exist. Rather neoclassical economics as defined in terms of the tools, models, and discourse of its price theory has always been with us. Finally, the twenty-nine tools and models are currently taught to every mainstream economist in their core graduate microeconomic theory courses as well as taught in undergraduate microeconomic theory courses.[2] Since the core tools and models and associated discourse (in conjunction with the deductive-formalist methodology) underpin virtually every book, article, and model that utilizes neoclassical microeconomic theory, they constitute the minimum standards of what the profession expects every new PhD economist to know[3] (Klamer and Colander 1990; Hansen 1991; Kasper et al. 1991; Krueger et al. 1991; Knoedler and Underwood 2003).

While neoclassical doctrinal continuity existed in American economics throughout the twentieth century, it was not necessarily one of harmony. Within neoclassical economics there was accepted and encouraged contested theoretical knowledge, that is, pluralism. The controversy over the supply curve and the rise of imperfect/monopolistic competition circa 1930, pricing and the marginalist controversy circa 1940s, the controversy over the different theories of the firm circa 1960s, and the rational expectations revolution circa 1970s are well-known examples of this internal pluralism. There were also the not-so-well controversies over demand theory circa 1940s–1960s and the economics of information circa 1950s onwards that involved the Chicago School, Cowles Commission, and the MIT crowd that also demonstrated the existence of pluralism within neoclassical economics (Mirowski and Hands 1998; Mirowski 2007). However, pluralism was not extended to alternative

Table 1.1 Neoclassical price theory/microeconomics in the twentieth century as represented in American textbooks[*]

	Time Periods			
	1899–1910	*1911–40*	*1941–70*	*1971–2002*
Tools and Models				
Economics defined as the allocation of scarce resources		5 (19)	(81)	37 (86)
Scarcity, scarce factor inputs	9 (75)	23 (88)	24 (77)	31 (72)
Production possibility frontier			7 (33)	36 (84)
Opportunity costs	5 (42)	12 (46)	18 (58)	33 (77)
Demand Side				
Utility/diminishing marginal utility	12 (100)	22 (85)	26 (84)	43 (100)
Maximize utility	8 (67)	18 (69)	28 (90)	43 (100)
Utility functions, indifference curves, marginal rate of substitution			21 (68)	43 (100)
Income/substitution effects			20 (65)	43 (100)
Individual consumer/market demand curve	11 (92)	26 (100)	31 (100)	43 (100)
Price elasticity of demand	7 (58)	22 (85)	31 (100)	43 (100)
Production and Costs				
Production function			15 (48)	39 (91)
Single input variation, marginal products	12 (100)	25 (96)	29 (94)	43 (100)
Law of diminishing returns	12 (100)	26 (100)	30 (97)	39 (91)
Proportional input variation, returns to scale	1 (8)	2 (8)	14 (45)	34 (79)
Isoquants, marginal rate of technical substitution			11 (35)	36 (84)
Marginal costs: $MC = Px/MPx$	3 (25)	12 (46)	31 (100)	42 (98)
Firm/market supply curve	11 (92)	25 (96)	30 (97)	42 (98)
Markets				
Perfect, pure, or free competition	10 (83)	24 (92)	31 (100)	43 (100)
Profit maximization	6 (50)	22 (85)	31 (100)	43 (100)
Marginal cost = price	1 (8)	10 (38)	31 (100)	43 (100)
Imperfect/monopolistic competition		7 (27)	31 (100)	40 (93)
Firm demand curve		6 (23)	29 (94)	42 (98)
Marginal revenue = marginal costs (or equivalent)		7 (27)	31 (100)	42 (98)
Oligopoly with firm demand curve			19 (61)	34 (79)
Kinked demand curve			17 (55)	27 (63)
Game theory			6 (25)	32 (74)
Distribution and General Equilibrium				
Marginal productivity principle	6 (50)	14 (54)	26 (84)	30 (70)
Wage rate = MP_L x Price, Profit = MP_K x Price	10 (83)	18 (69)	27 (87)	42 (98)
General equilibrium			17 (55)	30 (70)
Pareto–efficiency/optimality			8 (26)	31 (72)
Total Number of Textbooks	12	26	31	43

Note:
[*] The list of textbooks examined is found in Appendix A.1

contesting approaches except to one heretical challenger, Institutional economics in the inter-war period (Morgan and Rutherford 1998). Consequently, as far as most scholars are concerned, there existed no real theoretical challengers to neoclassical economics in the twentieth century. What is denied to exist, denied to having an intellectual and community history is what this book of essays is about: non-neoclassical-heterodox economics and its history as a community of non-neoclassical-heterodox economists.

Heresy, blasphemy, and heterodox economics

To write the history of non-neoclassical economics is to write about its theoretical ideas and applications, its social system of work, and its activities as a community of non-neoclassical economists. But, in relation to neoclassical economics, what is non-neoclassical economics, a non-neoclassical economist and, moreover, what is a community of non-neoclassical economists? To answer these "comparative" questions, let us take an unusual step and first consider the difference between heresy-heretic and blasphemy-blasphemer in the context of church and the state. A church is a body of religious arguments and ideas that are accepted by a community of believers who have the capability of imposing social penalties, such as shunning or ostracizing, upon members who have strayed from the approved path. While such penalties are unpleasant, they are not life-threatening or involve prison sentences. However, when the church becomes the state's church, its "infallible" judgments and statements regarding spiritual matters are accepted and supported without question by the state. Therefore a symbiotic relationship emerges where dissenting religious views can be interpreted as an attack upon the state and a criticism of the state can be interpreted as an attack upon the church. Consequently, more severe penalties, such as death or prison terms, can be imposed on wayward members as well as on non-members on the grounds that their errant beliefs are treasonable not just to God but also to the state since they may lead to questioning its legitimacy, and undermine social morality, stability, and the natural order of society. So the entrance of the state into the arena of belief transforms differences of views and opinion with their social-personal implications into a matter of life, death, and imprisonment, thereby creating the issue of non-conformance and tolerance. The state, rejecting tolerance in terms of personal conscious and liberty, becomes the protector of particular religious views, shielding them and their votaries from criticism and ridicule by upholding and perhaps imposing spiritual and participatory conformity and when they fail by establishing that dissenting activities are illegal and hence subject to state-decreed legal penalties.

Heresy, as broadly understood, is partial intellectual deviation from a given body of ideas and arguments. More specifically, in the context of church and state, heresy is theological or doctrinal deviation from the religion of the state church. For example, in Anglican orthodoxy qua the Church of England in the sixteenth and seventeenth centuries, a heretic was an individual who advocated particular theological or doctrinal deviations, such as denying the Trinity of the Father, the Son, and the Holy Spirit, rejecting the baptism of infants and children, or rejecting transubstantiation and even predestination, while still believing in God and other components of Christianity. The spiritual penalty for being an Arian, Socinian, or Anabaptist was excommunication and the secular penalty carried out by the state included imprisonment, death, and the public burning of written works. However, with the growth of religious tolerance—that is the growing perception that heretics such as Quakers, Baptists, Moravians, Catholics, Jews, and Unitarians were moral, peaceful citizens and therefore did not threaten the power of parliament, the sovereign or the established church—the acceptable religious community in Britain became diverse and the still heretical ideas vis-à-vis the church became viewed as erroneous or peculiar opinions to be tolerated and perhaps appreciated but not punished by the state. Yet in a diverse milieu of theological ideas and practices, it is possible for the religion of the established church to evolve over time so that one-time heretical ideas become accepted and heretics become fully accepted into the church's community.

In contrast to heresy, blasphemy entails the total rejection of a body of ideas and their replacement with ideas that are completely different. More specifically, in the context of church and state, blasphemy is the profaning and denying the truth and value of an established religion, its sacred beings, texts, and institutions to be replaced by their secular counterparts. In short blasphemy is treason against God. Consequently, a heretic is a believer who holds some dissenting views; while the blasphemer is a non-believer who explicitly, through reasoned arguments, wit, and ridicule, rejects the state religion and its sacred doctrines and institutions.[4] Because the rejection of the state church is viewed by the state as seditious, that is, as inciting a breach in the public order and as attacking its sovereignty, the basis of its laws, and the social morality underlying its legitimacy especially with regard to the lower classes and impressionable societal groups, it has always established and maintained penalties for blasphemers. The penalties, derived from state legislation (since the church's spiritual penalty of excommunication is ineffective for an individual that already rejects it), are based on what the blasphemer has spoken and/or written. They are also based on the manner in which the blasphemous material is presented as interpreted by the devotee experiencing the material.[5] With legal penalties at hand, such as death, imprisonment, fines, and loss of civil rights, the defenders of the faith have not fought shy of using the state's judicial system to endorse their religion and protect their deity. So, through its blasphemy laws, the state rejects tolerance for a segment of its citizens by denying the legal validity and implicitly and subtly denying the social acceptability of a particular form of discourse through restricting freedom of speech and engagement in knowledge. The result is that undesirable ideas and arguments are suppressed. Clearly, one litmus test of how far the state, church, and society embraces diversity and tolerates blasphemous ideas is the extent of its blasphemy laws (or conversely its tolerance laws) relative to the civil rights of its citizens (Levy 1993; Lund 1995a; Nash 1999).

As with a church, there are mainstream, heretical, and blasphemous economists.[6] In the twentieth century, mainstream economists have generally treated their heretical brethren with tolerance, partly because they ascribed to many of the same theoretical tools and models and accompanying discourse and partly because many theoretical advances in mainstream theory started out as heretical ideas.[7] Thus often one-time heretical economists become, without selling-out, well-respected mainstream economists. Also, as with church and state, mainstream economists have attempted to suppress the economic ideas and arguments of blasphemous economists, whom they do not generally consider their brethren at all. The methods they used range from social penalties to penalties imposed by academic institutions and the state. The social penalties included shunning, ostracizing, and discrimination, especially when the blasphemous economist was a member of the same professional association. In the latter case, neoclassical economists used organizational power to prevent the hiring of blasphemous economists, to deny them tenure, or to directly get them fired for teaching blasphemous material. They also directly and/or indirectly used the power and the authority of the state to impose penalties, which included denying blasphemous economists government research funds, firing and blacklisting thus preventing blasphemous economists from practicing their trade, and legally sanctioning definitions/descriptions of economics and economic theory that again excluded blasphemous material, with the outcome that blasphemous economists were not allowed to teach their theory and ideas in university classrooms. Although there does not actually exist economic blasphemy laws, the intolerance of mainstream economists combined with power derived from state-embracing professional associations and the latter's incestuous relationship with state institutions which gives them access to their state-derived power, has in all but name produced them over the course of the twentieth century. So given the intolerant and hostile attitudes of mainstream economists, it is a wonder that blasphemous economists actually existed in sufficient numbers and long enough to produce a blasphemous economic theory and a community of blasphemous economists. But it happened.

Blasphemous economic theory is characterized on the one hand by its disregard and rejection of not some but *all* the theoretical tools and models and accompanying discourse as well as the methodology that constitutes neoclassical price theory; hence, blasphemous theory rejects and denies the truth and value of neoclassical theory, its sacred laws, methodology, and texts. On the other hand, its explanations of economic events utilize non-neoclassical theoretical tools and models and employ a non-neoclassical discourse and methodology. Thus blasphemous economics and its theory can take on many guises, but the one that is the central concern of this book is *heterodox economics.* That is heterodox economics refers to specific economic theories and community of economists that are in various ways an alternative to neoclassical economics.[8] Consequently, it is a multi-level term that refers to a group of economic theories—specifically Post Keynesian-Sraffian, Marxist-radical, Institutional-evolutionary, social, feminist, Austrian, and ecological economics—that hold to various degrees blasphemous positions vis-à-vis mainstream economics; to a community of *heterodox economists* who engage with and are associated with one or more of the heterodox approaches and embrace a pluralistic attitude towards them without rejecting contestability and incommensurability among the theories; and finally to the development of a coherent *heterodox economic theory* that draws upon various theoretical contributions by heterodox approaches which stand in blasphemous contrast to mainstream theory and from which *heterodox economic policy* recommendations can be drawn.

Heterodox economic theory

The discipline of economics is about developing theoretical explanations of the provisioning process, which consists of the real economic activities that connect the individual with goods and services. The mainstream explanation focuses on how asocial, ahistorical individuals choose among scarce resources to meet competing ends given unlimited wants and explains it using fictitious concepts and a deductivist, closed-system methodology. In contrast, heterodox economics differs from mainstream economics not simply because it finds its *asocial* theoretical explanation of the provisioning process unsatisfactory, but also how it reaches this conclusion. In particular, the heterodox critique and rejection of mainstream theory is not a disparate collection of individual critiques. Rather, it is a concatenation of different heterodox critiques that generate its dismissal; and in doing so, the concatenated critique also provides the basis for making heterodox economics quite distinct from mainstream economics. That is, the demarcation of the conceptual and theoretical boundaries of neoclassical theory is done in terms of core propositions, such as scarcity, preferences and utility functions, technology and production functions, rationality, equilibrium, methodological individualism, and positivist and deductivist methodology. Starting with these propositions, it is well known that it is not possible to generate internally coherent explanations or stories or parables of market activity at either the micro or the macro level; and even if particular stories (represented in terms of models) of market activities are accepted, such as general equilibrium, game theory, or IS-LM, they have been shown, on their own terms, to be theoretically incoherent and empirically unsupported. Although the internal and story-as-a-model critiques show that neoclassical theory is incoherent, they do not by themselves differentiate neoclassical from heterodox theory. This, however, can be dealt with in terms of specific heterodox critiques of the core propositions, such as those noted above and the theoretical stories they promote. In particular, each of the heterodox approaches that are part of heterodox economics has produced critiques of particular core propositions of neoclassical

theory, while each core proposition has been subject to more than one heterodox critique; in addition, the multiple heterodox critiques of a single proposition overlap in argumentation. Finally, because of the overlapping and
interweaving of the heterodox critiques, they provide a general critique and
dismissal of the core propositions that leads to a rejection and denial of the
truth and values of mainstream theory, its laws, methodology, and texts. This
foundational rejection of neoclassical theory is also the basis for making
heterodox economics distinct from neoclassical economics (Rizvi 1994; Lawson
1997; Keen 2001; Ackerman and Nadal 2004; Lee and Keen 2004; White
2004; Petri 2004; Palacio-Vera 2005).

To illustrate this, consider the heterodox critiques of the neoclassical concept of scarcity. The Post Keynesians (Bortis 1997) argue that produced
means of production within a circular production process cannot be characterized as scarce and that production is a social process; while Institutionalists (DeGregori 1987) reject the view that natural resources are not
socially created to enter into the production process; and the Marxists
(Matthaei 1984) argue that the concept is a mystification and misspecifica-
tion of the economic problem—that it is not the relation of the individual to
given resources, but the social relationships that underpin the social provisioning process. The three critiques are complementary and integrative and
generate the common conclusion that the concept of scarcity must be rejected as well as the neoclassical definition of economics as the study of the
allocation of scarce resources among competing ends in light of unlimited
wants. Other similar heterodox critiques of the core propositions in neoclassical theory exist and arrive at similar conclusions. Together the three
critiques—internal, story as a model, and core propositions—form a concatenated structured heterodox critique that rejects and denies the truth and
value of neoclassical theory, its sacred laws, methodology, and texts; and by
accepting and promoting the critique, heterodox economics has engaged in
blasphemy, that is treason against mainstream economics.

Since the intellectual roots of heterodox economics are located in heterodox traditions that emphasize the wealth of nations, accumulation, justice,
social relationships in terms of class, gender, and race, full employment, and
economic and social reproduction, the discipline of economics, from the
heterodox perspective, is concerned with explaining the process that provides
the flow of goods and services required by society to meet the needs of those
who participate in its activities. That is, from a heterodox perspective, economics is the science of the *social* provisioning process, and this is the general
research agenda of heterodox economists. The heterodox explanation involves
human agency in a cultural context and social processes in historical time
affecting resources, consumption patterns, production and reproduction, and
the meaning (or ideology) of market, state, and non-market/state activities
engaged in social provisioning. Thus heterodox economic theory is a theoretical explanation of the historical process of social provisioning within the
context of a capitalist economy. Therefore it is concerned with explaining

those factors that are part of the process of social provisioning, including the structure and use of resources, the structure and change of social wants, structure of production and the reproduction of the business enterprise, family, state, and other relevant institutions and organizations, and distribution. In addition, heterodox economists extend their theory to examining issues associated with the process of social provisioning, such as racism, gender, and ideologies and myths.

Given the definition of heterodox economics as the science of the social-provisioning process and the structure of the explanation of the process combined with the pluralistic and integrative proclivities of heterodox economists, there have emerged a number of elements that have come to constitute the provisional theoretical and methodological core of heterodox theory. Some elements are clearly associated with particular heterodox approaches as noted by Phillip O'Hara:

> The main thing that social economists bring to the study (of heterodox economics) is an emphasis on ethics, morals and justice situated in an institutional setting. Institutionalists bring a pragmatic approach with a series of concepts of change and normative theory of progress, along with a commitment to policy. Marxists bring a set of theories of class and the economic surplus. Feminists bring a holistic account of the ongoing relationships between gender, class, and ethnicity in a context of difference. ... And post-Keynesians contribute through an analysis of institutions set in real time, with the emphasis on effective demand, uncertainty and a monetary theory of production linked closely with policy recommendations.
>
> (O'Hara, 2002b: 611)

However, other core methodological elements, such as critical realism, non-equilibrium or historical modeling, and the gendering and emotionalizing agency, and core theoretical elements, such as the socially embedded economy, circular production, and cumulative change, emerged from a synthesis of arguments that are associated only in part with particular heterodox approaches.

The core methodological elements establish the basis for constructing heterodox theory. In particular, the methodology emphasizes realism, structure, feminist and uncertain agency qua individual, history, and empirical groundness in the construction of heterodox theory, which is a historical narrative, an analytical story, of how capitalism works. The theory as a historical narrative does not simply recount or superficially describe actual economic events, such as the exploitation of workers; it does more in that it analytically explains the internal workings of the historical economic process that, say, generate the exploitation of workers. Moreover, because of its historical nature, the narrative is not necessarily organized around the concepts of equilibrium/long period positions and tendencies towards them.[9] Because the narrative provides an accurate picture of how capitalism actually works and changes in a circular and cumulative fashion, heterodox economists can use their theory to suggest alternative paths future economic events might take and propose relevant economic policies to take them. In constructing the narrative, they have at the same time created a particular social-economic-political picture of capitalism.

The core theoretical elements generate a three-component structure-organization-agency heterodox economic theory. The first component of the theory consists of three overlapping interdependencies that delineate the structure of a real capitalist economy. The first interdependency is the production of goods and services requires goods and services to be used as inputs. Hence, with regard to production, the overall economy (which includes both market and non-market production) is represented as an input–output matrix of material goods combined with different types of labor skills to produce an array of goods and services as outputs. Many of the outputs replace the goods and services used up in production and the rest constitute a physical surplus to be used for social provisioning, that is for consumption, private investment, government usage, and exports. A second interdependency is the relation between the wages of workers, profits of enterprises, and taxes of government and expenditures on consumption, investment, and government goods as well as non-market social provisioning activities. The last interdependency consists of the overlay of the flow of funds or money accompanying the production and exchange of the goods and services. Together these three interdependencies produce a monetary input-output structure of the economy where transactions in each market are a monetary transaction; where a change in price of a good or the method by which a good is produced in any one market will have an indirect or direct impact on the entire economy; and where the amount of private investment, government expenditure on real goods and services, and the excess of exports over imports determines the amount of market and non-market economic activity, the level of market employment and non-market laboring activities, and consumer expenditures on market and non-market goods and services.

The second component of heterodox theory consists of three broad categories of economic organizations that are embedded in the monetary input–output structure of the economy. The first category is micro market-oriented, hence particular to a set of markets and products. It consists of the business enterprise, private- and public-market organizations that regulate competition in product and service markets, and the organizations and institutions that regulate the wages of workers. The second is macro market-oriented and hence is spread across markets and products, or is not particular to any market or product. It includes the state and various subsidiary organizations as well as particular financial organizations, that is, those organizations that make decisions about government expenditures and taxation, and the interest rate. Finally the third category consists of non-market organizations that promote social reproduction and include the family and state and private organizations that contribute to and support the family. The significance of organizations is that they are the social embeddedness of agency qua the individual, the third component of heterodox theory. That is, agency, which are decisions made by individuals, concerning the social provisioning process and social well-being takes place through these organizations. And because the organizations are embedded in both instrumental and ceremonial institutions, such as gender, class, ethnicity, justice, marriage, ideology, and hierarchy as authority, agency as the individual acting through organizations affect both positively and negatively but never optimally the social-provisioning process.

Community and the history of economics

The history of economics is not simply an intellectual history, that is, a history of economic ideas. Those ideas are held by individuals who developed and propagated them among a community of scholars and other interested people. Thus, the history of economics is an interwoven, interdependent narrative of ideas and community. Without the history of community, there cannot be a real understanding of how and why the theory developed the way it did. Consequently, the history of any particular economic approach, such as neoclassical, heterodox, or Post Keynesian economics, cannot be grounded solely in ideas—it cannot just be an intellectual history. It must also include a story of the creation of identity and with it the creation and development and change of the community of economists engaged with the ideas. From this perspective, the history of Post Keynesian economics does not begin in 1936 with Keynes and the publication of the *General Theory*, but in the 1970s with the formation of a community of self-identified Post Keynesian economists in the United States who in part drew upon his ideas (see Chapter 5). Similarly, the history of heterodox economics does not start with Ricardo, Marx, Veblen, or Keynes, but in the 1960s and 1970s with the formation of various but mostly separate communities of heterodox economists and then in the 1980s and 1990s with their slow integration as heterodox economists increasingly took on multiple, merging heterodox identities (see Chapter 10).

Central to this approach to the history of economics is the concept of "community." Community is being used here as a way to encapsulate the intellectual and social organization of a science. That is, sciences are social systems of work that produce particular outputs called scientific knowledge, which are explanations and understanding of some set of real-world phenomena. However, scientific knowledge is fallible and perhaps historically contingent and hence can be contested; thus it is not some immutable objective stock that grows quantitatively. Rather scientific knowledge is a partially demarked body of knowledge that changes unpredictably and qualitatively. In short, what constitutes scientific knowledge has both a subjective and a "community approval" component. In this respect, scientific knowledge is a product of an elaborate intellectual and social organization which constitutes the system of work that is, for the most part, embedded in educational systems and their employment markets known as academic departments. The essential characteristics of a science are that its participants within this system of work see their activities as communal and hence consider themselves as a member of a community of scientists, and that the scientists control the way work is carried out, the goals for which it is carried out, and who is employed to carry it out.[10] This further implies that participants engaged in a particular science (or scientific field) are dependent at least to some degree on each other in the production of scientific knowledge. One component of this dependency is in terms of being able to use another scientist's research and the second is working on common issues that are relevant to achieving the goals of the scientific community. The former requires that the scientists and their research meet community-based acceptable research standards including competently utilizing acceptable research techniques; while the latter requires the existence of a community consensus on what are the goal-dependent central issues for research so as to ensure, without administrative directive, colleagues are also working on the same and/or broadly supportive issues. Thus the structure of dependency essentially determines the structure of the system of work that produces the scientific knowledge relevant to meeting the goals of the community. And those possible scientists that do not "fit" into this structure of dependency, do not produce the right kind of knowledge, can be marginalized and excluded from the community, but still exist within the field or they can be cleansed from the field altogether. Hence, it is possible for the marginalized in a scientific field, such as economics, to form their own within-the-field community of scientists and at the same time having to contend with efforts from the dominant community to eliminate them from the field completely.

Several factors affect the structure of dependency, including the nature of the audience for which the scientific output is intended; the degree to which control over the means of production of the scientific knowledge (including the equipment, the techniques, and the laboring skills), the format by which scientific knowledge is reported, and the communication outlets such as journals, are concentrated in the hands of a few or many; the role of individual and institutional reputations in affecting both the production of scientific knowledge (and particularly what is accepted as scientific knowledge) and the goals of such knowledge; and the role of state power and other organizational power outside the science community in legitimizing, supporting, or otherwise affecting particular reputations, goals, and scientific knowledge.[11] Variations in the impact of the factors on the structure of dependency and on the goals of scientific knowledge produce quite different social systems of scientific work. Hence it is possible to have a scientific field whose social system of work is controlled by an elite, is hierarchically structure, is centralized, has a high degree of participant dependency, and is legitimized and supported by state-organizational power and monies that has an incestuous and evolutionary relationship with the elite. And it is also possible to have a scientific field whose system of work is populated by numerous local schools that are not hierarchically structured, have a low degree of participant dependency, and are not legitimized and supported by state-organizational power and monies. Thus the intellectual and social organization of a scientific work, that is the community of scientists, is not naturally given for any scientific field, but is historically and consciously determined by its participants and recipients of its scientific knowledge (Whitley 1986, 1991, and 2000; Pickering 1995; Ropke 2005).

Intellectual and social organization of economics

Economics is a scientific field that can be divided into at least two distinct theoretical approaches, neoclassical economics and heterodox economics, where the object of analysis—the economy and the (asocial/social) provisioning process—and a material (as opposed to a religious or mystical) approach to explanation and understanding are the only things in common to both approaches.[12] Superficially it would appear that economics is a field with a low degree of structural dependency and hence produces diffused, locally coordinated knowledge. But this is incorrect since it is possible to view the neoclassical and heterodox approaches as separate sub-fields within the field of economics, each with its own structure of dependency and hence social system of work. One manifestation of this is that the core mainstream journals (see Table 2.3 on page 45) form a closed self-referencing group. That is to say, these journals cite other core mainstream journals and vice versa; but these journals in general do not cite core heterodox journals (see Lee and Harley 1998; Lee 2008; Appendix A.10), especially ignoring the Marxist, Institutionalist, and interdisciplinary journals.[13] Thus mainstream economists who publish in the core mainstream journals are influenced only by those journals and are ignorant of any views that are not carried by them. In contrast, heterodox economists devote part of their research time to understanding what the mainstream economists are saying, to criticizing their theoretical and empirical arguments, and to explaining why there needs to be an alternative theoretical approach. It follows that many of the articles by heterodox economists which are published in heterodox journals are concerned with issues in mainstream economics. Heterodox economists are also concerned with issues within heterodox economics and therefore write articles dealing with them which appear in heterodox journals. The heterodox journals reflect (hence empirically verify) this twofold agenda by citing both mainstream and heterodox journals. In particular, the percentage of citations imported on average from mainstream journals by the generalist and specialized heterodox journals (see Table 11.1 on page 213–16) range from 4.2 percent 13.1 percent per year which is generally greater than the percentage of citations imported from heterodox journals each year (see Appendix A.10).[14] On the other hand, core heterodox journals cite each other extensively (see Appendix A.27). Hence, core heterodox journals also form a self-referencing group, but which is more porous and open than the core mainstream journals.

So overall, economics consists of two well-defined sub-fields—mainstream economics that completely separates itself from heterodox economics which has its own body of knowledge, but still engages with the mainstream. While it is possible for a scientific field to comprise alternative sub-fields that exist harmoniously, this is not the case in economics. From its beginning as a scientific sub-field and community of scholars, neoclassical economics has not adopted an intellectual pluralistic attitude but has utilized organizational power and other forms of social control in an ongoing effort to eliminate heterodox economics in its many forms from the field of economics (see Chapters 2, 4, 6, 8 and 9). Heterodox economics has, in contrast, adopted a pluralistic attitude while at the same time developing its own distinctive body of knowledge.

Neoclassical economics

Although the methodology of neoclassical economics is grounded in methodological individualism and promotes the individual actor over social interaction and social norms, the actual work activity that produces neoclassical scientific output is socially organized. The structural organization of the work activity is derived from the theoretical organization of neoclassical economics. That is, neoclassical theory is arranged in a hierarchical manner. At the top is the theoretical core that comprises primary theoretical concepts and propositions that are accepted unconditionally.[15] From them, synthetic theoretical propositions are deduced. For example, the concepts of relative scarcity, rationality, optimization, and preference structure and the propositions of convexity, equilibrium, exchange, and technology combine to produce the synthetic propositions of demand curves, supply curves, and market equilibrium. The synthetic propositions in turn are the basis for deriving "lower" level propositions that directly engage issues derived from the economy and the provisioning process. They are embodied in applied economic research whose generation of empirical (as opposed to theoretical) scientific knowledge is not used to evaluate the core concepts and propositions or even the synthetic propositions.

For this hierarchical theoretical organization to be possible, it is necessary for economists at all levels of economic research to know and work with the same theory, have the same research standards, and utilize the same research techniques. It is also necessary that they accept the same broad goals and for the more specific issues for research the same set of theoretical propositions. These two requirements are achieved through the homogeneous teaching and intellectual inculcation of graduate students. That is graduate students in neoclassical graduate programs are uncritically introduced to a pre-established body of theory, while simultaneously shielded from criticism as well as alternative ways to "do" economics. Hence they are deliberately not provided the intellectual capabilities to critically evaluate neoclassical theory and, furthermore, are pointedly discouraged from ever criticizing it; but at the same time imbued with an attitude to exclude and cleanse from economics all views and approaches that are not those they have been taught. Consequently, work involving the theoretical core and resulting synthetic propositions is accepted as eventually having relevance for lower level production of scientific knowledge; and research at the lower levels utilize directly and/or indirectly the scientific output generated at the higher level. This hierarchical dependency structure works well when accompanied by a hierarchy of intellectual deference in that economists working at the different levels do not expect their research to question the theory coming from a higher level or to be given the scholarly recognition awarded to the higher level research; and they do not expect that they should have the same scholarly reputation as those economists doing research at a higher level.

For this dual hierarchical dependency structure to work, mainstream economists must respect the hierarchy and maintain their places without question. This social control is, in part, achieved through the process of community indoctrination that starts when graduate programs teach their students what the hierarchy is and that they should defer to it. Specifically, as part of their graduate education, economic students are taught to discriminate among types of scientific knowledge and accordingly value some more than others. Because this differential valuation is extended to the economists who produce the knowledge, there is also discrimination among economists in that some are considered more valuable than others. This is strongly reinforced through the control and allocation of jobs, access to the material resources needed to carry out research, and access to journals and publishers through which research that is more or less in conformity with neoclassical theory is made known and disseminated. Thus built into this "neoclassical" hierarchical dependency structure are discriminatory relationships that are widely accepted as "natural," the way things are to be, and hence are not seen as discriminatory. In this context, the ranking of journals and departments (see Chapters 2, 8, and 9) is designed to visibly reflect, reinforce, and internalize its existence without explicitly acknowledging the existence of the discriminatory relationship. Thus the discriminatory hierarchy of neoclassical economics is transformed into a community concern about reputations based on invidious distinctions in which the production of something more than minor or trivial scientific knowledge is an unintended and irregular by-product. (Beed and Beed 1996; Lee 2006)

Heterodox economics

For a community of heterodox economists to exist, it must be grounded in a social system of work that produces scientific or economic knowledge that contributes to the understanding of the economy and the social provisioning process. Moreover, its system of work is largely embedded in educational systems and their employment markets. Like in neoclassical economics and other scientific fields, economic research and employment can be found in a variety of non-educational institutions, such as governments, trade unions, and advocacy organizations. But the reproduction and expansion of the community is tied to academia. As noted above, a social system of work implies that the participants are dependent on each other for the production of scientific knowledge. Thus, the criteria for a community of heterodox economists to exist is that individual heterodox economists must see themselves as supporting a differentiated body of theory that is largely an antithetical alternative to neoclassical economic theory and partake in social networks and institutions that are outside those which make up the community of neoclasscial economists—see Chapter 10.[16] How strong or weak the community is, in part, is a function of how dependent heterodox economists are on each other's research and on the extent to which they work on common research goals; and, in part, dependent on the degree of integration of their social activities. Yet, irrespective of the degree of its cohesiveness, being a member of the heterodox community means advocating heterodox economic theory as well as engaging in social activities to ensure that the theory continues to be advocated independently of any individual member. In addition to the system of work that grounds the community, there are two social structures—social networks and organizations—that supports and promotes heterodox economic theory and hence contributes to bringing the community together. In particular, the social network glues together the heterodox theory with its supporting organizations and system of work in such a way so as to create a community of heterodox economists.

As with the mainstream, the social system of work for heterodox economists is department-based in that the economics department is the local employment market, establishes the career structure, is the organizational locale for teaching students and training future economists, and is the site for the production of scientific knowledge that must be publishable in refereed journals, books, and other reputable outlets. Consequently, heterodox economists are relatively indistinguishable from their neoclassical brethren except for their scientific output. This blasphemous difference, however, brings the individual heterodox economist under attack if she/he works in a predominantly neoclassical department; and brings heterodox departments under attack by university administrators (and often times supported by neoclassical economists) who are concerned about department rankings and the production and teaching of "improper" or low-value knowledge.

The social system of work for heterodox economists also differs from the mainstream in two distinct ways. First, although heterodox economic theory is still in the process of being developed, its theoretical content is not hierarchically organized and hence not hierarchically valued. Thus any contribution to the development of the theory, that is to explaining from a heterodox perspective, the economy and the social provisioning process is equally valued. As a corollary there is not a hierarchy of valued heterodox economists based on their particular contributions. A second corollary is that publishing outlets are not valued-ranked but are considered different-but-equal value. Consequently publishing outlets are chosen because of their subject matter that they publish. With non-hierarchical theory, and theory contributions, economists, and publishing outlets equally valued, it is not possible to hierarchically rank heterodox economic departments. Rather departments are evaluated within the heterodox community on the basis of their overall contribution to the development of heterodox economics and the community as a whole, including the production of scientific knowledge, the education of students and training of economists, the development and support of institutions, and the participation in the social network (see Chapter 11). A second difference concerns dependency in terms of being able to use other heterodox economists' research. Although they have the common goal of explaining the social provisioning process, heterodox economists have only gone part of the way of melding and synthesizing their different theoretical approaches and arguments. Hence not all heterodox scientific knowledge can be drawn upon by all heterodox economists. This makes for research and teaching uncertainty to be sure, but it also creates research and teaching opportunities that are directed towards reducing the uncertainty.

Complementing the social system of work are organizations, that is, social arrangements organized to produce specific outcomes that support and promote heterodox economic theory. Relevant institutions include journals, book publishers, professional associations and informal groups, and universities and research institutes with their undergraduate and graduate economic programs. The importance of these organizations is that they sustain through their material property, financial support and organizational activities, various intellectual centers within the heterodox community. The centers, connected by various social networks, provide the positive critical rivalry necessary for intellectual creativity within the community. The migration of members of the community among the materially based centers and the interaction of members from different centers at conferences, seminars, and over dinner means that heterodox economists with different views come face-to-face, interact, and engage in intellectual creativity; it also means an intermeshing of focus and issues.

Finally, the social network of heterodox economists consists of direct and indirect social relationships between heterodox economists. The relationships or social ties include correspondence; intellectual and social interactions at conferences, in seminars, or with students—such as teacher–student relationship; and belonging to the same mailing lists, subscribing to and publishing in the same journals, attending the same conferences and seminars, and supporting a common course of action. Thus, a social network produces a connected and integrated body of specialized individuals who develop a common set of arguments, are concerned with a common set of questions and topics, and develop common standards for judging the arguments, answers, and discourse. In other words, the network acts as a chain of intellectual discourses where intellectual interaction through face-to-face situations at seminars, in conferences, or over dinner brings together the intellectual community; focuses members' attention on and builds up vested interest in their own theoretical, historical, applied, and empirical topics and problems; and ties together written texts and lectures that are the long-term life of the community and gives its distinctiveness. The concatenated discourse that emerges from the face-to-face interaction keeps up the consciousness of the community's agenda and purpose by transcending all particular occasions of the interactions—that is, the discourse that emerges ensures that the community's purpose and agenda continue to be advocated independently of any individual member of the community or any specific face-to-face interaction. The discourse also has another impact in that it is the communicative process that creates thinkers within the community (Lloyd 1993; Wellman and Berkowitz 1997; Collins 1998).

Plan of the book

As noted previously, the history of heterodox economics is not just the history of heterodox economic theory; and nor is it only the history of systems of work, organizations, and networks. Rather, since the material requirements for producing scientific knowledge, organizations and networks affect the development of theory, and since theory has an impact on the type of networks, organizations, and systems of work that emerge, the history of heterodox economics draws on both and is thus an emergent synthesis of theories, systems of work, organizations, and networks. But such a history is complex and multi-faceted in that it requires the integration of biographical-intellectual studies with organizational histories, histories of the system of work, and histories of economic thought. It also requires historical reconstruction of social networks, embedding the community's history in its social-political-economic context, and most importantly a delineation of the process by which blasphemous ideas and scholars emerged and the methods then used by the mainstream to suppress them. For the writing of the history of heterodox economics, this hostile environment means that the community's history is initially one of economists coming to understand themselves as a group, in spite of opposing pressure, supporting a body of theory that is an antithetical alternative to neoclassical economic theory, developing systems of work, supporting organizations, and social networks necessary for the community to emerge so as to undertake its most important function that of producing scientific heterodox knowledge while defending themselves and their workplaces, organizations, and networks from continual attack by mainstream economists. Once the heterodox community emerges, its history changes into one of the intellectual and social production of knowledge within the context of a hostile environment.

To write a history of heterodox economics is not currently possible, given the complexity of the undertaking combined with the lack of extensive detailed studies on the components of the history. In particular, there are few detailed history of thought studies of the various heterodox approaches that formed the beginnings of heterodox economics in the 1960s and 1970s; and there are even fewer detailed community studies, although Tiago Mata's dissertation (Mata 2005) on Post Keynesian and radical political economics brilliantly redresses this omission. To redress this imbalance, the essays in this book are not concerned with the intellectual history of heterodox economics. Rather they concentrate on community studies of two different heterodox communities—Post Keynesian and Marxian-radical—that contributed to the emergence of heterodox economics and of the contested economic landscape they had to contend with; and of the emerging community of heterodox economists in the 1990s. The absence of studies of other heterodox approaches, such as Institutional, social, and feminist economics, is not due to their unimportance, but to the author's particular interests and participation in heterodox economics, as noted below. For similar reasons, the studies are restricted to the United States and the United Kingdom. Doing community studies requires that the researcher become "immersed" in the community he or she is studying. As a result, carrying out a study is quite time consuming (every one of the studies in this book took at least two years to complete and some took up to four years). Moreover, each heterodox community is distinct enough so that knowledge acquired of one community is not really transferable to another. What this means is that a single researcher cannot carry out all the community studies necessary to produce an overall history of heterodox economics. As with all important research endeavors, the end can only be reached with a little (or a lot) of research help from friends and colleagues.

In Part I, the four essays pertain to the United States and examine and recount the dominance of neoclassical economics and the near-suppression and cleansing of heterodox economics from American universities in the twentieth century (Chapter 2), the rise of radical economics from 1945 to 1970 (Chapter 3), the contested landscape of American economics in the 1970s (Chapter 4), and the emergence and establishment of Post Keynesian economics from 1971 to 1995 (Chapter 5). The four essays in Part II changes country and deal with heterodox economics in the United Kingdom starting with the contested landscape of British economics from 1900 to 1970 (Chapter 6), the development of heterodox economics in Britain 1970–96 (Chapter 7), and the impact of the Research Assessment Exercise and other state-based initiative on neoclassical and heterodox economics, 1989–2003 (Chapters 8 and 9). Finally, in Part III the first essay (Chapter 10) deals with the emergence of the community of heterodox economics from 1990 to 2006 and its current state as of 2006. The second essay (Chapter 11) deals with the very controversial issue of developing a methodology for ranking heterodox journals and departments and its importance for the future of heterodox economics.

Not knowing their own individual and collective history has resulted in heterodox economists—and this includes myself when I first started this project—not knowing who and what they are as well as not being able to fully understand the nature and implications of the contested academic landscape in which they practice their craft and seek to influence the thinking and acts of the society at large. One reason for this estrangement is that the stories, tales, news reports, articles, recollections, interviews, oral histories, letters, unpublished papers, and data that constitute the empirical grounding, the components of the history of heterodox economics are scattered, isolated, not public and therefore not generally known to heterodox economists.[17] Thus, one of the objectives of this collection of essays is to bring together this material so heterodox economists are made aware of it and even examine it. This is accomplished by the extensive use of notes, a large number of references, and an Appendix consisting of primary and secondary data.[18] Thus the extensive citations found in the notes and throughout the book combined with the primary and secondary data empirically ground the stories I am telling as well as providing the reader access to the "raw material." It is hoped that the reader does take advantage of this and examine the "raw material" for this is probably the best way to become acquainted with the history to which your contemporary activities are connected.

There is one final issue about writing the history of heterodox economics and that is the perspective of the storyteller. The essays that follow are told from a variety of perspectives—that of a historian with no first-hand knowledge of stories being told (Chapters 2, 3, 4, and 6); that of a heterodox economist too young to know first hand the early histories of the sub-communities that make up the heterodox community but is well acquainted with their recent histories through participant-observation (Chapters 5 and 7); and finally that of a current participant-observer (Chapters 8–11). Each perspective has its strengths and drawbacks, the most obvious of the latter being that the stories told will not necessarily accord with the memory of particular events held by individual heterodox economists. For example, as a consequence of being a graduate student at Rutgers University in the late 1970s, I use the informal knowledge acquired to help define and delineate what are early Post Keynesian events and who are Post Keynesian economists. The reconciling of different perspectives is a difficult task, made more complicated by the absence of life histories of many of the participating economists and the different weighting of particular events. All that is hoped for is that the methodology produces historical and contemporary narratives, that is, stories, that seem plausible and perhaps convincing to the reader and provides heterodox economists with a sense of their own history and an appreciation of the heterodox community in which they exist.

Part I

Heterodox economics in the United States

2 The contested landscape and dominance in American economics in the twentieth century

Following the implications of Table 1.1, the question that is examined in this chapter is did the near hegemony of neoclassical economics in the twentieth century or more specifically the 130-year period from 1870 to 2000 arise because it was the "better mousetrap" or were there other factors involved? That is, was the period characterized by doctrinal harmony or was it contested? And if it was contested, how did neoclassical economics maintain its dominance—was it indeed a better mousetrap or were other factors at work? To answer the question, it is necessary to start with the rise to dominance of neoclassical economics 1870 to 1900 and its organizational-academic dominance from 1900 to 1970, followed by an examination of the contested landscape and heretical theory from 1900 to 1940 and from 1945 to 1970, and ending with the use of department and journal rankings as the social-control mechanism through which neoclassical dominance was maintained from 1970 to 2000.

Rise to dominance of neoclassical economics, 1870–1900

The classical (or English) political economy that dominated American economics and was taught to students in 1870 consisted of fundamental assumptions—universal self-interest and existence of private property, maximum wealth balanced against sacrifice, and frictionless markets—and various theoretical arguments, such as labor-cost of production theory of value, capital as stored-up labor, wage-fund theory with its subsistence or iron law of wages, and inverse relationship between rents and profits and wages (or between profits and wages). Accompanying the theory was an extended discourse on the virtues of free competition and self-interest for the creation of wealth, frictionless markets, and harmony of the social classes and the existing distribution of income and wealth; and the discourse itself was grounded in a method that was static, deductive, non-empirical, and given to pronouncing natural laws that were valid for all times, lands, and societies.[1] In 1870 the acceptance or rejection of the theory qua discourse determined whether one was an economist or not. However, by the late 1870s the discourse (but not theory to the same degree) was beginning to divide along political lines. One group of economists believed that unchecked, unregulated economic growth with the accompanying centralization of economic power did not undermine the country's republican foundations while the second group of economists did think so and therefore advocated government regulation of economic growth. Accompanying the bifurcated discourse in the 1870s were numerous, widespread, and violent strikes, economic depression, growth of cartels and large enterprises, destructive competition, and the awareness of poverty and destitution especially in rapidly growing cities.

This economic disorder, known as the Social Problem, prompted many concerned young men to study political economy as well as to be open to new ways of thinking. They were sympathetic to socialism and welcome the emerging historical approach to economics articulated in Germany and elsewhere with its emphasis on history, historicization of theory, induction and the empirical grounding of theory, empirical research, and an organic view of the state and the economy that emphasizes state involvement in the economy. The methodological and political differences generated a controversy between the old *orthodox* classical political-economy school and the new *heterodox* historical political-economy school, one not centering on classical value theory *per se*, but on method, policy, workers' rights relative to capital, and the capability of classical theory to deal adequately with economic reality. However, the Haymarket incident in 1886 combined with increasing violent labor strikes, demonstration for the eight-hour day, the rise of prairie populism, and the increasing popularity of Henry George's single-tax movement and Edward Bellamy's Nationalism movement startled many of these young historically oriented economists. Moreover, there was the spread of classical-based Georgist and Marxian economic theories with their extensive theory of rent that had land yielding unearned value and theory of profits based on the exploitation of workers among the laboring classes thus raising the spectra of a class war. With their ingrained belief of American exceptionalism[2] being challenged, these economists stopped their advocacy of socialism and other progressive reforms and embraced (more or less) the capitalism of the status quo. At the same time they and others, including Henry Adams, John B. Clark, Edwin Seligman, Alvin Johnson, Richard Ely, Frank Taussig, Thomas Carver, John R. Commons, and Frank Fetter, began searching for 'safe' research topics and for an alternative economic theory where land, capital, and labor created value in the same manner, the distribution of income was based on the contribution of land, capital, and labor, and competition, supply and demand, and the market process tended to produce harmony among the classes and the best economic results[3] (Jones 1988; Mason 1982; Barber 1988c, 1988d; Rozwadowski 1988; Cookingham 1988; Henderson 1988; Goldman 1944; Ross 1991; Bernard 1990; Collier 1979; Plehn 1924; Furner 1975; Betz 1988; Hodgson 2001; Gaffney and Harrison 1994).

Weaken by the earlier controversy, the offending theoretical content of classical political economy, such as the labor theory of value and the wage fund, was dropped, the analyses of rent and the cost of producing goods were reformed to be consistent with the marginal utility approach to value, and the marginal productivity theory of distribution developed. In addition, the useful parts of the theory, such as its abstract nature, deductive method, and universal laws were directly adopted. The resulting synthesis, most notably produced by Alfred Marshall in his *Principles of Economics*, was neoclassical price theory.[4] Although the issues of historical method and the advocacy of social and state intervention in the economy still remained, the theory was infused with the virtue of markets. Hence, the acceptable range of advocacy was narrowed to improving the existing capitalist market economy as "realistically" delineated by the theory. Consequently, it was quickly adopted by all American economists, Thorstein Veblen, the Georgists, and the Marxists excepted.[5] Thus, the transformation of American economics took place within a relative short period of time, from 1885 to 1900, as American economists switched from employing the term 'political economy' to identify their subject matter and courses, using classical political economy texts, and having students read Adam Smith, David Ricardo, and Mill to employing the term economics, using neoclassical texts, and having students read Marshall and other neoclassical economists. As a result, circa 1900–10 all American universities and colleges were teaching neoclassical price theory in their introductory and basic economic courses as well as in their graduate economic courses where Marshall's *Principles of Economics* was one of the standard texts—see Table 1.1 for the theoretical topics covered.[6]

Not only were economists looking for a new theory, but the political environment of universities also hastened the transformation. The conservative nature of universities and political economists who taught meant that the one alternative to neoclassical economics, that is Marxian economics, was simply not taught and not considered as an alternative theoretical explanation of capitalism, that students were warned not to read George's *Progress and Poverty*, and that in the view of Seligman no thoroughly trained economist could ever advocate George's single tax. In particular, the marginalism vs. socialism debate that took place among British and European economists, socialists, and intellectuals from the period of 1870 to 1930 did not take place in the United States.[7] Rather being repositories of "sound opinion," nearly 90 percent of universities and colleges did not offered various elective courses on socialism, communism, and social reform and reconstruction of industrial society where the theoretical arguments of Marx and George could be critically evaluated. But those 10 percent that did generally had as one purpose of the course to convince students that their theories were wrong. In addition, given the politically charged times, conservative university administrations, business-dominated university trustees, academics, and outsiders attacked liberal and progressive economists, and blacklisted radical economists—but not in all cases. Thus, it was not a time to recklessly engage in activities inside or advocacy outside the university that would upset the status quo in any manner, such as being a proponent of unsound opinions such as the single tax, favoring trade unions and free trade, or being a supporter of socialism, bimetallism, or the wrong political party: teaching and advocating arguments that 'undermine' the moral basis of the social order or the economic security of property rights and business interests was dogmatically unacceptable.[8] What all sought was an economic theory that would promote the status quo and hence be appropriate to teach to students; and the professionalization of economists who then would only engage in the 'scientific' objective study of economic problems.[9] Their intellectual souls, their academic freedom, their advocacy for a better world exchanged for acceptability, respectability, and money—this was the devil's bargain accepted by nearly all American economists by 1900, with the result that heterodox-radical colleagues were, with their implicit approval, pressured to conform, silenced or cleansed from the academy. This is well illustrated at Columbia where as a lecturer Seligman opposed Henry George's candidacy for Mayor of New York in 1886 was advanced to an adjunct professorship in 1888 over Daniel De Leon, also a lecturer, who supported George's candidacy. Columbia made it clear to De Leon that he was not wanted and so he left in 1889. So threaten with stunted careers, dismissal, and blacklists, many heterodox-radical economists, such as Ely, Bemis, and Commons, became quiet and/or moved politically to the right (Barber 1988b, 1988c, 1988d, 1988e; Jones 1988; Rozwadowski 1988; Sass 1982, 1988; Cookingham 1988; Adelstein 1988; Henderson 1988; Seretan 1979; Bender 1993; Church 1974; Dorfman 1949; Carlson 1968; Plehn 1924; Lampman 1993; Barrow 1990; Gaffney and Harrison 1994; Goodwin 1973; Bernard 1990; Laughlin 1892; Furner 1975; Goldmann 1944; Lipset 1975; Parrish 1967; Ross 1991).

With advocacy and its implied ethical or *ought* driven agenda minimized or replaced in favour of the scientific or objective study of *what is* agenda, the paramount issue facing economists circa 1900 was one of determining what or which economic theory objectively explained the *is*. For the theory that explained the *is* also directs and limits the advocacy, the *ought*. The emerging neoclassical price theory objectively explained how the *is*, the capitalist market system, worked and that it worked well but not perfectly in providing for the material well-being of individuals and society. And this, in turn, constrained advocacy to promoting economic and social policies that would improve the workings of the existing capitalist system. On the other hand, Marxian economic theory provided a much darker understanding of the capitalist system and therefore promoted advocacy to radically alter capitalism and perhaps entirely replacing it with a socialist commonwealth. Thus, neoclassical economics could not exist harmoniously with Marxism (or as it turned out with other heterodox theories) since its emergence and development were underwritten with business and state money, power, and status because of its social importance—that of intellectually and ideologically defending the existing capitalist system. So fused together in neoclassical economics by 1900 was a research agenda to objectively explain how capitalism worked with the ideological agenda that promoted capitalism. This latter agenda in turn ensured that neoclassical economics was disposed to be anti-pluralistic and to use any means to suppress and cleanse heterodox economists and ideas from the academy and society at large. Hence, American economics in the twentieth century can be characterized as a very uneven hundred-year war for the theoretical soul of economists and with it the minds and souls of politicians and the general public.

Institutional dominance of neoclassical economics, 1900–70

With less than 10 percent of the professoriate critical of neoclassical theory in 1900, the impact of the near exclusivity of the teaching of neoclassical price theory at American universities and colleges by 1910 meant that the majority American PhD economists turned out over the next three decades would also be neoclassical economists. More specifically, from 1904 to 1940, one study has the number of candidates preparing PhD dissertations at 5590 distributed among 51 PhD-granting institutions—see Table 2.1. The leading twenty-two institutions had nearly 96 percent of the doctoral candidates for the period 1904 to 1910 and 92 percent of the candidates for the period 1904 to 1940. In addition, in a second study covering fifty-six institutions, they produced 90 percent of the 1844 doctorates in economics for the period 1926 to 1940. Except perhaps for Wisconsin and Pennsylvania, none of the twenty-two departments were known for their deviation from neoclassical price theory over the period of 1904 to 1920; and from 1920 to 1940 only Wisconsin, Columbia, and Texas were known for their deviation from the mainstream. So it is plausible to conclude that from 1904 to 1940 less than 10 percent of the sixty-six different institutions supporting doctoral dissertations in economics exposed their students to heretical economic views, and less than 30 percent of all doctoral candidates and 20 percent of all doctorates in economics were exposed to heretical economic theory.[10] This ensured that existing graduate and undergraduate economic departments retained their neoclassical orientation, as their new recruits would largely be neoclassical economists who would assign neoclassical textbooks to their students.[11] Moreover, departments whose theoretical orientation were a little blurry in the first decade or in any of the following three decades did not long remain in this unsettle state. Pressure to teach the theory taught at leading universities, such as Harvard, to be up to date, and to be on the leading edge of theory meant that 'deviant' departments soon corrected themselves, with Texas being the exception; and if they did not correct themselves, as in the case of The Brookings Institution, they were simply shut down.[12] As a result, the percentage of economic professors critical of neoclassical theory declined to probably less than 5 percent by 1940. Thus, in terms of price theory, by 1940 virtually all American universities (except Texas) were more than mere teaching the same thing, and they were drilling it into their students. Hence it mattered little whether a graduate student

Table 2.1 Leading American economic departments with Ph.D. programs and doctoral students, 1904–40

Doctoral Programs 1925, 1932	Candidates Preparing Ph.D. Dissertations 1904–10[a]	Candidates Preparing Ph.D. Dissertations 1904–40[a]	Ph.D. Dissertations Accepted, 1925–26 to 1939–40[d]
Brown	–	15	4
Chicago	31	754	111
Columbia	81	1171	194
Cornell	24	234	136
Harvard[b]	55	564	221
Illinois	4	174	120
Iowa	1	95	51
Johns Hopkins	13	141	44
Michigan	4	110	52
Minnesota	1	191	56
Missouri	–	12	5
New York	–	53	22
Northwestern	1	101	94
Ohio State	1	140	53
Pennsylvania	16	353	94
Princeton	7	97	36
Stanford	4	83	48
Texas	–	19	17
UC-Berkeley	3	136	90
Virginia	–	41	31
Wisconsin	38	522	140
Yale	23	148	41
Other	14	436	184
Total	321	5590[c]	1844

Sources: Hughes 1925: 14; Hughes 1934: 204; Froman 1930: 237; Froman 1942: 818; Forman 1952: 603; Marsh 1936; and *Doctoral Dissertations Accepted by American Universities, 1933–34 to 1939–40*.

Notes:
a For the time period 1904–40, a total of fifty-one American institutions provided information about candidates preparing Ph.D. dissertations. In addition to the leading twenty-two institutions there were American, Brookings Institutions, Bryn Mawr, Catholic, Clark, Colorado, Denver, Duke, Fordham, Georgetown, Indiana, Institute of Economics, Kansas, Kentucky, Nebraska, North Carolina, North Dakota, Oklahoma A&M, Pittsburgh, Southern California, St. Louis, Syracuse, Utah, University of Washington, Vanderbilt, Washington and Lee, Washington University, West Virginia, and Western Reserve.
b Includes Radcliffe College.
c Excludes the number of candidates for Toronto and McGill Universities which are located in Canada.
d For the time period 1925/26–39/40, a total of fifty-six American institutions provided information about accepted Ph.D. dissertations. In addition to the leading twenty-two institutions there were American, Brookings Institutions, Bryn Mawr, Boston University, Catholic, Cincinnati, Clark, Colorado, Duquesne, Duke, Fordham, George Peabody, Georgetown, George Washington, Indiana, Iowa State, Kansas, Louisiana, Maryland, Massachusetts State, Michigan State, Nebraska, North Carolina, Pennsylvania State, Pittsburgh, Purdue, Rutgers, Southern California, St. Louis, Syracuse, Temple, University of Washington, Vanderbilt, and Washington University.

attended Columbia, Wisconsin, Pennsylvania, Princeton, Yale, Michigan, Harvard, or Chicago, as he or she was trained in the same neoclassical price theory.[13] What differences remained between departments after 1940 centered on the degree of sophistication at which the theory was taught.

Responding to the increasing demand for up-to-date textbooks, the theoretical developments that occurred in the 1930s—such as economics defined as the allocation of scarce resources, indifference curves, isoquants, marginal revenue equals marginal cost, monopolistic (imperfect) competition, and the kinked demand curve—were rapidly introduced into textbooks at all levels in the 1940s and 1950s and have remained there ever since—see Table 1.1 on page 3. Consequently, over time departments adopted quite similar standards in the teaching of price theory to undergraduate and graduate students. In short, neoclassical economics, to the exclusion of Marxism and other heterodox approaches, was taught at American universities and colleges from 1900 to 1970: with exception of the inter-war period to some degree, there was neither pluralism in nor transformation of American economics.[14] Hence a reasonable guess is that less than 6 percent of the 12,625 PhD in economics turned out from 1920 to 1970 were trained in any systematic way in a heterodox price theory. This, in turn, had the knock on effect of ensuring that, in the face of emerging heterodox price theories after 1970, neoclassical price theory continued to be nearly exclusively taught in graduate economics programs until the end of the century (Mason 1982; Carlson 1968; Lee 1990; Brazer 1982; Ginzberg 1990; Bowen 1953; Huntington 1971; Cookingham 1987; Harmon and Soldz 1963; Rutherford 2001, 2003a, 2006; Harmon 1978).

Contested landscape and heretical theory, 1900–40

The dominance of neoclassical price theory by 1910 did not mean that the economic landscape was uncontested. From 1900 to 1940 (and after) there circulated among farmers, workers, immigrants, migrants, the unemployed, and the dispossessed, numerous popular tracts, pamphlets, newspapers, and books that made reference to, were only understandable in terms of, or directly discussed the classical political economy of Marxism (or socialism) and Georgism. In addition, cheap editions of *Capital* and other writings by Marx, Engels, and Lenin, and of *Progress and Poverty* were widely available by the 1930s and were bought and studied. Finally, reacting against their professors' disinterest or even hostility, university and college students set up clubs to study socialism and social reform including the single tax. For a more serious and in-depth study of Marxian and socialist theories, schools, institutes, and workers' colleges were established outside of colleges and universities. The sponsors of these alternative educational forums included the Socialist and Communist Parties, who wanted to educate their members and perspective members, members of trade unions, workers at shops and factories where trade union efforts were under way, members of working-class organizations, and individuals with socialist sympathies.[15] In all cases, some form of Marxian theory was taught to students and taught in a manner that made it clear that it was an alternative to bourgeois or neoclassical price theory.[16] The Georgists also established schools to educate followers and others on the economics of the single tax.[17] The basic course offered, "Fundamental Economics," was based on *Progress and Poverty, Science of Political Economy*, and other writings by George. The degree of sophistication at which the theories were taught in all these schools and colleges varied greatly partly because of diverse educational level of the students and because many of the teachers were self-educated, part-time volunteers. But the point is that in this educational environment, neoclassical theory was contested, although from a great distance and largely out of sight of most neoclassical economists (Kornbluh 1988; Graham 1990; Teitelbaum 1993; Cornell 1976; Sinclair 1923; Schwartz 1984; Altenbaugh 1990; Howe and Coser 1957: 429; Clancy 1952; Lipset 1975; Hellman 1987; Cohen 1990; Gettleman 1993; Horn 1979).

Complementing the underground contested economic landscape for this period was the ebb and flow of constraints on and intolerance towards socialism and other sorts of radicalism and progressivism on and off campus. In the pre-1917 period, progressive academics, including economists, ran into difficulties. They were labelled anarchists, radicals, or socialists if they displayed an interest in socialism in general or became involved in the Progressive movement and were not hired, dismissed, or pressured, as were Adams and Ely, to modify their views, were threaten with controls on their teaching and what they said outside the classroom, and had promotions delayed by damning reports from their conservative students.[18] The emerging conception of academic freedom in this period was not one of unconstrained freedom of intellectual engagement and discourse, but one of management and constraint: academics had academic freedom as long as they did not seriously deviate from the moral and political values of the status quo. So long as an economist did not espouse socialism, teach Georgism, or delineate destructive criticism of the existing order, they had complete academic freedom.

Moreover, college administrators put pressure on students not to establish *socialist* clubs but rather *social reform* or *social sciences* clubs; and did not permit the clubs to invite socialists and other radicals to speak at their campus meetings. Once the United States entered the First World War and then the Russian Revolution occurred, constraints and intolerance increased dramatically, which the American Association of University Professors fully encouraged and supported. Anti-war, radical, unpatriotic, and non-conventionally thinking professors (who probably also did not respect the ordinary decencies of discourse among gentlemen) were dismissed or not rehired as they should not be permitted to influence students and the intellectual life of the nation by calling into question the existing economic, social, or political conventions; student socialist and social reform/sciences clubs were attacked verbally in the press, shut down, or made very difficult to operate so that by

1922 few clubs (many now called Liberal Clubs which belonged to the Intercollegiate Liberal League formed in 1921) existed on any American campus while radical speakers were prevented from speaking on campus; students were disciplined or expelled for writing realistic descriptions of economic conditions or inviting radical speakers to campus; and faculty who underwrote club activities were let go when the club invited unacceptable speakers, such as progressive economist Robert Dunn who spoke on famine in the Soviet Union.[19] In addition, during the Red Scare of 1919–20, universities and colleges, such as Barnard, Wellesley, Radcliffe, Chicago, Yale, Vassar, and Smith, were denounced as hotbeds of Bolshevism and radical institutions because the writings of Marx and Engels were required reading for their students; established academics, such as Ross, Commons, and John Dewey were branded parlor Reds while others were discharged from their institutions for their political beliefs and writings, because they agreed to speak at a Socialist Party rally, or sympathized with the ideas and agenda of the Industrial Workers of the World or even the Non-Partisan League; trustees and presidents in cooperation with the business community set up spy systems in their universities and colleges to identify the radical, un-American professors and students for dismissal; and a movement was launched to scrutinize economic textbooks for breaches of loyalty. Finally, professors and instructors who questioned the interests of (or were questioned by) powerful business groups were harassed, suspended, dismissed, pressured into resigning; economic departments with too many progressives (as at the University of Washington) were restructured and placed in conservative business schools; and businesses threatened not to donate to universities that retained faculty with radical economic views.[20] American campuses were after 1924 non-political, with liberal academics (at least the ones who were left) cowed into silence, afraid to talk about Marx or anything radical, and students staunchly Republican, materialistic, and regarded college as the first step towards a job in the corporate world. In economics, departments stopped teaching courses on socialism opting for safer ones on economic theory, and managed the discourse in the social-problem courses so as to not violate the range of social-political values acceptable to the status quo (or in plain English liberal discourse was acceptable but radical discourse was not); in contrast there were no objections to courses extolling the virtues of capitalism taught by professors whose salaries were paid by the business community.

The non-political academic scene slowly became radicalized with the onset of the Great Depression and the increased prospects of war due to the rise of fascism. Both students and professors became interested in regulatory New Deal economic policies and in Marxism and became associated in some manner with the Communist Party and other left-wing and progressive organizations. Students held outdoor rallies for peace and formed clubs to examine all the views and issues surrounding the Great Depression and other social ills of American society as well as international questions. They invited outside speakers to speak on unemployment, the Harlan County coal strike, the Communist Party platform, Soviet art, and other topics. However, utilizing the power vested in *loco parentis* (which essentially granted university and college administrators almost absolute legal authority over their students), presidents and deans clamped down on the political activities of their students and their socialist and progressive clubs by barring controversial speakers from campus and through expulsions, suspensions, and dismissals (or threats thereof).[21] In addition, anti-radical, conservative trustees, presidents, and deans spied on their students, collecting information about their political affiliations, activities, and ideas. They then turned this information over to the Federal Bureau of Investigation (FBI); and by 1941 the FBI had dossiers on tens of thousands of American university students. Moreover, as many college administrators and professors believed it improper and unprofessional for faculty to engage in political activism on campus or to be members of the Communist Party, such instructors and professor were dismissed or simply not hired.[22] Finally, outside political and business pressures in the form of House Un-American Activities Committee inquiries, FBI surveillance of professors, loyalty oaths, state investigations of communists in state colleges and universities resulting in the firing of 'communist' professors, requests for firing particular progressive professors, and complaints by private citizens contributed to producing a more conservative, intolerant atmosphere on campus.[23] So by 1940 it can be argued that American academia as well as American society at large had become, relative to 1900, less tolerant of progressive-socialist-radical ideas and the individuals who espoused them.[24] And to show that they were in step with the less tolerant American society, the American Association of University Professors stated that a professor could only claim the protection of academic freedom if he/she exercised *appropriate* restraint in his/her writings and public talks, with appropriateness implicitly 'defined' as not upsetting the status quo to the extent that grave doubts are raised concerning his/her fitness for their academic position (Horn 1979; Trachtenberg 1920; De Leon and Fine 1927; Beale 1936; McMahon 1989; Fine 1930; Gruber 1975; Tap 1992; Beauregard 1988; Barrow 1990; Sinclair 1923; Saltmarsh 1991; Mathews 1973; Dugger 1974; Foster 1967; Peach 1966; Ross 1991; Solomon 1980; Goldman 1944; Sass 1982; Cheyney 1940; Coolidge 1921; Murray 1955; Lydenberg 1977; Mallach 1970; Lipset 1975; Allen 1986; Cohen 1993; Gettleman 1982; Schrecker 1986; Rutkoff and Scott 1986; Leberstein 1993; Vatter 1999; Mason 1982; Phillips 1989; Cross 1967; Dowd 1994; Hall 1989; Lowen 1997; Sturgeon 1986; Keen 1999; Bernstein 2001; Rudy 1996; Earnest 1953; Mitgang 1988; Jones, Enros, and Tropp 1984; AAUP 1941).

Inter-war heterodoxy: institutionalism and administered prices

The secular increase of intolerance outlined above had a counterpart within economics with regard to theory. As previously noted, neoclassical economists had banned and continued through the inter-war period to ban Marxism (and all that is Bolshevism) and Georgism from the classroom and acceptable economic discourse. On the other hand, the iconoclastic and critical comments regarding neoclassical price theory from Veblen and others were tolerated if not appreciated. However this restrictive tolerance and show of pluralism slowly declined as neoclassical economists became increasingly true believers. Hence, it became accepted that one might question aspects of neoclassical theory from an internal, friendly critic perspective; but to question it as a general proposition was not acceptable. Thus by restricting legitimate criticisms to those who held the same general beliefs, the same theory, neoclassical theory became more entrenched among economists and their students—but it produced heretics and blasphemers as well. Suggestive of this transformation were Harvard's Charles Bullock intolerant tirades concerning Veblen and his criticisms of neoclassical theory in the 1920s and Allyn Young's suggestion that Veblen was not really an economist in the first place. More representative of the transformation was the reaction of neoclassical economists to the emergence of Institutional economics.

Since the introduction of the German historical approach to American economics in the 1870s, there were numerous attempts to broaden economics beyond its price theory to include history, sociology, politics, and psychology, which, however, failed.[25] In addition, since the 1890s, neoclassical price theory was buffeted with criticisms, partially drawn from Darwinism, anthropology, and philosophy, about its narrow scope of inquiry, its mechanistic-deductive-static method of inquiry, its inadequate psychological, cultural, and historical foundations, and its non-concern with pressing social problems. Drawing on and synthesizing these two strands, Walton Hamilton in 1918 set out a research agenda for the development of an institutional approach to economic theory. The approach was heretical but not blasphemous for Hamilton's agenda was not to repudiate neoclassical price theory per se, but to give it a better, more modern conceptual-empirical grounding and refocus and enlarge its domain. Within a few years Hamilton's agenda had evolved into an Institutionalist research program[26] that was being pursued by a well-defined network of self-identified Institutionalist economists and highly sympathetic fellow travelers.[27] While Hamilton pursued a teaching agenda at Amherst College and the Brookings Graduate School that virtually excluded any formal training in neoclassical price theory and was clearly anti-neoclassical, Commons, Wesley Mitchell, John M. Clark, and other Institutionalists almost from the beginning made repeated statements that they were not disparaging neoclassical economists or repudiating neoclassical price theory but were trying to make the latter better. However, the neoclassical true believers still belittled their work, rebuked them for wasting their time about concerns with method, and applied professional pressure to have them retreat from their association with Institutionalism. Moreover, whenever an Institutionalist made an isolated iconoclastic statement, the response of the neoclassicals was that it was harmful and should be publicly retracted. Finally, because of their advocacy of scientific and politically detached inquiry, neoclassical economists disapproved of the Institutionalists' promotion of a political economics. So instead of bearing or even welcoming the heretical intellectual ferment generated by Institutionalism, neoclassical economists were intolerant of it.[28] As a result, many of the interwar Institutionalists minimized or ceased to advocate their views and quietly readopted their research to the language of neoclassical price theory; others, such as Hamilton, left economics altogether; and then there were those who found government work more rewarding and ceased to contribute to the building and development of Institutionalism.[29] The intended outcome of these changes was that graduate students ceased to identify or even have the possibility to identify with Institutional economics. Thus by 1930, Hamilton's brash heretical shout for the institutional approach to economic theory had become a mild calling; and by 1940 a heretical whimper little differentiated from neoclassical price theory. In fact, by 1940 many neoclassical economists had come to see Institutionalism and neoclassical theory as quite compatible, albeit with different emphases[30] (Gaffney and Harrison 1994; Emmett 1998; Carlson 1968; Young 1925; Jones 1988; Sass 1982; Ross 1991; Mayhew 1987; Hamilton 1918a, 1918b, 1919; Parker 1919; Hammond 2000; Gruchy 1947; Bernstein 2001; Hodgson 2001; Rutherford 1997, 2000a, 2000b, 2001, 2002, 2003a, 2004; and Kaufman 2007).

Beginning in the 1920s and more rapidly in the 1930s, American neoclassical price theory was transformed and expanded: general equilibrium began to creep in, monopolistic competition and the marginalist revolution transforms the discussion of costs, pricing, prices, the business enterprise, and competition, and theory began to inform empirical research. The extension of the theory enabled it to absorb many of the Institutionalist atheoretical case studies on the business enterprise and competition. However, the extension of the theory exposed it to criticism, especially in the areas of enterprise pricing and the behavior of prices. In 1932 Gardiner Means began his fifty-year attack on neoclassical price theory with the observation that the rise of the modern corporation and the theoretical implications it entailed rendered the theory obsolete and a new replacement theory had to be constructed. His subsequent empirical and theoretical work on prices in the 1930s led him to articulate his heterodox doctrine of administered prices. The blasphemous nature of his work was quickly recognized by neoclassical economists who responded accordingly. One response was the administered price controversy of the 1930s, which was largely an attempt to either empirically dismiss Means's research (and hence his doctrine) or to show that administered or inflexible prices could be entirely accounted for within neoclassical price theory. Although both responses individually failed in their objective, together they achieved the desired outcome: convincing neoclassical economists that Means's doctrine of administered prices did not pose any threat to their theory. A second response, which was closely associated with the controversy, was to subject Means to monetary and professional penalties, beginning in 1933 with his Harvard PhD committee rejecting the initial draft of his dissertation apparently because it contained an attack on neoclassical price theory and ending in 1940 when the neoclassical American Keynesians pushed him out of his job at the National Resources Planning Board.

The concern with administered or inflexible prices combined with the marginalist extension of neoclassical price theory prompted numerous research projects, many of which raised blasphemous questions among neoclassical economists about the gap between reality and neoclassical price. Moreover, Hamilton's work on prices and price polices of enterprises suggested that real-world pricing could not be captured at all by neoclassical theory; while Edwin Nourse's price-policy research supported and extended Means's work of administered prices. Finally, some economists drew upon their own business experience to reject marginalist theory as explaining how enterprises set prices. The reaction of neoclassical economists was to either claim as a question of belief that enterprises did in fact use marginalist pricing procedures when setting pricing or, as Edward Mason did to Hamilton, dismissed the research as completely uninteresting and irrelevant to the concerns of economists. However, try as they might, the neoclassical economists could not prevent the emergence of blasphemous ideas about enterprise pricing behavior—it took the post-war marginalist controversy to suppress the blasphemy and penalize its supporters[31] (Lee 1984, 1997, 1998; Lee and Samuels 1992; Hamilton and Associates 1938; Mason 1939).

The severe reaction of neoclassical economists to the blasphemous ideas of Veblen, Hamilton, Means, and others did not result in their complete suppression. Rather it helped create a fragmented academic-intellectual environment where blasphemous Institutionalist ideas, such as culture, institutionalized patterns of behavior, holistic methodology, and instrumentalism, remained separate from Means's blasphemous work on administered prices. Moreover, in hindsight, Means's administered prices and Keynes's discussion of the role of investment and money in the economy were completely compatible. However, since the American Keynesians were welded to neoclassical price theory, the integration of administered prices with Keynesian theory did not happen (Rutherford and DesRoches 2008). In short, all the components were available in 1940 to create a relatively complete heterodox economic theory that could replace neoclassical theory; but the marriage never took place. So it would have been possible for the history of American heterodox economics to begin in the 1930s; but in fact it does not begin until the 1960s. Between 1940 and the 1960s was an interregnum.

Post-war economic landscape: McCarthyism, conservatism, and modernism, 1945–70

In the post-war years, three different forces affected the landscape of American economics. The most dramatic of these was the anticommunist hysteria that silenced an entire generation of radical and progressive American academics, including economists. Moreover, the emerging conservative pro-business anti-government political and social climate affected liberal economists in terms of what they taught and what they wrote in textbooks. The final force was the modernization movement where economic departments consciously redesigned their programs to ensure that the most up-to-date versions of neoclassical economic theory were taught using the appropriate mathematical tools. As a result, all that was taught in this post-war period was neoclassical economic theory while the descriptive-Institutional oriented approach became less emphasized and nearly disappeared.

During the post-1945 anticommunist hysteria some states passed laws designed to exterminate communism and communists and made the teaching of communism illegal. More specifically, over thirty states required academics at public universities to take loyalty oaths;[32] and those who would not take them for whatever reason, including on grounds of conscience, lost their jobs. Across the United States, universities, including both administrators and academics, jump on the McCarthyite bandwagon (either on their own volition, on the behest of philanthropic foundations, the military, Central Intelligence Agency, or other government units, or both) and held that "extreme" academic freedom was unacceptable and should be restricted to what was generally socially acceptable.[33] As a consequence, this meant that being a Communist Party member made an academic an unfit teacher and hence was sufficient grounds for not hiring, for dismissal, and for denying tenure or promotion:

> ... conspiracy is an avowed method employed by the Communists. No member of an academic community can properly claim the right to instruct the youth of the nation to embrace a philosophy which advocates the violent overthrow of free government. This is beyond the bounds of academic freedom. Secondly, membership in the Communist party, or adherence to its principles, carries with it an obligation which makes a person ineligible for membership in a free academic community, since a Communist is subject to party discipline, and anyone under such intellectual control is not intellectually free. His mind is closed by the doors of Communist doctrine. He may not pursue truth wherever it may lead. He is, therefore, unfit for membership in any academic society.[34]

(McGrath 1954a)

This was later extended to cover situations where academics invoked the Fifth Amendment to refuse answering such questions as naming names or denying that they were communists; were fellow travelers; or were just plain radical, progressive, or unusual, such as supporting the New Deal and New Deal-type economic policies, government regulation, national economic planning, civil rights, labor unions, Consumer Union, National Lawyers Guild,

Henry Wallace's 1948 presidential campaign, signing petitions for amnesty for Communist Party leaders, or being a Unitarian or a homosexual.[35]

These actions by universities were possible because administrators actively co-operated with the FBI and in many cases asked the FBI to vet potential hires, professors going up for tenure, and all tenured faculty and make recommendations about hiring and firing.[36] They were also not resisted (at least to any great extent) by their academic staff for a variety of reasons including that some staff were American Legion and FBI informants and collaborators while others feared reprisal by the university administration.[37] Moreover, many of the professional associations to which academics belonged either collaborated with the FBI, such as the American Anthropological Association and the American Economic Association (AEA) or were deliberately passive and ineffectual, such as the American Association for University Professors.[38] Consequently very few progressive, radicals, or communists were hired or remained employed by American universities;[39] and a blacklist actively and jointly maintained by the universities, individual academics, and the FBI ensured that a radical dismissed by one university was not hired by another.[40] To avoid the withdrawal of research funds or escape attacks, harassment, social ostracism, or the inevitable dismissal or denial of tenure, many progressive academics left academia voluntarily, took academic positions outside the United States,[41] restricted and censored the content of their lectures (such as not teaching Keynesian economics or as not to appear pacifistic, atheistic, or unpatriotic) since classes were monitored by students and police informers, advised graduate students to do safe, conventional dissertations so as to avoid red-baiting from committee members, avoided talking to student groups about socialism, and/or at the least metaphorically voluntarily blowing their brains out by re-directing their own research and publications to safe, more conventional areas.[42] Then there were others where the stress led to heart attacks or alcoholisms that contributed to premature deaths; or who attempted suicide or succeeded or were shot by anti-communist fanatics.[43] The academy's general (but not universal) acquiescence to and participation in anti-Communist hysteria silenced an entire generation of radical and progressive academics, snuffing out nearly all *radical* and even mildly critical evaluation of the American way of life.[44] By 1960, with exceptions, campuses across the United States for the most part bulged with silent professors who shied away from opening the minds of their students and were mute about racial discrimination and their country's military activities abroad. The attacks on radical academics finally ended only because there were no more to attack, although Stanford continued its decade-long attack on Baran until his death in 1964 to persuade him to leave, while in 1965 Harvard did try to fire Sam Bowles for refusing to sign an oath of loyalty to the U.S. Constitution, Shaffer restricted his mid-1960s search for an academic post to states and institutions that did not require loyalty oaths, and in 1968 the University of California-Riverside refused to hire Victor Perlo for reasons supposedly independent from his position as the chief economist of the Communist Party.[45] Loyalty oaths themselves were finally declared unconstitutional in 1967, although the U.S. government still used the McCarran-Walter Act to prevent Marxist-radical economists from entering the country[46] (Schrecker 1986, 1998; Diamond 1992; Matthews 1953; Lewis 1988; Breit and Culbertson 1976; Goodwin 1998; Donnelly 1985; Phillips 1989; Rutkoff and Scott 1986; Dowd 1997; Vatter 1999; Hollingsworth, 2000; Dugger 1974; Klein 1980; Munk 1992; Struik 1993; Novick 1988; Zinn 1997; Keen 1999; Ohmann 1997; Nader 1997; Price 2004; Selcraig 1982; Warne 1993; Fariello 1995; Lydenberg 1977; *Newsletter on Intellectual Freedom*, September 1957: 10; Sturgeon 2002; Jones 2002; Shaffer 2002, 2004; Weisskopf 2002; Horn 1999; Lowen 1997; Sorenson 1980; Sherman 2006; Arestis and Sawyer 2000).

Concurrent with the anti-communist hysteria, heterodox economists were subject to two additional censures. The first was the view that free enterprise was an important basis for intellectual progress, with the implication that academic economists should believe in free enterprise as well as sell it by teaching it to their students. Supported by the business community (which also completely endorsed the anticommunist dismissals of radical and progressive academics), this view came across as anti-government, anti-union, and anti-economic planning. Thus heterodox, Keynesian, and New Deal-type economists were attacked who taught Keynesian macroeconomics or Institutional economics, criticized neoclassical theory as being anti-labor and anti-farmer, advocated some kind of government involvement in the economy, supported organized labor, and were critical of the organization, operation and methods of large business enterprises.[47] The opening salvo came in 1948 when Lorie Tarshis's introductory textbook *The Elements of Economics*, was attacked by the business-oriented McCarthyite National Economic Council for providing a Keynesian view of the macro economy and presenting Keynesian pro-government interventionist policies. A letter-writing campaign was also organized to get colleges to ban the use of the textbook in economic courses as well as to have Stanford to dismiss Tarshis. The campaign succeeded in destroying the market for the book. A comparable but much less successful campaign was directed at Paul Samuelson's textbook *Economics*, for the similar reasons that it had a strong Keynesian bias and was likely to be adopted by those who advocated government involvement in the economy.[48] The next salvo occurred at the University of Illinois in 1950, when conservative economists, with McCarthyite attitudes towards Europeans, liberals, and macroeconomics and mathematics, attacked department chair Everett Hagen. The reason for the attack was that they did not like the way he was directing the department and the fact that they were losing students to the younger "Keynesian" economists. The attack spilled onto the young, newly hired "Keynesian" economists, such as Eisner, Leonid Hurwicz, Don Patinkin, and Franco Modigliani, who were branded "pinks" or "reds" by the local press.[49] In 1951, the Texas state legislature called for the firing of Ayres because he argued in front of students that the current hostility towards government was fostered by an uncritical acceptance of the ideology of free enterprise and contributed nothing to an understanding of the development of capitalist society. By the mid-1950s, these kinds of attacks had started to decline, in part because universities objected to them and defended their professors, although some salvos did continue into the 1960s.[50] Consequently, the business community altered its strategy and essentially began to bribe economic departments to adopt its conservative position by offering money for department chairs and other scholarly activities.[51]

The second censure that heterodox economists faced resulted from their disinterest or opposition to being respectable neoclassical economists. The wartime work of economists in the context of the United States war-command economy strangely enough convinced them and post-war economists of the validity of neoclassical price theory and of the usefulness of formalistic and mathematical discourse. Moreover, in the Cold War years neoclassical theory in general and specialized areas such as linear programming and game theory received significant amounts of financial support from Washington as well as from foundations because they contributed to the "objective" needs of national defense. Consequently, in this post-war public affirmation and anticommunist context, economic departments wanted to avoid the reputation of being weak in theory and mathematical training, to ensure that their students did not leave complaining that they had not receive a good graduate education, and to be at the theoretical forefront of the discipline or at least be respectable. Continuing the trend of the 1930s of hiring up-to-date neoclassically trained theorists, departments from 1945 onward into the 1970s made clear decisions to hire well-trained neoclassical theorists with proselytizing, anti-pluralistic attitudes to transform the way economic theory was being taught to its undergraduate and graduate students. More specifically, intermediate theory courses in micro and macro were introduced and in some cases with a mathematical economics course as a prerequisite; mathematical economics courses became required for undergraduate majors; graduate theory courses became more mathematical; some degree of mathematical preparedness was expected of incoming graduate students; and graduate students were taught that a true scientific economist was one that discarded ideological biases, became detached and objective, and accepted the conclusions of logic and evidence. As a result economic departments became less eclectic and pluralistic and more neoclassical-theoretical in tone, attitude, and research, eventually to the extent that no alternatives were present or tolerated (such as at Chicago or Virginia). This was most noticeable in departments, such as Columbia, Wisconsin, Berkeley, and Ohio, which had a significant number of Institutionalists and fellow-travelers at the beginning of the post-war period but nearly none by 1970.

In addition, the AEA made significant efforts during World War II and after to increase the technical-mathematical competence of its members so that they could contribute to the concerns of the military and professionally to public policy discussions. It was realized that this would require a change in the training of graduate students, with an increased focus on a common core of theory supported by extensive training in mathematical and statistical techniques.[52] With these forces in place, over time the criteria for appointments, tenure, promotion, and salary increases gradually became how well one was versed in the technical-mathematical exposition of neoclassical theory and how well one could utilize that theory in articles that were then published in leading mainstream economic journals.[53] The rapidity with which this transformation occurred meant that both mainstream and heterodox economists who, over a ten-year period, had not kept (or would not keep) up with the advances in theory and techniques and were not active in research and publishing in the leading journals quickly suffered a relative decline in income, status, and respect as economists within their department and the profession at large (and in some cases ceased to be in the opinion of their colleagues functioning economists at all because they were anti-theory and their papers "did not contain a single graph or equation"). As a result their teaching gradually became restricted to areas outside of theory and incompatible with the conservative market ideology embodied in the theory, such as the history of economic thought, transportation, utilities, or economic planning. Heterodox economists suffered the additional fate of not even being employable.[54]

The outcome of the political repression of the post-war years in conjunction with the repressive dominance of neoclassical economists ensured the near complete suppression of Marxian economic theory and the continual decline towards the extinction of Institutional economics—as acknowledged by Bronfenbrenner (1964) and seconded by Davis (1965), as Fels (1975) noted that the economics department at Vanderbilt had not for the period 1948 to 1976 hired a Marxist economist, and as George Stigler stated:

> It is indeed true that a believer in the labor theory of value could not get a professorship at a major American university, although the reason would be that the professors could not bring themselves to believe that he was both honest and intelligent.

> (Stigler 1959: 527)

Consequently, no top-ranked doctoral program and most of the other doctoral programs, except Texas, Maryland, Oklahoma, and Utah, exposed (or wanted to expose) their students to Marxism, Institutionalism, and other heterodox approaches, although it did start to happen by the end of the 1960s (see Table 2.2 and Appendix A.6). So the neoclassical dominance and anti-pluralism of the pre-war period continued into the 1960s, which meant that of the 10,784 doctorates produced from 1941 to 1970 (see Appendix A.3), probably less than three percent had any real exposure to heterodox economics. More specifically, of the top ranked doctoral programs, only Columbia, Michigan, Yale, and Harvard had any significant promotion of

Table 2.2 Leading American economic departments with Ph.D. programs and doctoral students, 1962–74

Doctoral Programs 1959, 1966, 1970	*Ph.D Dissertations Accepted, 1962–74*
Brown	77
Carnegie-Mellon	52
Chicago	244
Columbia	314
Cornell	200
Duke	132
Harvard	439
Illinois	248
Indiana	137
Iowa State	227
Johns Hopkins	75
Michigan	201
Michigan State	207
Minnesota	206
MIT	232
North Carolina	47
Northwestern	131
Pennsylvania	301
Princeton	138
Purdue	222
Rochester	65
Stanford	178
UC-Berkeley	387
UCLA	108
Vanderbilt	71
Virginia	96
Washington	83
Washington (St. Louis)	63
Wisconsin	371
Yale	234
Subtotal	5486
Total	9265

Sources: Keniston 1959: 129; Cartter 1966: 34; Roose and Andersen 1970: 58; Harmon and Soldz 1963: 74–84; Harmon 1978: 112–13; and Appendix A.2.

heterodox economics in the late 1960s up to 1974. These top programs produced 5,486 doctorates in economics from 1962 to 1974 or 59 percent of the total number of doctorates in economics produced. Since a majority of the graduates of the top doctoral programs go on to staff the top and lesser tier doctoral programs, these near-totally trained neoclassical economists (with near-complete ignorance of heterodox economics) ensured that, in spite of the social upheaval of the 1960s, what was taught in more than 80 percent of the doctoral programs across the United States over the next thirty years was near exclusively neoclassical theory. (Fones-Wolf 1994; Schrecker 1986; Donnelly 1985; Goodwin 1998; Backhouse 1998; Phillips 1989; Sandilands

2001; Root 1956; Iversen 1959; Samuelson 1998; Colander and Landreth 1998; Selcraig 1982; Solberg and Tomilson 1997; Barber 1997a, 1997b; Modigliani 2001; Breit and Culbertson 1976; Rutherford 2000b; Stigler 1959; Stern 1963; Brazer 1982; Sass 1982; Cross 1967; Huntington 1971; Cookingham 1987; Adelman 1990; Bowen 1953; Blaug 1999; Bernstein 1990, 1995, 1999, 2001; Lampman 1993; Lowen 1997; Bronfenbrenner 1993; Jones 2002; Shaffer 2004; Schmid 2004; Kaufman 2004; Dowd 2002; Samuels 2002; Weintraub 2002; Snavely 1967; Jensen 2001; McCumber 2001; Krueger et al. 1991; Hansen 1991; Kasper, et al. 1991).

Maintaining institutional dominance: neoclassical economics and the ranking game, 1970–2000

The social upheavals in the 1960s generated space and opportunities for economic departments with doctoral programs with heterodox components to emerge in the 1970s onwards. Neoclassical economists could have tolerated this small amount of pluralism, but they did not. With the ending of the Vietnam and the Cold War and the mainstreaming of the Civil Rights, women, and gay rights movements, the traditional mechanisms that neoclassical economists relied on to help cleanse economics of heterodoxy no longer were available. Moreover, intellectual bullying of heterodox-interested graduate students, denying appointments, reappointments, and tenure to heterodox economists, red-baiting, and professional ostracism/discrimination were only somewhat effective as a control mechanism (see Chapter 4). Hence a new mechanism of social control was needed, one that appeared external to the discipline and at the same time eliminated or constrained the few departments with heterodox proclivities that emerged since 1970 and reduced the likelihood that more would emerge. As it turned out, the most potent social-control mechanism was the ranking of economic journals and departments since it provided an "objective" criteria for attacking heterodox economists and cleansing economic departments and graduate programs of heterodoxy.

Around 1970, the Institutionalists (and other heterodox economists) and neoclassical economists in the economics department at the University of Houston engaged in a struggle for control—see Chapter 4, note 22. As part of the struggle, William Moore (1972, 1973) produced the first comprehensive and influential ranking of economic journals and departments as a way to legitimize the cleansing of the department of Institutionalist economists (Lower, 2004).[55] Separately, as noted above, in the post-war period American economic departments made clear decisions to hire well-trained neoclassical theorists with proselytizing attitudes to transform the way economic theory was being taught to its undergraduates and graduate students. Consequently, by the 1960s and into the 1970s, departments in many different universities had improved so much—having highly trained faculty publishing in the "conventional" top journals and the new journals and instituted doctoral programs, that it was not completely clear who were the top department qua doctoral programs or what were the top journals. The uncertainty as to which were the top departments was, initially, a concern of government agencies and private foundations that needed a mechanism to evaluate requests for funding projects. However, by the 1980s, universities were using rankings to decide whether departments should exist, be reorganized, or abolished. Moreover, departments, university administrators, and grant-giving institutions began to base their tenure, promotion, salary, and grant decisions on the prestige (which was equated with the quality of scholarship) of the journals in which one published. In this context, it quickly became realized that Moore's ranking exercise could be used for a similar purpose, that of determining which were the top neoclassical journals and departments and which were not (Lee 2006).

Ranking journals and departments

Underlying the desire to rank departments and their doctoral programs was the fundamental assumption that economic-specific knowledge was broadly uncontested; that is, the professors and practitioners in economics generally accepted only neoclassical economics and hence produced relatively homogeneous scientific output. Without this assumption of knowledge homogeneity, department-program rankings would be largely meaningless. However, by adopting department performance indicators which are based on the assumption, it becomes easy to use the indicators to rank some departments and their programs as "less than adequate," "marginal," or "not sufficient for doctoral education" without wondering whether the ranking was due to intellectual bias against anything heterodox in nature. But to use only informed opinions (as was done in the pre-1973 department rankings—see Tables 2.1 and 2.2) invited skepticism of whether they actually identified the high scholarly productive departments. Thus quantifiable measures, such as total publications, publications per faculty, and citations per faculty, were sought. But correlations between department ranks based on informed opinion and publications suggested they were less than a near perfect match—that is, when using "crude" quantitative measures, it was possible for non-prestigious departments and the economists within them to equal if not outperform their prestigious rivals (Crane 1965: 714). Therefore, the high-ranking-reputation accorded to Harvard's economics department, for example, was still insufficiently "objectively" grounded, which left open the possibility that a lowly regarded economics department but with a sufficient number of publications, pages, and/or citations could be its "objective" equal. To reduce this possibility, a "journal quality index" was needed which established that the journals selected and ranked for the publication-based ranking of departments represented scholarly quality and hence were prestigious journals. This was achieved by selecting "blue ribbon" journals based on author institutional affiliation, subjective evaluation such as "everyone would agree are core, mainstream, highly respected, quality journals," and/or by utilizing a citation count. As a result, the use of quality journals and their rankings to rank departments produced nearly the same results as informed opinion, in part because the "journal quality index" was generated by the same informed opinion.

Coats (1971) suggested that nine journals (see Table 2.3) constituted the top and leading economic journals. Given the existence of numerous old and new economic journals and unconvinced by Coats's arguments, some twenty-one different articles producing twenty-three different rankings emerged over the next thirty years identifying the blue-ribbon, core, mainstream economic journals—see Appendix A.3. Although different criteria were used in the selection of the journals and in ranking of the journals selected, the outcome was a relatively stable hierarchy of high-quality important and low-quality unimportant economic journals. This is illustrated by reference to the list of the twenty-seven top journals generated by Diamond (1989). The list includes both the nine journals of Coats's 1971 list, the eight blue-ribbon journals identified in 1995 by Conroy and Dusasky (1995), and seventeen of the top journals of the most recent ranking—see Table 2.3 below. Moreover, from eight to twenty-two of the Diamond List journals are included in each of the 22 lists of top journals in Appendix A.3 while nine appear on 75 percent or more of the lists and fourteen appeared on over half of the lists. Thus, there is a significant degree of commonality between the various lists; and embedded in the various lists is a core of nine top journals that does not change.

From the 1920s to the 1960s, there existed an informed opinion as to who were the top economic departments with doctoral programs—see Table 2.4. However, as noted above, this view was open to question by the 1960s, hence the onslaught of fifteen department ranking studies that produced nineteen different rankings. Yet, although different criteria were used in the selection of the departments and in ranking of the departments selected, the outcome was a relatively stable set of top departments. That is, reputation-based and publication-based rankings and identification produced the same top economic departments. Moreover, this continuity among the top departments existed over time, as is illustrated in Table 2.4 which compares the top economic departments in 1925 and 1934, in 1959–70, and in 1995 to 2003. The minimal amount of variation in top-ranked departments is also be deduced from the fact that over the period of 1959 to 2003, fifteen departments appeared among the top twenty-five departments on 16–19 of the rankings, while another nine appeared on 11–15 of the rankings[56] (Lee 2006).

Rankings and heterodox economics

Together, the journal and department ranking studies establish that top departments publish in quality economic journals and quality journals publish economists from the top departments. This "empirical" fact along with

Table 2.3 Stability in top neoclassical journals, 1969–2003

Coats's List (1971)	Diamond's List (1989)	Kalaitzidakis et al. (2003)
*American Economic Review	*American Economic Review	*American Economic Review
Economica	Brookings Papers	Economic Journal
Economic Journal	Canadian Journal of Economics	*Econometrica
*Econometrica	Economica	Economic Letters
*Journal of Political Economy	Economic Inquiry	European Economic Review
*Oxford Economic Papers	Economic Journal	*International Economics Review
*Quarterly Journal of Economics	*Econometrica	Journal of Econometrics
*Review of Economics & Statistics	Economic Letters	Journal of Economic Literature
*Review of Economic Studies	European Economics Review	*Journal of Economic Theory
	*International Economic Review	Journal of Labor Economics
	Journal of Development Economics	Journal of Monetary Theory
	Journal of Econometrics	*Journal of Political Economy
	Journal of Economic Literature	Journal of Public Economics
	*Journal of Economic Theory	*Quarterly Journal of Economics
	Journal of Financial Economics	Rand Journal of Economics
	Journal of International Economics	*Review of Economics & Statistics
	Journal of Labor Economics	*Review of Economic Studies
	Journal of Law and Economics	
	Journal of Mathematical Economics	
	Journal of Monetary Economics	
	*Journal of Political Economy	
	Journal of Public Economics	
	Oxford Economic Papers	
	*Quarterly Journal of Economics	
	Rand Journal of Economics	
	*Review of Economics & Statistics	
	*Review of Economic Studies	

Source: Derived from Appendix A.3 and Coats (1971).

Note: * The Blue Ribbon Journals of Conroy and Dusasky (1995)

Table 2.4 Leading American economic departments with Ph.D. programs, 1925–2003

	Hughes (1925, 1934)	Keniston/Carter/ Roose-Andersen (1959–70)	Currently (1995–2003)*
	Brown	Brown	Brown
	Chicago	Carnegie-Mellon	Boston University
	Columbia	Chicago	Carnegie-Mellon
	Cornell	Columbia	Chicago
	Harvard	Cornell	Columbia
	Illinois	Duke	Cornell
	Iowa	Harvard	Duke
	Johns Hopkins	Illinois	Florida
	Michigan	Indiana	Harvard
	Minnesota	Iowa State	Maryland
	Missouri	Johns Hopkins	Michigan
	New York	Michigan	Minnesota
	Northwestern	Michigan State	MIT
	Ohio State	Minnesota	New York
	Pennsylvania	MIT	Northwestern
	Princeton	North Carolina	Ohio State
	Stanford	Northwestern	Pennsylvania
	Texas	Pennsylvania	Pittsburg
	UC-Berkeley	Princeton	Princeton
	Virginia	Purdue	Rochester
	Wisconsin	Rochester	Stanford
	Yale	Stanford	Texas
		UC-Berkeley	UC-Berkeley
		UCLA	UCLA
		Vanderbilt	UC-San Diego
		Virginia	Wisconsin
		Washington	Yale
		Wisconsin	
		Yale	
Total Number of Doctoral Programs	53	71	108

Source: Appendix A.4; Hughes 1925, 1934.

Note:
* Derived from Rankings N through S in Appendix A. 4

evidence from the ranking and collateral studies establishes that mainstream economics in the latter twentieth century is a class-structured as well as a hierarchical dependency structured science (Lee 2006). Consequently, the top departments qua class dictate what the appropriate graduate training is and controls access to the top journals and hence the production of neoclassical scientific knowledge. Thus scientific knowledge in economics is class-based and hence socially constructed in that it must exhibit the social characteristics most appropriate for the continued dominance and social control of economics by the top departments (Braxton 1986). Therefore, it is unsurprising that of the twenty-three journal ranking studies only nine included heterodox journals (since their knowledge is unimportant to mainstream economists); and the six journals—*Cambridge Journal of Economics, Journal of Economic Issues, Journal of Post Keynesian Economics, Review of Radical Political Economics, Review of Social Economy,* and *Science and Society*—ranked in the studies generally fell into the lower 40 percent of all ranked journals (see Appendix A.5).[57] And it is also unsurprising that the rankings of the twenty-one economic departments whose graduate programs had heterodox economics components suffered. That is, of the of the nineteen department rankings only thirteen cover "all" doctoral programs so as to include all the doctoral programs with heterodox components; of these, eight were based on publications while five were based on informed opinion; and of the eight publication-based rankings, only two included heterodox journals. The outcome is that, based on the eight department publication-based rankings, the eight departments with a major heterodox component from 1970 to 2000[58] got ranked generally in the lower 40 percent of all ranked programs and their rankings fell over time. Hence by the end of the century they were all but one (the University of Massachusetts at Amherst) ranked in the lower 25 percent (see Appendix A.6).[59] In addition, the thirteen departments with minor heterodox components in their doctoral programs[60] suffered declines in their rankings from 1959 onwards as long as the heterodox component was maintained in the doctoral program and in the department as a whole; but once the heterodoxy was dropped then their rankings improved dramatically— see Appendix A.6.[61]

The implication of the above is that the rankings of journals and departments proved an effective mechanism to control, contain, and suppress heterodox economics because the decisions to do so were locally undertaken and seen as "objective." That is, a university and/or economics department decides to increase its ranking and hence adopts policies to do this, which include positively discriminating in terms of hiring, promotion, and research strategies towards mainstream economists and their research, with the knock-on effect of increasing the neoclassical content and reducing the heterodox content of its undergraduate and graduate programs. Consequently, heterodox economists in the department are marginalized, while those who leave are not replaced and no new ones are hired. While Houston (as noted above), Texas, and Connecticut utilized rankings in this manner (see Chapter 4), the most recent example is Notre Dame.[62] In this case, the Provost of Academic Affairs, Dean of the College of Arts and Letters, and the chair of the economics department (who is a neoclassical economist) argued that the heterodox component of the economic graduate program combined with the heterodox economic research and publications in unranked heterodox journals by many of the professors had resulted in a low department ranking among U.S. economic programs at research-doctorate universities. More specifically, it was argued that publishing in top neoclassical journals was necessary for an economics department to achieve a ranking that was better than its current (1993) ranking of 81 out of 107 research-doctorate programs (see Appendix A.6). In addition, it was argued that only neoclassical economics was real scientific knowledge and hence the only kind of knowledge that appears in top journals, policy makers and the business community listen to, should be taught to undergraduates, and should be used to really train graduate students.[63] Fully imbued with the anti-pluralism spirit, their solution (which was supported by many of the neoclassical economists with the phrase "there is no viable alternative to the mainstream") was to exile the heterodox economists to a dead-end undergraduate department and create a new economics department founded on intellectual biases in which only "the very best neoclassical economists whose research ... is routinely published in the leading economic journals" will be recruited. The leading journals were suggestively defined as "the premier economics journals, or at least the top 20 journals, in the last decade." However, as suggested above and in Lee (2006), publishing in top neoclassical journals is difficult for economists in non-top twenty-five departments; and given the stability of the top twenty-five departments, entry into this elite or even the top forty is simply not a possibility for Notre Dame (Fosmoe 2003a, 2003b; Gresik 2003; Goldberger et al. 1995; The University of Notre Dame, Academic Council meeting, March 20, 2003—http://provost.nd.edu/academic-resources-and-information/ac_minutes/documents/3-20-03.pdf; Donovan 2004; and "Proposal about Economics at Notre Dame," March 17, 2003).

By the final decade of the twentieth century, the hegemony of neoclassical theory in doctoral programs (as well as undergraduate programs) was seemingly so complete that the American Economic Association Commission on Graduate Education in Economics simply did not recognize that economic theories other than neoclassical economic theory existed, while also noting that graduate programs in the United States were virtually identical in terms of the core theory taught at both the graduate and undergraduate level.[64] Such intellectual insularity was the end product of the century-long intolerant, anti-pluralistic attitude that promoted the repression of heterodox economics and its complement of indoctrinating students with neoclassical theory. These two forces also did something more: their interaction decisively and deliberately shaped American economics—its theory, culture, and attitude towards heterodox economic theory—for the second half of the twentieth century and beyond.[65] As suggested by Table 1.1 on page 3, students were taught from textbooks that only presented neoclassical price theory; and over time the deliberate sub-text conservative political message became more conservative, more overt, and more *ought*. Advocacy now became acceptable for economists because it was confined to a conservative agenda that reinforced the status quo. Moreover, economists consciously avoided grand theorizing and sought concrete projects, directed their intellectual efforts towards refining neoclassical theory without concern of how well it was grounded in real economies, and stood aloof of political advocacy by accepting the political, social, and economic status quo, thereby maintaining their century-old agreement of being ideological apologists for the business community and capitalism. Silent on social-economic issues and intellectually closed to different ways of doing economics, they reject pluralism by belittling heterodox economists (and their Ph.D. students) whose theories they opposed with taunts of non-rigorous and being brain-dead; turning out future economists with no (or at least a biased) historical understanding of their discipline and no awareness of heterodox economic approaches; promoting a repressive classroom environment where critical questions were not welcomed and responses were intended to bully students into a submissive silence; and rejecting dissertations and theses if they contained heterodox views. But such a dark cloud does have a silver lining and this was the emergence and embattled existence of heterodox economics in the United States that occurred in the last half of the twentieth century which shall be the focus of the next three chapters.

3   Radical economics in post-war America, 1945–70

The Socialist and Communist party schools that survived the inter-war period briefly blossomed in the post-war years, but were shut down by McCarthyism.[1] Still, while in existence, they promoted extensive interest in Marxian economic theory that was complemented and extended by academic scholarship. Moreover, the decline of McCarthyism in the 1950s and the collapse of the Communist Party in 1956 created intellectual room for the rise of dissent movements and thinkers, the culmination of which was the New Left movement in the 1960s. In the more questioning and dissonance atmosphere of the 1960s, radical scholarship emerged, Marxian scholarship re-emerged, and a critical perception of neoclassical economic theory developed. It was from this potent mixture of dissonance and criticism that radical economics and the Union for Radical Political Economics emerged in 1968.

Marxism and the parties schools, 1945–57

The long-standing Rand School of Social Sciences continued to operate until 1956. While McCarthyism was not the direct cause of its closure, the intellectual climate it created sharply reduced the number of students from a high of 13,000 in 1946 as well as the already low interest in Marxian economic theory. Similarly, the various schools supported partially or wholly by the Communist Party thrived with over 12,000 students taking courses in the peak years of 1947–48.[2] Economic courses offered by the schools included the American economy in the twentieth century, economic problems of the war, fundamentals of trade unionism, history of modern economic thought, economics of American industry, Soviet economy, monopoly capital after World War II, economics of socialism, economics of US foreign policy, imperialism, economics of US agriculture, and Keynes and Marx, as well as courses in Marxian political economy and advanced seminars on the first and third volumes of *Capital*. For example, the introductory political economy course at the Weydemeyer School covered topics on commodity production, labor theory of value, price and value, theory of profits, and economic crisis. Throughout the course neoclassical price theory was critically evaluated, and special attention was paid to refuting Keynes.[3] Moreover, the course on the development of modern economic thought at the Jefferson School for Social Science started with mercantilism and then dealt with the physiocrats, classical political economy, and ended with neoclassical economics and current trends in economic thought; while the course description for "Marxism vs. Keynesism" read as follows:[4]

> A critique of the theories of John Maynard Keynes and his followers. Keynesism as the dominant economic ideology of monopoly capitalism. How the social democrats, the liberal bourgeoisie and the reactionaries use Keynesism. Does Keynesism add anything new to economic theory? Tactical questions in relation to Keynesism in the labor movement. *Previous study of Marxist political economy is required.*
>
> (Jefferson School for Social Science, 1954 Summer Catalogue: 10)

However, the advent of Truman's loyalty order in 1947 which placed all the schools (and only these schools) on the Attorney General's subversive list precipitated a significant drop of students; and the passage of the McCarran Subversive Activities Control Act in 1950 produced a further drop in attendance. Finally, the Federal government used the McCarran Act to make the schools, on penalty of fines and prison, register as Communist-front organizations, knowing that the process involved would destroy them. Thus by 1957 none of the schools remained in existence[5] (Fariello 1995; Cornell 1976; Shannon 1959; Ginger and Christiano 1987; Sherman 2006; Klein 1980; Jefferson School 1953, 1955; Committee on Un-American Activities 1957; Cohen 1993; Gettleman 1990, 1993, 2001).

The various schools supported by the Communist and Socialist parties did more than just provide instruction in Marxian economic theory; they also generated a potential network of "academics" that had an abiding interest in it. For example, from 1942 to 1954 over fifty individuals taught economic courses at the School for Democracy and its successor, the Jefferson School for Social Science. While most instructors were not trained as economists and many only taught one or two courses, there were nine individuals who taught on a regular basis for six or more years and hence had more than a passing interest in Marxian theory.[6] Extrapolating from the Jefferson School experience to all the schools run by the Communist Party, the potential number of individuals in the United States, circa 1950, with an abiding if not scholarly interest in Marxian economic theory was at least 150[7] (course listings, Jefferson School of Social Science 1944–54).

Science and Society, *Monthly Review*, and Marxian scholarship, 1936–60

Complementing, supporting, and extending the grassroots interest in Marxism were the scholarly journal *Science and Society* and the magazine *Monthly Review*. First appearing in 1936, the agenda of *Science and Society* was the promotion and extension of Marxist scholarship. Being an independent Marxist journal that accepted different interpretations of Marxist theory, it quickly obtained a circulation of 4,000 by 1941 and nearly 10,000 by 1946. Because of the multi- and inter-disciplinary nature of Marxism, only a small number of articles, communications, and book reviews were written by economists and dealt with economic topics. During the first four years before the collapse of the "Popular Front" in 1940, twelve different American economists published in or were editors/contributing editors of the journal.[8] Articles ranged from an insightful discussion of the economics consequences of Keynes,[9] Institutional economics, and Marx on the corporation to computing the rate of surplus value and delineating the economic strength of the Soviet Union; and the economic books reviewed included *The Structure of the American Economy* by Gardiner Means, *Full Recovery or Stagnation* by Alvin Hansen, and *Political Economy and Capitalism* by Maurice Dobb.

The Popular Front collapsed in 1940 as a result of the Hitler–Stalin Pact and this changed atmosphere prompted many of the Marxist-heterodox economists associated with the journal to disassociate and to reject Marxian economic theory. At the same time, the United States' entry into the Second World War meant that others became involved with war-related activities that consumed all their time and energy. Consequently, of all the pre-war economists only Paul Sweezy and Anna Rochester remained associated with *Science and Society*; but four new economists contributed to the journal which published articles on social security, productivity and exploitation, labor theory of value, Keynesian economics, and Marxism and recent economic thought (see Appendix, A.7, column C, and A.8, columns A and B). Thus, complementing the grassroots interest in Marxian theory in 1950 were at least ten academic economists who could introduce students to Marxian economic theory (see Appendix, A.7, columns B, C, and H). McCarthyism, as noted in the previous chapter, nearly destroyed this collective scholarly interest in Marxism. Most of the academic economists who displayed any interest in Marxism were affected by it, such as being dismissed from their positions, driven to attempt suicide, and otherwise harassed (see Appendix, A.7, column G); and this extended to the editors of *Science and Society*, as all but one of them lost their teaching positions. Moreover, given the climate of fear, contributors ceased contributing to the journal while others used pseudonyms.[10] Although a desperate situation existed, the scholarly study of Marxian economic theory did not cease. Fewer academic economists published in the journal in the 1950s, but this was offset by an increase in the number of non-academic economists publishing there (see Appendix, A.7, columns D and I, and A.8, column C). Topics of the articles included welfare economics, falling rate of profit, value and price, and capital accumulation.[11]

Complementing *Science and Society* was the emergence of *Monthly Review* in 1949. Leo Huberman and Sweezy established *Monthly Review* as an independent socialist magazine devoted to analyzing, from a socialist point of view, developments in domestic and foreign affairs. Since subscriptions rose from 450 to 2,500 in 1950 (and 6,000 in 1954), the *Monthly Review* quickly became a forum for scholarly qua popular articles on domestic and foreign issues informed in part by Marxian theory and the center of many discussions among Marxists and similar interested fellow travelers. Moreover, Huberman published articles on the fundamentals of Marxian theory, such as surplus value, accumulation, and monopoly. In addition, Sweezy published a number of articles in which he developed his theory of monopoly capitalism, while Paul Baran published articles on economic development and Marxism. But beyond this, there were relatively few articles on or informed by Marxian economic theory by other economists.[12] This was due, in part, to the popular orientation of the magazine and, in part, to the continual suppression of Marxism and the fear it generated. In the early issues, authors' names were not put on articles because fear of economic and social reprisals; and teachers' names were not put on the *Monthly Review* mailing list. Moreover, from 1949 to 1960 and up to 1967, there was at least one article a year by an economist using a pen-name.[13] Yet, in spite of the political risk, ten different American academic economists published in the *Monthly Review* in the 1950s (see Appendix, A.7, column E)[14] (Burgum, et al. 1941; Goldway 1986; Parry, et al. 1986; Phelps 1999; Clecak 1968).

Emergence of dissonance and the new left movement, 1945–60s

In response to the Cold War after 1945, a number of peace groups emerged, such as the Marxist-oriented Committee for Non-Violent Revolution and the Gandhian-oriented Peacemakers. In 1957 the Committee for a Sane Nuclear Policy was founded for the purpose of demonstrating and lobbying for disarmament or a nuclear test-ban treaty among the great powers. Moreover, the growing post-war civil-rights movement challenged state-supported segregation which had, as an unintended consequence, a liberating effect on many people, including college students, regarding the social *status quo*. Finally, although the anti-communist crusade destroyed most of the left-wing organizations in the United States, the Communist Party and various small left-wing political sects and their university student organizations managed to survive to some degree. However, with Khrushchev's 1956 speech detailing Stalin's atrocities, the Party collapsed; and this, combined with the factionalism among the other left-wing parties and their largely inactive student organizations, meant that for the first time since the 1930s no single party dominated the American left. As a result pluralism and intellectual openness on the left emerged. These activities and events together helped produce an environment that supported magazines of the left, such as *Dissent* (1954) and *Liberation* (1956), dissident academics and intellectuals, and doubts about the labor theory of value and hence the possibility to re-examine Marxian economic theory.[15]

The dissident academics and intellectuals played an important role in this process. The contribution of some, such as Lewis Mumford, consisted in the continuing articulation of the radical and critical traditions they had adopted in the more questioning decade of the 1930s. Others, such as Paul Goodman, C. Wright Mills, William A. Williams, Galbraith, Allen Ginsberg, and Mary McCarthy, attacked the mid-century consensus view of American history, the alleged pluralism of American polity, and the unequal affluence, complacency, conformity, and suburbanization of American society. Engaging in dissenting partisanship, they emphasized the lack of meaningful work, the emptiness of material consumption that produced widespread alienation, the class and gender nature of American society, the existence of a power elite, and the militaristic nature of the United States. Finally, there were the dissidents, such as Erich Fromm and Herbert Marcuse, who developed humanist interpretations of Marxism as a way to rescue it from the grasp of Stalinism. Complementing the dissidents was the beginning of a vibrant counter-culture that had different values and promoted alternative intellectual activity than that found in mainstream American culture. Together the above influences and forces generated young university-age men and women who were, if not angry, at least dissatisfied with the subtle existential oppression imposed by mid-century America and hence disposed to alternative possibilities and solutions.

Circa 1960 American campuses bulged with students who attended overcrowded and impersonal lectures and found their inaccessible professors silent on racial segregation, hawkish on American foreign policy, and bullish about the American way of life. In addition, the traditional forms of socializing and the ways of building networks of friends became less legitimate. Finally, as a legacy of the anticommunist scare, most universities maintained tight social and political control over student activities, including bans on progressive-left speakers, such as, in the case of the University of Texas, Eleanor Roosevelt and Adlai Stevenson, and adhering to state bans on teaching communism. Many students simply bought into this less than perfect situation. They were indifferent to ideas in the classroom or to political and social events but were interested in their social life and in making grades and seeking credentials for employment and status in corporate America. Others, however, sought alternative ways of improving their campus lives. They favored jeans, wore longer hair, and went to coffee houses off campus where they talked politics, philosophy, and literature. Revitalizing student politics and engaging in student protests to address these issues was one way; another way was to get involved in meaningful political activism. Thus these disenchanted young men and women who threw away their first vote on communist or socialist candidates became involved in the civil-rights movement through which they saw discrimination, illiteracy, poverty, and hate that they had never experienced. They also became aware of the Vietnam War and hence became involved in the anti-war movement. Together these activities turned the disenchanted into angry young men and women who engaged in campus protest against the war, racial segregation, and restrictions on the freedom of speech.[16] And it was these individuals who became attracted to campus activist groups in the late 1950s and later to the newly formed Student Peace Union (1959), Young People's Socialist League (1960), and Students for a Democratic Society (1960), and the emerging New Left movement. Further events of the 1960s, such as the Cuban missile crisis, uprising in the black urban ghettos, the continuation and expansion of the Vietnam War, and the May 1968 student uprising in Paris stimulated the growth of the New Left. In response to these events, the Students for a Democratic Society (SDS) established the Economic Research and Action project (1963–65), which involved SDSers trying to organize the ghetto poor in Newark, Chicago, and other Northern cities. Moreover, the SDS as well as other New Left groups responded to President Johnson's bombing of North Vietnam in early 1965 with protest meetings and rallies that in turn lead to teach-ins, first starting at the University of Michigan and then spreading to more than thirty universities.

While the factors generating campus activism led students to examine Marxism, Marxist theory and ideology played a minor role in the New Left movement up until 1965. This was due, in part, to interest in other ideas and ideologies such as existentialism, anarchism, syndicalism, and utopianism; and, in part, to the pervasive desire to engage in direct action activities that would change the system. Moreover, interest in Marxism was mostly directed at Marx's concept of man and alienation rather than at his economic theorizing, since the language of the latter seemed hollow and tied to the past by its association with the discredited leftists of the 1930s. Finally, there was an indigenous American radicalism deeply embedded in American thought that railed against large corporations, Wall Street, and the exploitative nature of free enterprise and the status quo.[17] As a result, the young activists initially preferred to call themselves liberals or radicals, not socialists, Marxists, or leftists. However, by the mid-1960s as a result of the mounting conservative backlash, their self-identification terminology moved predominately towards radical with a clear leftish hue, but still not socialist or Marxist. To adopt the latter label meant for the movement activists accepting a particular body of ideology-theoretical ideas to the exclusion of others; and they simply had no interest in doing so.

By the mid-decade, there was a growing uneasiness among some SDSers that the SDS and the movement lacked positive alternatives and ideological foundations to challenge and replace capitalism and its corporate liberalism ideology. Hence they began to pay attention to the work of the French Marxists, Ernest Mandel, Andre Gorz, and Serge Mallet. In addition, the SDS opened its newsletter, *New Left Notes*, to economic articles utilizing Marxian and radical economic analysis.[18] Finally, in June 1966 it set up the Radical Education Project (REP) to provide competent research on the issues of left program and theory to educate student activists, and to extend the movement beyond college students.[19] To achieve this end, it established research and study groups in areas such as education and the university, the ghetto, labor, Latin America, imperialism, political economy, and the power structure in local communities.[20] It also published literature and study guides on various themes including Marxism, established *Radicals in the Professions Newsletter*, sponsored conferences to bring dispersed radicals together, and ran a speakers' bureau. But knowledge of Marxian political economy among the participants in the New Left remained minimal and somewhat incoherent because there was no established mechanism by which they could learn it.[21] Consequently the older participants who had time to pick up Marxism in an ad hoc way could not really communicate with the younger ones who had not been able to do so. Thus, most New Left participants maintained the position that Marxian political economy was not essential to revolutionary theory or for revolutionary consciousness. Instead the popular view was that large numbers of people are organized around obvious issues, not whether the rate of profit falls or the distinction between absolute and differential rent (Unger 1974; Isserman 1987, 1988; Langer 1989; Monhollon 2002; Wynkoop 2002; McMillian 2000; Zinn 1969; O'Neill 2001; Downing and Salomone 1969; Billingsley 1999; Rossinow 1998; Bunting 2002; Rudy 1996; Sale 1974; Schiffrin 1968; Horowitz 1968).

Radical and Marxian economics, 1960–70[22]

As noted in the previous sections, scholarly discourse on Marxian economic theory existed throughout the 1950s, in spite of the repressive conditions. Aside from the articles and discussion found in *Science and Society*, *Monthly Review*, and *Dissent*, there were Du Bois clubs and self-study Marxist groups (many of which were spied upon by the FBI) scattered in cities, colleges, and universities around the country that were led by individuals generally trained in subjects other than economics. In addition, some university student could attend the lectures of radical-Marxist economist, such as Baran, Davis, Niebyl, Sweezy, Dowd, Shlakman, Montgomery, and others (see Appendix, A.7, columns H and I). However circa 1960 saw the beginning of increasing grassroots interest in radical-Marxian economic theory that came into full bloom by the end of the decade. For example, there was a Economics Study Group in New York City at which *Alfred Evenitsky* read the paper "Monopoly Capitalism and Marx's Economic Doctrines" before it was published in *Science and Society*.[23] Moreover, socialist and communist clubs began springing up on campuses (quickly followed by the local FBI opening a file on them). Concurrently, there was the emergence of the New Left and the journal *Studies on the Left*.[24] Established as a radical history journal whose purpose was to challenge the 1950s consensus view of American history, *Studies* published articles dealing with the economic, political, and social development of the United States. By 1962, this purpose crystallized into the "corporate liberalism" thesis. The thesis drew upon, in part, Marxist theory and addressed the Marxist concern about the links between economic and political power in a capitalist economy. Consequently, the journal published a number of economic articles and book reviews that had some bearing on the thesis. For example, James Becker wrote an extraordinary article in which he combined Keynes, Means's administered prices doctrine, Institutionalist literature, and aspects of Marxian theory to produce a good first approximation of the economic theory underlying the corporate liberalism thesis. There were also articles discussing the need for community unions to carry on the struggle against corporate capitalism as well as book reviews of Baran and Sweezy's *Monopoly Capitalism* and Gillman's *Prosperity in Crisis* that criticized their Marxian-Keynesian interpretation of the American economy (Schiffrin 1968; Langer 1989; Evenitsky 1960; Wynkoop 2002; Bronfenbrenner 1964, 1973; Wiener 1989; Sherman 2006; Buhle 1990; Mattson 2003; Becker 1963, 1966; O'Connor 1964a, 1964b; Lebowitz 1966).

The radical-Marxist economic articles (which drew upon the breath of heterodox-radical-Marxian economic theory) and reviews in *Studies* contributed to the growing number of similar articles and reviews also appearing in *Science and Society*. Significantly, many of the articles dealt with theoretical issues that were central to Marxian theory, such as articles on the falling rate of profit, Marxism and monopoly capital, reproduction and crisis, productive and unproductive labor, imperialism, and value theory. *Monthly Review* also carried substantive articles on imperialism, economic stagnation and monopoly capital, economic planning, monopoly, and corporations, although written in a more popular style for intellectuals and activists. Moreover, Baran and Sweezy's use of facts combined with a particular utilization of Marxian theory in *Monopoly Capital* (1966) to examine economic stagnation and monopoly capital (later supplemented by the work of Harry Magdoff and Harry Braverman which produced a distinct approach to Marxism, known as the Monthly Review school, the first of its kind in the United States) was well received by those in the movement. *Monopoly Capital* quickly became the book to read, discuss in study groups, and recommend to radical friends.[25]

This increased scholarly interest in Marxian economic theory mirrored the general rise of interest in Marxism. In 1964 a number of young faculty members at Rutgers University and the Polytechnic Institute of Brooklyn felt that there were enough left academics to hold a conference where particular issues and themes could be addressed from a socialist perspective. Thus a call for papers was sent out announcing a Socialist Scholars Conference (SSC) for socialist scholars of all kinds. The response was overwhelming, with around one thousand scholars and activists attending the first conference in 1965. The SSC continued for another five years, with the last conference in 1970.[26] Because historians established the SSC and the subsequent steering committees consisted of academics and scholars from across the social sciences and humanities, the Conference theme of socialist scholarship covered a diverse set of historical, literature, political, and economic topics or subjects addressed from those perspectives. The topics of the economic papers included imperialism (Magdoff 1967), third world workers (Sweezy 1967), and workers and revolution (Mandel 1968).[27] There were also papers on administrative corporatism, economic imperialism, and the political economy of Ernest Mandel. In addition to the SSC, radical historians began to find Marxism a useful tool in starting their research, as illustrated by the founding in 1967 of the SDS-sponsored journal of the history of American radicalism *Radical America*. The editors of the journal not only voiced their support of Marxism, they also published articles on reading Marx and Mandel's Marxist economic theory.

The final set of forces supporting the growth of interest in specifically Marxian economic theory emanated from the Communist Party, which was slowly recovering from the disastrous years of the 1950s. In 1964 the historian Herbert Aptheker established The American Institute for Marxist Studies (AIMS) for the purposes of encouraging Marxist and radical scholarship in the United States and bringing Marxist thought into the forum of reasonable debate to produce meaningful dialogue among Marxist and non-Marxist scholars and writers. Its major activity was publishing a newsletter that provided bibliographical information on publications and dissertations that dealt in some way with Marxism and the Soviet Union.[28] It also sponsored symposiums on various topics, including one in 1965 on Marxian methodology in the social sciences; but economics was not one of the disciplines represented and discussed. A second activity was the establishment of the Center for Marxist Education in New York City in 1969. The purpose of the Center was to fill the "serious theoretical gap in the tremendous activist [New Left] movement which has arisen in reaction to the poverty, racism, violence, corruption and degradation which characterizes life today in capitalist United States." In its first year, it offered classes on various topics in revolutionary theory including monopoly capitalism and political economy. Taught by Perlo, the monopoly capitalism course entailed a close study of American monopoly capitalism.[29] The course on political economy, taught by Party members who had no apparent training in economics, dealt with the origins and basic features of capitalism, labor theory of value, exploitation, accumulation of capital, causes and consequences of economic crises, imperialism, state monopoly capitalism, and the general crisis of capitalism[30] (Goldway 1986; Sharpe, et al. 1966; Davis 1961, 1962; Evenitsky 1963; Sherman 1970; Meek 1961; Clecak 1968; Tonak and Savran 1987; Baran 1957; Baran and Sweezy 1966; Magdoff 1969; Braverman 1974; Phelps 1999; Wynkoop 2002; Barkan 1997; Fischer, et al. 1971; Wiener 1989; Gilbert 1968; Levine 1969, 1970; *AIMS Newsletter* 2.6, November–December 1965: 2; and Mattick 1969).

The various Marxist and radical journals, Socialist Scholars Conferences, and the educational activities of the Communist Party provided a rich and multi-faceted intellectual and activist environment for radical-Marxists. Through these outlets and activities, it was possible for like-minded economists to publish and engage in radical-Marxist discourse independently of mainstream economists and their journals.[31] However, the number of core radical-Marxist economists in the 1960s prior to the formation of the Union for Radical Political Economics remained relatively small at twenty-six with another twenty-four as fellow travelers.[32] Moreover, the outlets and activities did not provide the specialist forums at which the economists could discuss topics of particular interest to them. And nor did they provide the academic base that was needed to assist the younger economists in their academic careers. To overcome these problems but at the same time staying within and enlarging this alternative intellectual environment, young radical-Marxist economists established in 1968 the Union for Radical Political Economics.

Emergence of the union for radical political economics, 1965–70

In July 1967, the SDS-Radical Education Project hosted a conference on Radicals in the Professions that focused on the questions that were being discussed by radicals in academia and other professions everywhere: was it possible to be a radical in the professions and should radical academics try to work within academia or devote their time to the movement? The conference was well attended; consequently a second conference for radicals in the professions was held in January 1968.[33] The discussion at this conference dealt, in part, with how radicals could influence their graduate departments and with developing radical professional groups. Two months later, in March 1968, a New University Conference was held with the purpose of establishing a national organization for radical faculty and graduate students.[34] With such ideas in the air, it is not surprising that over the next two years young radical academics established radical caucuses within the American Anthropologists Association, Political Science Association, American Sociological Association, the Modern Language Association, and the American Psychiatric Association, with the common objectives of getting "radical" sessions on the national conference programs and influencing the outcomes of the business meetings. Over time, working from within either resulted in accommodation by the existing organization, as in the case of the Modern Language Association; or in non-accommodation resulting in moves by the radicals to set up an alternative organization, as in the case of the American Historical Association and the founding of the *Radical Historians' Newsletter* (1970) and later the Mid-Atlantic Radical Historians' Organization (1973) and its journal *Radical History Review* (1974). Economics was not immune to this, but with a difference. Instead of first forming a radical caucus within the AEA and lobbying for their own program space, the young radical economists directly established their own independent opposition organization, the Union for Radical Political Economics (URPE). The explanation for this abrupt rupture with the AEA is found in the diverse set of forces supporting radical-Marxian economics in the 1960s. The first was the role of *Studies on the Left, Science and Society*, and *Monthly Review* in promoting scholarship in radical-Marxian economic theory, followed by the Socialist Scholars Conferences and *Radical America*, both of which promoted socialist scholarship. Finally, the Communist Party promoted Marxism through scholarship and popular education. While important for the growth in interest and scholarship in radical-Marxian economics, they did not meet the academic needs of young radical economists. So taking their destiny in their own hands, they established URPE (Attewell 1984; Sale 1974; Ericson 1975; Skotnes 2001; Lemisch 1989; Novick 1988; Wiener 1989; Sachs 1967; Nickerman 1967; Booth 1968; Morris 1968; Brown 1968; Gordon, et al. 1969; Wolfe 1971; Nicolaus 1973; Bloland and Bloland 1974).

At the University of Michigan, the angry young men and women coalesce into a cadre of activists and radicals who became involved in the SDS. In particular, Michigan economic graduate students, such as Howard Wachtel and Michael Zweig, became involved in the SDS early on; and in 1966, another Michigan economics student, Barry Bluestone, became involved in the SDS-related Radical Education Project, also located at Michigan. The concern of these (and other) graduate students was that they felt that the neoclassical economic theory they were being taught failed to address important real-world problems.[35] On 24 March 1965, less than two months after American warplanes had begun systematic bombing of North Vietnam, Michigan had the first teach-in in the United States on the Vietnam War. Nearly three thousand students participated in the teach-in, which consisted of lectures and discussion sessions and lasted throughout the night. Out of the experience there emerged, a year later in April 1966, a Free University at which a number of seminars were given, including one on "Modern Political Economy." The seminar prompted a number of the economics graduate students who attended it to explore new issues, ideas, and approaches to economic problems and related social issues. Recognizing the need for continuing contact and discussion, a series of three meetings were held in January 1967 to further delineate the subjects economics failed to examine and to explore the implications of such an undertaking.[36] The concern raised by participants was that the socialization of young economists through the tenure process put pressure on them to do conventional mainstream research; but if they decided not to pursue mainstream research they quickly would become isolated. To deal with both negative consequences, it was felt that some kind of group was necessary, as it would provide a social network for the sharing of a similar critical approach to economics, provide intellectual stimulation, and help members avoid being diverted from their social concerns into the normal pursuits of academic economists.[37] Establishing such a group would require finding an amendable economics department and become members of it. As this would take time to accomplish, an interim solution was pursued—that of establishing an identifiable group of individuals pursuing economic and social questions compatible with modern political economy.[38]

Following nearly two years of discussion, influenced by the formation of the New University Conference, and at the height of the student rebellion, a meeting was called to discuss the establishment of an ongoing radical economics organization. A five-day Radical Economics Conference was held at Michigan from September 4 to September 8, 1968. It was attended by a small group of twelve graduate students and faculty members, all of whom were affected and influenced by the civil-rights movement, Vietnam War, feminist movement, and the New Left. Included in the group were Bluestone, Kelman, Wachtel, and John Weeks from Michigan, Zweig from SUNY Stony Brook, Ted Behr and Peter Bohmer from MIT, Michael Reich from Harvard, and others from Eastern Michigan, Miami University, and the Institute for Policy Studies.[39] After much intense discussion the participants emerged from the conference with the agenda of forming an "on-going organization of new left economists committed to radical teaching, research, and organizing both within educational institutions and within the movement itself." As a result, a Radical Economics Secretariat was established at Michigan that, in turn, developed a prospectus for The Union for Radical Political Economics.[40]

The prospectus began with a short synopsis of the poverty of mainstream economics that can be summarized as "The Living Dead: Life Without Compassion:"

> We have been called to accept,
> to discuss, to analyze
> the status quo and its needs for hegemony.
> Let us work for its continuance and not
> question its effects.
> For our responsibility is to the biding of the
> supplier of our paychecks and not humanity.
> And compassion for and commitment to
> > the starving
> > the sick
> > the estranged
> > the oppressed
> > the imprisoned
> is irrelevant to
> > our research
> > our teaching
> > our advocacy
> > our identity as economists.

It then argued that a new type of economist was needed:

> An economist concerned with the important problems of the world in which he lives and works; an economist willing to jettison the irrelevant and incorrect portions of the received doctrine, while at the same time willing to embark upon the arduous task of constructing a new economics.
> (Wachtel 1968: 18; also see Zweig 1968)

Recognizing that this new economist could not emerge without some help from his/her friends, the prospectus proposed the establishment of a new organization of economists that would promote an interdisciplinary approach to social problems and the resurrection of the political economist, new courses that reflected the urgencies of the day, a new set of priorities for economic research and joint research, and economic analysis for the needs of the movement. The prospectus closed with the warning that without the existence of an organization for radical political economists, the pressures of society and the mainstream socialization of university and government employment would eventually convert them into supporters of the status quo.

The first activity of the Secretariat was to sponsor a New England Radical Economics Conference, organized by Behr and held at MIT in mid-November.[41] The success of the conference, at which there were over 120 participants, prompted the Secretariat to hold a nationwide conference in Philadelphia on December 19–21, 1968 and distribute the following announcement to about 250 campuses:

RADICAL ECONOMICS CONFERENCE
A national radical economic conference sponsored by the Union for Radical Political Economics will be held in Philadelphia Dec. 19–21. This is an effort to bring together academic economists, non-academic economists, Movement organizers, and other interested persons to discuss "radical economics" and establish a firm basis for a national organization of radical economists. Some of the topics to be discussed are (1) a radical critique of contemporary economics (2) radical teaching and research (3) poverty problems (4) economic development and imperialism (5) the economics of democratic control (6) the relevance of Marxist, neo-classical, and institutional economic analysis to current problems.

(*New Left Notes*, December 11, 1968: 6)

The Philadelphia conference was also a success with over 150 participants from fifty different universities and organizations and as many diverse political perspectives in attendance.[42] At the conference business session, URPE was formally established as a nationwide professional organization, independent of the American Economics Association, with an executive committee charged to oversee the publishing of working and occasional papers, the establishment of a newsletter through which to disseminate information to its members, and the establishment of a quarterly bulletin, which eventually became the *Review of Radical Political Economics*, for the publication of scholarly papers (Unger 1974; Menashe and Radosh 1967; Brazer 1982; McMillan 2000; Wachtel 1968; Wachtel and Bluestone 1969; Bluestone 1969; Wachtel and Vanderslice 1973; Reich 1995; Arestis and Sawyer 2000; Mata 2005; URPE 1969; *AIMS Newsletter*, November–December 1968: 2).

Once formed, URPE and its members quickly undertook activities to develop an ongoing community of radical economists outside of the mainstream community and its socializing influences. In particular, at the local and regional level, regional and area organizers were appointed, local chapters and collectives established such as the New York chapter (1969), the American University collective (1969), and the Wright State University collective (1970), and at least six regional conferences were held at American University, MIT, University of California-Berkeley, University of Michigan, and Oberlin College. At the national level, a national conference to be held in August was established for the purpose of activist and theoretical discussions and for URPE people to get to know each other. In addition, there were activities at the annual Allied Social Sciences Association meetings, starting with Zweig who lead a couple of seminars of the "radicals economics group" at the 1968 meetings; staging a "counter-convention" at the meetings the following year with the theme of "towards a radical political economics" consisting of eight sessions, seventeen papers, and two panel discussions; and finally at the 1970 meetings, putting on a session on radical approaches to the teaching of economics followed by four workshops, some films and a party.[43] These activities, through their intellectual, activist, and social discourse, brought and bonded together radical economists by establishing community-wide goals and values. To support and reinforce this emerging community, URPE used its newsletter to disseminate information about local, regional, and national activities, to announce the establishment of graduate economic programs that contained radical components, to identify economic departments that hire radical economists,[44] to carry course outlines of interest to its members,[45] and to promote radical economic and political discourse. Finally, the establishment of the *Review of Radical Political Economics* provided an outlet for scholarly papers written by members of URPE that was, most importantly, an alternative to the mainstream journals.[46] Consequently, URPE membership increased from less than fifty in December 1968 to 300 plus by February 1969 to over 950 members by mid-1971 (and over 1600 members by mid-1975).

Complementing the organizational and social building of URPE was the development of a *pluralistic* radical intellectual milieu compatible with the URPE prospectus. The membership of URPE included both academics and activists (many times combined in the same person). Consequently, much of the discourse among the membership focused on how to combine radical scholarship with working for the movement. The concerns were evident in conference topics and papers and interchanges in the *Newsletter*.[47] More specifically, the concern with radical scholarship focused on critiques of neoclassical economics and the development of a radical-heterodox (at least to some degree) economic theory; while the concern with activism focused on advocacy economics. The resolution to this potentially divisive discourse came in terms of scholarly work on pressing social and economic issues. That is, the critique of neoclassical economics produced the consensus that, as currently articulated, it could not adequately deal with the social and economic problems that were of concern to the movement. Hence, the contribution of URPE economists to the movement would be the theoretical and empirical investigations of the problems of imperialism, unemployment, gender, class divisions, racism, education, poverty, crime, health, housing, transportation, inequality, and the environment, and the advocacy of radical solutions. Since most economists in URPE were educated in economic departments that taught only neoclassical economic theory, their knowledge of Marxist economic theory and other heterodox theoretical frameworks was meager at best. Keeping with the pluralistic, co-operative ethos of URPE, a multi-faceted theoretical discourse emerged whose purpose was the development of a radical (not necessarily Marxian or more specifically the *Monthly Review* approach to Marxism) economic theory that could then be used to better inform the investigation of social and economic problems and their solutions.[48] This interactive, synergistic relationship between activism and theory generated by 1970 a distinct radical intellectual milieu that bound together all members of URPE, whether they are academics, activists, or both[49] (*URPE Newsletter* 1969–71; Behr 1969b; Anonymous 1969; Michelson 1969a, 1969b; Bronfenbrenner 1970a; Ulmer 1970; Salmans 1970; Hymer and Roosevelt 1972; Worland 1972; Francis 1972; Weaver 1970; Franklin and Tabb 1974; Mata 2005; Attewell 1984).

The response of neoclassical economists to the emergence of radical economics and URPE was, as will be shown in Chapter 4, one of antagonism and bewilderment. They were also bewildered as to what radical economics was if it was not Marxian economics and who were radical economists if they were mot Marxists. Without a historical perspective and awareness of the darker side of American society, politics, and academia, they did not realize that post-war radical economics and the identity of radical economists was plausibly the bastard child of McCarthyism. That is, the Marxists and radical-heterodox economists that emerged from McCarthyism felt attacked, suppressed, and emotionally drained. With their scholarly community and supporting institutions in tatters and the near absence of Marxist economics being taught in universities, the gradual re-emergence of a broadly critical radical economics in the 1950s drew upon a broader range of economic arguments.[50] While the older economists who were trained prior to 1945 still adhered to a dogmatic Marxian theory, the few younger economists were more theoretically pluralistic in their outlook. The older economists provided links to the past: to the old (Soviet-style) Marxist legacy of the 1930s and 1940s and to the institutions and journals that supported it. But as time went on, these links faded more into the background or simply became less prominent as the older economists began retiring from the field and the younger economists, many of whom had not been introduced to Marxian theory in any systematic manner, focused their attention on the events of the 1960s and the new intellectual ideas and new journals that emerged at the same time. Consequently, the activities of the 1960s, such as AIMS and the Socialist Scholars Conferences, that were linked to traditional Marxism had a small impact on the establishment of URPE and on the emerging radical economists.[51] Specifically, the initial active membership of URPE was mostly academics, that is, they were members of academic institutions (sixty-two out of seventy or 88 percent of the URPE members listed in A.9, columns H and I in the Appendix). As noted above there were fifty radical-Marxist and fellow traveler economists in the 1960s prior to the formation of URPE; however, only eleven participated in its formation and early activities. Thus, on the one hand, the formation of URPE dramatically increased the number of radical-Marxist economists by over 100 percent; but on the other hand, URPE's connection with the previous generation of radical-Marxist economists and the influence of this generation on URPE was next to minimal.[52] In short, radical economics, radical economists, and URPE emerged without a past in part because McCarthyism was successful in weakening the dominance of Marxism among American leftists and radicals. And it is this historical legacy combined with the insistence on the pluralism of ideas and theories as well as a life of commitment to activism for dealing with the social-economic problems facing Americans that defined and hence constituted radical economics and the identity of radical economists in 1970, which is so well captured in the following passage recited by University of Texas students in 1961 who embraced a "life of commitment":

> We have been called to live:
> to be responsive and sensitive; …
> Let us take upon ourselves the urgencies of the world, …
> enable us to be responsible: …
> to the people of this world
> may we have compassion for
>> the starving
>> the sick
>> the estranged
>> the oppressed
>> the imprisoned.

(Rossinow 1998: 75)

4 The contested landscape of American economics, 1965–80

Dominance of neoclassical economics

By 1970 there were over 15,000 American economists, most of who were neoclassical economists and belonged to the AEA. Because of the repressive dominance of neoclassical economists and because of the pre- and post-war repression of heterodox economics and economists, neoclassical economists shared membership in a tightly knit hierarchically-arranged community. This community accepted a single relatively homogeneous body of ideas or theories, shared the same set of standards—theoretical, technical, and empirical—for evaluating research and hierarchically ranking publications, engaged in a network of inter-institutional and interpersonal ties that promoted communication, reciprocated employment and conference participation opportunities, and rejected or suppressed all else.[1] Clearly, the neoclassical community circa 1970 institutionalized the anti-pluralism, red scare-repression, and the McCarthyism values of the previous seventy years. But it did more; it institutionalized what can be called "thinking like an economist." That is, to think like an economist is to use chains of deductive reasoning in conjunction with neoclassical models to help understand economic phenomena. It includes identifying tradeoffs in the context of constraints, tracing the behavioral implications of some change while abstracting from other aspects of reality, explaining the consequences of aggregation, and using equilibrium as a theoretical organizing concept. To violate this neoclassical creed, to not think like a neoclassical economist, is not to be an economist at all. Fortunately for neoclassical economists, most students that entered the Ph.D. programs in the 1950s to the middle 1960s were intellectually incapable of critically reflecting on what "thinking like an economist" should be. Lacking a free intellect and having a mind never opened to alternative theoretical approaches, these economics graduate students could only pursue truth where their professors let them. Ironically, this made them (and only them) perfectly fit for membership in the economics academic community.

The homogeneous nature of the body of theory held by the neoclassical community was revealed in a survey of the present state of economics that was published in 1970 (Ruggles 1970a). In the survey, the discipline was defined in terms of understanding how the economy operated; and, by completely ignoring the existence of heterodox economic theory, this understanding was conceived solely in terms of the mechanisms by which scarce resources were allocated, prices determined, income distributed, and economic growth took place. Moreover, it was argued that the economic theory which delineated this understanding provided much of the unity of the discipline. And within economic theory, it was microeconomic theory, as represented in terms of core tools and models in Table 1.1, which was the central core on which economics as a whole was based. Finally, it was argued that "The acquisition of this understanding has been cumulative, and there now exists a well-established core of economic theory and an economic accounting framework which provides the economists with his basic working tools" (Ruggles 1970b: 11).

The survey faithfully reported the existing consensus among neoclassical economists as to what constituted economics and the usual standards of honest, unbiased scientific work. Thus, any negative criticism in terms of not examining important and pressing social-economic problems, of the esoteric-irrelevant nature of economic theory and its mathematical models, and of the conservative bias of neoclassical economic theory and neoclassical economists or suggestions that economics needs to be completely rebuilt on a different theoretical foundation was met with forceful, denigrating rebuttals, snide comments (such as that critics rarely seem to do any real research), and the claim that nearly all was right with economics. So, as a community, it is not surprising that neoclassical economists felt that heterodox economists had a faulty understanding of neoclassical economic theory, were technically deficient and their theories technically inferior to neoclassical theory, and held ideologically-slanted political and social values that led them to accept out-dated and erroneous theories and at the same time prevented them from understanding how markets really worked and from doing any real research.[2] Of course the irony of this attitude was that the concurrent capital controversy showed that neoclassical economists had a faulty understanding of their own theory. In fact, by the late 1960s, neoclassical economists seemed to be very much on the defensive as some graduate students were asking them impolite questions such as "please define capital" and they resented it. Hence, it is not surprising they would lash out stating that heterodox theory lacked scientific rigor and was non-quantifiable, while heterodox economists "pandered to the prejudices and abilities of dumbbells, who can't understand any other variety" (Bronfenbrenner 1973: 5).[3] Thus, if heterodox economists and the mush they called theories were to be taken seriously, neoclassical economists argued, they would have to become more neoclassical in language, technique, theorizing, and style; and if they refused, then their tenure as academic economists should be brought to an end and as a result their theoretical mush would deservedly disappear from economics. Given this intellectual climate, by not accepting the terms offered and, at the same time, persisting in developing an alternative theory, open-minded, inquisitive economic graduate students (heterodox or not) as well as outright heterodox economists faced intellectual bullying, hostility, rejection, if not outright reprisals in terms of fewer academic appointments, limited tenure and promotion prospects, fewer publications, and denial of access to sessions at the annual conference of the AEA[4] (Siegfried, et al. 1991; Weintraub 2002; McCumber 2001; Heilbroner 1970, 1971; Eagly 1974; Ruggles 1970b; Leontief 1971; Schultze 1971; Gurley 1971; Olson and Clague 1971; Tobin 1973; Blackman 1971; Heller 1975; Lindbeck 1977; Bach 1972; Bronfenbrenner 1970b, 1973; Solow 1970a, 1970b, 1971; Sowell 1993; Reder 1982; Lebowitz 2002; Hunt 1972; Meranto Meranto, and Lippman 1985; Shapiro 2005).

In spite of the changing social and political environment and the rise of the New Left in the 1960s, American economic departments largely maintained an anti-radical, anti-protest feeling, along side its pro-free enterprise position. In particular, unlike professors in English, philosophy, history, and other disciplines, most economists did not become involved in civil rights and anti-war activities on campus. Rather it would seem that they accepted to some degree the anti-civil rights, the non-existence of racism, anti-communism rhetoric that permeated society at large.[5] Moreover, they believed that neoclassical economic theory and its applications to the real world should be accepted by students without question or discussion. However, some students found it sterile and innately conservative. So they doubted and questioned the theory only to be slapped down by the professor with denigrating phrases, such as "perhaps you should study neoclassical theory and learn it thoroughly before you criticize it" or "if you continue to have these doubts about the theory, perhaps you should drop out of economics."[6] Undaunted by the intolerant atmosphere in the classroom, they searched elsewhere for readings and syllabuses in economics that would be fresher and more challenging than the one they were using. They found Sweezy and the *Monthly Review*; and the Marxist organizations contacted were happy to respond. But these efforts did not undermine the restricted approach to economic presented in the theory classes. These conservative, intolerant, anti-pluralistic attitudes held by neoclassical economists in nearly all economic departments (and in the neoclassical community at large) towards doubts, criticisms, and the movement combined with the dominance of neoclassical economic theory in terms of teaching, research, and disciplinary status made it difficult for radical-Marxist, social and Institutional economists to obtain academic appointments in the period of high demand for academic economists the 1960s to the mid-1970s, especially at Ph.D.-granting institutions.[7]

Even before trying to obtain teaching positions, potential heterodox economists faced a hostile academic environment where administrators (prompted perhaps by the FBI) and most faculty viewed them as possible disrupters and believed that they would use their teaching positions to indoctrinate students in one particular view point, use political tests for hiring and granting tenure and promotion, and use the university to promote a political agenda. The depressing irony that this was precisely what universities and mainstream academic economists had been doing for the entire twentieth century and especially since 1945 was not lost on them. This discriminatory and hostile environment was for radical academics and heterodox economists in particular captured in the pity phrase: "two radical academics is one too many and one heterodox economist is one too many." In addition, heterodox economists trying to obtain teaching positions for the first time also had particular problems because the institutions to which they were applying would receive letters of recommendation saying that they were troublemakers.[8] But even if heterodox economists obtained appointments, these two factors meant that they faced harassment, received warnings about engaging in political activities, and, in any case, were often denied reappointments and/or tenure, an outcome that frequently occurred in other academic disciplines as well.[9] The most publicized event in this latter regard occurred at Harvard when in 1972 its economics department denied tenure to Sam Bowles and reappointment to Arthur MacEwan on the grounds that radical economics was not a significant contribution to economics, with the result that, by 1974, four of its five radical economists had left.[10] Similar events occurred at Yale University where in 1969–70 Stephen Hymer was refused tenure and promotion after he made a public commitment to Marxism, at the University of Massachusetts at Amherst when in 1972 Michael Best was denied reappointment because he was not an economist with promise since he intended to publish in the *Review of Radical Political Economics*, at San Diego State College where in 1973 Peter Bohmer was fired for being a radical economist, at Idaho State University where in 1973 Ron Stanfield was not reappointed solely because of his radical views, at San Jose State University where in May 1974 three heterodox economists, David Landes, Gayle Southworth, and Andy Parnes, were replaced by four conservative neoclassical economists and Douglas Dowd was continually threaten with dismissal by its President, at St. Mary's College where in 1974 Eugene Coyle was denied tenure for not teaching traditional microeconomics in the usual uncritical manner, at University of Massachusetts-Boston where in 1975 Paddy Quick's contract was not renewed because of her political activities, and at Stanford in 1975 when Foley was denied tenure because of his growing interest and research in Marxian economics.[11]

Harassment, red-baiting, discrimination, and exclusion of established and/or tenured heterodox economists by their neoclassical colleagues and conservative administrators also occurred.[12] Much of this took place within the department in the form of limiting their possibility of teaching heterodox economic material to undergraduate and graduate students. In particular, since 1945 history of thought, economic history, and labor economics were courses in which undergraduate and graduate students were introduced to radical-heterodox issues and theories. As a result, departments often eliminated courses in history of economic thought and economic history from the course offerings, prevented heterodox economists from teaching economic theory courses, and either blocked or attempted to block the introduction of heterodox courses and/or specialized field in heterodox political economy (or the common euphuism of "alternative approaches" preferred by mainstream economists) into the undergraduate and graduate programs.[13] Moreover in some cases when a field in heterodox economics or "alternative approaches" was established, the neoclassical faculty introduced additional conditions for students who wanted to do the field, such as demonstrating competency in neoclassical theory beyond the first-year comprehensive examinations (without a reciprocal requirement being placed on those doing the field in economic theory).[14] And in other cases, departments simply discriminated against students who took heterodox fields when allocating teaching and research assistantships.[15] In addition, there were whispering campaigns to direct students away from heterodox economists and their courses; biased promotion panels to block advancement; and favoritism in the allocation of department resources.[16]

Outside the department, heterodox economists faced discrimination against their research and their writings. Quite bluntly, for example, research proposals submitted to the National Science Foundation were summarily rejected as not dealing with economics with a reminder that NSF money was only for neoclassical economists. As for their writings, papers critical of core tools, models, and discourse of neoclassical economic theory or challenging the findings of prominent neoclassical economists stood less and less of a chance of being published in mainstream journals.[17] Moreover, papers whose heterodox topics were not of interest to neoclassical economists or whose style was literary also stood little chance of being accepted by mainstream journals—they would simply be described as "not very good papers." Consequently, most heterodox economists eventually did not bother to submit their papers to these journals.[18] Finally, the program of the annual conference of the AEA at the annual meeting of the Allied Social Science Associations (ASSA) was arranged by the President-elect, as opposed to being derived from an open call for papers. This meant that it was not possible for "outsiders" to have sessions at the annual conference, unless the President-elect invited them. As this rarely happened, heterodox economists by the late 1960s felt increasingly discriminated against and hence increasingly excluded from the annual conference.[19] In short, "life among the econ tribe" for heterodox economists circa 1970 was far more difficult and brutish than Leijonhufvud could ever imagine; and often short, for ostracism was frequently practiced by the tribal elders and their supporters[20] (Lazonick 1973; URPE 1972, 1973a, 1973b, 1973c, 1973d, 1974a, 1974b, 1975a; Christiansen 1974; Lipset and Riesman 1975; Rudy 1996; Lifschultz 1974; Stanfield 2002; Ward 1977; Walsh 1978; Foley 1999; Tarascio 1999; *AIMS Newsletter* 1.3 (November–December, 1965: 4–7); Colfax 1973; Dowd 1974, 1997; Fusfeld 1997; Aslanbeigui and Choi 1997; Barber 1997b; Aslanbeigui and Naples 1997a; Shepherd 1995; Johnson 1971b; Yonay 1998; Arestis and Sawyer 2000; Borts 1981; Bernstein 2002; Blecker 2002; Bunting 2002; Dawidoff 2002;

Golden 1975; Quick 2002; Davidson in King 1995a; The Carnegie Commission on Higher Education 1973a, 1973b, 1973c; Coyle 2002; Loube 2003; Mata 2005; Davidson 1972c; Leijonhufvud 1981).

Building heterodox economics in the 1970s

The contested landscape of American economics did not consist solely of the efforts of neoclassical economists to suppress the threat of heterodoxy. There were positive efforts in the 1970s to build heterodoxy, such as the ongoing efforts by heterodox economists to build and expand the activities of URPE and the Association for Evolutionary Economics (AFEE) as well as the efforts to revive and develop the Association for Social Economics (ASE) and in 1979 the formation of the Association for Institutional Thought (AFIT) in 1979.[21] Moreover, there was in the 1970s the sustained effort by Post Keynesian economists to build Post Keynesian economics (which is discussed in Chapter 5). Finally, there was in the 1970s a wide range of localized efforts—some successful and some not—by heterodox professors and graduate students in economic Ph.D. and M.A. programs to create, in one way or another, a friendly and supportive academic and social environment in which to study heterodox economics, to teach heterodox economics, and to do research in heterodox economics.[22]

Directing our attention to these latter efforts, one outcome was to have heterodox economics as a major component of the graduate program.[23] This was achieved at the eight departments shown in Table 4.1 by similar means. First, none of them were identified or ranked among the top economic departments in the 1960s—see Table 2.4 and Appendix A.6. Thus, there was

Table 4.1 Economics PhD programs with a major heterodox component, 1970–80

University	Fields					URPE Chapter	PhD Graduates 1971–80
	PE	*IE*	*SE*	*PKE*	*ME*		
American	×					×	20
Colorado State-Fort Collins			×			×	58
New School	×					×	46
Notre Dame	×						53
Rutgers				×	×		59
Texas	×	×	×			×	55
UC-Riverside	×	×	×			×	35
UM-Amherst	×						29

Sources: Owen and Glahe 1974; Owen and Antoine 1977; Owen 1979; Owen and Cross 1982; Stanfield 2002; Swaney 2002; Brazer 1982; Bernstein 2002; Rosser. 2002.

Notes:
PE = Political Economy; IE = Institutional Economics; SE = Social Economics; PKE = Post Keynesian Economics; ME = Radical-Marxian Economics.

no well-established high-rated mainstream reputation to deal with.[24] Second, with the exception of Texas who had a heterodox graduate program from as early as 1940, in each case, the major impetus came from the heterodox economists, some times supported by the university administration (as at American, Amherst, and Rutgers), and not vigorously opposed (and perhaps even supported) by the non-heterodox economists. Probably the best-known example took place at Amherst. In 1972, the economics department at Amherst was in turmoil; so the administration decided to resolve it by creating a pluralist economics department. Meanwhile, ever since the late 1960s radical economists had been on the lookout for an economics department where they can get hired as a group and teach Marxian economics. When the possibility at Amherst arose, a group of radical economists was organized and hired in block by Amherst to establish a program in political economy and Marxism: Stephen Resnick and Richard Wolff were hired in 1973 and Bowls, Gintis, and Rick Edwards were hired in 1974. By 1976 Amherst had ten "Marxist" economists, the largest and most visible group of radical economists at a single university at the time. However, before Amherst there was American. In 1964, Charles Wilber, who was trained as an Institutionalist at Maryland, joined the department. Subsequently, James Weaver, also an Institutionalist from Oklahoma, was hired. Together, they invited Sweezy to speak in 1965, which was not viewed favorably by the rest of the faculty. But with the rise of the New Left, student activism qua campus revolt, a friendly dean, and a hire of an additional Institutionalist from Maryland, the graduate curriculum became less oriented towards neo-classical theory.[25] In 1968 Wilber and Weaver went to the Radical Economics Conference in Philadelphia to recruit heterodox economists which resulted in the hiring of Howard Wachtel (1969) and Larry Sawers (1969). It was after their arrival that work began on developing a political-economy track in the graduate program was launched in 1971. By the mid-1970s, there were at least six professors who identified as Marxists and enough radical graduate students to maintain an URPE chapter.

In some cases, the Ph.D. program was directly altered (as at American, New School, Amherst, and Notre Dame) in which heterodox economics became part of the core theory courses. In others (such as at Rutgers) a cohort of heterodox economists, courses, and graduate students was built up before a heterodox field was established. Finally, there were cases, such as UC-Riverside, where the initial efforts were directed at establishing a field in, say, political economy, which comprised two or three courses taught by two or three heterodox economists. But over time the number of heterodox economists increased as well as heterodox course offerings generally outside the field.[26] In all cases, with the increase in the number of heterodox economists, heterodox courses, and graduate students interested in heterodox economics, its role in the graduate program became more secure and pervasive.[27] This, in turn, led to more academic and social activities that made the departments with their graduate programs an exciting place to do heterodox economics. As a result, heterodox economics became a major and relatively secure component of these eight Ph.D. economic programs by 1980 (Lifschultz 1974; Walsh 1978; Resnick 2003; Lee 2000a and Chapter 5; Colander 2001; URPE 1971, 1972, 1973d, 1978b; Sherman 2006; Phillips 1994; Stanfield 2002; Hamilton 2004; Swaney 2002; Zwerdling 1978; Wachtel 2004; Weaver 2004; Wilber 2004]

In addition to the eight heterodox economic programs, there were another thirteen departments, five of which were top ranked and the other eight not ranked at all, in which heterodox economics formed a minor component of their Ph.D. programs—see Table 4.2 and Appendix A.6. Some of the non-ranked departments, such as Oklahoma, Maryland, and Utah, had from the 1950s a number of heterodox economists and a pluralistic ethos, while other departments, such as Tennessee, amassed a cadre of heterodox economists and a pluralistic ethos in the 1960s. Thus, although the programs did not have a specific field in heterodox economics, various graduate courses had hetero-dox content. However, this resulted in heterodox economics only being a minor component in the programs. In this context, the history of heterodoxy at Utah is quite interesting. The origin of the heterodoxy started in the early 1950s when heterodox-Marxist economists Robert Edminister, Lawrence Nabers, and Ernest Randa left California for Utah because the latter did not require its faculty to sign an oath of allegiance. Later in the mid-1950s Sydney Coontz, who was a Marxist, joined the department; and in the mid-1960s Allen Sievers who was a scholar of Marx and an ardent Institutionalist

Table 4.2 Economics PhD programs with a minor heterodox component, 1970–80

University	Fields					URPE Chapter	PhD Graduates 1971–80
	PE	*IE*	*SE*	*PKE*	*ME*		
Columbia	×						139
Connecticut	×	×					47
Maryland		×	×				83
Michigan	×					×	162
Nebraska		×					56
New Hampshire	×						6
Oklahoma							32
Stanford	×					×	152
Temple	×	×					28
Tennessee							39
UC-Berkeley	×					×	171
Utah							
Yale	×					×	184

Sources: Owen and Glahe 1974; Owen and Antoine 1977; Owen 1979; Owen and Cross 1982; Stanfield 2002; Swaney 2002; Brazer 1982; Bernstein 2002; Rosser. 2002.

Notes:
PE = Political Economy; IE = Institutional Economics; SE = Social Economics; PKE = Post Keynesian Economics; ME = Radical-Marxian Economics.

joined the department. Consequently from the 1950s to 1980, the department and its graduate program was theoretically diverse, with some faculty being mainstream, others being some variety of Institutionalism, and some being historically-oriented economists sympathetic to various approaches to political economy. Thus while "anti-mainstream" was a significant theme of the graduate program and graduate students were introduced to sophisticated methodological and theoretical critiques of neoclassical economics, there was not a specific focus on heterodox economics. This changed in 1978 when the department restructured the graduate program and hired four Marxist economists: E. Kay Hunt, Peter Philips, Michael Carter, and Susan Carter. Since then, heterodox economics has become a major component in the department's graduate program.

In other departments, such as UC-Berkeley, Michigan, Columbia, Stanford, and Yale (and non-ranked University of New Hampshire) graduate students (many who belong to URPE and were members of the local URPE chapter) worked with a couple of heterodox faculty members to convince the relatively open-minded mainstream faculty to hire heterodox economists and establish a heterodox field comprising of two or three courses.[28] The efforts at Yale are of particular interest. In the 1960s Resnick (1963), Stephen Hymer (1964), and David Levey (1967) were hired and there was some pressure by younger faculty to hire a senior person to teach Marxism. But at this time there were few radical graduate students at Yale and little push for courses on Marxian-radical economics, although Levey was allowed to do a seminar on *Capital* vol. I and teach a Marxist-tinged course on the "Structure of the American Economy." This changed in 1970 when the incoming class of first-year economic graduate students included a number of radicals, such as Laurie Nisonoff, Heidi Hartmann, Bob Cherry, and Marianne Hill.[29] Their interests and agitation, supported by Resnick and Hymer, eventually led, in the face of growing intolerance from the late 1960s, to the hiring of David Levine in 1972 and the development of a field in "alternative approaches" that was available to the 1974 class that included Michael Bernstein, Carol Heim, Marcellus Andrews, and Julie Matthaei.[30]

The existence of the field provided the catalyst for additional academic activities such as heterodox seminars, bringing in visiting heterodox economists, and heterodox doctoral dissertations as well as social activities. A good example of this was Stanford. Around 1972, the URPE chapter helped to establish a graduate field in Alternative Approaches to Economic Analysis, but there was only one tenure member of the department, John Gurley, to staff it. Additional pressure by the URPE chapter in 1974 to increase the staffing for the field correlated with Donald Harris getting tenure. The field consisted of three courses: the history of economic thought, Marxian economics, and value, distribution, and growth. In addition there was a very active seminar with presentations by faculty, by visiting professors such as Hyman Minsky, Paul Davidson, Alessandro Roncaglia, Alfredo Medio, Pierangelo Garegnani, and Krishna Bharadwaj, and by students who used it to hone their dissertation proposals. After the seminar, the participants went out to dinner at a Chinese restaurant. Moreover, many of the participants in the field often went to the seminars put on by the URPE chapter at Berkeley. Heterodox economists who took the field and participated in its extended activities included Steven Fazzari, Tracy Mott, Jane Knodell, Warren Whatley, Nilufer Cagutay, and Robert Blecker.[31]

Finally, beyond the twenty-one Ph.D. graduate programs with heterodox components, there were a number of Ph.D. programs with one or two courses in heterodox economics, perhaps complemented by an URPE chapter, but otherwise heterodox economics was for the most part marginalized. For example, at Harvard Stephen Marglin offered a bi-annual course in political economy and was supported by Lazonick (and later by Schor), while at Michigan State Robert Solo offered a bi-annual course on "Organization and Control in the Political Economy," Warren Samuels taught courses on public expenditure and law and economics, Harry Trebing taught courses on public utility regulations and industrial organization, and Allan Schmid in the agricultural economics department taught Institutional economics in a course on "Economics of Public Choice" which was cross-listed with economics.[32] However, it should be noted that the presence of heterodox-institutional economics at Michigan State was pervasive, even if low-keyed. Consequently, its impact on heterodox economics is frequently not recognized.[33] In addition, Wisconsin offered a bi-annual course in Institutional economics and had an URPE chapter while at MIT Michael Piore and Lance Taylor influenced graduate students simply through the courses they taught. Supplementing the three tiers of Ph.D. programs were at least ten M.A. programs that offered fields and courses in political economy, Institutional economics, and social economics. The M.A. programs with Institutionalist fields, courses, and/or ethos included California State University-Fresno, University of Missouri-Kansas City, North Texas State University, and the University of Denver. Other M.A. programs with a heterodox field, course, and/or ethos included De Paul University (social economics), Renesselaer Polytechnic Institute (political economy), St. Mary's University (social economics), Butler University (political economy), University of Nevada-Reno (political economy and social economics), and Roosevelt University (Post Keynesian economics and Marxism).[34]

In spite of the contested landscape, the positive efforts to build heterodox economics in America were successful—whereas in 1950 there were the few, the isolated, the suppressed, by 1980 there existed national and regional heterodox organizations and conferences, Ph.D. and M.A. programs that trained heterodox economists, heterodox journals and publishers that published heterodox economic books, and an open social network of heterodox economists. Moreover, from 1976 to 1995, the twenty-five Ph.D. programs produced Ph.D.s who published 501 articles in three major American heterodox journals, *Journal of Economic Issues, Journal of Post Keynesian Economics*, and *Review of Social Economy*—see Appendix A.11. Such a significant achievement was unknown in the history of economics and not duplicated in any other academic discipline. Thus, the emergence of heterodox economics as a relatively permanent contestant in American economics by 1980 was the reward to those heterodox economists, faculty and graduate students alike, who took the initial steps of breaking with the mainstream and thereby incurring their wrath in the hope of building a better, more pluralistic economics.

But in a contested discipline, relative permanence does not mean the continuance of heterodox economics in a particular department. When, as in the 1980s and 1990s, administrative support, graduate student support, and/or the number of heterodox economists decline combined with growing opposition from non-heterodox economists, the heterodox components of doctoral programs are more likely to be threaten with elimination. For example, even through there was significant student support, the decline of administrative support and the number of heterodox economists in the department resulted in an attempt to eliminate heterodoxy at UC-Riverside in the 1980s and a successful effort to eliminate heterodoxy at Rutgers by 1987. Perhaps the most widely used tactic to eliminate or reduce the heterodoxy in a graduate program was simply to deny the material resources needed to maintain it. One approach was to deny tenure to the heterodox professors teaching the heterodox components, which directly resulted in the demise of heterodoxy at Yale in 1980 and contributed to the demise of heterodoxy at Rutgers by 1987. A second was to remove heterodox economists from important positions in the department and eliminate the heterodox course offerings while a third approach was not to replace heterodox professors who taught the heterodox components when they leave or retire, which contributed to the demise at Texas (1980), Oklahoma (1985), UC-Berkeley (mid-1990s), Tennessee (1990s), Stanford (1990), Michigan (1992), Rutgers (1987), and Maryland (late 1980s). Sometimes the latter approach was justified on the grounds that a good graduate program requires the development of its mainstream relative to the heterodox components with the result that heterodoxy tended to be marginalized in the program, as has happened at the University of New Hampshire in the 1990s.

However, an underlying current that tended to reinforce both tactics was the ranking of departments in terms of their adherence to and exposition of neoclassical theory. For example, at Texas, the combination of retirements and deans wanting a high-quality, that is high-ranking, department meant that perspective faculty members must have doctorates from the top doctoral programs and be neoclassical economists as well. Consequently the hires from the 1970s onwards were nearly all neoclassical economists from top programs: so that by 2002, 82 percent of the faculty had doctoral degrees from top programs including Harvard, Yale, Princeton, Pennsylvania, Cornell, Columbia, Brown, Chicago, UC-Berkeley, Stanford, Duke, Northwestern, Johns Hopkins, Wisconsin, Michigan, and MIT. Hence, the Texas graduate program ceased to have any significant heterodox content by the 1980s; and at the same time the ranking of Texas went from adequate plus in 1970 to a top 25 department by the mid-1990s—see Appendix A.6. Similarly, after receiving a ranking of 84 out of 107 doctoral programs in the 1993

National Research Council study, Connecticut decided to significantly emphasis mainstream components of its program and to marginalize the heterodox components, accomplished by hiring only mainstream economists. More generally, drawing from the evidence in Appendix A.6, the seven departments—Columbia, UC-Berkeley, Maryland, Michigan, Stanford, Texas, and Yale – that were ranked from to top 25 to adequate plus for the period 1959 to 1970 and maintained or significantly improved that ranking through to the 1990s had eliminated heterodoxy from their doctoral programs by the mid-1990s. In addition, the two departments—Connecticut and Rutgers—who were non-ranked in 1970 and decided to improve their rankings had eliminated heterodoxy in their programs by 1995 and 1987 respectively. In contrast, the eight departments—American, CS-Fort Collins, UC-Riverside, UM-Amherst, New Hampshire, New School, Notre Dame, and Utah—who were non-ranked in 1970 and whose rankings declined through to the 1990s retained or increased the heterodox component to their doctoral programs.[35] Thus, it is clear that the rankings of departments is directly and/or indirectly detrimental to the existence of heterodoxy in doctoral programs, as the recent destruction of heterodoxy at Notre Dame which was in part legitimized by reference to department rankings attests to. The issue of department ranking will be discussed further in Chapter 11 (Brazelton 2004; Mayhew 2002; Adams 1994; URPE 1970, 1972, 1973b, 1974a, 1975a, 1976, 1978a, 1980a; Blecker 2002; Fazzari 2002; Bernstein 2002; Weisskopf 2002; Fisher 2002; McDowell 2002; Lifschultz 1974; Wolff 2002; Resnick 2003; Matthaei 2004; Levey 2004; Nisonoff 2004; Weisbrot 2004; Sturgeon 2002; Hamilton 2004; Minkler 2004; Poirot 2002; Campbell 2002; Hunt and Sievers 2004; Schaniel 1992; Elmslie 2004).

5 The history of Post Keynesian economics in America, 1971–95

Post Keynesian economics did not emerge in a vacuum; rather there existed organizations and social networks, such as URPE, Association for Evolutionary Economics (AFEE), and the Association of Social Economics (ASE) that helped its birth and development. Although each of the associations and their journals represented a different orientation towards economic theory and policy, they had more in common with each other than they had with neoclassical economics. In particular, their critiques of neoclassical economic theory were broadly similar and their topics for economic inquiry were clearly overlapping. Moreover, while their particular methodologies, theories, and style were different, they were in many ways compatible. Finally, many economists in each association were open to dialogue and social interaction with other heterodox economists. These three factors together meant that an open and friendly environment existed in which Post Keynesian economics could develop. It also meant that by the late 1980s many heterodox economists borrowed inspiration and theory freely from all four approaches—a point that will be further discussed below and in Chapter 10. Apart from URPE, AFEE, and ASE, there were also five individuals—Paul Davidson, Alfred Eichner, Jan Kregel, Edward Nell, and Sidney Weintraub—who were the key players that brought Post Keynesian economics to life in America.[1] Eichner began thinking of himself as a Post Keynesian as early as April 1969, just two months after he had started correspondence with Joan Robinson. This identification grew over the next two years along with his mastery of and confidence in the emerging Post Keynesian paradigm as a result of his continual correspondence and debate with Robinson. By April 1971 Eichner began wondering whether the time was ripe for a Post Keynesian revolution in the United States.

Starting in 1958, Sidney Weintraub began discarding many of the accoutrements which made up neoclassical economics. In their places he substituted his aggregate supply and demand analysis, mark-up pricing, and endogenous money supply. By the mid-1960s he saw himself as unorthodox; and by 1972 he realized his view of economic theory was quite different from that entertained by neoclassical economists and his view of good economic theory was not incompatible with the theories and arguments coming out of

Cambridge, England. As an unreconstructed Keynesian, he was open to a Post Keynesian revolution. Paul Davidson took his graduate education at the University of Pennsylvania where he came under the influence of Weintraub just as the latter began breaking with neoclassical macroeconomics and going back to Keynes. Thus, he also became interested in Keynes's approach to macroeconomics and money. In the early 1960s Davidson began work on Keynes's finance motive through which he obtained, in his view, an insight of the true role of money in the Keynesian revolution. This eventually led to an article on the topic published in 1965 that, in turn, boosted his confidence to integrate monetary analysis into Keynes's general theory. His first attempt along this line was an article on money and growth in 1968 in which he presented his alternative approach. The response Davidson expected from his neoclassical brethren never materialized; thus he decided to write a book that would systematically present his views on money and employment so that they could not be overlooked. During this same period, Davidson began corresponding with Robinson, first over the topic of the demand for finance and then expanding to include expectations, uncertainty, equilibrium, and capital accumulation. The frank discussion prompted him to take study leave in Cambridge in 1970–71 where he intended to write his book on money and employment. The year was an intense learning experience as Davidson argued and discussed with Robinson and other Cambridge economists virtually every point in the book he was writing. By the end of the year, he had completed the manuscript which was published in 1972 as *Money and the Real World*; the book marked the beginning of Post Keynesian monetary theory. The year at Cambridge also convinced Davidson that whatever differences he had with Robinson and the economic theorizing at Cambridge, his work was much more compatible with that than what passed as neoclassical macroeconomics.

Edward Nell was introduced to the capital controversy and the Cambridge criticisms of neoclassical economics while at Oxford in the late 1950s. This background combined with his fundamental interest in economic growth and social change propelled him to both examine the inadequacy of neoclassical economic theory while at the same time fashion a replacement theory synthesized from Marx, Robinson, and other heterodox economists. The first fruits of this life-long project came in 1967 with the publication of "Theories of Growth and Theories of Value." In 1969 he became a professor at New School for Social Research (now The New School) where he promptly initiated steps to revitalize the economics department by making it a center for heterodox economic theorizing. Jan Kregel took his first two years of graduate education at Rutgers University (1966–68) where he came under the influence of Davidson. Wanting to do his Ph.D. dissertation on the developments in economic theory at Cambridge, he went to England for the 1968–69 academic year. Armed with an introduction from Davidson, Kregel took tutorials from Robinson as well as engaged in extensive discussion with other Cambridge economists. The outcome of his year in Cambridge was the first draft of his dissertation which was revised and accepted by Rutgers, at the insistence of both Davidson and Robinson, for his Ph.D. in 1970; it was published the following year as *Rate if Profit, Distribution and Growth: two views*. However, Kregel was interested in more than comparing and contrasting Cambridge economics with neoclassical economics; he wanted to reconstruct economic theory, combining Keynes's short-period theory of effective demand with Kalecki's sectorial modeling of the economy and the Cambridge extensions of the theory to the long-period. Thus he was open to a Post Keynesian revolution and his contribution to it was *The Reconstruction of Political Economy: an introduction to Post-Keynesian economics* (1973), the first textbook on Post Keynesian economic theory (Lee 2000a; King 2002, 2005b; Davidson 1965, 1968, 1972b; Davidson in Arestis and Sawyer 2000; Turner 1989; Nell in Arestis and Sawyer 2000; Nell 1967b; Colander 2001; Kregel 1971, 1973).

Creating a social network of Post Keynesians, 1971–80

The beginning—December 1971

Throughout the 1960s, Robinson made several trips to the United States, lecturing on the capital controversies, methodology, and the shortcomings of neoclassical economics. Many of her visits were at the request of graduate students and young economists, which she went out of her way to honor in part because she felt that this was the only way to gain a foothold among American economists. Her 1971 visit to America was no different. Robinson was positively received by younger heterodox-inclined economists and graduate students. But then there were the many horror stories told by graduate students who felt that they could not protest against neoclassical economics lest they lose their financial support; and at the same time their neoclassical professors would not defend the neoclassical theory they made their students learn. When Robinson was at Columbia University in November, Eichner and Luigi Pasinetti talked with her about this lamentable situation. Eichner suggested that a possible way forward would be to set up a meeting between Robinson and sympathetic economists at the upcoming ASSA meetings in New Orleans to discuss a possible program of action. Robinson agreed to this; so Eichner wrote a letter that she signed which invited the recipient to a meeting on December 28, 1971 to discuss the above situation and ways to remedy it.

The letter was sent to between twenty and thirty economists, of whom seventeen attended the meeting, including Davidson, Eichner, Kregel, Hyman Minsky, and Nell—see Table 5.1. Since the economists who attended the meeting came from different backgrounds and held different perceptions as to what needed to be done, the meeting itself was a confusing affair and quite traumatic for Eichner who thought that a consensual solution to the situation was easily obtainable.[2] However, there was agreement on one point:

everybody at the meeting felt that the *American Economic Review* (AER) was closed to heterodox economists and that something should be done about it. Eichner took this small window of opportunity to write about this matter, in the name of the group, to John Kenneth Galbraith in his role as President of the AEA.[3] More importantly, Eichner used the issue of the AER to create common ground between the members of the group for the longer term project of developing an alternative to neoclassical economics through means of regular communication. To this end, he initiated the communication by asking the members to respond to a series of questions on alterative economic theories, whereupon the replies would be sent to all members of the group. Finally, he asked the members whether they knew of other economists who "would be interested in joining this effort to supplant the conventional neo-classical analysis," and, asked, if so, whether they would send him their names and addresses so that he could add them to the mailing list. These latter two activities by Eichner constituted, in the United States, the beginning of Post Keynesian economics as an identifiable body of ideas supported by a network of economists and organizations (Lee 2000a; Turner 1989; Davidson 1970c; Pasinetti 1992; Sherman 1994).

The term "Post Keynesian"

In the 1950s and 1960s, the term *post-Keynesian* was used in a chronological sense to loosely describe a wide range of post-*General Theory* developments in macroeconomics and monetary theory.[4] It was also used more specifically in the United States to denote the synthesis between Keynesian macroeconomics and neoclassical microeconomics. The term as representing the neoclassical synthesis first came to prominence in 1954 with the publication of *Post-Keynesian Economics* edited by K. Kurihara. This usage was adopted by various economists, including Paul Samuelson, who used it in his introductory economics text *Economics*. Moreover, at the same time Eichner was setting up the New Orleans meeting, Daniel Fusfeld was writing an article on the post-Keynesian synthesis and its collapse.[5] But changes were afoot. In 1959 Robinson used the term in a chronological sense, but also to refer to her theoretical work and that of her Cambridge colleagues, such as Nicholas Kaldor. Later Adrian Wood (1968) used post-Keynesian in a combined chronological sense as well as referring to the body of theory associated with the Robinson–Kaldor models of the economy. However, Wood did not think that the term represented something very different from the term "neo-Keynesian," which was widely used by Cambridge economists. But Robinson viewed neo-Keynesian as referring to neoclassical Keynesianism and preferred to use Anglo-Italian to denote the Cambridge–Kalecki–Pasinetti line of theorizing which she supported. Thus from 1968 to 1972 the three terms were apparently used interchangeably by economists in Cambridge as well as by interested Americans. Davidson, for example, used Anglo-Italian in his 1969–70 correspondence with Robinson, but in *Money and the Real World*

(1972b) used neo-Keynesian. (King 2002; Fusfeld 1972; Wood 1968; Robinson 1969a, 1969b; Davidson 1969a, 1969b, 1970a, 1970b; Elliott and Cownie 1975; Sherman 1975; Mata 2005; Lee 2000a)

In a letter to Robinson in April 1969, Eichner mentioned that he was making his students familiar with "the post-Keynesian Robinson-Kaldor type of growth model." This was one of the first uses in the United States of the term post-Keynesian to denote a body of theory that extended Keynes' theory of effective demand into the long period.[6] Later in April 1971 he wrote to Robinson mentioning the post-Keynesian theory of income distribution; and in another letter that same month, he wondered if "the time is ripe for a post-Keynesian Revolution" in the United States. Therefore, it is not surprising that Robinson, who had substituted post-Keynesian in place of Anglo-Italian by late 1971, suggested the name post-Keynesian economics at the New Orleans meeting to identify the theoretical orientation and activities of the group. However, this was rejected (with the consequence that the group remained initially nameless[7]), partly because the economists who attended the meeting had different views of what an alternative to neoclassical economic theory should be. The objection could have also been due to the fact that the term was, as noted above, already used to denote the neoclassical synthesis. In spite of its neoclassical connotations, Eichner continued to use and promote the term in his work, papers presented at conferences, and newsletters sent out to like-minded economists. Moreover, as noted above, Kregel used the term in the title of his book *The Reconstruction of Political Economy: an introduction to Post-Keynesian economics* (1973) as well as in two articles published in 1972 and 1974 in the *Bulletin of the Conference of Socialist Economists*. Finally, with the publication of Eichner's and Kregel's 1975 *Journal of Economic Literature* (JEL) article "An Essay on Post-Keynesian Theory: a new paradigm in economics" the term became widely accepted as the name for the new paradigm (Lee 2000a; King 2002; Kregel 1972, 1974; Mata 2005; Eichner and Kregel 1975).

Once the term post-Keynesian had been accepted as the name, there arose the issue of whether it should be spelled post-Keynesian or Post Keynesian. The controversy, however, was not really about spelling *per se* but about what the different spellings represented. The former stood for the narrow Cambridge line of inquiry advocated by Eichner; the latter, on the other hand, represented a broader line of theorizing advocated by Davidson which included the Cambridge approach as well as those of the fundamental Keynesians, Institutionalists, and radical economists. Over time, Davidson's position became widely accepted by American Post Keynesians, especially the younger ones who were largely ignorant of the spelling controversy.[8] Consequently, by circa 1980 the controversy had run its course and either name (although the "Post Keynesian" spelling was used most often) became generally accepted as representing the broad view of what constituted Post Keynesian economics (Lee 2000a; Davidson 1980c; Mata 2005; Wilber and Jameson 1983).

Social-network building, 1972–80

To establish Post Keynesian economics, Eichner's first step was to start a "newsletter" in January 1972 to inform the participants at the New Orleans meeting as well as subsequent economists who "joined" the group about its current and forthcoming activities. Eichner saw the newsletter as a mechanism by which to "build up a sense of awareness that those of us who are dissatisfied with neo-classical theory are neither alone nor without positive alternatives" (Lee 2000a: 123), that is to build a social network of Post Keynesian economists.[9] With the help of Nell, his second step was to arrange an URPE session at the 1972 ASSA Toronto meetings to discuss the papers being prepared for Nell's anti-neoclassical textbook[10] and the issue of whether the theoretical differences among Post Keynesians, Marxists and neo-Marxists, and Institutionalists hindered the development of any common body of economic theory as an alternative to the neoclassical paradigm. The title of the URPE session was "The Possibility of an Alternative to the Neo-Classical Paradigm: a dialogue between Marxists, Keynesians, and Institutionalists," with papers given by Eichner and Hyman Minsky; the discussants included Fusfeld, Frank Roosevelt, Don Harris, Martin Pfaff, Nell and David King.[11] Over fifty people attended the session and its outcome suggested that, while there were differences between the various groups, they were not necessarily irreconcilable, at least in Eichner's eyes:

> I [Eichner] would like to add that the session reinforced my belief that it is possible to develop an alternative to the neo-classical paradigm, that the differences between Marxists, neo-Marxists, Keynesians, post-Keynesians, institutionalists and grant economists are not necessarily irreconcilable. At the same time, however, the development of an alternative paradigm will not be easily accomplished, especially since the members of the various schools insist on emphasizing entirely different types of problems. This tendency to talk past one another was certainly evident in Toronto. Still, the fact that the different groups tend to emphasize different types of problems does not mean that they are in fundamental disagreement with one another. Only if the dialogue among them continues will it be possible to find out for certain one way or the other.
>
> (Lee 2000a: 145)

At the business meeting following the panel discussion, it was agreed that the group adopt the name Political Economy Club and that dialogue should continue in local political economy clubs established for this purpose.

The high hopes that Eichner voiced at the Toronto meetings evaporated over the next several months. First, he was unable to establish a political economy club in New York City, and none was established elsewhere.[12] Moreover, he realized that there were too few Post Keynesians and too little Post Keynesian literature to make a significant impact on the American economics profession. Finally, he felt that his attempt to promote a basis for a common point of view had failed. However, with Robinson's encouragement, Eichner regained his determination to promote Post Keynesian economics, now tempered with a more realistic perception of how difficult it would be. With Nell's help, an URPE session was put together for the New York 1973 ASSA meetings around the theme "Post-Keynesian Theory as a Teachable Alternative Macroeconomics."[13] Attendance was good, but Eichner realized that additional sessions were needed to acquaint American economists with the approach and thereby enhancing the social network of Post Keynesian economists. Not conceding defeat, he got a paper accepted for the 1974 Atlantic Economic Association meeting which he considered significant as it was another opportunity to make Post Keynesian theory better known to American economists. The paper he gave was an early version of his 1975 JEL article "An Essay on Post-Keynesian Theory." Attendance at the session was limited but Eichner was not disappointed as a number of copies of the paper were taken. Finally, he got a place on an URPE session, "Alternative Approaches to Economic Theory," at the 1974 ASSA meetings.[14] He gave a more up-to-date version of the Atlantic paper which was tailored for the URPE audience. Although the Marxists attacked the theory for its implied support for liberal economic policies, its non-critical analysis of capitalism, and its un-Marxian demeanor and emphasis on commodities, Eichner felt that the large audience which attended the session went away with the impression that Post Keynesian theory was beginning to emerge and that they should know something about it. This openness of URPE to Eichner, Nell, and Post Keynesian economics was based on its core value of pluralism. Although few founding members of URPE (and 1960s radicals) displayed any interest in Post Keynesianism (see Table 5.1 column H and A.12 in the Appendix), the pluralism ethos ensured that papers on or related to Post Keynesian topics were given at URPE sessions from 1975 to 1983.[15] More importantly, the URPE sessions and the conference party provided a social framework in which Post Keynesians were able to mix with radical and other heterodox economists.[16] This interaction produced intellectually stimulating interchanges which led to close and warm working relationships between many Post Keynesians and Marxists in the 1980s and 1990s. The close working relationships may have been in part due to the Marxists (and radicals) becoming more open to social-democratic or liberal policy solutions to economic problems, and the Post Keynesians more open to radical changes in social and political organizations and institutions. For whatever reasons, it has resulted in the melding of many views, so that from 1978 to 1995 at least twenty-two Post Keynesians were also wearing a Marxist-radical hat, up from four in 1971 to 1978—see Table 5.1 and Appendix A.12, columns L. and M. (Sherman 1976, 1994; Wilber and Jameson 1983; Lee 2000a; Dowd 1998)

The creation and dissemination of Post Keynesian literature, Eichner felt, was a necessary step to build an enduring social network of Post Keynesian economists. Thus in the February and November 1973 and March 1974 newsletters he promoted Nell's forthcoming textbook and Robinson's and John Eatwell's recently published textbook *An Introduction to Modern Economics* (1973).[17] In addition, Eichner and Nell compiled a Post Keynesian economics bibliography that was distributed at the 1973 URPE session and sent out with the newsletter. Finally, Eichner asked Kregel to collaborate with him on a paper on Post Keynesian economic theory. The intent of the paper was to be a guide and an introduction to Post Keynesian theory, thus providing the means and stimulus for American economists to read the literature on their own. Consequently, Eichner felt it was necessary in the paper to emphasize what Post Keynesians had in common rather than what they argued about among themselves. The paper, titled "Post-Keynesian Theory: the new paradigm in economics," was submitted to the JEL in July 1974. Mark Perlman, the editor of the JEL, found the paper interesting but reported that it needed polishing. With Perlman's sympathetic guiding of the revision process, a revised paper was eventually accepted and published in December 1975. (Lee 2000a)

By 1976 the social network of Post Keynesian economists was becoming established. But Eichner realized that without some sort of organizational support it was vulnerable. Thus in Fall 1976 he established a seminar on Post Keynesian theory at Columbia University. Its purpose was to bring together a wide range of Post Keynesian economists to work out just what Post Keynesian economics was and to determine effective ways to disseminate Post Keynesian economics in the United States. The first seminar took place in October 1976 with Eatwell giving a paper on taxation, distribution, and effective demand, where he combined Kalecki's analysis of effective demand with Sraffa's system of price equations. In the following seminars, Weintraub talked on prices and income distribution, Davidson on the Marshallian roots of Post Keynesian economics, Basil Moore on endogenous money, and Harvey Gram on von Neumann growth models. Although the initial seminars were well attended, the long distances that many had to travel, combined with the tremendous divisions which emerged between the participants, meant that attendance fell off and the last seminar was in December.[18]

With the demise of the Post Keynesian seminar, Davidson decided to concentrate his efforts on holding a one-day conference. Thus a planning meeting was organized in January 1977 where Davidson, Eichner, Kregel, Moore, and others discussed and decided on the conference theme, topics, papers, and speakers. The theme of the conference was Post Keynesian theory and inflation, and its purpose was to be "a forum for the exchange of ideas and scholarship by those economists whose work falls within the tradition established by Keynes, Kalecki, Robinson, Kaldor, and Sraffa."[19] Held at Rutgers University in April 1977, the conference had sessions on the monetary aspect of inflation, the international dimension, incomes policy as a stabilization device, and beyond Post-Keynesian theory: the unexplored issues. Participants included Davidson, Eichner, Kregel, Nell, Minsky, Moore, and Weintraub, as well as Lorie Tarshis, John Burbridge, Robin Marris, Lawrence Seidman, Stephen Rousseas, and Geoff Harcourt.[20] Over eighty economists attended and in spite of differences of opinion and temperamental behavior, Eichner and Davidson judged it a success (Lee 2000a; Rotheim in King 1995a; Eichner 1976a, 1976b, 1977; Davidson 1978; Ogata 1981).

The social network of Post Keynesian economists which had emerged by the Rutgers Conference was three-tiered. The first tier consisted of ten economists—Davidson, Eichner, Kregel, Minsky, Moore, Nell, Rotheim, Rousseas, Sherman, and Weintraub—who were involved in or had attended at least two Post Keynesian 'events' between 1971 and 1977 and also subscribed to and/or was on the editorial board of the *Journal of Post Keynesian Economics* (JPKE) when it was founded in 1978—see Table 5.1. As a group, they created Post Keynesian economics in America. The second tier also consisted of ten economists—see Table 5.1—who were involved in two Post Keynesian events, including subscribing to the JPKE. While their interest in Post Keynesian economics may not have been as strong or as developed as the first-tier economists, their participation in the social network was important for its development. The third tier consisted of over three hundred economists who were part of the social network to the extent that they were interested in Post Keynesian economic theory, as indicated by subscribing to the JPKE. Many would have also attended various Post Keynesian events and/or have received Eichner's newsletter. Whatever their association with the social network, their presence made its establishment a success.

Building organizational support for Post Jeynesian economics, 1977–82

Journal of Post Keynesian Economics

By 1977 the process of creating a social network of Post Keynesian economists was almost complete, but without supportive organizations it was vulnerable. As noted above, the first attempt at developing a supportive institution was the seminar on Post Keynesian theory that Eichner established at Columbia University in Fall 1976. When that stopped, Davidson turned his organization-building efforts to holding a one-day conference on Post Keynesian theory and inflation at Rutgers University in April 1977. Although the conference itself did not provide long-term institutional support, it did provide the impetus needed to establish the *Journal of Post Keynesian Economics*. At the time of the New Orleans meeting in 1971 (and even before that), Weintraub and Davidson had discussed ways to broaden the ideas of Keynes among American economists. In particular, Weintraub had tried to start a "Post Keynesian" network of economists and associated journal in the 1960s; and in 1969–71, when chair of the economics department at the University of Waterloo, he had plans for developing a Post Keynesian department and a journal. Thus, Weintraub was very responsive to the idea of a

Table 5.1 Social network of Post Keynesian economists, 1971–78

Name	A	B	C	D	E	F	G	H
E. Applebaum					×		×	
T. Asimakopulos	×						×	
P. Davidson	×				×	×	×	
A. Eichner	×	×	×	×	×	×	×	
D. Harris	×	×						
J. Kregel	×			×	×	×	×	
F. Lee						×	×	
R. Lekachman	×						×	R
H. Minsky	×	×				×	×	
B. Moore					×	×	×	
E. Nell	×	×	×		×	×	×	
M. Pfaff	×	×						
I. Rima					×		×	
F. Roosevelt		×		×				U
R. Rotheim					×	×	×	
S. Rousseas					×	×	×	R
L. Seidman						×	×	
H. Sherman	×			×			×	R, U
L. Tarshis						×	×	
S. Weintraub					×	×	×	

Notes:
A: 1971 New Orleans meeting
B: URPE Session at the 1972 ASSA Meetings
C: URPE Session at the 1973 ASSA Meetings
D: URPE Session at the 1974 ASSA Meetings
E: Post Keynesian theory seminar at Columbia University, 1976
F: Conference on Post Keynesian Theory and Inflation, Rutgers University, 1977
G: Charter subscribers and initial editors of the JPKE, 1978
H: Associated with radical economics (R) and/or URPE (U)

journal based on Keynes' ideas rather than on neoclassical Keynesianism. He also realized that a journal was needed as a way for Post Keynesians to engage in the intellectual give-and-take necessary to develop their theories. However, nothing happened until 1977.

In 1976, Eichner invited Weintraub to a planning session for the Rutgers conference. Weintraub turned the invitation down on the grounds that he was interested in doing something far larger than participating in a local gripe forum, such as producing an alterative to the major economic journals. However, his participation in the conference convinced him that there was enough interest in Post Keynesian economics to make it possible to actually establish an alternative journal. Writing to Galbraith in May 1977, Weintraub stated:

> I would very much like to see a new journal established here that could make some dent, if not break, the Establishment stranglehold. The AER has become hopeless and will remain so under the present and, I fear,

subsequent editors. Most others are hardly better, with a few even worse. Pretentious symbols, perfect foresight, and stationariness or steadiness largely preoccupy them, with obeisance to authority a prerequisite and lines combed for heresy.[21]... There should be some place for an issue-oriented publication.

(Weintraub 1977b)

He concluded the letter by asking Galbraith for his views on the proposal. In his response, Galbraith agreed with Weintraub and suggested that the journal might be called "A Journal of Post-Keynesian Economics." He also outlined how the journal proposal should be put together and that he would help raise money for its establishment. The response from Galbraith immediately prompted Weintraub to sound out Davidson about financial support from Rutgers University. Then, in short order, Weintraub and Davidson produced proposals first for a "Quarterly Journal of Post-Keynesian Economics," then for the "Post-Keynesian Economic Journal," and finally for the "Journal of Post Keynesian Economics."

By the end of July the financial-material support at Rutgers for the journal had been promised and a journal prospectus drafted to be sent out with letters soliciting contributions, editorial aid, and support from others. The letter and prospectus was sent to those who attended the Rutgers conference as well as to many others, both in the United States and overseas. The response was substantial and mostly positive.[22] Small and not-so-small contributions were received from over sixty economists and non-economists and Galbraith personally match that amount with a contribution of $1000.00. Weintraub and Davidson used the money raised to persuade Myron Sharpe[23] of M. E. Sharpe, Inc to publish the *Journal of Post Keynesian Economics* (JPKE), with the first issue coming out in Fall 1978.[24] Within twelve months the number of subscribers exceeded 1300, which meant that the JPKE was financially solvent (and profitable for Sharpe), its long-term prospects secure, and, most importantly, it could provide enduring organizational support for the social network of Post Keynesian economists (Minsky 1974; Eichner 1977; Weintraub 1974, 1977a, 1977b, 1977c, 1977d; Galbraith 1977a, 1977b; Davidson and Weintraub 1977a, 1977b, 1977c; Davidson 1977, 1978, 1998; Mata 2005; King 2005b).

Post Keynesian economics at Rutgers

As noted in the previous chapter, by the mid-1970s a great many university and college economic departments and over twenty graduate economic programs spread around the United States contained heterodox economists, offered courses in heterodox political economy, provided support for graduate students pursuing doctoral dissertations using heterodox economic theory, and had graduate seminars at which heterodox economists were invited to speak. These university departments and their graduate programs

provided valuable, although indirect, support for the social network of Post
Keynesian economists; but direct organizational support in terms of graduate programs was really needed. In 1974, Davidson was appointed as the
area-wide chair of the economics discipline at Rutgers. At the time, Rutgers
consisted of five colleges—Rutgers, Douglass, Livingston, Cook, and University College, each with their own low-rated mainstream department.
Motivated by the publicity that the University of Massachusetts-Amherst
received for establishing a "radical" economic department, the Provost
charged Davidson with the task to differentiate economics at Rutgers from
the mainstream departments, such as Princeton. Thus, he began promoting
the graduate program at Rutgers University as a place to study Post Keynesian economics. He also obtained the blessing of the President to establish
the JPKE at Rutgers and with the assistance of Kregel, and later Eichner,
worked on establishing a center for Post Keynesian economics at Rutgers. In
1977 under Davidson's guidance, Kregel was appointed as chair of the
Livingston College economics department, where he promoted Post Keynesian economics by hiring Nina Shapiro in 1978 and Eichner in 1980 and
bringing in Alessandro Roncaglia (1978) and Sergio Parrinello (1978) as
visiting lecturers.[25] Davidson, Kregel, and Eichner organized seminars on
Post Keynesian economics, inviting Rutgers heterodox economists as well as
outside heterodox economists, such as Wassily Leontief, Geoff Hodgson,
John Cornwall, Paolo Sylos-Labini, and John Eatwell, to speak; they also
organized one-day conferences. By 1982, Davidson, Kregel and Eichner had
achieved their objective of making Rutgers known as the place to study Post
Keynesian economics in the United States (Davidson 1980a, 2003; Lee
2000a; Ogata 1981).

Publishing and other organizational activities

Eichner realized that books on Post Keynesian economics needed to be
published if it was going to survive and spread. With the publication of
A Guide to Post-Keynesian Economics in 1979 he began a publishing partnership with M. E. Sharpe that subsequently resulted in the appearance of
nineteen books related to Post Keynesian economics over a ten-year period.
The purpose of the partnership was, in part, to provide a publishing outlet
for young and newly emerging Post Keynesians. It also provided Eichner
with a forum to encourage and help young Post Keynesians, thereby
strengthening and developing the social network of Post Keynesian economists. Finally, there were two less successful efforts, one by Eichner and the
other by Davidson and Weintraub, to build supportive organizations. In
1978, Eichner set up The Center for Economic and Anthropogenic Research
(CEAR) for the purpose of carrying out the modeling and econometric
research that eventually went into his last book *The Macrodynamics of
Advanced Market Economies* (1991). It served as a focal point in that Eichner used it to draw some of the Post Keynesian graduate students at Rutgers

into his macrodynamics project. Not only did they undertake specific projects, they also gained research skills, a deeper understanding of Post Keynesian theory, and an appreciation for the need to empirically ground and test the theory.[26] CEAR did get some external funding from The New York Times Co. and the Conservation of Human Resources, but it was generally a letter-head operation funded out of Eichner's own income. Eichner did apply for a number of National Science Foundation grants but was turned down each time because of the Post Keynesian orientation of his research proposals.[27] In 1980–81, Davidson and Weintraub attempted to organize an ongoing semi-annual international conference on economic policy analysis. The purpose of the conferences was to highlight to the media that liberal national and international policies existed, as well as developing practical economic policies. However, they were unable to obtain the necessary financial support (Lee 2000a; Kuttner 1985; Davidson 1980a, 1980b, 1981; King 2005b).

Progress and disappointment in the development of Post Keynesian economics, 1978 to 1995

From 1978 to 1995, the interaction of the network of Post Keynesians with supportive organizations—such as the JPKE and the three heterodox associations and their journals and conferences—resulted in a significant increase in the number of identifiable Post Keynesians at all three tiers. The JPKE provided a recognizable publishing outlet for members of the network, as well as a way for economists to enter it. In addition, appointments to its managing board of editors identified important contributors to Post Keynesian economics, thereby making the network more visible. Finally, subscribing to the JPKE provided a way for many economists to visibly enter the network. However significant the contribution of the JPKE was to the expansion of the Post Keynesian network, it was not more important than the interaction between the pluralist tendency of second- and third-generation Post Keynesians and their heterodox brethren. The framework for this interaction is found in UPRE, AFEE, and ASE and their support for Post Keynesian economics.

Mutual aid and building Post Keynesian economics, 1970s to 1983

As noted above, URPE opened its conferences to Post Keynesians and to papers that would be of interest to them. This pluralistic characteristic of URPE was also found in its journal *Review of Radical Political Economics* (RRPE). Early on the RRPE carried articles on heterodox theory, especially Marxian theory, on applied topics, on imperialism and related issues, and on the developing frontiers of radical political economics such as welfare economics and the economics of the family. As a consequence of this pluralism, RRPE published articles (and book reviews) on and relating to Post Keynesian economics, starting with Nell (1972) on the Cambridge controversy, continuing with Shapiro (1976) on the neoclassical theory of the firm and ending with Willi Semmler (1981) and David Kotz (1982) on mark-up pricing, monopoly, inflation, and crisis.[28]

When Warren Samuels became editor in 1971, the *Journal of Economic Issues* (JEI) also started carrying reviews of books on radical and Marxian economics and, with a short lag, also published articles on radical and Marxian economics. Similarly, beginning in 1971, AFEE's program of the annual meeting included papers on Marxism and from a Marxian perspective and discussants with radical or Marxist orientation. Given this relative openness to radical heterodoxy, AFEE extended the same warm reception to Post Keynesian economics. The JEI first carried reviews of books with Post Keynesian themes, such as *A Critique of Economic Theory* by E. K. Hunt and Jesse Schwartz (1974), *An Introduction to Modern Economics* by Joan Robinson and John Eatwell (1976), and *The Intellectual Capital of Michael Kalecki* by George Feiwel (1977). The first article on Post Keynesian economics was Nina Shapiro's "The Revolutionary Character of Post-Keynesian Economics" (1977), followed by others in 1978 and 1980 which dealt with Post Keynesian themes, such as Keynes, monetary production, growth, and financial instability. This introductory stage was completed when Robert Brazelton, in his article "Post Keynesian Economics: an institutional compatibility?" (1981a), concluded that there was room for useful communication between the two schools.[29] Although the program at AFEE's annual meeting covered topics of interest to Post Keynesians, it was not until the 1979 meeting that papers first appeared with a clear Post Keynesian orientation. Subsequent meetings in 1980, 1982, and 1983 included papers dealing with Post Keynesian economics.[30] The meetings also facilitated social interaction between Institutionalists and Post Keynesians, whether at the Veblen–Commons award luncheon, at the evening social, over a bite to eat, or commenting on papers. As a consequence by 1983 some Institutionalists, such as Brazelton and Wilber, felt that a synthesis was occurring which could best be described as Post-Keynesian Institutionalism (Samuels 2003; AFEE 1965–83; Wilber and Jameson 1983; Gruchy 1984, 1987; Tool 1998; Stanfield 1998; Brazelton 1998).

In 1941 a group of Catholic economists had established the Catholic Economic Association (CEA). In the following year they founded its official journal, the *Review of Social Economy* (ROSE). The interest of economists in the CEA was the evaluation of the assumptions, institutions, methods, and objectives of economics in light of Christian moral principles. Beginning in the late 1950s, there was a concern among the members that membership was declining. This eventually led to a change in name in 1970 to Association for Social Economics (ASE), and new objectives were adopted so as to facilitate the inclusion of all economists interested in formulating economic policies consistent with a concern for ethical values in a pluralistic economy and the demands of personal dignity. The concerns of the members and the contents of the ROSE did not immediately change with the change of name. However, with its doors open to all social economists, it was not long before Institutionalists and other heterodox economists joined the ASE. As a result, an alliance emerged between the solidarists[31] and left Catholic social economists, such as William Waters who was the editor of the ROSE and Stephen Worland, and the left Institutionalists such as William Dugger, Ron Stanfield, and Wilber. Consequently, in the latter part of the 1970s an increasing number of articles in the ROSE were being written by heterodox economists, such as Dugger (1977, 1979), Stanfield (1978, 1979), and E. K. Hunt (1979, 1980), who were interested in broadening the scope of social economics beyond its Catholic roots. These developments eventually led to the publication in the ROSE of the first article dealing with Post Keynesian economics, by Elba Brown in 1981, "The Neoclassical and Post-Keynesian Research Programs: the methodological issues." The evolution of the sessions at the annual meeting generally followed the same course as the articles published in the ROSE. Sessions on regulation, social insurance, quality of life, education, the equity of the price system and social justice dominated the meetings throughout the 1970s and various Institutionalists found their way on the program either as presenters or discussants. However, the significant change at the annual meeting came in 1983 when Dugger, as the program chair, focused the sessions on power in the social economy. Institutionalist economists figured prominently among the sessions and for the first time Post Keynesians presented papers[32] (Gruenberg 1991; Divine 1991; Roets 1991; Solterer 1991; Worland 1998; Peterson 1998; ASE 1970–83; Dugger 1993; Danner 1991; Waters 1993; Davis 1999).

For mutual aid to make the contribution it did in the formative years of Post Keynesian economics, it was necessary for Post Keynesians to reciprocate with openness and pluralism. Without a doubt, during the 1970s Davidson, Eichner, Kregel, Nell, and Weintraub were always open to working with other heterodox economists, and their attitude was also characteristic of many other lesser-known Post Keynesians in the 1970s, such as Arthur Grant. Grant was a student of Weintraub in the 1950s when the latter began to break away from neoclassical economics. His academic career mostly involved teaching undergraduate and master's-level economics students, first at Drexel University and then at Roosevelt University in Chicago. Beginning in the 1960s with the Cambridge capital controversy, Grant took an interest in both the critique of neoclassical economic theory and the attempts, either by radical economists or Post Keynesians, to fashion an alternative to it. By the mid-1970s, he had read many of the books and articles by Sraffa, Pasinetti, Nell, Robinson, Kregel, Kalecki, Adrian Wood, Eichner, and Weintraub as well as Marx and various Marxian economists. Moreover, he subscribed to the JPKE, RRPE, and the *Cambridge Journal of Economics*. Finally, by 1977 he was using Robinson and Eatwell's *An Introduction to Modern Economics* as his text for his intermediate undergraduate macroeconomics course; teaching his graduate students Post Keynesian economic theory;[33] and refusing to teach his students neoclassical price theory on the grounds that the theory was simply wrong. What Grant brought to Post Keynesian economics was a pluralistic attitude, in that he did not think that it could adequately developed without taking on board contributions from Marxian economics. In particular, he found Marx's falling rate of profit thesis a good explanation for stagflation and his labor theory of value as a way to include social content. One of his objectives was to "tie up post Keynesian thinking with Marxian and show that there is at least a way in which both lead to the same consequence insofar as the rate of profit is concerned" (Grant 1978d). The outcomes of his attempt were two articles in the JPKE on monopoly power and reproduction crisis in 1979 and 1982 respectively[34] (Plotnick 1983–84; Grant 1977a, 1977b, 1978a, 1978b, 1978c, 1978d, 1978e, 1979a, 1979b, 1979c, 1979d, 1982).

Rise and fall of Post Keynesian economics at Rutgers, 1977 to 1987

The combination of an emergent Post Keynesianism and Rutgers as a center for it meant that students with a background and specific interest in Post Keynesian economics began applying to the Rutgers graduate economics program. In the decade from 1977 to 1987, over fifteen students who entered the program became intimately involved in Post Keynesian economics and worked closely with Davidson, Eichner, Kregel, and Shapiro, and other Post Keynesian and heterodox economists. Some, such as Miles Groves and myself, were directed to the program by Eichner, while others, such as William Milberg, Fernando Carvalho, and Andrea Terzi came because of the JPKE and Davidson's reputation.[35] As a group, they were an eager lot, seeking out Post Keynesian theory wherever it was—attending classes given by Eichner, Davidson, Kregel, and Shapiro, writing class and seminar papers on Post Keynesian economics, requesting special classes and meetings with their professors, and establishing their own seminars on Post Keynesian economics.[36] In addition, they attended and participated in the Post Keynesian seminars noted above. The seminars were lively affairs with hard but friendly questions; and many times afterwards, Eichner, Davidson, Shapiro, and Michele Naples went out with the graduate students to a local restaurant for dinner and engaged in further discussions. Many of the students first presented their research leading to their dissertations during the after-dinner discussions. Finally, they were academically inclined in that with the encouragement of their professors they produced articles which appeared in economic journals before they obtained their Ph.D.[37]

In 1979 the neoclassical economists in Rutgers College began attacking Davidson, the JPKE, and Post Keynesian economics in general seemingly on the grounds that they did not want Rutgers to have a Post Keynesian reputation. This negative attitude was extended to the hiring of Eichner and to graduate students when they requested that a field in political economy be added to the graduate program. When Eichner arrived at Rutgers in 1980, he inquired as to why Post Keynesian theory was not part of the theory core of the graduate program. This led to a committee being established to examine the core curriculum of the graduate program. The outcome was the committee recommended that the theory core remain as it was and that Post Keynesian theory should not be included as part of it. By pressing the point, Eichner contributed to the mounting backlash against the Post Keynesian and other heterodox economists, which by this time produced such a hostile environment that some graduate students were already thinking of leaving the program. However, it was when the University decided to abolish the separate colleges and amalgamate the separate departments in May 1981 that the situation began to degenerate rather quickly. Within a short time, Kregel had left Rutgers (after he was told that he had to teach accounting courses) and the remaining heterodox economists were excluded from teaching on the graduate program; in particular Davidson was prevented from teaching the first semester graduate macroeconomics course because it was claimed that he was not competent to do so; and without the protection of Livingston College, Eichner was prevented from teaching an undergraduate course on macrodynamics. Moreover, the existence of Post Keynesian activities were kept from entering graduate students, while older graduate students were told they should not work with Eichner and the other Post Keynesian and heterodox economists. The outcome was that Shapiro and Naples were denied tenure, Beneria left when she found out that she was paid less than comparable male neoclassical economists in the department, Street retired and was not replaced, and Davidson and the JPKE left for the University of Tennessee; and at the same time heterodox graduate students left the program.[38] By autumn 1987 Eichner was the only Post Keynesian economist left at Rutgers. With these changes, the organizational support for Post Keynesian economics at Rutgers collapsed; and with Eichner's death in 1988, Post Keynesian economics disappeared from Rutgers altogether (Lee 1980, 1981a, 1981b, 1981c, 2000a; Kregel 1979; Kuttner 1985; Milberg in King 1995a; Terzi 1998; Carvalho 1998; Efaw 1998; Colander 2001; King 2005b).

Growth of Post Keynesian economics, 1978 to 1995

In spite of the Rutgers debacle, Post Keynesian economics continue to grow and expand. In particular, URPE, AFEE, and ASE continued their support. With their conference programs at the annual ASSA meetings open to Post Keynesian sessions and to Post Keynesian economists, the awareness of Post Keynesian economics among heterodox economists increased. As indicated in Table 5.2, from 1984 to 1995, they provided conference space for thirty-six Post Keynesian sessions and 158 other sessions, with URPE providing the most conference support with twenty-four Post Keynesian sessions and ninety-four other sessions that included Post Keynesian economists. The support of AFEE and ASE was also substantial, and their growth offset the

Table 5.2 URPE, AFEE, and ASE support for Post Keynesian economics at the annual ASSA meetings, 1984–95

Year	Post Keynesian Sessions			Other Sessions with Post Keynesian Economists			Total
	URPE	AFEE	ASE	URPE	AFEE	ASE	
1984	0	0	0	4	3	2	9
1985	2	2	0	10	1	1	16
1986	3	0	0	4	3	1	11
1987	5	1	0	12	2	3	23
1988	2	0	1	10	5	3	21
1989	1	1	1	10	3	2	18
1990	3	0	0	10	2	2	17
1992	4	1	0	10	4	2	21
1993	1	1	1	8	5	3	19
1994	2	1	0	8	6	4	21
1995	1	1	1	8	6	1	18
Total	24	8	4	94	40	24	194

Source: ASSA 1984–95.

slight decline in URPE's support. Lastly, the number of sessions at the annual meetings where heterodox economists could be exposed to Post Keynesian themes and arguments averaged about nineteen. In addition to conference support, the editors of the JEI, ROSE, and RRPE accepted articles and communications on Post Keynesian themes and concerns and/or by Post Keynesian economists. From 1984 to 1995 they published 181, or a yearly average of fifteen, Post Keynesian articles and communications. Finally, from 1984 to 1995 a total of twenty Post Keynesians were invited or elected to be on the editorial boards of the JEI, ROSE, and RRPE—see Appendix A.12, column N.

The open, pluralistic attitude of AFEE, ASE, and URPE was reciprocated by Post Keynesians. Of the eighty-five of the highly active Post Keynesians for the period 1978 to 1995, twenty-five were members of AFEE, nine of ASE, and seventeen of URPE, while thirty-nine, eighteen, and twenty-one had published in the JEI, RSE, and RRPE respectively. In addition, forty-six participated in non-Post Keynesian AFEE, ASE, and URPE sessions, while thirty-seven participated in Post Keynesian AFEE, ASE, and URPE sessions. Together, sixty-five of the eighty-five (or 76 per cent) Post Keynesians were involved to some degree with other heterodox economists and their ideas—see Appendix A.12, columns F, H–O. This pluralism, combined with the support of AFEE, ASE, and URPE, meant that all their members were exposed in some degree to Post Keynesian economic theory, themes, and concerns. As their combined membership was, circa 1990, approximately 1700, the pluralistic impulse had expanded the number of economists with at least a passing interest in Post Keynesian theory from three hundred to nearly a thousand—see Appendix A.24.

Finally, although Rutgers as a center for Post Keynesian economics lasted less than a decade, its influence on the development of Post Keynesianism continued. First, its Post Keynesian-heterodox graduates published from 1976 to 1995 28 articles in the JPKE as well as six in the JEI, three in ROSE, and four in RRPE—see Appendix A.11. In addition, from 1984 to 1995 Balakrishnan, Deprez, Efaw, Gaynor, Groves, Milberg, Terzi, and Lee and four of his students participated in approximately sixty URPE, fifteen AFEE, and one ASE sessions. Moreover, Deprez, Lee, and Milberg achieved significant positions within the Post Keynesian social network, ranging from being an editor, publishing in, and/or subscribing to the JPKE, to participating in Post Keynesian and non-Post Keynesian AFEE, ASE, and URPE sessions, attending the bi-annual Post Keynesian Workshop, and publishing in and/or subscribing to the JEI, ROSE, and RRPE—see Appendix A.12. Finally, and most significantly, after moving from Rutgers to the University of Tennessee, Davidson established, with the University's assistance, an ongoing series of Post Keynesian Workshops, starting in 1988 and continuing to the present day.[39] The 1988, 1990, and 1993 Workshops had a total of 188 participants, including 35 different American Post Keynesians (as well as seven other American heterodox economists), and the presented papers covered such topics as the distribution of income, the business enterprise ands profits, monetary theory and policy, and endogenous money and the interest rate. More importantly, it provided an organizational framework by which old members of the Post Keynesian network could renew and strengthen their social ties as well as a way for new members to enter the network.

Through their active participation in other heterodox associations, their proclivities to participate in conferences and publish articles, the Post Keynesian workshop, Post Keynesians were able to maintain an active social network and open it to new members as well; and as a result, the number of highly active Post Keynesians increased from twenty for the period 1971 to 1978 to eighty-five for the period 1978 to 1995. The seven Post Keynesian "events" indicated represented in columns A–G in Appendix A.12 are the best set indicators of whether an individual is an active participant in Post Keynesian economics. Thus, it is possible to identify thirty Post Keynesians who were involved in or committed to at least four of them, and to identify fifty-five additional Post-Keynesians who were involved in or committed to two or three events. So over the period 1978 to 1995 there were eight-five significantly active Post Keynesian economists, which represented a four-fold increase in the number of participants in the network since 1978. Thus, the combination of highly active Post Keynesians and their pluralistic tendency and the openness of heterodox economists and their associations resulted in more than a three-fold expansion of the core and extended social network to over 1100 "Post Keynesian" economists. So, in spite of the loss of Rutgers, Post Keynesian economics experienced significant expansion from 1978 to 1995.

Part II

Heterodox economics in the United Kingdom

6 The contested landscape of British economics, 1900–70

Introduction

Like in the United States, the landscape of British economics is a contested one. Beginning in the 1870s, classical political economy came under increasing criticism from adherents to the heterodox historical political economy school and the emerging neoclassical school. Moreover, the rise of interest in socialism and land nationalization by the working class and accompanying interest in Marxian economics and Georgism produced a significant negative response by the capitalist class and social elite. In particular, the interplay between working-class interest in Marxism and the upper classes efforts to rid the workers (and other interested people) of this pernicious interest produced an extraordinary contested history of heterodox economics in twentieth-century Britain up to 1970. On the one hand, there was the forty-year attempt to establish a community of independent working-class education with Marxism as one of its key components that was organizationally grounded and had teachers, students, books, and schools; and then there was the forty-year effort by the upper classes to prevent such a community from existing. At the same time, there was effort among academic economists to exclude Marxism and other heterodox approaches from taking hold in university economic departments and being taught to students. Thus by the 1950s, neoclassical economics dominated both the instruction to workers and university departments, although there were some rumblings of opposition. But the 1960s saw cracks in the status quo, a crisis in economics, and the beginning efforts to create anew a community of heterodox economists, the fruits of which will be shown in the following chapter. The rest of this chapter will embellish the above historical sketch of the contested landscape of British economics, starting with a prologue on working-class education, Marxism, and upper-class reaction in the three decades prior to the twentieth century.

Adult education was a feature of British society since before 1800; however, working-class education was another matter. The political agitation of the 1790s lead to workers reading, thinking, and discussing among themselves, the outcome of which, in the early 1800s, contributed to the emergence of the English working class and the perception that their interests were different from their social-economic betters. Thus education within and for the working class consisted of obtaining "really useful knowledge," that is knowledge that both educated and contributed to their social and economic emancipation. Such knowledge, which could only come from workers themselves, was an embedded concatenation of political knowledge that explained everyday experiences such as why the state attacked trade unions, a social explanation of society, and political economy that included both the study of economic history and economic principles that addressed such questions as poverty, exploitation, and co-operation. In contrast, the upper classes feared the consequences of workers obtaining really useful knowledge.[1] Thus they thought that workers should be educated to understand that their interests coincided with their interests and that workers and capitalists were engaged in a cooperative venture; and the teaching of political economy was considered one way to achieve this. The adult school movement from 1800 to the 1840s was carried out with this in mind, while from 1820 to 1850 Mechanics' Institutes were established throughout Great Britain with the intention to produce in a round-about-way a more skilled labor force that would identify with the interests of the upper classes.

The 1850s marked the emergence of secularism in Britain, a movement consisting of the working and lower middle classes whose mission was a radical restructuring of society by peaceful means. The fundamental view held by secularists was that religion was nonsense and promoted social practices and mores that were exceedingly harmful to men, women, and children. Thus, their aim was to discredit Christianity and those social institutions that depend upon it. Questioning a central pillar of society lead to two related outcomes: the first was the questioning of other central and sacred pillars of society and the second was a powerful desire to be educated. Freethought and education—a deadly combination for the status quo. Therefore, secularists formed secular and freethought societies throughout Britain where weekly lectures were held on wide-ranging topics and libraries were established for members' use. In the early 1880s, membership in the societies reached its peak, for another cause that excited the working classes began to emerge—that is socialism. Initially they co-existed in that secularists could either be in favor of socialism or individualism; and given their adherence to freethought, they invited champions of both views to debate their merits at their meetings while also ensuring that their libraries stocked their books.[2] However, the aims and objectives of secularism, while compatible, were different so eventually there was a split with the former fading into the background. Still it was due to their inquisitiveness and adherence to freethought that secularists, through their societies, enabled socialisms to be introduced to the working classes[3] (Johnson 1979; Shapin and Barnes 1977; Tyrrell 1969; Fieldhouse 1996a; Royle 1980; Simon 1965; Macintyre 1980).

The last twenty years of the nineteenth century witnessed the rise of trade unionism, working-class politics and a drift of workers away from the Liberal Party, and consequent interest in socialism (and in Georgism and land reform). As part of the process, there was an emphasis on education as a way to change workers' outlook on the economy and their position and role in society, which included learning about Marxism and socialism. One venue was lectures (outdoors and indoors) given by members of the Socialist League, Social Democratic Federation, Fabian Society, and various local socialist societies to working-class audiences across Britain. In addition, publications on Marxism and socialism directed at the working class became widespread.[4] With the availability of literature, it was not long thereafter that socialist groups revived the tradition of independent working-class education and formed discussion and study classes whose texts included *Capital, Wage, Labour and Capital*, and *The Socialist Catechism*. What drove many to take up studying Marxism was the need for economic knowledge that would enable them to direct their own trade-union activities without depending on the mainstream political parties for guidance and most importantly to challenge capitalism in the workplace and work for revolution and the emergence of socialism.

Reactions to the spread of Marxism (and Georgism and land reform) among workers varied among the upper classes. Attempts were made by the authorities to directly prevent freedom of speech and assembly relative to open air lectures, but in the end they failed due to protests by the working class. Another approach was a sustained effort to discredit Marxian theory (and its Ricardian foundations), especially the labor theory of value and its corollary that the origin of profits was in the exploitation of labor, and replace it with theories whose central tenet was that exchange value was determined solely by utility or demand. The critique was largely aimed at the educated classes and the labor aristocracy, as it was carried out in journals that were too expensive for most workers to purchase.[5] Thus, it had one significant outcome in that Marxian theory was largely dismissed as a legitimate theoretical account of capitalism and hence it should not be taught as part of regular instruction at universities and university colleges, although many of them had lectures on the history of socialism and on the shortcomings of Marxism. As a result, the way was cleared for the uncontested rise to dominance of the teaching of Marshallian supply and demand theory at British universities.[6]

Since workers were unaffected by this "high-brow" critique, a third approach to combating Marxism in the working classes and saving the country from revolutionary socialism was the university extension movement. Started in 1873, the movement involved Cambridge, Oxford, and (indirectly) the University of London using university graduates to deliver 12–13 lecture (week) and later 6-lecture courses to both working class and middle class and professional men and women located in towns and cities across Britain. They consisted of lectures to large audiences, smaller discussion classes, essays, and readings that led, over a two or three year period, to a certificate, which could be used to gain entry into a university. The economic courses selected by the local extension committees to offer to students were proposed by industrialists for their workers or by the extension lecturers themselves. In either case, because the extension lecturers in economics were "trained" in a modified Millian classical political economy or were absorbing the emerging Marshallian theory with its embryonic marginal productivity theory of distribution, their lectures ranged from promoting harmony of class interests and sympathy for the richer classes, mild praise of trade unions, advocating some forms of government intervention into the economy, to the folly of defying economic laws that proscribed the effectiveness of industrial disputes to raise wages (which was what the industrialists wanted drilled into their workers).[7] Whatever the theme of the course, it was made clear that mild to radical reform (such as state protection of workers and municipal ownership of water, gas, and local trams and buses) was preferable to the unnecessary and dangerous radical transformation of society advocated by revolutionary socialists and Georgists.[8] Such lectures were popular with workers in the 1870s, but the declining economic circumstances of workers in the 1880s and 1890s found their popularity fall, in part because they cost too much to attend, in part because of the rise in the interest of socialism, and in part because the theory taught had little connection to their everyday life.[9] Thus for much of the 1880s to 1900, lecturers had to increasingly contend with students and audiences that forsook the fundamental principles of economics and ascribed all the current social ills to the existence of capitalism, the predominance of machinery, and private ownership of land.[10] So in the end, the failure to quell working-class interest in Marxism meant that at the beginning of the twentieth century there existed a potential cadre of workers waiting for "formal" schooling in Marxism (Simon 1965; Willis 1977; Coats 1963; Jepson 1973; Kadish 1982, 1986, 1987, 1990, 1993; Tribe 1990; Goldman 1995; Burrows 1978; Koot 1987; Stigler 1969).

Working-class engagement with Marxism, 1900–940

In the first decade of the twentieth century, interest in socialist ideas was growing among young adults in various industrial centers in Britain; and in tandem many cheap socialist writings were available. While many attempted by themselves or with friends to understand, for example, the first nine chapters of *Capital*, it was difficult going. Hence, there was an increasing demand for tutors to guide the studies and organize classes or study groups. For example, in Scotland, the Social Democratic Federation and later the Socialist Labour Party ran classes on economics which included reading and working through *Wage, Labour and Capital*, *Value, Price and Profit*, and parts of *Capital*. Moreover, in many Welsh mining villages in the South Wales Mid-Rhondda coal fields, miners' libraries were established as early as 1880 and by circa 1905 were the focal point of miners interested in Marx and Marxian economics, an interest that lasted through the 1930s.[11] Thus, there clearly was a demand to learn about Marxism and socialism (Simon 1965; Cooke 2006; Macintyre 1980; Heal 1973; Francis 1976).

Two responses arose to meet the demand. One was to provide tutors, lecturers, and courses that would direct workers away from Marxism, revolutionary socialism, and class conflict towards reforming the capitalist system but without altering its primary social relationships—and this approach was undertaken by the Workers' Educational Association (WEA). A second response was that the working class created their own educational institutions, such as labor colleges, to educate the tutors and lecturers who would then go back to their villages and trade unions and teach—this became known as the Independent Working Class Education (IWCE) movement. Generated by the same demand for Marxism, the two responses engaged in uneven struggle for the educational soul and vision of the future of trade unions and the working class, a struggle that essentially ended by 1940 with a victory for the liberal educational philosophy of the WEA.

Workers' Educational Association and Marxism, 1903–40

Because many local organizing committees were dominated by middle-class people and the costs of putting on lectures and courses were entirely financed by local fees, the university-extension movement increasingly provided six-lecture popular, literary courses that were based on giving lectures to large audiences of 150 or more followed by more intensive discussion classes of fifty students or more. Being excluded from local organizing activities combined with high fees resulted perhaps in only a quarter of the students being working class; and the large lectures and discussion classes combined with the shorter courses worked against maintaining university standards.[12] Into this context stepped the WEA in 1903, which had as its purpose the making of university education more readily available specifically to the working class, an orientation that some extension lecturers did not like. Initially, it did so by supporting and promoting university-extension courses, but was not very successful because the courses were too expensive for working-class people and too short for the work to be of university standard. However, the financial hurdle was overcome in 1907 when at the Oxford Joint Conference on Education of Workpeople, the government through the Board of Education and/or the local educational authorities agreed to provide the WEA with grants to cover in part the cost of the tutorial courses while the university offering the course would cover half of the costs; the WEA would then cover the remaining costs with donations from individuals, trade unions, co-operative societies, and other miscellaneous sources. As a result, within a few years nearly all the universities and university colleges sponsored tutorial classes.

Initially, joint committees were established to oversee the tutorial classes. The committee consisted of university representatives and workers representing the local WEA. The local WEA would request a course such as economics or industrial history, engage with the local educational authorities and the Board of Education concerning the grant for the course, and the university involved would select the lecturer for the course (although the local WEA could request a particular lecturer) who would, in conjunction with the local WEA, determine its content. The lecturer would generally possess a university degree or a diploma, such as the Oxford Diploma in

Economics and Political Science; and increasingly the university degree was in economics. In addition, the lecturer was employed as a member of staff by the university as a lecturer, college tutor, or professor in a specific department or by the university's joint committee on nearly a full-time basis in teaching tutorial classes; or was directly employed by the joint committee on a full-time basis but not as a member of the university.[13] Similar to the university-extension classes, the tutorial classes lasted three years with 24, two-hour classes per year, were limited to about thirty students, and consisted of lectures, discussions, essays, and extensive reading. Later in the 1920s, universities started establishing extra-mural departments that would specifically oversee the tutorial classes and included all full-time tutorial lecturers; and the departments would work with the WEA to put on courses.[14] In either case, the academic standard of the classes were to be such that upon its completion, the student would have done university-standard work and hence have a chance to qualify for entry into a university. More specifically, a student who completed a tutorial class in economics would have the background to embark upon and obtain, for example, the Oxford Diploma of Economics and Political Science with an additional year of work or enter a university such as Oxford and obtain a degree in Philosophy, Politics and Economics.

Initially, the economics classes were so arranged that for the first two years the student studied the economic history and industrial structure of Great Britain, while the third year was devoted to analyzing the current working of the British economy, especially its distribution of income and wealth. Later, economic history was dropped and theory was pushed to the first year followed by applied topics and topical issues, such as international economics, for the next two years. Economic theory was used to frame the discussion and analysis and the one promoted by the WEA was Marshall's supply and demand theory. In the early years the assigned books included Alfred Marshall's *Principles of Economics* and *Economics of Industry*, supplemented by Henry Seager's *Introduction to Economics*, Edwin Seligman's *Principles of Economics*, and Charles Gide's *Principles of Political Economy*, all which presented the same theory as found in Marshall but with slightly different exposition. However, in the inter-war years Henry Clay's general textbook *Economics: an introduction for the general reader* was often the main text assigned, supplemented by Marshall, Hubert Henderson's *Supply and Demand*, and others—see Roy Harrod's 1920s syllabus in Appendix A.13.[15] In either case, Marshall's theory was presented as "objective truth" in that no fundamental criticisms of it were presented and discussed.[16] Although it was the theory students were expected to know, they were also introduced (perhaps) to Marx, such as reading the first nine chapters of *Capital* supplemented by Henry Hyndman's *Economics of Socialism* and followed by Eugen von Bohm-Bawerk's critique *Karl Marx and the Close of his System*; to A. D. Lindsay's dismissal of the labor theory of value in his popular WEA book *Karl Marx's Capital*; or to a five-page or less questionable critique of the labor theory of value as in Clay's book or Seligman's text.[17] The point of the digression and critique was not to have an objective and balanced discussion but to reject the labor theory of value and its explanation of profits as surplus value, the notion of class conflict as it pertained to the division of the surplus and to the social control of the working class by the capitalist class, and the concept of the social surplus itself: for as Seligman (1909: 369) argued, "The opposition to ordinary profits emanates from those who deprecate the entire constitution of modern industrial society. According to Marx, ... " Thus, from the beginning, the general theory orientation of economics as taught in WEA tutorial courses was neoclassical economics, as represented by Marshall and subsequent developments.[18]

It is in this context of putting on tutorial courses that the educational ethos of the WEA becomes important. From the beginning, there were two somewhat competing educational ethos within the WEA. One was education for self-emancipation or the pursuit of knowledge for its own sake, not specifically for achieving material, social, or political ends such as altering class relationships.[19] The second, supported by G. D. H. Cole and R. H. Tawney, was education for emancipation of the working class and social transformation-improving society along reformist lines as opposed by revolution. From 1903 to the Second World War, the two ethos worked together but also competed with each other; but in the end it was the self-emancipation ethos that dominated. Consequently, over time lecturers increasingly conveyed their material impartially, objectively and without political or religious bias with the aim of stimulating students to think for themselves, to be critical of authorities and sources of information, and to be able to argue all points of view dispassionately. Thus, students were equipped with critical objectivity of which the government greatly approved. By making Marshall's theory the main theoretical approach taught in the economic classes while at the same time dismissing Marxian theory, the WEA made it clear to the students which approach was considered objectively, scientifically superior.[20] This outcome was consistent with the educational ethos that progress both in educational and industrial matters could only be accomplished through class co-operation and not through any fundamental social upheavals, a clear case of the interweaving of politics and education.

By restricting the economics taught to Marshall's theory, the WEA ensured with deliberate forethought that it would not equipped students with the knowledge that would lead to "revolutionary" emancipation and social change or what was called "spurious knowledge and bogus remedies." In other words, the WEA did not diminish radicalism or the desire for socialism per se, but it did affect the kind of socialism desired. That is, by presenting the economics that it did, the issue of socialism was focused on particular problems and issues, such as the distribution of income or the lack of competition, and how to solve them without unduly affecting the social relationships underpinning British capitalism. Larger social questions, such as the existence of private property, class and hierarchical authority, wage slavery, and the class origins of profits, were ignored since the kind of economics presented in the classes avoided the issues. In particular, revolutionary socialism was dismissed. Thus, the socialism desired was that of the individual and the education that was received made the tutorial students feel alive intellectually but did not lead the individual to study Marxian theory or to engage with revolutionary socialism.[21] However, because the WEA had classes in economics and economic history there was always the possibility students would be introduced to some unacceptable "Marxist" theory. Hence, a constant vigilance was maintained by central and local government as well as by the WEA. This was done in one of four ways: the government accusing the WEA of spreading revolutionary ideas (as it did in 1917) and the WEA responding that it did not, but then redoubling its efforts to police its tutors; local authorities and the business community made it known to the WEA that they wanted objective, non-political studies, while others made their dislike for socialists known and the WEA taking it into account when developing classes and selecting tutors; by the central and local authorities controlling, overseeing, and removing (or threatening to) the WEA grant;[22] and by having most tutors on short-term contracts and hence liable to dismissal at any time, thus making them vulnerable to pressure to maintain political and economic neutrality if not orthodoxy.

Clearly, the WEA played a significant role in restricting the spread of Marxist theory among the working class; that is, it help confine economic thinking among workers and students to Marshallian price theory with its emphasis on markets and adjustments to preserve the status quo. More significantly, in contrast to the favorable treatment it awarded orthodox economics and economists, the WEA deliberately did not promote itself as an academic site where Marxist economists could teach and conduct research that would lead to academic, textbook, and popular publications. In short, the WEA contributed significantly to the efforts by government and the educational community to contest, counter, and disinfect the working class of Marxism[23] (Fieldhouse 1977, 1983, 1990, 1996c, 1996d; Goldman 1995; Jepson 1973; Blyth 1983; Harrop 1987; Feis 1920; Mansbridge 1913; Thomas 1922; Young 1992; Rose 2002; Simon 1965, 1990a; Duncan 2003; Cooke 2006; Steedman 2004; Macintyre 1980; Lewis 1993).

Ruskin College and Marxism, 1899–1940

Established in 1899, Ruskin College was the first residential college in Britain devoted specifically to the higher education of working men and women. Its purpose was not simply education as a mind-broadening experience that would be useful for trade unionists, but an education that would reduce class differences and conflicts. Hence, there was an attempt from the beginning to have all teaching done impartially without any political orientation by which it was meant no positive support for socialism. The first tutor and lecturer in economics at Ruskin was H. B. Lees-Smith, appointed in 1899 just after graduating from Oxford. Consequently his knowledge of economics consisted of knowing Mill supplemented by some Marshall and embedded in a historical-empirical context, all the hallmarks of Oxford political economy circa 1900. Therefore, from the beginning of Ruskin College, the economic theory taught as the principal way to explore and understand capitalism and current social problems was a Millian version of supply and demand increasingly supplemented by Marshallian developments. While the first Ruskin students did not seem to object to such an approach, by 1905 when miners, especially from South Wales, started entering Ruskin, there was a sharp reaction.[24] Coming with previous knowledge (however rudimentary) of Marxian economics, especially the labor theory of value and its explanation of the origins of profits, obtained from reading books and attending Marxist study groups at the miners' libraries, these students wanted further and more in-depth instruction, but instead were taught Millian-Marshall supply and demand with its marginal utility theory of value. Such theory they believed and argued was capitalist propaganda that smoothed over class conflict and hence not really useful knowledge from a working class perspective.[25]

In 1907, Lees-Smith left Ruskin for a professorship in public administration at University College, Bristol, but before leaving, he hand-picked Henry Sanderson Furniss to replace him as the tutor and lecturer in economics. Furniss's Oxford degree (1893) was in history where he read some economic theory and economic history, but in 1905 he returned to Oxford where he studied for and obtained the Diploma in Economics in 1906. However, as noted below, reading and attending lectures for the Diploma did not entail much if any engagement with Marxian theory. Hence at the time of his appointment, Furniss had read almost no works on socialism and Marxism. Thus his lectures on economic theory (which he tried to keep free from bias) were centered on Marshall's supply and demand theory, but also included a critical engagement with Marxism and a refutation of the labor theory of value. In addition, in lectures on other economic topics and engagement with economic problems, Furniss sought to make students realize that they needed to be aware of ways, in addition to the socialist viewpoint, to examine the issues. The year that Furniss started at Ruskin, the incoming class included Welsh miners and engineers, all of who were familiar with socialism and had at least attempted to read Marx. So they were looking forward to studying Marx and the labor theory of value and thus obtaining really useful knowledge that would enable them to return to their towns and trade unions as tutors and lecturers. Hence, their surprise and dismay at being taught what they considered to be capitalist economics resulted in agitation to be taught, in a non-prejudicial manner, Marxian economic theory.[26]

This discord contributed to the Ruskin strike of 1909 that pitted the College's impartial liberal approach to education against the advocacy that the College's teaching should be aimed at the needs of the working class with a distinct emphasis on socialism and Marxian theory.[27] The outcome of the strike and the events leading up to it was the formation of the Plebs League, the Central Labor College, and the Independent Working Class Education movement—see below. However, for the purpose here, the strike did not alter the teaching of economics at Ruskin. It continued to be "bourgeois" economic theory in the first year and topics and issues in the second, such as foreign trade, income distribution, public finance, and industrial problems. In 1909 the Diploma of Economics (renamed the Diploma of Economics and Political Science) was opened to working-class people. Since the economic theory taught at Ruskin was virtually the same as that taught for the Diploma, Ruskin students started taking it and continued to do so throughout the inter-war period.[28] Moreover, the economic tutors at Ruskin after Furniss—Percy Ford (1919), Grace Coleman (1920–1925), Alfred Plummer (1925–1937), and Henry Smith (1937–1939)—increasingly based their teaching on Marshall's *Principles of Economics*, supplemented and extended with Philip Wicksteed's *The Common Sense of Political Economy*, Joan Robinson's *Economics of Imperfect Competition*, and Edward Chamberlin's *Theory of Monopolistic Competition*, which they considered a more scientific approach to analyzing capitalism and explaining how prices, wages, and profits were determined.[29] So by 1940, Marx and Marxian economics was mostly ignored in economic lectures that became increasingly attuned to the requirements for obtaining the Diploma rather than the needs of trade unions and the labor movement.[30] Thus Ruskin College turn out the students that could not be tutors for the Marxian study groups back in their villages or serve their union effectively. Rather, as with the WEA, Ruskin students turned away from revolutionary socialism and became increasingly interested in solving particular problems without affecting the underlying social relationships (Young and Lee 1993; Craik 1964; Furniss 1931; Pollins 1984; Lewis 1976, 1993; Francis 1976; Yorke 1977; Jennings 1977; Chester 1986; Hader and Lindeman 1929; Drews and Fieldhouse 1996; Goldman 1995).

Labor colleges and the Independent Working Class Education movement, 1910–40

The Independent Working Class Education (IWCE) movement was an effort to direct and promote the education of the working class independently of state approved and supported organizations, specifically universities and university colleges, WEA, and Ruskin College. The rationale was that the state, being the handmaiden of the capitalist class, would direct, approve, and promote unuseful and misleading education that would direct workers away from revolutionary socialism by, in part, teaching Marshallian economics instead of Marxian economics. The beginning of the IWCE movement was in 1908 when students at Ruskin College formed the Plebs League. Its platform was to promote independent working-class education and its initial goal was to transform Ruskin into a real labor college, that is a college which was controlled by the labor movement through affiliation with trade unions and other organized labor bodies and their representation on its governing committee. However, as it became evident that Ruskin was not going to change, the students turned their efforts to establish in 1909 a residential college—the Central Labor College (CLC). Once established, the Plebs League promoted the establishment around the country of "Plebs" branches that would start classes in economics, industrial history, and sociology which would become affiliated with the CLC.[31]

The Plebs League enthusiasm for IWCE and the existence of the CLC galvanized workers' and socialist societies in Sheffield, Liverpool, Scotland, and elsewhere who were already engaged in educational activities to establish their own labor colleges or at least classes affiliated with the Plebs League or the CLC. Independent of the Plebs League and CLC-affiliated classes, there were other activities in working-class education. In Scotland for the period from 1900 to 1914, members of the Socialist Labour Party had to attend a class in Marxism as a precondition for joining. The Socialist Party of Great Britain and the British Socialist Party also conduct similar classes; while freelance socialist propagandists earned a living by lecturing on Marxism to local socialist societies, many of who were unaffiliated with any party. An example was Scotland's John Maclean who began teaching Marxian economics and industrial history classes for the Social Democratic Federation in 1906 and from 1908 to 1916 taught economics from a socialist standpoint in evening continuation classes; and then in the winter of 1917 taught a Marxian economics class of 500 students in Glasgow and six additional classes in nearby towns. In addition, his colleague James MacDougall taught classes in Paisley and Lanarkshire, while in 1916 the Socialist Labour Party in Glasgow held classes on Marxian economics and industrial history and in 1919 Arthur Woodburn started a small class in Edinburgh that called itself the Marxian School of Economics which complemented the nineteen Plebs-affiliated classes in Marxian economics and industrial history in Glasgow. Thus, by 1920 there was not a working-class community in Great Britain that was not touched by IWCE classes and especially classes in Marxian economics—see Appendix A.14.

As the number of labor colleges and classes proliferated there arose a concern of how to coordinate the provisioning of working class education. In 1921, a scheme was adopted by the various colleges (except the CLC) and representatives of the Plebs League to set up the National Council of Labour Colleges (NCLC) that would act as a coordinator among the providers of IWCE. Initially, the NCLC oversaw some seventeen labor colleges and some twenty labor college class groups (see Appendix A.14). This expanded over the next fifteen months to ninety-one colleges and class groups; and by 1924–25, there were 102 colleges and 37 class groups. To better organize the provision of IWCE better, the NCLC eventually organized the country into thirteen divisions, each with its own under-paid organizer whose charge was to organize, advertise, and sometimes teach classes, work with local trade unions, recruit local tutors, raise money, keep student records, give occasional lectures and make frequent speeches, and much more.[32] From 1921 to 1929 IWCE was organized such that the CLC was the residential college that educated students, many who became NCLC organizers while others became voluntary tutors and lecturers at the provincial labor colleges and classes that were overseen by the NCLC. With the demise of the CLC in 1929, the NCLC, its district organizers, and affiliated non-residential labor colleges became the sole providers of IWCE to 1940 and beyond into the post-war years.[33]

The purpose of the IWCE movement was to provide workers a really useful education that would aid them in their struggle for social and industrial emancipation and the transformation of society into a socialist new Jerusalem. To accomplish this, tutors first needed to be educated in Marxism and industrial history; and second they needed to return to their towns and villages and workplaces to organize and offer courses on Marxian economics and industrial history through local labor colleges and class groups. As the only residential labor college, the CLC, from its formation in 1909 to its demise in 1929, uniquely performed the first task of educating tutors. In particular, like Ruskin, the CLC had a two-year program. In their first year, students initially took a thirteen-week lecture course on elementary economics which was complemented by a course of industrial history. In the period 1909–16, the course covered elementary Marxian economics, starting with the scope of political economy, modes of production, and value and ending with money, capital, surplus value, and wages—see Appendix A.14 for similar provincial courses. However, over time, the course changed in response to the changing capabilities and interests of the students. So in the period 1919 to 1929, the course was extended to twenty-six weeks divided into elementary Marxism for the first half and history of economic thought and a critique of neoclassical economics in the second half. The readings for elementary economics initially included *Wage, Labour and Capital*, *Value, Price and Profit*, and parts of *Capital* as well as supplemental texts, such as the Mary Marcy's *Shop Talks on Economics* and Noah Ablett's *Easy Outlines of Economics* first serialized in *The Plebs Magazine* from April 1909 to January 1910 and later published in 1919. In the 1920s, the main text was *An Outline of Economics* by William McLaine which was a more developed version of *Easy Outlines*. It included the usual readings by Marx and extended the readings to include Louis Boudin's *Theoretical System of Marx*, Marshall's *Principles* and *Industry and Trade*, and Denis Robertson's *Study of Industrial Fluctuations*.

The objective of the elementary course was to provide students with the background to tackle *Capital*, which was the advanced course in economics. That is, in their second year, students took another 24-lecture course on political economy (1909–16) and on advanced economics (1919–29). The former course consisted of a detailed study of the first volume of *Capital*, while the latter course included more advanced aspects of Marxian economics and material on money, stock exchange, trusts, banking, international exchange, and foreign trade—see Appendix A.14.[34] The readings for the course included Marx's *Critique of Political Economy* and *Capital* (all three volumes), Henry Macrosty's *The Trust Movement in British Industry*, various government reports on trusts published by the Anti-Profiteering Committee under the Standing Committee on Trusts, and Hobson's *Evolution of Modern Capitalism*.

For the CLC to be successful, it was necessary for its students to return to their towns and villages and teach their fellow workers Marxian economics. To prepare them for the task, the CLC encouraged second-year students to undertake some tutorial work around London and at provincial classes. The provincial classes to which the CLC tutors returned were organized in terms of labor colleges or simply just classes associated with Plebs branches and later the NCLC. Like the CLC, the point of the provincial labor colleges was to educate workers for industrial and political struggle, with the difference that the workers were generally not full-time students but directly engaged in the workplace. Consequently, economics had to be taught "fundamentally from the Labour standpoint. Otherwise we ought to send our students to the Capitalist Universities. Our students must make the writings of Marx and Marxian scholars the basis of their studies ... " (Maclean 1916: 8).[35] But this education was not at the expense of excluding the study of Marshall, "the pontiff of present-day capitalist Economics, or the other great writers who have influenced or are to-day moulding economic thought" (Maclean 1916: 8). Hence, IWCE as carried out by the labor colleges and through the NCLC included both Marxian and Marshallian economics, with the emphasis on the former and a critical evaluation of the latter.

The provincial CLC and NCLC classes were modeled after the CLC classes. In particular, the early provincial CLC classes were one and a half hours a week for twenty-six weeks and the students had to write two essays a week. Later the NCLC classes lasted for twelve meetings and each meeting was two hours long. The class would open with the tutor giving a short exposition, followed by a student reading a couple of pages from, for example, *Value, Price and Profit*, and ending with class discussion and questions presided over by the tutor; however, written work was not required. Keen students were encouraged to become branch lecturers and eventually class lecturers, which meant they were encouraged to read extensively and develop good notes.

The cadre of economics lectures and tutors that emerged from the IWCE movement acquired a basic understanding of Marxian economics and an awareness of Marshallian economics. The economic lecturers at the CLC—Ashcroft, Mainwaring, Sims, Reynolds, and Robertson—had training in Marxian economics supplemented with in-depth study of *Capital* and related literature. The same can also be said of the provincial economic tutors, many of who attended CLC while others learned Marxian economics at the provincial labor colleges or through CLC–NCLC postal courses. In all, this cadre of over fifty and perhaps over two hundred economic lecturers and tutors constituted a far flung quasi-academic community where Marxian economics with the theory of choice for teaching and discussion—see Appendix A.14. Initially linked centrally to the CLC and later to the NCLC, the community consisted of labor colleges and affiliated courses that were geographically spread across the working-class communities of Great Britain and which were tied together through *The Plebs Magazine* (later renamed simply *The Plebs*). *Plebs* was a generalist journal for the IWCE movement that carried a wide range of articles, notices, and other information for students and tutors alike, including economic articles, book reviews, and translations-reprints of material such as extracts from *Capital* and letters on economics by Joseph Dietzgen—see Appendix A.14.

Although a quasi-academic community of Marxist economists existed outside the academy, the constraints it faced limited its effectiveness in teaching Marxian economics to the working class and its scholarly capabilities to broaden, enrich, and develop the theory. Most lecturers and tutors had a good basic understanding of Marxian economics, but depth was mostly limited to the three volumes of *Capital* plus supplemental readings, such as Lenin's *Imperialism*. Although a short summary might appear in *The Plebs*, the contributions of Hilferding, Kautsky, Trotsky, and Bukharin did not to any significant extent become part of the general teaching of Marxian theory. Still, their understanding of Marx and Marxian economics was as good if not better than any Cambridge economics tripos graduate understanding of Marshall and Marshallian economics.[36] On the other hand, the lecturers and tutors understanding of Marshallian economics was at least rudimentary, but did not include the theoretical developments associated with imperfect competition and Keynes in their lectures and tutorials; they were familiar, however, with marginal utility theory and understood the marginal productivity theory of distribution and did teach it and repudiated it at the same time.[37] Consequently, the concentration of Marx and Marxian economics made the teaching look to some students quite dated even though it was not.[38]

The community's scholarly engagement with Marxism was checkered. Because most of the provincial tutors had full-time non-academic jobs, they were limited in opportunities to engage in scholarship; and those who taught for a living had to teach so much to survive that they also did not have time to engage in positive critical scholarship. Thus, at times their Marxian economics became stale, dogmatic, and mechanical; but when time and energy permitted, they did read new textbooks, such as Bogdanoff's *A Short Course of Economic Science* (1925), and articles from *The Plebs* on Marxian economics and how to teach it, on national and international economic crises, and on the industries of Britain—see Appendix A.14. As a result, only a few—Ablett, Casey, Crick, Maclean, and Mainwaring—actually published a book or an article on Marxian economics; and none was able to engage with the developments in crisis theory and the modeling of the breakdown of capitalism. In addition, they entertained critiques of Marxian economics and especially the labor theory of value, even when poorly argued as the case with a very young Maurice Dobb (1922). The community as a whole generally accepted the soundness of the theory and rejected or ignored the various critiques associated with the "transformation problem." This was not due to provincialism of the community, that its members were ill-educated, or that the theory was believed to be true based on personal experience, although each point has an element of truth. Rather Marxian economics, in spite of its alleged theoretical flaws, provided a better understanding of the capitalist economy than did Marshallian price theory. Hence the alleged flaws were overlooked and/or minimized, especially when they were flouted by employers and propertied classes as part of their attack on militant workers and their efforts to improve their lot in life and make a more equitable and just society.[39]

It is clear that at least for the period 1909 to 1940, the IWCE movement did succeed in providing a really useful education for workers. A cadre of at least 200 Marxist-trained economics tutors was created and they did return or remain in their towns and villages teaching economic classes at the local labor college. However, success was hard won and, in the end, temporary. The nasty political warfare with the Communist Party of Great Britain, opposition to Marxism by conservative trade unionists who by the mid-1920s controlled many trade unions, economic decline of the Welsh coal-fields, the failure of the 1926 General Strike, and the Great Depression all contributed in various ways to the demise of the CLC, the inter-war decline in economic classes and students, and the shift away from Marxism to training courses for trade unionists by the NCLC.[40] But there was also a more particular reason: the continual opposition by the State, business community, and the WEA to the teaching "false economics" of Marxism to the working class. For example, workers that attended informal classes on Marxism, went to the CLC, or took classes at a local labor college were singled out by employers and denied employment—an outcome that cost the CLC the support of some trade unions who expected the students they financed to return and contribute as educators. In addition, the Board of Education made sure that Local Education Authorities' adult education classes did not have attributes of labor college classes, such as emphasis on social and economic issues, while local authorities prevented the NCLC from using state school rooms for classes and restricted or prevented the use of Plebs textbooks in their adult education classes. Moreover, the business community and the WEA promoted the use of university extra-mural classes in Marshallian economics to attack and "snuff out" the Marxian economic classes of the local labor colleges. Faced with such a broad and sustained attack for promoting and teaching a particular economic theory (a situation that the supporters of Marshallian economics never had to face), it is unsurprising that by 1940, the IWCE movement had ceased to be promoting an education that aided the working class in their struggle for social and industrial emancipation (Simon 1965, 1990b; Craik 1912, 1964; Thomas 1922; Hader and Lindeman 1929; Phillips and Putnam 1980; Young 1992; Millar and Lowe 1979; Kershaw 1910; Atkins 1981; Duncan 1992; Jones 1984; Cohen 1990a; Macintyre 1980; Maclean n.d.; Lewis 1984, 1993;

Tsuzuki 1983; Steele and Taylor 2004; McIlroy 1996; Cooke 2006; *The Plebs Magazine* 1909–39, various issues).

Communist Party and workers' schools

Formed in 1920, the Communist Party of Great Britain (CP) did not immediately attempt to establish its own schools to teach Marxism; rather they initially co-operatively engaged with the Plebs League, CLC, and the NCLC. However, the honeymoon was short-lived and soon dissent, disruption, and name-calling emerged which resulted in the CP withdrawing its participation in the IWCE movement. Yet at the local level where the party did not sponsor their own educational classes, communists participated in NCLC classes and even taught Marxian economic courses at labor colleges as a practical way of providing long-term study in Marxian economics. Although many CP members felt that NCLC classes were entirely adequate, the CP did attempt after 1924 to establish an alternative to the labor colleges, but it mostly involved Party training that emphasized immediate political action rather than an academic-educational approach to teaching Marxism.[41] Finally, in the early 1930s, the CP decided to publish a number of guides for a Marxist study course on political economy.[42]

To mark the fiftieth anniversary of Marx's death, the CP decided in 1933 to establish the Marx Memorial Library and Workers' School in London. The School's remit was to provide a range of courses, lectures, and other educational activities concerning Marxism, Soviet Union, and the CP. For the first year, the School gave a three-term course on political economy that covered the three volumes of *Capital* which included lectures and tutor-led study circles. It continued for the next couple of years, but then was discontinued because of the lack of students. Then in 1938 it offered a five-week course by John Strachey on "Political Economy." During the war, the School continued to publish syllabuses and study guides and train tutors to lead study circles at factories as well as offering extension courses on political economy. In 1943, Dobb's syllabus on "Economics of Capitalism" was published and sold 12,500 copies in just over twelve months. Similar to the previous syllabuses and study guides he had written, this was divided into lessons and provided guidance to study circles in the form of questions and supplemental material. In addition, there was R. Page Arnot's "Introduction to Political Economy."[43] Shortly after the establishment of the School, the Marx House School in Manchester was established by three ex-tutors of the South-East Lancashire Labour College in January 1934.[44] The founders offered a two-year training course that would transform the student's previous knowledge into scientific reasoning. The first year of lectures covered the sciences and sociology, while the second year was given to lectures on political economy, the works of Marx, Engels, and Lenin, and the struggle of the contemporary revolutionary movement. However, it never obtain enough students or tutors to be viable and so closed in 1938. But in 1940 a second

Marx House School was opened and it offered training courses as well as a ten-lesson correspondence course in political economy. In 1945, the CP realized that the Marx Schools in London and Manchester could not really complete with the WEA and NCLC which were also recognized as friendly associations, and thus closed them and ceased to be a provider of classes in Marxian economics. In the end, the CP's contribution to promoting an education that aided the working class in their struggle for social and industrial emancipation was not very significant; however, through Dobb's positive research into Marxian economics, the teaching of Marxian economics improved considerably (at least in terms of study guides) (Lewis 1993; Macintyre 1980; Miles 1984; Cohen 1990b; Dobb 1943; Arnot 1942; *Marx House Bulletin: Organ of the Marx Memorial Library and Workers' School*, issues January 1935, August 1941, October 1941, and February 1945).

Engagement with Marxism inside the university, 1900–45

At the turn of the century, historical economics and to a much lesser extent Marxism were components of economic teaching in British in universities and colleges. In Cambridge, socialism as a doctrine was a component of the Moral Sciences Tripos, but it (and Marxism) had no place in the Economics and Politics Tripos when it was established in 1903. In fact Marshall excluded the teaching of Marxian theory at Cambridge.[45] Similarly, at Oxford in the period prior to 1914, theory lectures were a combination of Mill and Marshall. In addition, there were lectures on socialism, capital and labor, and history of economic thought. Moreover at the provincial university colleges, such as University College at Nottingham, the elementary course on the theory of value (price) circa 1915 was structured along the lines of Marshall's *Economics of Industry*.[46] By the 1920s, interest in historical economics had declined to the vanishing point, but the teaching of Marx and socialism increased. In 1921, Oxford established a honours degree in Philosophy, Politics, and Economics with an examination paper in capital and labor (reflecting the concern over class harmony or class conflict) and an examination paper based on prescribed books which for economics formed the core of the history of economic thought and covered Smith, Ricardo, List, Marx, and Jevons. Therefore lectures were offered on the "relations of labour and capital," "Karl Marx, *Capital*," "labour problems and theories of wages," and "social progress in the last forty years." The lectures on Marx were, however, not supportive but highly critical. In particular the lectures by H. W. B. Joseph on "Marx's Theory of Value" (1922) and by A. D. Lindsay on "Karl Marx, Capital" (1925) were dismissive of the labor theory of value and hence his explanation of the origin and distribution of profits and of the existence of class conflict. However, in 1928, the capital and labor examination paper was dropped and replaced by one on advanced economic theory (which was defined as neoclassical theory). As a result, lectures on the problems of capital and labor cease to be given—no more labor problems and conflict between capital and labor. Then in 1933, the prescribed books examination papers were dropped and replaced by papers which included the works of Smith and Ricardo, public finance, and statistical measurement of national income. Hence lectures on Marx quickly cease to be given. What remained were lectures on Marshallian neoclassical economics, as represented in the works of A. C. Pigou, J. Robinson, A. Kahn, and R. Harrod.[47]

So by 1939, neoclassical economics had achieved a near-hegemonic victory at Oxford: gone was the Oxford historical and applied approach to political economy that was one of the driving forces behind the establishment of Oxford's distinctive Honour School in Philosophy, Politics, and Economics; and gone were prescribed reading and lectures on Marx and Marxism. The teaching of Marx and Marxian economics was also absent at virtually all other British universities and university colleges—there is no evidence of Marxist economists being employed at any other university except Leeds and Cambridge or lectures on Marxian economics being given at other universities including Cambridge. Even when presented in a positive light by an economist, such as H. D. Dickinson (Leeds), the labor theory of value was rejected and the rest of Marx's theoretical contributions were interpreted in terms of neoclassical theory. Moreover, even Dobb (Cambridge) attempted to meld together Marshall and Marx in the 1920s, which earned him the reputation of an "exponent of Bolshevism à la Marshall" (Ashley and Saunders 1930: 42). However, in the 1930s, he left Marshall behind and began to examine Marx in his own terms and from the perspective of classical political economy which culminated with the publication of *Political Economy and Capitalism* in 1937. At this same time he informally engaged with Cambridge students about Marxian economics, something that did not happen elsewhere.[48] Finally there were Sraffa's 1928–31 Cambridge "Lectures on the Advanced Theory of Value" in which he rejected Marshallian price theory, argued that classical political economy was an alternative to Marshallian economics, and advanced his interpretation of classical political economy based on the concepts of surplus, physical real costs, and asymmetrical treatment of distributional variables. Although pregnant with the possibility of producing an economic theory different from Marxian and neoclassical theory, this was not recognized by Cambridge lecturers and students. This absence of Marxism or any other kind of non-neoclassical theorizing from the thinking and awareness of British economists in the inter-war period was legitimized by the widespread adoption of Marshall's continuity thesis which asserted that the entire history of economic theory led with little deviation to the neoclassical theory taught and espoused since 1900.

Along with the rise to dominance of Marshallian neoclassical theory, British economics became, as a result of a number of powerful institutional forces, increasingly homogenized. One was the Royal Economic Society that actively promoted itself as the economic society for all British economists, while discouraging the view that there should be other competing or alternative associations for British economists.[49] The second institutional force was the role of *The Economic Journal* in projecting what constituted economics and the forefront of economic research. Although the "neoclassical theory" content of the journal grew slowly over time, by the 1930s it was clear that what constituted acceptable economic theory was neoclassical economic theory broadly interpreted. The "true-believer" use of neoclassical theory and methodology, irrespective of the particular topics to which it was applied, was the defining characteristic of a young British economist in the 1930s, as starkly evident by the articles published in the newly formed *Economica* (1921) and the *Review of Economic Studies* (1933).[50]

The third less obtrusive but extremely powerful institutional force was the role of examinations and external examiners from Cambridge and the London School of Economics in ensuring that non-neoclassical material was not taught at provincial institutions. For example, a student entering University College, Southampton in the 1930s to read economics under Percy Ford (former economics tutor at Ruskin College) would in fact be reading for a University of London external degree. Thus the economic content of the degree would be determined by the University of London and particularly by the London School of Economics. Consequently the student would read material by Wicksell, Knight, Marshall, Keynes, Pigou, Hayek and Robbins, but not Marx or any historical, institutional, or Marxian economist. Moreover, the lecturers would have to lecture only on the neoclassical material being prescribed so as to not disadvantage their students when it came to exams, since the examinations were set by the University of London. The situation at Southampton was not different from the situations faced by university colleges elsewhere. Even if an economics department at a provincial institution could determine its own content, the role of the external examiner would generally ensure that the content did not stray too far from neoclassical economics. The final force concerned the appointments of professors and lecturers in that the status of Cambridge and later the London School of Economics ensured through the letters of reference that only proper neoclassical economists were appointed (Groenewegen 1995; Young and Lee 1993; *Oxford University Gazette*, 1900–39, various issues; Chester 1986; Koot 1987; Kadish 1982, 1989; Middleton 1998; Wood 1959; Pollitt 1988; Tribe 2000; Coats 1967; Lee 1993; King 1988; A. Robinson 1990; Collard 1990; Turner 1989; Dickinson 1936–37; Ashley and Saunders 1930; Dobb 1922; Meek 1977; Bellamy 1986–87; Macintyre 1980; Marcuzzo 2001, 2005; Signorino 2005; Kurz and Salvadori 2005).

From neoclassical dominance to cracks in the status quo of British economics, 1945–75

In the post-war period, the IWCE movement did not revive and the NCLC moved away from providing a really useful education needed to understand

and change society towards providing specialized training in trade unions matters. As a result, the teaching of Marxian economics by the NCLC declined throughout the period until 1964, when the NCLC was absorbed by the Trades Union Congress and its teaching of Marxian economics ceased altogether. But this was not entirely the fault of the NCLC. By 1945 many unions and the TUC were dominated by right-wing trade unionists who opposed Marxism. Hence there were purges of trade-union officials who were communists and attacks upon any educational/training provisions that seem to deal with Marxism and were provided by CP members. Moreover, when the TUC sponsored training schemes through universities, such as Glasgow, the London School Economics, and Leeds, the economics taught was most assuredly neoclassical economics (which the tutors believed was the truth) with no Marxian economics in sight (much to the disgruntlement of the workers taking the lectures). Moreover, the WEA continue to monitor and constrain the teaching of any kind of Marxism. In light of the emerging Cold War, the McCarthyite attitudes of WEA officers who did not believe that communists could be objective teachers, and anti-communist TUC and state officials who threatened the WEA with the withdrawal of grants and other financial support, the WEA actively restricted the employment of tutors who were members of the CP or fellow-travelers. Consequently, the working class and its associated educational organizations were no longer a possible source on which to develop a community of Marxist economists which could challenge the community of neoclassical economists that were largely located in universities; and attempts to do this in the turbulent 1960s and 1970s were stillborn or ended after a couple of years.

This raises the question of whether British universities could be a possible site on which to develop an alternative community of economists that could challenge neoclassical economics. In general, from 1945 through the 1960s British economics and what was taught at universities was some variant of the reigning neoclassical economics. In particular, there existed no association of economists or other institutional arrangement around which critics of and dissenters from neoclassical economics could gather and develop a collective existence. Rather as relatively isolated academics, they had little or no support within academia. If they severely questioned or challenged the orthodoxy or attempted to provide a anti-neoclassical theory, they were singled out for attacked and marginalization, as in the cases of Philip Andrews and George Richardson. Moreover, just being a Marxist meant that promotion was denied, as happened to Ronald Meek when teaching at the University of Glasgow in the 1950s. Thus they stood little chance against the cleansing and discriminatory proclivities of the mainstream.[51] Finally, there existed an element of conformity within British economics which impressed upon British economists that they were all colleagues who belonged to the same economic association, the Royal Economic Society; and the Royal Economic Society portrayed itself as the only institution for all British economists. Consequently, even if individual economists did disagree with neoclassical theory they did not, at least in the period 1945 to the mid-1960s, see themselves as so different from their neoclassical colleagues to feel that their interests would be best served by establishing a new economic association or a new economic journal[52] (McIlroy 1990a, 1990b, 1990c, 1996; Fieldhouse 1985; Young and Lee 1993; Newman 2002; Lee and Irving-Lessmann 1992).

Heterodox economics research

Of course there were discernible non-Marxist and Marxist heterodox economics research agendas being carried out by individuals in British universities. One non-Marxist agenda was Andrews's theory of competitive oligopoly which he developed throughout this period. In addition, he supervised doctoral students (for example Harry Edwards) while George Richardson indirectly contributed to it and in the process help develop the doctrine of normal cost prices. However, the doctrine made no impact on British economics.[53] A second heterodox research agenda was in Marxian economics most notably carried out by Dobb, Meek, and Ronald Bellamy, the only Marxist economists in British universities in the 1950s, from 1945 to 1956. The agenda started with the publication of Dobb's *Studies in the Development of Capitalism* in 1946 which lead to extensive theoretical and historical debate among historians in the Communist Party Historians' Group.[54] The next significant event was the writing, by a group of Marxist economists headed by John Eaton (whose real name was Stephen Bodington), of *Political Economy: A Marxist Textbook* (1949).[55] The text, written at the level of a first-year Oxbridge undergraduate and as comprehensive as Marshall's *Principles*, covered all of Marxian economics, starting with the historical setting of capitalism and ending with the advance to socialism. Moreover, from 1945 up to 1957, the Marxist journals *The Modern Quarterly* (new series 1945–53) and *The Marxist Quarterly* (1954–57) contributed to the Marxist research agenda by carrying articles on left-wing Keynesianism and full employment (Dobb 1950; Singh 1956), on the labor theory of value, Marxist crisis theory, monopoly capital (Bellamy 1956), Keynes and Marx (Meek 1950–51), and important book reviews (Dobb 1952; Bellamy 1955, 1957). Finally, Meek engaged in a historical study of the labor theory of value that culminated with the publication of *Studies in the Labour Theory of Value* in 1956. While this decade of research in Marxian economics was highly productive, it did not have any noticeable impact on British economics and on the teaching of Marxian economics to university students.[56] It came to an end in 1956–57 with the Soviet Union's crushing of the Hungarian uprising and Khruschev's speech detailing Stalin's atrocities.[57]

Related to the Marxian agenda but clearly distinct from it was a third research heterodox research agenda initially started under the name of left-wing Keynesianism and evolved into a less politically-charged name of Post

Keynesian economics in the 1970s. The beginning of left (or social democratic) Keynesianism was with Joan Robinson's 1942 (1991) essay on Marxian economics followed by a number of essays in which she argued that full employment was not possible without common ownership of the means of production, national economic planning, price controls, and a national investment policy. Then there was Kalecki's 1943 article on the "Political Aspects of Full Employment" which was, in turn, followed by William Beveridge's *Full Employment in a Free Society* (1944) and Oxford economists' *The Economics of Full Employment* (1945). Left-wing Keynesians, drawing upon Kalecki's representation of Keynes's theory of effective demand, argued that economic activity, hence the level of output and employment, was determined by consumption, private investment, and government expenditures; and then, drawing on the Hansen–Steindl stagnation thesis, argued that private investment would never be sufficient to generate full employment.[58] Thus, they pointed out that full employment could be achieved by increasing military expenditures and expenditures supporting imperialism; but more humane economic policies could be pursued that would achieve the same results, such as producing a more equal income distribution that would promote consumption or increasing government expenditures on social programs, social infrastructure, and nationalized industries. That full employment could be achieved without significantly altering the relationship between capitalists and workers earned it the enmity of Marxists and the CP.[59] But on the other hand, since the theoretical basis of left-wing Keynesianism had some similarities with Marxian theory, it was or at least could be incompatible with neoclassical theory.

Although pregnant with heterodox possibilities, left-wing Keynesianism place in British economics declined with the emergence of the Cold War and the corresponding anti-communist/McCarthyism rhetoric and actions from the 1940s onwards to the point that, while it may have been taught at a number of universities, it only existed at Cambridge as an ongoing research program. Thus, it was in Robinson's work on generalizing the *General Theory* culminating with the publication of *Accumulation of Capital* (1956), Kaldor's work on alternative theories of distribution and economic growth, and Luigi Pasinetti's work on growth and distribution but without the political edge that left-wing Keynesianism survived. The final heterodox research agenda that emerged after 1945 was associated with Sraffa's *Production of Commodities by Means of Commodities* (1960) rehabilitation of the surplus approach. In this case, after 1960 Dobb and Meek and numerous Cambridge students (see Chapter 7) used Sraffa to engage with Marx and vice-versa while Pasinetti drew upon Sraffa to launch a lifetime research project into structural surplus models and economic growth and change.[60] Of the four post-war heterodox research agendas mention, three were largely if not entirely located at Cambridge; and this was especially the case in the 1960s. Thus, the co-existence in the 1960s of Marx, the surplus, accumulation of capital, and distribution and of Dobb, Kaldor, Pasinetti, Robinson, and

Sraffa drew post-graduates and visitors to Cambridge and excited students already at Cambridge—see Appendix A.15. This had a significant impact on the emergence and development of heterodox economics in Britain from 1970 onwards (Lee 1998; Eaton 1951; King 2002, 2004b; Dobb, 1949, 1950, 1955, 1969, 1970b; Bellamy 1981; Howard and King 1992, 2004; Kaldor 1956, 1978; Pasinetti 1974, 1993, and in Arestis and Sawyer 2000; Robinson 1956).

New Left and student activism, 1956–75

The New Left emerged in 1956–57 as a result of the shattering impact on the Communist Party and the British Left in general of Khruschev's speech denouncing Stalin's crimes, of the suppression of the riots in Poland, of the Suez Crisis, and of the Hungarian uprising. Consequently, a wider field for socialist politics came into being where non-aligned Marxists could fight for socialism outside the Communist Party. Joining in the fight were middle-class non-aligned "angry young men and women" who rejected the complacency of post-war Britain as well as the single-lane road to socialism via nationalization and centralized state planning. The evolving view from the New Left was that socialism meant more than simply material well-being; it also meant social equality and an improved quality of life. This intellectual ferment produced a growing disenchantment with the traditional presentation of Marxian economic theory as well as with the arguments that Keynesian techniques could produce a more humane capitalism; but at the same time it produced a renewed interest in Marxism and more particularly in socialist economics. The questioning of tradition and authority in the fight for socialism became a hallmark of the New Left; it also became a characteristic of the articles published in various New Left publications, culminating in the *New Left Review* (1960) (Chun 1993; Kenny 1995).

Independent of New Left political activities, the latter half of the 1960s saw a particular upsurge of radical activism both outside and inside universities. With the election of a Labour government in 1964, many expected the development of economic policies that would maintain economic growth and which would move the UK closer to socialism. However, the period of 1964 to 1970 was dominated by the introduction of wage and price controls to deal with inflation, the perception of slow economic growth, cuts in social expenditures, devaluation, and attempts to curb the power of trade unions and the ability of workers to engage in strike action. In addition, there were international issues regarding Rhodesia and South Africa and white-minority rule and support of the United States in Vietnam as well as domestic issues about immigration and Northern Ireland which simultaneously raised questions about the degree to which the Labour government supported imperialism and racism. Collectively, these issues and events produced a radicalizing effect on students and younger academics in higher education.

Inside the university sector students began questioning the constitutional and disciplinary procedures by which universities had hitherto operated. This involved, between 1967 to 1975, sit-ins at nearly all of the forty-four universities and a few polytechnics as well as rent strikes, boycott of classes, and paint-spraying of buildings. The expansion of the university sector both in terms of the number of universities and the number of students generated a less academic-collegial oriented environment; students felt estranged from their lecturers and tutors while both the students and the teaching staff felt estranged from those who ran the institutions. In particular, decisions were made and imposed on students and staff alike without any consultation or consideration. Moreover, in some cases, such as at Warwick, decisions made by the University (largely without consultation with the staff) tended to favor particular areas that were closely connected to local business interests; the outcome of which meant that students and staff in the more academic less business-oriented areas had to cope with a declining physical environment and under-stocked libraries. In some cases, students were left without student unions. These imprecise but deeply felt grievances and issues eventually erupted into student activism (which in various universities and polytechnics was supported by some of the teaching staff and governors). The spark often came from an unexpected source, such as the appointment of a new Director at the London School of Economics or a supplement in *The Times* touting science at Warwick tailored to the needs of industry; but once the activism-opposition started, the harsh response (at least in student eyes) by the universities generated additional student activism. One outcome of the student activism was that students and the younger staff took an increasing interest in radical politics which opposed the capitalist system; and for students interested in economics and budding post-graduate economists this translated into an interest in Marxism as well as in critiques of neoclassical economic theory (Williams 1970; Bagnall and Cox 1973; Radice 1973c; Childs 1997; Stewart 1989; Dahrendorf 1995; Thompson 1980).

Complementing the rise of student activism was the breakdown in the homogeneity of economics departments across universities and polytechnics. That is, the rapid expansion of higher education in the 1960s to 1973 with the establishment of new universities and thirty polytechnics and the expansion of undergraduate and post-graduate student numbers provided space and opportunity for the appointment of critical, dissenting, radical, or Marxist professors and lecturers. From 1964 to 1974, the number students pursuing single and joint honours degrees in economics increased by over 125 per cent, the number of post-graduate degrees awarded in economics increased by nearly 300 percent, the number to teaching posts increased by over 100 percent. Because the need to appoint many economists within a relatively short time span, it became possible for the likes of Andrews and Meek to be appointed as professors and heads of economic departments at provincial universities established since the 1950s. In addition, appointments for lectureships became relatively easier for younger radical-Marxist economists, especially at the new universities in the 1960s and later at the new polytechnics in the 1970s and early 1980s[61] (Stewart 1989; Middleton 1998; Coats and Booth 1978).

Crisis in mainstream economics

Perceptions of the state of economics and economic theory from 1965 to 1975 was one of crisis; but the crisis envisaged varied among economists. One view sought the origin of the crisis in the abstract and unrealistic demeanor of the rapidly evolving, mathematized neoclassical theory that was incapable of answering important economic policy questions. A variant of this view was the concern that the increasingly abstract economic theory was losing its grounding in the real world because its assumptions lacked empirical validity. And this concern was increasing because economists seem uninterested in developing new empirical data designed to validate their assumptions and enrich their understanding of the workings of the economy; and because it appeared that econometrics could not provide reliable, stable results supporting predictions derived from the theory, the case frequently cited being the Phillips Curve. A second view of the crisis focused on the theoretical inadequacy of the Keynesian neoclassical synthesis to account for inflation and more generally stagflation.[62] This perceived inadequacy provided room for heretical forms of neoclassical theory, that is monetarism, to challenge the theoretical and policy status quo.[63] The challenge was interpreted by many economists as a crisis qua counter-revolution; and the solution was a better developed and more logically coherent neoclassical theory. In particular, the Keynesian neoclassical synthesis became viewed as theoretically incoherent, with the result that it eventually was replaced by rational expectations and New Keynesian macroeconomics.

For most economists, the crisis was an internal issue in that the existing body of neoclassical economic theory, while generally sound, had some problems that needed ironing out. Thus, there was no loss of faith in the theory or in the capability of economists to use the theory to discuss, analyze, and resolve important policy issues. However, for others the crisis arose precisely because of a loss of faith in neoclassical economic theory. Most of these economists agreed that neoclassical economic theory as it stood could not deal with real-world problems, that it was too abstract and not grounded in the real world, and that it was generally irrelevant to many important economic issues. In addition, they also believed that fundamental problems existed with the theory. For example, the Cambridge economists' extension of Keynes into the area of value, distribution, and economic growth produced both models and results that were different from neoclassical growth models and results, thus suggesting the orthodox modeling of economic growth was wrong. Moreover the capital controversy revealed that important aspects of aggregate neoclassical theory were logically incoherent. Finally, the methodological contributions of Keynes in terms of uncertainty, expectations, and historical time suggested that the static equilibrium nature of neoclassical economic theory rendered it fundamentally incapable of explaining how the real economy actually worked (Postan 1968; Worswick 1972; Leontief 1971; Phelps Brown 1972; Anon 1973; Bleaney 1996; Johnson 1971a; Robinson 1972; Radice 1973c; Knapp 1973; Beckerman 1976; Middleton 1998).

No one of these problems by themselves resulted in an economist losing faith in neoclassical economics, but as a collective they did, although it took time and a great deal of soul searching. Moreover, economists took an even longer period of time before taking a positive step of explicitly rejecting neoclassical theory entirely and developing a non-neoclassical economic theory. Thus, it was easier for economists to argue that neoclassical economic theory was irrelevant or "rubbish"; however, it was much harder for them to take break with it entirely and develop an alternative. The break was not only with the theory; it was also with societal body of economists. In short, those who took this route were not only blasphemers; they were also located beyond the pale. That some economists could contemplate such a break implies that the crisis in economics went far deeper than the problems with theory would suggest. In particular, neoclassical economic theory as well as the organizational and institutional arrangement of economics in Britain collectively faced in the 1960s the beginnings of a challenge by an alternative theory with its own organizational and institutional arrangements.

Moving away from mainstream economics

The Marxian economics that was articulated and taught in the inter-war years was seen by many as not capable of providing cogent, critical insights to the workings of post-war British capitalism, the economic developments in third world countries, or the economic problems facing socialist economies. Moreover, to some, Marxian theory appeared stagnate and flawed and it could only be revitalized through some kind of synthesis with mainstream economics.[64] With the advent of the New Left and its questioning of tradition and authority, the angry ones, such as Perry Anderson, Michael Barratt Brown, Robin Blackburn, Ken Coates, John Hughes, Meek, Joan Robinson, Bob Rowthorn, and Anthony Topham, opened Marxian economics to new interpretations and developments, including Sraffa's *Production of Commodities* and subsequent research emanating from it. Moreover, they drew upon Veblenian, Galbraithian, and other non-Marxian radical-popular critiques of capitalism.[65] Finally, they critically evaluated shortcomings of economics in general, such as being a purely technical discipline where economic categories were not saturated with social significance; of neoclassical economic theory, such as its reliance on methodological individualism, ignoring social-economic power, and being unable to take account of historical time or secular history; and of the practitioners who blithely design economic policies based on theory without first even inquiring whether the theory and the actual economic conditions mesh—the case particularly noted being Kaldor's tax policies for underdeveloped countries. Finally, they criticized Keynesian theory along with indicative planning and income policies because they could not provide solutions to the bourgeois problems of growth and inflation and because they ignored the more fundamental issue of the exploitation of workers produced by capitalist social relations. The outcomes of this flowering of openness, criticism, inquisitiveness, and eclecticism were increasingly sophisticated debates on economic issues and policies and the beginning of a more robust Marxian economic theory which could be considered a body of economic theory in its own right as well as a replacement for neoclassical economic theory as it provided a better theoretical understanding of capitalism.

Supporting the theoretical developments were various organizational developments. Quickly emerging were new publishing outlets that were not associated with the Communist Party. In particular, New Left journals were established, including *The New Reasoner* (1957–59), *University and Left Review*[66] (1957–59) and *New Left Review* (1960). Later the *New Left Review* (NLR) created its own publishing house, New Left Books (1970).[67] The significance of the NLR was that it quickly evolved from a popular forum into an academic journal devoted to developing Marxian theory. In particular, the early economic articles were eclectic and non-technical; and topics included imperialism, left-wing Keynesian critique of post-war capitalism, review of contemporary Marxist economics, and a discussion of the rate of exploitation from a Sraffian perspective. However, by the late 1960s, articles concerned with Marxian theory or from a Marxian perspective began to dominate.[68] Thus the NLR became an important outlet in the Britain for articles concerned with or utilizing Marxian economic theory. Moreover, in response to the growing interest in workers' control, the Institute for Workers' Control was established in 1968 as a loose organization for putting on conferences and publishing pamphlets about various aspects of workers' control. Finally, many of the economists and political economists of or around the New Left —including Barratt Brown, Blackburn, Coates, Hughes, Robinson, and Rowthorn—held university appointments. These developments provided the beginning of an institutional basis from which to challenge British economics as well as suggesting an alternative institutional arrangement for economics that was a seamless thread from academia to applied policy developments in trade unions (although this latter possibility never materialized). These kinds of developments made it possible for the first time for some British economists to actually think about seeking an alternative framework to the status quo of British economics (Chun 1993; Kenny 1995; Meek 1955; Dickinson 1963; Blackburn 1966, 1969; Samuel 1960; Hall 1960; Robinson 1965; Kaldor 1964; Anderson 1969; Howard and King 2004; Williams 1976–77).

7 Heterodox economics in Britain, 1970–96

As noted in the Introduction, the complexity of the history of heterodox economics combined with the lack of extensive detailed studies on components of the history means that it is not yet possible to produce a general history of heterodox economics or a generalized historical identity of heterodox economists. Some detailed studies have been produced on specific heterodox theories and on the organizational and institutional components of the history and thereby have contributed to creating a historical identity for heterodox economists. This chapter is a further contribution to this agenda in that it reconstructs the historical emergence of Marxian-Post Keynesian-heterodox economics in terms of identity, institutions, and organizations in Britain from 1970 to 1996. The first section sets the historical stage by covering the rise and fall of the efforts to develop Marxian-heterodox economics within the Conference of Socialist Economists from 1970 to 1975. Cast out into the intellectual wilderness, the second section deals with the non-Cambridge and Cambridge efforts to create a Post Keynesian-heterodox identity and institutional and organizational support for that identity from 1974 to 1988. The third section deals with the fruits of these efforts, that is the creation and activity of Post-Keynesian Economics Study Group, of the Malvern conferences, and of the development of various publishing outlets from 1988 to 1996.

Conference of Socialist Economists and Heterodox Economics, 1970 to 1975

By the mid-1960s there were a number of students studying economics while at the same time partaking in socialist politics. Their activities lead them to reject, for socialist reasons, the neoclassical economics they learnt in class as well as becoming skeptical of the reformist aspects of the economics of Keynes and the left-wing Keynesians of the Cambridge school. However, the combination of politics and the student uprising in France in 1968, the Cambridge capital theory controversy, and the economics of the Cambridge school prompted many to become interested in "socialist" economics. Moreover, in 1967 Raymond Williams, Stuart Hall, and Edward Thompson (with help from many colleagues) produced a pamphlet called *May Day Manifesto*. It opened with the observation that the Labour Party was no longer just an inadequate agency for socialism; rather it was now an active collaborator in the process of reproducing capitalist society. The *Manifesto* then went on to tie the various existing single-issue campaigns to a critique of capitalism; and finished with the argument that the campaigns needed to become part of a unified movement. With the help of still more colleagues, including Bob Rowthorn and Tom Wengraf, the pamphlet was revised and reissued the following year as the *May Day Manifesto 1968*. One of the arguments forcibly pushed in the *Manifesto* was the necessity for socialists to build new organizations from which to press their alternative policies and demands; and one of its principles was that people on the left should be able to discuss openly with each other (Williams 1968, 1979; Rustin 1980; Rowthorn 1967; Chun 1993; Kenny 1995).

In the spring of 1969, there were two conferences —one sponsored by the Institute of Workers' Control and the second by the May Day Manifesto Group and others called the National Convention of the Left—which drew together over 600 activists from a variety of left-wing organizations and campaigns, including young (and old) New Left-socialists-radicals economists. At the conferences young "socialist" economists got together to discuss various issues about the current economic situation in Britain. This positive experience prompted them to think about a conference of socialist economists where they could concentrate on the problems of political economy without the constraints of political parties or the antagonisms by mainstream economists.[1] Hugo Radice, a Cambridge post-graduate economics student and who was present at both conferences, quickly acted upon this sentiment. In June 1969 he sent a flyer to his economic colleagues at Cambridge announcing a meeting to look at the possibility of developing an alternative approach, particularly a socialist alternative approach, to mainstream economics:

[ECONOMICS OR POLITICAL ECONOMY?]
Many of us who study or teach economics feel that much of our subject matter is irrelevant and meaningless in the face of the intense social and economic problems of the world. For the most part, economics takes the existing capitalist system for granted, and is concerned solely with making it work more 'efficiently', or with making marginal adjustments which are totally inadequate. Furthermore, economists persistently deny that economic problems are inevitably social and political problems as well.

For committed socialists, economics as it is currently practised is seen as clearly supporting the status quo, both ideologically and practically. For many others, it is just totally divorced from the realities of mass starvation, imperialism, poverty, unemployment and inequalities of all kinds. It is easy simply to reject economics as 'bourgeois' or 'irrelevant', and to see political activity as of far greater importance than academic study. It is equally easy for those who have acquired some knowledge of Marxist theory to engage in theoretical discussion among themselves. What is harder, but absolutely necessary, is to develop a real alternative— a practical, living, developing political economy, devoted to the committed analysis of social and economic problems, challenging the existing capitalist system and its ideology, forming an integral part of our political practice.

It is true that in Cambridge alternative approaches are to some extent available. Neoclassical theory has been attacked and partially defeated, and many socialists work and teach here. But little of this filters through to the uninitiated. Much of the work being done is highly theoretical, and as yet has had little substantive effect on the courses being offered. Surely given the resources available it ought to be possible to begin working seriously and systematically at developing the socialist alternative?

(Radice 1969)

The meeting was attended by a number of economists, including Rowthorn, Ajit Singh, and possibly Sam Aaronovitch and Robin Murray; and emerging from it was the desire to have further meetings as well as a conference. Over the summer Radice, Rowthorn, Aaronovitch, and Murray decided, after consulting with other left-wing economists, to organize a Conference of Socialist Economists. Sending out a letter to any and all possible socialist or left-wing economists, they stated

In comparison with the vast mass of economic literature now being produced, socialist economists have contributed in only a very limited way to debates on outstanding theoretical questions and to the analysis of modern capitalism. In the knowledge that to make such a contribution requires a cooperative effort and opportunities for a full exchange of ideas, a group of us ... have worked out a programme for a first meeting. ...

(Rowthorn et al. 1969)

The conference was held on 10–11 January 1970 in London at the Marx Memorial Library and at the nearby National Union of Furniture Trade Operators Hall and was attended by over ninety individuals, mostly economists. There were three sessions, one on the capital-theory controversy, another on development economics, and the third on the internationalization of capital.[2] There was a fourth session for the discussion of future activities at which a committee, consisting of Aaronovitch, Murray, Radice, Geoff Kay, Bodington, Neil Lockwood, and Wengraf, was elected to plan a second conference on the economic role of the state in modern capitalism.

The committee began organizing the next conference and at the same time established a newsletter to keep interested economists informed as to what was going on with regard to the future conference as well as on matters of other interests, such as seminars, other conferences, and recent books and articles. In addition, a register of socialist economists was developed which included names, addresses and areas of interest for the purpose to help facilitate communication between economists working in the same field or in the same geographical area. The second conference took place at King's College, Cambridge, on October 17–18, 1970. The conference organizers introduced the economic role of the state as one of the most critical problems facing Marxists:

> With increasing socialization and centralization of the means of production has come increasing intervention and direct participation by the state in the economy in particular, but also in all other aspects of social life; thus the state bulks larger and larger in our analysis as well as in our political activity. As political economists, we must contribute to a clearer understanding of this problem by analyzing the nature and extent of the links binding the state to the capitalist economy. Such an analysis requires a continual interplay between a theory of the state, as a general framework of analysis, and empirical and historical studies of the specifics of the situation in Britain and elsewhere. This conference is intended to serve as a starting point for this important task.
>
> (Radice 1970)

The conference attracted some 140 participants which heard two papers at the opening session, one on the Marxist theory of the state by Wengraf and a second on the state in bourgeois economic theory by Lockwood. At the afternoon session, Barratt Brown, Bellamy, and Bill Warren gave three on different views of the role of the state in the post-war British economy. Another fifteen papers were disseminated as background reading. The concluding session of the conference dealt with future activities and it was here that the Conference of Socialist Economists (CSE) was established as a permanent organization.[3] In addition, it was agreed to examine the possibility of publishing a journal. Finally, given the intense debate over international business enterprises and their relationship to the state, it was decided that the CSE should hold the next conference in June 1971 on Britain and the European Economic Community (EEC).

Because of organizational difficulties, the conference was moved to December 1971.[4] In its place was held, in May 1971, a working CSE Conference where seven working papers on topics dealing with Britain and the EEC were presented. More importantly the participants at the conference established the working framework of the CSE. It consisted of a coordinating committee which managed the day-to-day activities of the CSE, oversaw the organization of the annual conference (which was carried out locally), and produced a newsletter; and an editorial group elected to run the *Bulletin of the Conference of Socialist Economists.*[5] A third component of CSE was the establishment of local CSE groups which would be encouraged to hold seminars or small conferences on more specialist topics. The emerging framework combined with a theoretically heterogeneous and pluralistic socialist membership meant that the CSE began its life as an open organization whose members were interested in a wide range of theoretical and applied issues from a Marxian or other left perspective[6] (Radice 1970, 1971a, 1972b, 1973c, 1980; Rowthorn, et al. 1969; Aaronovitch, Murray, and Radice 1969; Picciotto 1986; Bellamy 1970; CSE *Newsletter*, February 1970, April 1970, July 1970, January 1971, April 1971, and July 1971)

Developing Marxian-Heterodox Economics, 1971 to 1975

Once formed, the activities of the CSE contributed significantly to the building of social networks and institutions necessary for the development of Marxian-heterodox economics.[7] The purpose of the *Bulletin* was to provide a general forum for exchanging ideas by publishing conference papers, articles, and notes and reviews. Thus in its six years of existence, from 1971 to 1976, fifty-nine of the seventy-six articles published were on economic topics, and of the these seventeen dealt with Sraffa-value theory themes and two dealt with Post Keynesian themes; and all of them were original and a majority of them came from CSE conferences, day schools, and study groups. Moreover, the *Bulletin* quickly became an accepted academic journal with library subscriptions increasing from seven in 1973 to fifty in 1975 (see Appendix A.15), as well as an important academic publishing outlet for Marxist-heterodox economists.

The CSE also continued holding an annual conference. At the 1971 conference on Britain and the EEC, it was decided that the theme of the 1972 conference would be "The Marxist Theory of Crisis." However, it was eventually broadened to include Post Keynesian theory of capitalist crisis. Thus the conference theme became "The Nature of Capitalist Crisis" and it included papers on Marxian crisis theory, inflation, profitability, and the Post Keynesian theory of capital crisis, and a discussion on Marx vs. Keynes led by Joan Robinson and Rowthorn.[8] Following on from it a specialist conference was planned on "Marxian theory of money and finance" but was broadened to include radical Keynesian theory of money and the problem of inflation; hence, the conference transformed into one on money and inflation. About 70 participants heard papers by Kregel, Adrian Winnett, Rowthorn, Pat Devine, Meghnad Desai, and George Zis on topics ranging from Post Keynesian monetary theory to Marxian theory of inflation to monetarism; and after the conference closed Radice led a discussion on money and finance capital.[9] The 1974 CSE conference was on imperialism and approximately two hundred participants heard papers ranging from dependency theory, unequal exchange, and international monetary crisis to case studies of Brazil, South Africa, and Ireland. At the conference it was decided that the next one would have multiple themes instead of a single one. Thus the 1975 conference had three papers on Marx, money and inflation, one on housing, and one on the political economy of women.[10]

Besides conferences, the CSE supported various activities initiated by its members that contributed to the building of the heterodox community of economists. From 1972 to 1975 it supported fourteen day-schools on specialized topics ranging from capital theory, the teaching of economics, and the international economy to money and imperialism; and attendance generally ranged from twenty to over seventy participants—see Appendix A.15. Members also formed established six study groups as well as four local groups, Warwick, Sussex, and two in London—see Appendix A.15. Because economists dominated the CSE membership at this time,[11] traditional economic topics tended to dominate the activities.[12] However, the study group format did permit members to examine novel, fringe, and interdisciplinary areas, the political economy of women and housing groups being the best examples[13] (Radice 1972b, 1973a, 1973b; Conference of Socialist Economists 1972b; CSE *Newsletter*, 1973–76; Kregel 1972; Winnett 1973).

Sraffa-value-theory debate

In Cambridge in the 1960s Robinson, Dobb, and others argued that Sraffa's *Production of Commodities* provided a particular attack on the logical foundations of neoclassical economic theory and particularly the neoclassical theory of distribution. In June 1969, Barbara MacLennan at the University of Manchester invited Dobb to give a paper at the staff seminar on either Marx or Sraffa. Dobb agreed and in October gave a paper on "Theories of Distribution from Ricardo to Sraffa." The emphasis of the paper was on articulating the implications of what Dobb called the Sraffa system on understanding classical and neoclassical theories of distribution. So when asked to give a paper at the first CSE conference, he redrafted the Manchester paper providing a little more discussion of the implication of the Sraffa system for Marx, but otherwise the content remained the same. Nuti in his comments on Dobb's paper emphasized the critique of neoclassical production and distribution theory[14] (MacLennan 1969a, 1969b; Dobb 1969, 1970b; Nuti 1970a).

While CSE members appreciated the critical thrust of the Sraffa system regarding neoclassical economic theory, they were more interested in exploring its implications for Marxian economic theory, as suggested by Robinson in 1965 and hinted at by Dobb and Nuti:

> I should like to suggest for discussion, therefore, that a promising way of approaching the theory of distribution could be that of combining the Dmitriev–Sraffa relation between wage and profit rates with the little we know—not least from Marx—about the interaction of real and monetary phenomena.
>
> (Nuti 1970a: 6)

In particular many CSE members wanted to move beyond the eclectic theoretical analysis of contemporary capitalism, which they thought amounted to no more than radical Keynesianism, to a more coherent Marxian economic theory. However, what it would consist of was open to debate. Drawing on Sraffa's book, Dobb, Robinson, and John Eatwell argued that it might be possible to develop an alternative economic theory based on the surplus approach but independent of the labor theory of value and other questionable aspects of Marxian economic theory. Moreover, a close study of Sraffa's work led Ian Steedman to articulate the view that Marx's value theory and theory of profits suffered similar problems to those found in neoclassical theory.[15] This prompted others, such as Rowthorn, to question whether Marx after Sraffa was really Marxian economic theory. Thus, in May 1972 the first CSE day school was held at Cambridge on "Capital Theory and Marxist Political Economy."[16]

The purpose of the day school was to assist those who were not experts to relate the issues of the capital theory debate to the basic concepts of Marxist economics. Steedman[17] concentrated on the reswitching debate while Rowthorn[18] discussed the relation of the Sraffa system and the Cambridge school to Marxist theory; and Dobb summed up the discussion. Over seventy individuals attended the day school and took part in four hours of sustained discussion in which the initial disagreements were voiced that eventually evolved into an acrimonious split between Marxists and other heterodox economists. At the seminar Rowthorn took issue with the great claims articulated by Eatwell and Pieroangelo Gargnani about what could be done with the Sraffa system. He argued that the Sraffa system and the "Cambridge school" was limited to a critique of neoclassical economics and was unable to interpret what was actually happening in the economy; and that much of what was valuable in Marx's economics could not be formalized in a Sraffa system. However, what Rowthorn did not do at the seminar was address the issue of the logical validity of the Sraffian arguments regarding the falling rate of profit, transformation problem, and the labor theory of value. Given Rowthorn's emerging stature as a defender of Marxism, this omission had unfortunate consequences in that it became a weapon used by those who refused to admit that Marxism might have some theoretical errors in light of the Sraffa system to attack others who thought otherwise. Shortly thereafter, Rowthorn utilized the term neo-Ricardianism to denote the use of the Sraffa system to critique neoclassical economics.[19] The term was also used as a way of discourse to indicate that while the Sraffian system may have been a prelude to a critique of neoclassical theory, it certainly was not an advance forward to a better economic theory in spite of the comments held by various Cambridge economists and other followers of Sraffa. The intention of Rowthorn and others after him was to argue that Marxian economics was the only way forward. This was certainly in keeping with the views of some members of CSE, but it was quickly questioned.

The differences expressed at the day school did not disappear, but created a substantial controversy between the Marxists and the Sraffians. Steedman and Geoff Hodgson[20] used the Sraffa system to critically re-evaluate the labor value theory and the falling rate of profit as a first step towards making Marxian economic theory better. As this approach generated interest within CSE, a "Law of Value" conference was held the following year, June 1973. There was a large contingent from the University of Manchester including Steedman, Hodgson, Pat Devine, David Purdy and Mike Walsh, all of who held similar views regarding Sraffa, Marx, and value theory; and their main opponent was David Yaffe.[21] Most of the debate at the conference concerned Marx's theory of the falling rate of profit, with ancillary discussions of Marx's concept of law and empiricism. Both sides left the conference with their views in tact, but the Manchester group felt that they won the debate on points. Further research later that year by Steedman and Hodgson on the problem of joint production produced the anomaly of negative labor values. For them this meant the complete abandonment of the labor theory of value as well as the Marxian concepts and arguments of the rate of profit, capital accumulation and the falling rate of profit, and exploitation—see Hodgson and Steedman (1975), Hodgson (1974, 1976), and Steedman (1973, 1975, 1977). Consequently, they argued that Sraffa's physical quantities approach had to be taken on board by Marxists in the reconstruction of Marxian theory.

The path offered by Steedman and Hodgson for the reconstruction of Marxian theory was, however, not acceptable for a number of reasons to many members of CSE. Some members, such as Yaffa, simply did not believe that there were logical and analytical mistakes in Marxian theory or that it was possible to reconstruct Marxism if one or more of its central theoretical pillars were removed. Others, such as Fine and Laurence Harris, argued that Marx was correct on all counts, except for the transformation problem. So instead of trying to develop the Sraffa system to deal with production as a social process as well as value, fetishism, exploitation, and capitalist development, they preferred to "paper over the cracks," as Hodgson (1977) argued, and retain Marxian theory.[22] Finally, members of CSE agreed with Rowthorn that the Sraffa system had severe limitations for analyzing capitalism because of its preoccupation with exchange rather than production as a social process; that the method of the Sraffa system limited its capability of providing a critical theory of capitalism that corresponded to Marx's; and that the Sraffian approach did not clearly sustain the ideological vision and critical political perspective associated with Marxism.[23] So even though Marx may have been incorrect in some respects, the contributions of the Sraffa system was of little worth[24] (CSE *Newsletter*, March 1972; Radice 1972a 1972b, 1973c, 1980; Rowthorn 1980; "Seminar on Capital Theory and Marxist Political Economy" 1972; "Law of Value Conference" 1973; Hodgson, 1982, 1997, 2000; Steedman 1979; Howard and King 1992; Lebowitz 1973–74; Harcourt 1978; Yaffe 1994).

The unraveling of the Marxian-heterodox community

At the end of its first five years of existence, CSE had indeed contributed significantly to building the institutional and organizational components necessary for a community of Marxist, Post Keynesian, Sraffian, and Kaleckian or Marxist-heterodox economists to survive and thrive. The *Bulletin* was a recognized academic publishing outlet; and CSE was on the verge of developing other publishing outlets. Its annual conference combined with the day-schools, study and local groups, and involvement on its coordinating committee and/ or the editorial committee of the *Bulletin* produced a dense social network of heterodox economists. Thus it is possible to identify eighty-six individuals who participated in at least one of these activities (see Appendix, A.16) and a core of twenty-six economists who participated in three or more of these activities—see Table 7.1. What is striking about the table is that it includes Marxists (Fine, Rowthorn, and Yaffe), Post Keynesians (Kregel, Robinson, and Winnett), and Sraffians (Eatwell, Hodgson, and Steedman), that is the entire spectrum of Marxian-heterodox economists. So through its institution and organizational developments, CSE was able to bring together the entire spectrum of heterodox economists to explicitly engage in a variety of scholarly, academic, and professional activities that constituted Britain's first post-war community of heterodox economists.

Although the CSE created the institutional conditions for the community of Marxist-heterodox economists to exist, it failed to create a corresponding collective identity among its participants. One reason for this was the Sraffa-value-theory debate acrimoniously divided the CSE membership which consisted of a broad spectrum ranging from non-Marxists to fundamental Marxists that were anti-Sraffian. Thus there was the group at one end that supported Steedman, Hodgson, and the constructivist Sraffian position, a group at the other end that were anti-Sraffian, and finally the broad middle that found to some degree Sraffa complementary to Marx but were caught in the cross-fire of the debate. Illustrative of the ill-feelings generated by the debate was Fine and Harris's 1976 article "Controversial Issues in Marxist Economic Theory," in which they branded those who did not agree with them as neo-Ricardians or fundamentalist Marxists, terms which were clearly used in a disparaging sense (although they denied this—see Fine and Harris (1977). Like many others, they also branded neo-Ricardian theory as bourgeois economics as a way to dismiss it. On the other hand, both Steedman and Hodgson at times appeared to suggest that their opponents were bereft of logic and prone to believe rather than to think for themselves.[25] A second reason was the debate over the content of the *Bulletin*. One issue in the debate was the concern that it might become too academic/professional in approach and therefore too difficult for many CSE members to read. In addition, there was increasing demand for a portion of the *Bulletin* to be open to articles which analyze current topics; and finally there was pressure to expand the type of articles and material carried by the *Bulletin* beyond the narrow confines of economics and related topics. The outcome of the debate was that some CSE members like Steedman viewed the pressures as reducing standards; while to others it was altering the journal from economics to a more generalist one.

Table 7.1 Social network of Marxist-heterodox economists participating in three or more CSE activities, 1970–75

Name	A	B	C	D	E	F
S. Aaronovitch	×	×				×
M. Barratt Brown	×			×	×	×
R. Bellamy	×		×	×		
G. Catephores	×	×	×			×
P. Devine	×	×	×	×		×
M. Desai	×	×	×			
J. Duckworth		×			×	×
J. Eatwell	×	×	×			
B. Fine		×	×		×	×
L. Fishman			×	×		
J. Gardiner	×	×	×	×	×	×
A. Glyn	×	×	×	×	×	×
P. Hare			×			×
L. Harris			×		×	×
J. Harrison			×	×	×	×
G. Hodgson		×	×	×		
G. Kay	×	×	×		×	
R. Murray	×		×		×	×
G. Pilling			×	×		×
H. Radice	×	×	×	×	×	×
J. Robinson	×	×	×	×		
B. Rowthorn	×	×	×	×	×	
I. Steedman	×	×	×			×
B. Sutcliffe	×	×	×		×	
A. Winnett			×	×		×
D. Yaffe				×	×	×

Source: Derived from Appendix, A.16.

Notes:

A = Attended the January and/or October 1970 CSE Conferences and/or appeared on the July 1970 Register of Socialist Economists

B = Attended or requested details about the CSE Day-school on Capital Theory and Marxist Political Economy, May 1972

C = Published in the *Bulletin*, 1971–76

D = Presented a Paper at CSE Conference, 1971–75

E = Involved in a day-school (excluding B), local group, study group and/or appear on a speakers' list, 1971–75

F = Member of the CSE coordinating committee and/or the *Bulletin* editorial committee, 1971–75

The final reason for the failure to create a collective identity was that the membership of CSE changed in composition by 1976 so that economists ceased to be the dominant constituent. This change was visibly marked by the 1976 conference, whose theme was the labor process and was dominated by non-economic papers. Moreover, as the CSE became more made up of members whose interests were neither in economic theory nor in critically confronting Marxian theory, subsequent conference themes had less and less to do with economics, the proportion of CSE study groups, day schools, and seminars that dealt with economic theory, issues and topics declined.[26] Finally, from 1977 to 1990, only 27 percent of the articles published in the *Capital and Class* dealt with economic topics and issues, down from 78 percent for the *Bulletin*. As a result, economists who were critically disposed towards Marx and engaged with Post Keynesian–Sraffian approaches, who were disposed to producing high-quality academic economic articles, and who just like doing economics did not feel welcome in or able to identify with CSE and as a result left it, became inactive, or joined for a short while before leaving. This in turn made it unlikely that non-Marxian heterodox economists would join and identify with CSE; and the CSE responded by not encouraging engagement with Post Keynesian–Sraffian and other non-Marxist heterodox economists[27] (CSE *Newsletter*, February 1973, February 1974, February 1978 to April 1981; Mohun and Fine 1975; Radice 1973a, 1973b, 1973c, 1980; Conference of Socialist Economists 1972b; King 2000; Sawyer 2007; Devine 2007; Picciotto 1986).

In the wilderness: creating Post Keynesian-heterodox identity outside the CSE, 1974–88

Outside of the CSE in the early 1970s there were no national academic organizations that heterodox economists could identify with and be drawn to; there were no academic economic journals to which to submit papers; and there were no annual economic conferences or nationally-oriented seminars to attend.[28] In short, there were, outside CSE and with the exception of Cambridge, almost no local and no regional and national organizations in place in the early 1970s that could contribute to the creation of a Post Keynesian-heterodox identity. Thus, to purse the type of economics they found interesting, heterodox economists outside of CSE found it necessary to build the institutions and organizations step-by-step and in this process the foundations for a Post Keynesian-heterodox identity was laid. And this difficult task was made much harder because, except for a significant concentration at Cambridge and a smaller concentration at Manchester, Post Keynesian-heterodox economists were sparsely spread throughout the old university sector while the majority of them were located in the poorer, less reputable polytechnic sector.

Building institutions and organization outside of Cambridge

In the 1970s, economists not engaged with the CSE also became skeptical of neoclassical economics and were, in hindsight, groping their way towards a Post Keynesian-heterodox approach.[29] Because their skepticism often prevented them from obtaining employment in the university sector, many of them became employed in the polytechnic sector (see Chapter 6). Thus it is not surprising that the first attractor of skeptical qua heterodox economists outside of Cambridge was the polytechnic-based *Thames Papers in Political Economy*. Started by Thanos Skouras in 1974, it was a series of occasional papers appearing three times a year co-produced at Thames Polytechnic (now University of Greenwich) and at North East London Polytechnic (now University of East London).[30] The purpose of the *Thames Papers* was to stimulate public discussion of practical issues in political economy and to bring to the notice of a wider audience of economists controversial questions in economic theory.[31] This meant that papers presenting non-neoclassical approaches to both theoretical and policy questions of political economy dominated its publications since they had no easy access to publication otherwise.[32] The early publications reflected the broadly-heterodox perspectives of Skouras and the early members of the editorial board, such as George Hadjimatheou and Yannis Kitromilides, as not any one particular theoretical viewpoint was championed—see for example Robinson (1974), Harcourt (1975), Nore (1976), and Green (1977).

In 1978 there was a major change in the composition of the editorial board with Philip Arestis, Sami Daniel, and Klaus Heidensohn becoming members.[33] This change coincided with a perceptible shift towards publishing Post Keynesian-oriented papers, beginning with Chick's 1978 paper "Keynesians, Monetarists and Keynes: the end of the debate—or a beginning?" (1978a). In particular, Arestis became increasingly attracted to Post Keynesian economics as well active on the editorial board. When Skouras returned to Greece in 1983 to advise the Deputy Minister of National Economy, he became co-editor (and eventually editor) and took charge of the editorial duties. By this time Arestis was in contact with Alfred Eichner and had become a Post Keynesian economist with missionary zeal.[34] Consequently, the shift to Post Keynesian papers became noticeable. In 1982 the first paper with "Post-Keynesian" in the title was published (see Harcourt, 1982) and that was quickly followed by four similar titles over the next four years—see Eichner (1983), Moore (1984), Arestis and Driver (1984), and Davidson (1986).[35] In addition, nearly all the papers after 1986 until 1990 when *Thames Papers* ceased publication were written by Post Keynesian economists.[36] Thus for the 1980s *Thames Papers* was an important "local" publishing outlet for British Post Keynesians, but more importantly, it provided an institutional anchor for the development of Post Keynesian economics (Daniel 1999; Driver 1999; Skouras 1999).

A second development in this area was the establishment of the *British Review of Economic Issues* in 1977 by the Association of Polytechnic Teachers in Economics, which itself was established in 1972. The aims of the Association were to promote the development of economics teaching and to encourage research into economics in polytechnics and other institutions of higher education and the *Review* was started with this in mind. Skouras (1977–84) was the first editor and almost immediately he was publishing papers of interest to Post Keynesian-heterodox economists—see Chick

(1978b) and Arestis and Riley (1980). In 1983 the first paper with "Post-Keynesian" in the title was published (Dabysing and Jones 1983). Later, in 1985 Arestis (1985–88) became editor and the number of papers by and/or of interest to Post Keynesian-heterodox economists. Thus in a very short time, the *Review* became identified as a journal that would publish heterodox articles, with the result that by 1988 virtually every issue of the *Review* carried a heterodox-oriented article.[37]

In addition to journal publications, there were other activities that promoted Post Keynesian economics. First there were conferences, such as the one on "The Economics of Michal Kalecki: a symposium" in November 1979;[38] and in 1982 Arestis put on a Post Keynesian Conference at Thames Polytechnic at which Eichner gave a keynote address. Moreover, there was the Keynes Seminar, first organized in 1972 and held at the University of Kent on a biannual basis. The initial seminars included few Post Keynesian-heterodox economists, but this slowly changed starting in 1980 so that by the ninth seminar in 1989 they had a significant presence.[39] Finally, in October 1982, Arestis started a Post Keynesian research project on short period macro-econometric modeling of the British economy with Ciaran Driver also at Thames Polytechnic[40] (CSE *Newsletter*, October 1982; Thirlwall 1982, 1987; Hill 1989; Harcourt 1985).

Building Post Keynesian-heterodox economics at Cambridge

Although there was a concentration of Post Keynesian-heterodox economists at Cambridge in the 1950s and 1960s, they were not a harmonious group. Theoretical differences and personalities created schisms, isolated individuals such as Dobb, Richard Goodwin, and Richard Stine, and neglected the younger newly emerging generation of Post Keynesian-heterodox economists. Moreover, little care was taken in preparing their succession, so as Joan Robinson, Goodwin, Stone, Kaldor, and Kahn retired, their places were taken by mainstream economists. While this outcome resulted in the progressive decline of Post Keynesian-heterodox economics at Cambridge, the 1960s and early 1970s was a period of hope and change. At this time, Cambridge had many economists—staff, post-graduate students, and visitors—who were skeptical and/or identified their theoretical orientation as Marxist, Keynesian, Kaleckian, Sraffian, and perhaps Post Keynesian—see Appendix A.15.[41] As a whole, they were conscious that their intellectual engagement, scholarship, and theoretical and applied research were creating a "new economic analysis." These activities were supported outside of Cambridge by the CSE of which many engaged with (see Appendix A.16) and within Cambridge through seminars, workshops, and study groups. One example of a seminar was the 1969–70 Marxism seminar (which was still running a decade later). Its aim was to stimulate Marxist discussion of political issues within the Cambridge Socialist Society. There were a total of nineteen seminars covering the Marxist socio-economic critique of capitalism,

Marxist social philosophy, classless society, and the historical development of Marxism. In addition, in 1971 there was a seminar on the corporation in monopoly capitalism, a workshop on "British Capitalism Today," and a study group reading *Capital*. Finally, there was the Cambridge Political Economy Group which was established in the early 1970s to analyze the problems of the British economy from a Marxist perspective.

Responding to the pending move of the *Economic Journal* from Cambridge to Oxford (which took place at the end of 1976) and the consequence that the new editors would be more likely to reject papers critical of mainstream economics, the younger heterodox socialist economists—Eatwell, Singh, and Rowthorn—began thinking in late 1974 about establishing their own journal. Consequently, further discussions took place with Cambridge and non-Cambridge heterodox economists, including Hodgson, Steedman, Purdy, and MacLennan from Manchester. To ensure that the prospective journal remained under their control, a cooperative was formed in 1976, the Cambridge Political Economy Society (CPES), which would own and produce it.[42] The CPES was intended as a intellectual, organizational, and institutional focal point at Cambridge for the ongoing engagement in heterodox economics.[43] In particular, it was

> ... founded to provide a focus for theoretical and applied work, with strong emphasis on realism of analysis, the provision and use of empirical evidence, and the formulation of economic policies. This initiative springs from the belief that the economic approach rooted in the traditions of Marx, Kalecki and Keynes has much to contribute to the understanding and treatment of current economic and social issues: unemployment, inflation, the organization of production, the distribution of social product, class conflict, uneven development and instability in the world economy, the underdevelopment of the third world and economic and social change in socialist countries.
>
> (*Cambridge Journal of Economics*, 1.1, 1977)

Thus, in 1977 the *Cambridge Journal of Economics* (CJE) was founded for the purpose of publishing works engaged with these issues and approaches. Later in 1982, Eatwell, Murray Milgate, and Giancarlo de Vivo, under the CPES, established the *Contributions to Political Economy*, an annual whose objective was to publish "articles on the theory and history of political economy (that fell) within the critical traditions in economic thought associated with the work of the classical political economists, Marx, Keynes and Sraffa" (*Contributions to Political Economy*, 1, 1982).[44] Finally, in 1985, it set up a charitable trust for the education of the public in political economy and its main beneficiaries have been Cambridge post-graduate students in terms of grants and scholarships totaling more than a quarter of a million pounds. The CPES also sponsored a number of conferences. In particular, in November 1978, the CPES with the CSE and the *New Left Review* sponsored a conference on "Value Theory and Contemporary Analysis".[45] Then in 1983, centenary of Keynes's birth, the CPES organized a conference on methodological issues in Keynesian economics. It had sixty-three participants who listened to twenty papers on probability, rationality, expectations, econometrics, and Keynes's methodology, many of which were published in *Keynes' Economics: Methodological Issues* (Lawson and Pesaran 1985) [46] (The Seminars on Marxism 1969–70; Radice, 1971a, 1971b; CSE *Newsletter,* April 1978; Pasinetti, 2005, 2007; Singh in Arestis and Sawyer 2000; Kitson 2005; Mata 2006).

Identity, theory, and Post Keynesian-heterodox economics

What is of interest in the above discussion is that prior to the early 1980s, Post Keynesian economics in Britain did not signify a particular collection of arguments or identify a specific group of economists. Rather what generally existed was an attachment to particular names: Keynes-Keynesians, Kalecki-Kaleckians, and Sraffa-Sraffians.[47] Thus, heterodox economists became Keynesians, Kaleckians, and Sraffians as if they were distinctly different theoretical approaches which did not permit a common identification such as Post Keynesian but did allow a pluralist of theoretical dialogue and debate that now can be characterized as heterodox economics. This pluralist-heterodox attitude is aptly captured in Skouras' reminiscences about his editorial position at the *Thames Papers*:

> ... there was no opposition to Marxism but, at the same time, there was no precedence given to it either. Some of the first papers were Marxian. ... My editorial policy did not favour non-Marxian heterodoxy over Marxian work. What I objected to was the reproduction of platitudes, routine and inconclusive econometric "testing", pseudo-scientific quantification, doctrinaire navel-searching, banal arguments and pedantic and sloppy reasoning. Unfortunately, a lot of Marxian work shared some of these characteristics with run-of-the-mill neoclassical work. My main editorial concern was to find interesting papers that had something fresh to say on a theoretical or policy issue of some importance. ... As it turned out, heterodox views seemed to me to satisfy most often the conditions of novelty and relevance. Thus, pluralistic heterodoxy and a critical stance towards neoclassical economics emerge as the main editorial direction.
>
> (Skouras 1999)

The significance of Skouras's comments is that heterodoxy outside of CSE did not consist of any group of specific approaches, such as Institutional, social, evolutionary, or Post Keynesian. Consequently a Post Keynesian social network did not exist and in fact was not even contemplated. This rather diffuse view of heterodoxy also existed at Cambridge. There were the varied activities of the socialist economists and later the CSPE and the CJE, all of which touted the traditions of Marx, Kalecki, and Keynes, but did not mention Post Keynesianism. Hence a young economist, such as Tony Lawson in the 1970s, was only aware of differences between individuals and not at all aware of Post Keynesian economics *per se*:

> The CJE which I joined in 79 was Keynesian and still is. People there called themselves Keynesian. ... I'm not sure I often if ever heard the label Post Keynesian. ... The Cambridge I came into was Keynesian. ...
> (Lawson 2000)

The happenstance of four "events" in the early 1980s altered this. The first, as noted above, was the growing significance of Post Keynesian-heterodox economic activities outside of Cambridge as it coalesced around Arestis and the *Thames Papers* and *British Review of Economic Issues*. This was enhanced by a number of economists becoming interested in Kaleckian-Post Keynesian themes.[48] The second was the 1983 Keynes conference at which Chick, Sheila Dow, Geoff Harcourt, Hodgson, Lawson, and John Pheby all attended to discuss a common theme—methodology and inevitably Post Keynesian economics. A third event was Harcourt's return to Cambridge in 1982 to write an intellectual history of Keynes's students (see Harcourt 2006) and in the process began to explicitly promote Post Keynesian economics. He lectured to undergraduate and post-graduate students on Post Keynesian topics or at least on topics from a Post Keynesian perspective. He also had eight to eleven Ph.D. students at any one time, including Michelle Baddeley, Flavio Comim, Terry O'Shaughnessy, and Keiran Sharpe who became engaged with the UK Post Keynesian-heterodox community.[49] Finally, the project of the constructivist Sraffians to reconstruct economic theory—the protagonists in Britain were Eatwell, Hodgson, Lynn Mainwaring, Milgate, and Steedman—reached its high water mark in circa 1982–83 when it reached out to engage with Keynes's principle of effective demand as well as establishing a publishing venue for Post Keynesian-heterodox economists.[50] Thus Post Keynesian-heterodox economics was, by 1985, recognized by British heterodox economists at Cambridge and elsewhere as a significant research agenda in British heterodox economics and was identified as including the contributions of Keynes, Kalecki, Kaldor, Robinson, and Sraffa, that is all the heterodox approaches that existed in Britain except Marxism.[51] So by the mid-1980s, there existed at least seventy-five British economists who had engaged in some degree with Post Keynesian-heterodox economics—see Appendix A.17, columns B–E. Moreover, the CSE "contributed" to the emergence of Post Keynesian economics on two accounts. First, twenty-eight of the seventy-five economists participated in its early activities before becoming involved in Post Keynesian-heterodox activities—see Appendix A.17, column A. Second, because the CSE failed to maintain its interest in issues of economic policy and applied questions, a number of CSE economists established an alternative

Table 7.2 Social network of Post Keynesian-heterodox economists participating in two or more Post Keynesian-heterodox activities, 1974–88

Name	B	C	D	E
P. Arestis	×	×		×
P. Auerbach		×		×
V. Chick	×	×	×	×
K. Coutts		×	×	
F. Cripps		×	×	
S. Daniel	×	×		
M. Desai		×	×	
S. Dow	×	×	×	×
C. Driver	×	×		×
J. Eatwell	×	×	×	
W. Godley			×	×
J. GrahL	×	×		
F. Green	×	×		
G. Hadjimatheou	×	×		×
G. Harcourt	×	×	×	×
L. Harris		×	×	
J. Harrison	×	×		
S. Himmelweit		×	×	
G. Hodgson		×	×	×
A. Hughes		×	×	
J. Humphries		×	×	
J. Kregel		×		×
T. Lawson		×	×	
P. Lyandrou	×	×		
J. McCombie			×	×
S. Mohun		×	×	
P. Nolan		×	×	
P. Reynolds	×	×		×
J. Robinson	×	×		×
B. Rowthorn	×	×		
J. Rubery		×	×	
N. Sarantis		×		×
M. Sawyer	×	×		
A. Singh	×	×	×	
T. Skouras	×	×		
I. Steedman		×	×	
R. Tarling		×	×	
T. Ward		×	×	×
F. Wilkinson		×	×	

Source: Derived from Appendix A.17.

Notes:

B = Editorial board and/or publish in *Thames Papers in Political Economy*, 1974–90

C = Editorial board and/or publish in *British Review of Economic Issues*, 1977–88; in the *Cambridge Journal of Economics*, 1977–88; and/or in *Contributions to Political Economy*, 1982–88

D = CJE Value Conference (1978) and/or Keynes Conference on Methodology (1983)

E = Editorial board, published in, or subscribed to the *Journal of Post Keynesian Economics*, 1977–88 forum in 1980. Its importance was that through its annual conference (lasting until 1985) and publication *Socialist Economic Review*, a network of economists who promoted a mixture of Marxist and left Keynesian analysis emerged. And this network help maintain a collective interest in aspects of Post Keynesian-heterodox economics.[52] Finally, as indicated in Table 7.2, there was a "core" set of Post Keynesian-heterodox economists, about half located at Cambridge and the rest spread around Britain, and located in old as well as new universities (or polytechnics) (Eatwell and Milgate 1983; Arestis and Skouras 1985; Hodgson 1997; Lawson 2000; Sawyer 2007; Harcourt in Arestis and Sawyer 2000).

Post Keynesian-heterodox economics, 1988–96

Post-Keynesian Economics Study Group[53]

In 1988, Arestis and Chick successfully applied to the Economic and Social Research Council (ESRC) for a grant to finance a Post-Keynesian Economics Study Group (PKSG)[54] on the grounds "that the volume of research taking a broadly Post-Keynesian approach is now great enough to justify a Study Group." They visualized Post Keynesian economics as a distinctive theoretical approach that drew on the works of Keynes, Kalecki, Joan Robinson, Kaldor, and Sraffa and distinguished itself by "its insistence that history, social structure and institutional practice be embodied in its theory and reflected in its policy recommendations."[55] The establishment of the Study Group was the first heterodox organizational structure to emerge with the title of Post-Keynesian in Britain and hence constitutes the organizational beginnings beginning of Post Keynesian economics in Britain.[56]

To develop the PKSG, a mailing list was compiled in 1991 of 225 British economists that might attend its meetings and perhaps present a paper, while notices were placed in *Review of Political Economy* and the European Association for Evolutionary Political Economy *Newsletter* inviting foreign Post Keynesian-heterodox economists to present papers to the Study Group. The main activities of the Study Group from 1988 to 1996 consisted of half-day seminars with two or three domestic and/or foreign speakers five or six times an academic year and starting in 1991 one conference each year.[57] In addition, from January 1995 to December 1997, Dow produced seven issues of the *PKSG Newsletter*.[58] Over the period of 1988 to 1996, there were thirty-nine seminars, six conferences, and one post-graduate conference at which 177 papers were presented to an average audience of thirty-seven economists of which thirty-two were attached to British universities on virtually all methodological, theoretical, and applied topics that would interest Post Keynesian-heterodox economists, including papers drawing from Kalecki, Keynes, Marx, Sraffa, Hayek, and Weintraub, as well as papers that articulated theoretical and methodological critiques of Post Keynesian economics.

The seminars and conferences brought British Post Keynesian-heterodox economists together on a frequent basis so that they developed a "visual recognition" of their community and the intellectual discussions that took place during the meetings and social-intellectual discussions that took place in the pub afterwards furthered the development of the community:

> Undoubtedly a major attraction of the seminars has been their scholarship. One of the greatest pleasures for those who have attended the seminars has been their wide-ranging discussions between people who have read and thought about the issues raised. ... This scholarship is largely the outcome of what I feel is an important animating factor of our discussions, namely the participation of a wide range of people who do not regard themselves as Post Keynesians. I recall numerous Kaleckians, at least three Marxists, a couple of neo-Ricardians, one or two institutionalists, and at least one Austrian, who gave papers and took part in proceedings. Without them, the Post Keynesians (and indeed the participating Kaleckians, Marxists, neo-Ricardians and Austrians) would lose that friendly, but critical, input into their discussions, without which those discussions could easily degenerate into self-congratulation, complacency, shallowness, and clichéd thinking. With that input, all of us, Post Keynesians, Kaleckians, neo-Ricardians, Marxists, institutionalists and Austrians, have improved beyond measure the quality of our debates, thought and research. All of us have not only learned much about our own areas of interest but also extended the range of our thought and research.
>
> (Toporowski 1996: 3)

In addition, *PKSG Newsletter* was established to further integrate the community. It carried notices of conferences, seminars, interesting visitors to Britain, newsletters, journals, new books, and other Post Keynesian associations, abstracts of papers presented at the PKSG seminars and conferences, and news of members and their activities. The *PKSG Newsletter* also carried one sustained interchange between its members on the demise or future of Post Keynesian economics. When contemplating its establishment, Dow asked me to write a controversial piece on Post Keynesian economics for the first issue. Drawing on research I was doing on the impact of the United Kingdom Research Assessment Exercise on heterodox economics and heterodox economists (see Chapter 8), I wrote an article for the first issue on "The Death of Post Keynesian Economics?" The article was indeed controversial in that it elicited a number of responses for the next four issues.[59] In particular, the British Post Keynesians—Alistair Dow, Peter Riach, and Paul Downward—questioned the pessimism of the article, took exception to its stress on the need to teach Post Keynesian economics, and felt that Post Keynesian economics could survive and thrive in business schools; but they did not question the existence of the Post Keynesian-heterodox community and that it was a community worth maintaining.

When founded in 1988, the PKSG received a £6000.00 grant from the ESRC initially for the period October 1988 to March 1990, but extended it to November 1990.[60] At that point, it was discovered that the ESRC had suspended funding for all study groups. Thus Arestis and Chick approached the Royal Economic Society (RES) for funding of the Study Group's activities and received £900.00 for 1991. In addition, Edward Elgar, the publisher, contributed £1000.00 the conference on "Money and Finance in the Economic Restructuring of Europe, East and West" that took place in March 1992 for the opportunity to publish the conference volume.[61] Then in October 1991, the ESRC awarded the Study Group £10,000.00 for 1992 and 1993. Arestis and Chick applied for ESRC funding in 1993 and again was awarded a grant for 1994 and 1995; but the subsequent application for ESRC funding in 1995 for 1996–97 was not. At the time of the 1995 application, both Arestis and Chick stepped down as co-chair of the PKSG and Sheila Dow and John Hillard took their places. In light of the ESRC rejection, Dow and Chick submitted a funding application to the RES and received a partial grant for 1996.

Losing ESRC funding combined with Arestis and Chick stepping down prompted a rethinking and reflection about the activities of the Study Group. Out of the discussions with various members, including Dow, Chick, Vicky Allsopp, Downward, Bill Gerrard, Winnett, and myself, a number of proposed changes were articulated, accepted by the members of the Study Group, and put into action. First, the organizational locus of the PKSG was shifted to Leeds University where Hillard was located because he had support for the production and mailing of the *PKSG Newsletter* and for the Group's financial reimbursement for travel and other items. Second and more significantly, it was decided that some seminars would be located outside of London as a way to broaden and strengthen the PKSG membership and add strength to those departments where there was already a significant Post Keynesian presence;[62] that a post-graduate workshop be organized by the graduate students at Leeds;[63] and that there would be joint participation in seminars and conferences with other bodies.[64] Finally, there was a proposal for transforming the PKSG into an explicit Post Keynesian association. However, it was never acted on in part because of a concern for heterodox pluralism. That is, it was feared that some fellow-travelers, who had been so essential to the on-goings of the PKSG, would feel excluded and cease to participate. Rather it was suggested that an association with a name that was more broadly inviting be established as a way to maintain the Post Keynesian-heterodox community that had emerged in Britain by the mid-1990s; but such an association did not emerge until 1999 with the formation of the Association for Heterodox Economics—see Chapter 10 (Toporowski 1996; Ietto-Gillies 1997).

John Pheby and Post Keynesian-heterodox pluralism

A major contribution to creating and maintaining the Post Keynesian-heterodox economics community was the Great Malvern conferences in political economy organized by John Pheby from 1987 to 1996. The first conference arose because Lorie Tarshis mentioned to Pheby that he wanted to come to England in 1987 but needed an invitation to a conference. So he organized a small conference on the theme of "New Directions in Post Keynesian Economics," which took place in 1987 at Great Malvern, England.[65] Although intended as a one-off event, it was quite successful and the participants enjoyed the ambience and so demanded a second conference. This resulted in nine successive conferences to 1996 which was attended on average by twenty-one British economists plus a number of foreign economists who listened and commented on around fifteen papers over two and a half days. Very quickly, the Malvern conference gained a reputation as a venue where papers drawing on different heterodox approaches could be given and the ensuing discussion was both vigorous and friendly:

> ... the dominant theme running through Malvern has been a belief that heterodox economic paradigms have much to teach one another, and that economists with different perspectives can learn from one another if given the right environment. Malvern has provided that environment. It has been a place where all approaches to economic analysis have been welcome and respected, and where the insights from one tradition have met up with what Latakos has called "the hard core" beliefs from other paradigms. The results have been frequently contentious and sometimes synergistic, but they have always been illuminating.
>
> (Pressman 1996: 1–2)

This point was also frequently expressed by participants while at the conferences and afterwards upon reflection, as Lawson recalled: "It was the only forum I remember where ... approaches that might be classified as Post Keynesian, Austrianism, Institutionalism in the UK anyway, came together in one forum. ... " (Lawson, 2000).

In 1986 Pheby was in the process of contacting publishers about setting up a journal that eventually became the *Review of Political Economy* (ROPE). At this same time, the publisher of *Socialist Economic Review* withdrew its support, thus pushing Sawyer and others to approach other publishers, including Edward Arnold. Arnold responded with a journal proposal and hence the *International Review of Applied Economics* was established (with the first issue appearing 1987). This success prompted Pheby to also approach Arnold with the result that ROPE was established (with the first issue appearing in 1989).[66] Thus, one outcome of the 1987 Malvern Conference was that Pheby was able to obtain papers for the first issue of the journal as well as recruit several of the participants as members of the board of editors.[67] Following the pluralistic theme of the Malvern conferences the initial editorial policy of ROPE encouraged: " ... contributions from non-orthodox groups such as post-Keynesian, institutionalist, subjectivist and behavioural economists. However, submissions from a variety of economists doing creative work in the broad traditions of political economy will be welcome" (*Review of Political Economy*, 1.1, 1989). Over time minor modifications to it were made to specifically encourage submissions from the broad traditions of political economy or heterodox economics so that the 1996 editorial policy " ... welcomes constructive and critical contributions in all areas of political economy, including the Post-Keynesian, Sraffian, Marxian, Austrian and Institutionalist traditions" (*Review of Political Economy*, 8.2, 1996). Of the more than seventy-eight different British economists that participated in the conferences, sixty were part of the Post Keynesian-heterodox community. In addition, forty-five different British Post Keynesian-heterodox economists published in ROPE. Thus, because the Malvern conference–ROPE complex encouraged a broad engagement across the different approaches that made up the Post Keynesian-heterodox community, a total of seventy-five different Post Keynesian-heterodox economists interacted with within the Malvern conference-ROPE complex (see Appendix A.17, columns I–J)[68] (Pheby 1989, 1999; Lawson 2000; Sawyer 2007; Pressman 1996).

Supplementary support for Post Keynesian-heterodox economics

From 1989 to 1995, the *British Review of Economic Issues* under the editorship of Hadjimatheou (1989–92) and Reynolds (1992–95) continued its support as a publishing outlet for Post Keynesian-heterodox economists. Out of the twenty-one issues published from 1989 to 1995, there were 21 articles by Post Keynesian-heterodox economists, with perhaps the most interesting one being Downward's (1994) analysis of the evidence on business pricing. Moreover, between 1988 and 1996 there emerged three additional publishing outlets for Post Keynesian-heterodox economists that complemented the current existing ones, due largely to the efforts of Sawyer, Arestis, and Harcourt. One was the Edward Elgar book series "New Directions in Modern Economics" with Sawyer as series editor. The aim of the series was to present a challenge to orthodox economic thinking:

> It focuses on new ideas emanating from radical traditions including post-Keynesian, Kaleckian, neo-Ricardian and Marxian. The books in the series do not adhere rigidly to any single school of thought but share in common an attempt to present a positive alternative to the conventional wisdom. The main emphasis of the series is on the development and application of new ideas to current problems in economic theory and policy. It will include new original contributions to theory, overviews of work in the radical tradition and the evaluation of alternative economic policies.

The fourteen books that came out in the series from 1988 to 1996 included Pheby's *New Directions in Post-Keynesian Economics* (1989) and Arestis's *The Post-Keynesian Approach to Economics* (1992).[69] A second publishing outlet established was the *International Papers in Political Economy* (IPPE). It was planned to be similar in content, format, and style to the *Thames Papers*, which had ceased publication in 1990:

> We have decided to proceed with plans for IPPE as a result of the considerable interest from colleagues working in the non-orthodox traditions in economics in the publication of longer, more reflective essays. The Thames Papers ... are no longer able to satisfy this demand. Our intention in seeking to launch the IPPE would be to create an ethos similar to that previously associated with the Thames Papers but also to make the papers much more international in origin and orientation. We would be the managing editors of this series, and would appoint at least one person from the major countries to form an editorial board.
>
> (Arestis and Sawyer 1990)

From 1993 to 1996, nine issues were published, all on Post Keynesian-heterodox topics, including Singh (1995) on markets and economic development, Peter Howells (1995) on endogenous money, and Arestis and Sawyer (1996) on the Tobin tax. The third outlet was the book series "Aspects of Political Economy," with Harcourt as the series editor. Thirteen books were published in the series, which ran from 1987 to 1993, six by British Marxist-Post Keynesian-heterodox economists, including Ian Steedman's, *From Exploitation to Altruism* (1989a) and Paul Dunne's, *Quantitative Marxism* (1991).[70]

In addition to publishing support, Post Keynesian-heterodox economists also had other opportunities to present their material to interested audiences. Over the period of 1988 to 1996, a number of economists that attended PKSG activities also attended the annual CSE conference and many presented papers, especially under the quantitative Marxism theme overseen by Paul Dunne.[71] Additionally, Harcourt organized a Post Keynesian seminar at Cambridge that ran until 1998 when he retired.[72] Moreover, in 1990 the Cambridge realist workshop was born as a reading group. Lawson and research students Steve Fleetwood, Steve Pratten, Jochen Runde, and Clive Lawson initially got together to discuss philosophical issues; however, because they invited others to attend combined with word-of-mouth and the excitement about the topics discussed, it quickly grew to over 40 participants. By 1994, it had evolved to the point that individuals presented papers and then had to discuss and defend what they said. From 1994 to 1996, some fifty-eight papers were presented at the workshop and the presenters that were also engaged in Post Keynesian-heterodox activities included Lawson, Hodgson, Steve Parsons, Runde, Harcourt, David Young and Bernard Walters (Conference of Socialist Economists 1988–96; Lawson 2000; Cambridge Realist Workshop: http://www. econ.cam.ac.uk/seminars/realist/index.htm (accessed May 27, 2008)).

Finally, there was indirect support in the form of supervising doctoral students and post-graduate courses. From the beginning, doctoral students from University College London, Cambridge, School of Oriental and African

Studies (SOAS), and Stirling attended the PKSG; then circa 1995, doctoral students from Leeds began attending the seminars. In addition, circa 1994 nineteen economic departments had post-graduate courses which included either required and/or elective classes that included Post Keynesian-heterodox material (see Appendix A.20). While many of the classes existed in 1988 and others came into existence subsequently, there was no taught Post Keynesian-heterodox post-graduate course until 1993 when De Montfort University established a M.A. degree in economics. Its aim was to offer a range of classes which in their totality provided an alternative to neoclassical economics: "The programme presents a theoretical core which draws upon the various non-traditional schools of thought, such as Institutional economics, Marxian economics, Sraffian economics, and Post Keynesian economics" (Master of Arts Degree in Economics, De Montfort University, Leicester, 1994: 1, in the author's possession). As a result, like the doctoral students, students from the De Montfort program attended the PKSG seminars. Whether the post-graduate students were doctoral, M.Phil., or M.A. candidates, many often attended the PKSG meetings, some gave papers (such as Steve Dunn and Giuseppe Fontana from Leeds, Mario Gracia from Cambridge, and Rogerio Studart from University College London—see Appendix A.17), and others made significant post-1996 contributions to the PKSG.

Post Keynesian-heterodox community: organization and identity

By 1996, the community of Post Keynesian-heterodox economists was well established. The PKSG combined with the Malvern conferences and reinforced by the Cambridge realist workshop and CSE conferences constituted its organizational structure.[73] Supplementing it was the "publication structure," that is an array of heterodox journals and a book series that would publish Post Keynesian-heterodox material. Thus the two structures promoted institutional behavior in that economists within the community became increasingly habituated to attend Post Keynesian-heterodox activities; to read, subscribe, and publish in ROPE, CJE, JPKE, and other heterodox journals; and to buy Post Keynesian-heterodox books published by Edward Elgar. From 1988 to 1996, the number of British economists that were identified as potential members of the community was 467, of which 309 were actually engaged within it by partaking in at least one of its possible thirty-nine activities.[74] This is significantly greater than the seventy-five British economists that engaged in some degree with Post Keynesian-heterodox economics in the 1980s (see Appendix A.17) and more than the number of economists in the CSE in 1975 (see Appendix A.16). Of the 309 economists, 192 were more than minimally engaged (see Appendix A.17); and of these, sixty-three were significantly involved in community activities (see Table 7.3), which is more than the thirty-nine active Post Keynesian-heterodox economists in the early 1980s (see Table 7.2) and the twenty-six active Marxist-heterodox economists in the early 1970s (see Table 7.1).

Table 7.3 Social network of Post Keynesian-heterodox economists participating in three or more Post Keynesian-heterodox activities, 1988–96

Name	F	G	H	I	J	K	L
V. Allsopp	×	×	×				
P. Arestis	×	×	×	×	×	×	×
P. Auerbach	×	×	×				×
R. Ayres		×			×		×
V. Brown		×	×	×	×		
S. Cameron		×			×		×
V. Chick	×	×	×	×	×		×
B. Corry	×	×	×				
K. Coutts	×	×				×	
K. Cowling		×			×	×	
M. Desai	×	×	×			×	×
M. Dietrich	×			×	×		×
A. Dow	×	×		×			×
S. Dow	×	×	×	×	×	×	
P. Downward	×		×	×	×		×
C. Driver	×	×	×			×	
J. Foster	×			×	×		
S. Frowen		×	×	×			
C. Fuller		×	×			×	
B. Gerrard	×	×	×	×			
A. Ghatak		×	×	×			×
J. Gilbert		×		×	×		
M. Glickman		×	×				×
J. Grahl	×	×	×	×			
F. Green	×	×	×		×	×	×
G. Harcourt	×	×	×	×	×	×	×
S. Hargreaves-Heap		×	×	×	×		
J. Hillard	×	×	×	×			
G. Hodgson	×	×		×	×	×	
P. Howells	×	×	×		×	×	×
G. Ietto-Gillies	×	×	×		×		×
T. Lawson	×	×	×	×	×	×	×
F. Lee	×	×	×	×	×		×
B. Loasby	×	×	×				
L. Mainwaring	×	×		×	×	×	×
D. Mair	×	×	×	×	×	×	×
J. McCombie		×	×				×
J. Michie	×	×			×	×	
P. Mottershead		×	×				×
G. Palma	×	×				×	×
S. Parsons	×		×	×	×	×	
S. Pashkoff	×		×	×		×	
J. Pheby	×	×		×	×		×
C. Pitelis	×	×	×		×		×
P. Reynolds	×	×	×	×	×		×
P. Riach	×	×	×	×	×	×	×
J. Runde	×		×	×		×	
N. Sarantis	×	×	×				×
M. Sawyer	×	×	×	×	×		×

Table 7.3 (continued)

Name	F	G	H	I	J	K	L
A. Singh	×					×	×
F. Skuse	×	×	×				
C. Starmer		×		×	×		
I. Steedman	×	×	×	×	×	×	×
R. Studart	×			×	×		
A. Thirlwall		×				×	×
J. Toporowski	×	×	×		×		
A. Trigg		×	×				×
A. Tylecote	×	×	×	×	×		
J. Vint		×		×			×
B. Walters	×		×	×			
F. Wilkinson		×			×	×	
A. Winnett	×	×	×	×			
D. Young	×	×	×	×	×		

Source: Derived from Appendix A.17

Notes:
F = Presented a Paper at the Post-Keynesian Economics Study Group, 1988–96; contributed to its *Newsletter*, 1995–96; and/or contributed to the running of the Group
G = Post-Keynesian Economics Study Group Mailing List, 1991
H = Attended 2 or more of the 18 meetings of the Post-Keynesian Economics Study Group, February 1993 to November 1996
I = Presented a Paper at or Attended the Great Malvern Political Economy Conference, 1987–94
J = Editorial board and/or publish in the *Review of Political Economy*, 1989–96
K = Editorial board and/or publish in the *Cambridge Journal of Economics*, 1989–96; and/or in *Contributions to Political Economy*, 1989–96
L = Editorial board and/or publish in the *Post Keynesian Journal of Economics*, 1989–96; in *British Review of Economic Issues/Economic Issues*, 1989–95; and/or in *International Papers in Political Economy*, 1993–96. Also subscribe to the *Journal of Post Keynesian Economics*, *Journal of Economics Issues*, and/or *Review of Social Economy*.

Among the 63 active Post Keynesian-heterodox economists, fourteen stand out as making the community's identity—Arestis, Chick, Dow, Green, Harcourt, Howells, Lawson, Mainwaring, Mair, Reynolds, Riach, Sawyer, Steedman, and myself. Individually, they engaged across the thirty-nine activities and in six or seven of the different categories of activities. Moreover, they include the organizers and coordinators of the PKSG and the Cambridge realist workshop (Arestis, Chick, Dow, and Lawson), editors of the *PKSG Newsletter*, *IPPE*, *British Review of Economic Issues*, "New Directions," and "Aspects of Political Economy" book series (Arestis, Dow, Reynolds, Sawyer, and Harcourt), and pre-1980 heterodox 'activists' (Arestis, Chick, Green, Harcourt, Mainwaring, Riach, and Steedman). In addition, the fourteen economists gave papers and otherwise participated in community's seminar and conference activities, and published their work in the various Post Keynesian-heterodox publication outlets noted above. Thus their activities help produce and reproduce the organizational and publication structures of the Post Keynesian-heterodox community. Finally, because of their prominence within the community, they established both a dense set of relationships among themselves and an extensive set of relationships among other members of the community. Thus the fourteen economists provided a composite identity of Post Keynesian-heterodox economics: an intermingling of ideas by Keynes, Kalecki, Marx, and Sraffa with the ideas of other heterodox economists was represented in their published work and seminar conference discussions. This composite identity, which was supported and reinforced by community members at large, combined with the organizational and publication structures, defined the Post Keynesian-heterodox community in Britain in the 1990s.

8   Research Assessment Exercise and its impact on heterodox economics, 1989–96

Prior to 1986, the year of the first Research Assessment Exercise (RAE), funding for research in British universities was built into expenditures per student on the assumption that all academics were engaged in research and scholarship as part of their role as academics. Additional funds for specific projects were available upon successful application from the Research Councils according to the principle of dual funding. However, beginning in the 1970s, the University Grants Committee (UGC) found that the government grant for the funding of teaching and research in British universities was declining in real terms. Moreover, in the early 1980s the universities fell victim to heavy cuts in public expenditure and it became apparent to many administrators in the field that excellence in research could not be maintained without applying some principle of selectivity in funding. Somewhat reluctantly, therefore, the UGC agreed to a research selectivity exercise whereby research funds were distributed to different departments according to the UGC's assessment of its degree of excellence. The first exercise was an ad hoc affair with the UGC hurriedly appointing its assessors and only a small proportion of research monies dependent on their ratings.[1] The second exercise was carried out by the UGC in 1989 with a larger proportion of research funding dependent on the ratings of duly constituted subject panels to whom departments were to submit more refined applications; and in 1992, its successor, the Universities Funding Council (UFC), carried out a third exercise. In 1992, over 90 per cent of the UFC's research funds was distributed by its successors, the Higher Education Funding Councils (HEFCs) for England, Wales, Scotland, and Northern Ireland, according to the ratings of its subject panels and the pre-1992 universities had to compete for that money with the ex-polytechnics or the new universities. As for the 1996 RAE, British universities prepared their submissions in an even tighter financial climate brought about by an average of 5 percent reduction in real terms across the sector for 1996/97 (Universities Funding Council 1989; Phillimore 1989; Halsey 1992; Higher Education Funding Council for England 1993).

The first exercise seemed to have little impact on economists and their research. However, by the time of the 1989 RAE, the so-called "Diamond

List" of core mainstream economic journals (see Appendix A.18; also A.3) had been drawn up and there was a strong belief amongst British economists that this list was used by the assessors to inform their judgment of the quality of research in economics departments. Attempts were made to extend this list for use in the 1992 RAE, though this modified list remained, like its predecessor, "unofficial' (see Appendix A.18).[2] The existence of these lists, whether official or not, produced considerable discontent amongst British economists, for reasons not at all unrelated to the research rating received by their departments (Diamond 1989; Minutes of Conference of Heads of University Departments of Economics 4/11/89, 21/5/93, and 21/5/94).

At the 1994 Royal Economic Society Annual Conference a special session was held at which the chairman of the economics panel for the 1992 RAE, Anthony Atkinson, gave his view of what the panel did and also received questions from the floor. One question asked was how did the panel regard economic research that fell outside the domain of mainstream economics. The answer was, in part, that the assessors did not discriminate against heterodox research and that the RAE exercise should not be used by economic departments to discriminate against heterodox research. Atkinson went on to add that he did not believe British economists would actively discriminate against heterodox economists and their research. However, at the same conference a flyer appeared which announced that the University of Manchester was in the market for nine economists who would raise the School of Economic Studies research profile in mainstream economics (see *Guardian* March 29, 1994).[3] Advertisements for posts in other institutions subsequently appeared that similarly specified that applicants must be working within mainstream economics and linked this explicitly to either maintaining or improving their ranking in the assessment exercise.[4] Therefore, it seemed that economics departments were, in their hiring practices, discriminating positively towards mainstream economists and their research as a way to maintain and/or enhance their rating in the 1996 RAE; and that such practices implied a discriminatory attitude towards heterodox economists.

If the RAE had an impact on heterodox economics, what was it? In this chapter, three components of the question are examined. First, the methodology of the RAE and the role of peer review within it are delineated. Next, the extent to which the RAE economics panel fulfilled the criteria of peer review is explored. Lastly, the impact of the RAE on heterodox economics in the mid-1990s is examined. Chapter 9 continues the theme and examines the impact of the RAE on heterodox economics at the beginning of the twenty-first century.

Methodology of the Research Assessment Exercise

The methodology of the RAE was (and is) based on peer review, which can be defined as a system where the intellectual excellence of a piece of research is judged by a committee or panel of researchers working in, or close to, the field in question. For peer review to work it is necessary that each member of the panel be pre-eminent in the specialism(s) which they have to evaluate; that the preeminent panel members be selected from across the relevant academic community; that the actual method of selection is open, democratic, and involves as much of the academic community as possible; that involvement in peer review be voluntary as opposed to forced under threat of financial punishment; that feedback be provided automatically to all applicants; that an appeal system exists; that the panel be open to unorthodox and interdisciplinary research; and that the peers do not individually or as a group have an interest, financially or otherwise, in the outcome. The UGC fully accepted the peer review system since, in their view, there was no substitution for the sensitive and subtle judgment by experts in the field. Accordingly, it suggested that the choice of peers for the 1989 research assessment exercise be made with regard to "the range of specialized expertise needed to cover the spread of research in the subject area to be assessed;" to "the spread of institutions being assessed;" to "age and current active involvement in research;" and to "evidence of wide knowledge of the conduct of research in the relevant subject area" (Universities Funding Council 1989:15). The UFC and the HEFCs also adopted similar guidelines for the 1992 and 1996 assessment exercises (Advisory Board for the Research Councils 1990; Smith 1988a, 1988b; Universities Funding Council 1989; Lock 1985; Roy 1982; Hubbard 1995; Higher Education Funding Council for England 1994, 1995a; Griffith 1995).

Economics assessment panel and peer review

As carried out, the RAE violated a number of the criteria of peer review, such as no feedback was given to the departments in the 1989 and 1992 exercises as well as there being no appeal process, university academics and their departments were financially "forced' as opposed to volunteering to be peer reviewed, and the reviewers had a financial and a reputational interest in the particular and global outcomes. While serious omissions, they are of less importance relative to the process for selecting peers, peer capabilities of judging both orthodox and heterodox research, and peer interest in outcomes. It is clear that the UGC, UFC, and HEFCs were not in general very concerned that the methods of selection of the panel-peers were not open and democratic, about the issue of heterodox research, or that the peers had a theoretical interest in the outcome of their deliberations. But how did it work out at the micro-level, that is, at the level of the economic panel?

Economics panel-selection process

For peer review to work, it is necessary, as noted above, for the actual selection of the peers be open, democratic, and involve as much of the academic community as possible. However, the UGC, UFC, and HEFC were not concerned about this as they supported a process by which the economic panels for the 1989, 1992, and 1996 RAE were appointed that was not open or democratic in that the majority of economists had little say in, or understanding of, the selection process. The make-up of the 1989 panel consisted of two appointments by the UGC, four economists recommended by the Royal Economic Society (RES), one economist recommended by the Scottish Economic Society, two non-economists, and two observers from other panels. The economists appointed by the UGC were Charles Feinstein and Leonard Nicholson. In Feinstein's case, the UGC asked the RES to nominate someone for the chair of the economics panel and the Society proposed Feinstein. As for the other five economists, four were selected from a list of five names sent to the UGC by the RES. To obtain the five names, the Society solicited nominations from members of its standing committee of the Conference of Heads of University Departments of Economics (CHUDE).[5] The CHUDE Steering Committee considered all the nominations that came in and recommended to the RES Executive Committee what it thought to be a balanced slate of five names for transmission to the UGC. The five names put forward by the RES were Meghnad Desai, John Flemming, Kenneth George, James Mirrlees, and Alan Winters. Of these, Desai, Flemming, Mirrlees, and Winters were selected by the UGC for the panel. The fifth economist on the panel, Peter Sloane, was nominated by the Scottish Economic Society and supported by the CHUDE Steering Committee. The names of the panel assessors were not made public until after the exercise was completed (Minutes of the Conference of Heads of University Departments of Economics 5/11/88, 4/11/89; Standing Committee 25/2/89, 14/10/89; Feinstein 1995).

The selection of economists for the 1992 panel was slightly different in that the UFC did not directly appoint any of the panel members. Rather it solicited nominations for all panel members from subject associations, professional bodies, and learned societies, including CHUDE and the RES. Since the UFC's timescale from first seeking nominations for the assessment panels to announcing who the panel members were was only two months, the Steering Committee of CHUDE decided to seek nominations only from its members. Some seventy names were proposed by the heads, of which twelve or so commanded substantially more support than the remainder. Taking into account subject coverage and geographical spread, the Steering Committee selected eight or so names which they forwarded to the RES who in turn forwarded them to the Council. From the names submitted, the UFC and its economic advisors selected the chair for the economics panel, Atkinson, and then in consultation with Atkinson they selected the rest of the panel, which included Michael Artis, Frank Hahn, David Hendry, Ted Podolski, Peter Sloane, Nicholas Stern, and Alan Winters.[6] Hahn however declined to serve on the panel and Stern was unavailable to serve. After behind-close-doors discussions between Atkinson, Hendry, and Alistair Ulph (the chair of CHUDE), the former was replaced by James Malcolmson and the latter by Max Steuer.[7] The identity of the initial panel members was made known in July 1992 and updated later in November (Minutes of the Conference of Heads of University Departments of Economics 9/5/92, 7/11/92; Standing Committee 22/2/92, 19/9/92; Universities Funding Council 1992; Higher Education Funding Council for England 1993).

The selection of economists for the 1996 economics panel involved a three-step process. First, the four funding bodies, Higher Education Funding Council for England, Scottish Higher Education Funding Council, Higher Education Funding Council for Wales, and Department of Education Northern Ireland, drawing upon the advice of Atkinson, appointed Hendry as chair of the panel. At this same time the Steering Committee of CHUDE sought nominations from its members and the names of the five economists with the most nominations, that is, Philip Arestis, Hendry, David Greenaway, Malcolmson, and Sloane, were forwarded to Hendry for consideration. Hendry accepted the CHUDE list. Drawing upon the nominations submitted by other learned and professional bodies and in consultation with Greenaway, the Chairman of CHUDE, and Atkinson, Hendry also appointed John Beath, Anne Booth, Kenneth George, and Charles Goodhart to the panel. The identities of the panel members were made known in July 1995 (Higher Education Funding Council for England 1994, 1995a; Standing Committee 25/2/95, 15/5/95).

Peer review, judging research, and the economics panel

For the RAE to work, it was necessary that the method of assessment used by the various subject panels produced ratings that meant the same thing across all subject areas. It was also essential to the Exercise that the method of assessment used by a panel produced ratings which meant the same thing across all departments within a subject area. To achieve this, the members of the 1989 economics panel initially read all the submissions and gave each of them an independent mark.[8] Each department was also assigned one member of the panel who considered its submission in detail. A lengthy meeting was then convened where the individual submission marks were considered in conjunction with the department reports and a rating for each department determined. Similarly for the 1992 RAE, each submission was read by each panel member from which a provisional ranking of the departments derived. For the twenty borderline departments, each of them were allocated two panel members who also read and reported on the cited publications, as well as considering other aspects of its submission. This second evaluation was used to determine the final rating of the borderline departments. The 1996 economics panel largely followed the methods used by the 1992 panel (Griffith 1995; Higher Education Funding Council for England 1993, 1995b; Minutes of the Conference of Heads of University Departments of Economics 411/89, 21/5/93; Flemming 1991; Feinstein 1995).

The principal criterion in peer review and the RAE for selecting of economists for the economics panel should be pre-eminence in research in one or more of the subject areas in economics. While it is difficult to concretize preeminence in research, one indication of it, in light of the emphasis mainstream economists place on journal publications (see Chapter 2 and Lee 2006), is the number of publications a panel member has in core mainstream or heterodox journals. Therefore, using the *SSCI: Source Index* as the basis, it is possible to determine the number of journal publications of each of the 1989, 1992, and 1996 panel members published for the period 1966 to 1994, the percentage of the publications which appeared in core mainstream and heterodox journals,[9] and the percentage of core mainstream journals in which the publications occurred.[10] It is clear from Table 8.1 that a majority of the assessors on the 1989, 1992, and 1996 panels were well published and that, except for Arestis and Booth, over half of their publications appeared in core mainstream journals.[11] Thus, they would appear to fulfill the criteria of preeminence in mainstream research at the time the Research Assessment Exercises took place. Although Feinstein lacked journal publications, he had published and edited numerous books, primarily in economic history, and therefore can be considered well published. On the other hand, Nicholson had a long productive career beginning in 1940 with numerous journal and book publications; but by 1985 his publications had come to an end. Thus he did not fulfill the criterion of pre-eminence in research at the time of the 1989 Research Assessment Exercise. Further, given the absence of extensive journal or book publications by Podolski and Steuer, they did not fulfill the criterion of preeminence in research at the time of the 1992 RAE. Finally, both Beath and George published less compared with the other members on the 1996 panel, thus casting some doubt as to whether they fulfill the criterion of pre-eminence in research.

The second criterion for selecting panel members is subject coverage. Although, also difficult to concretize, Table 8.1 shows that none of the 1989, 1992, and 1996 panel members actually published in more than 36 per cent of the core mainstream journals, while, overall, the 1989, 1992, and 1996 panel members published in only 51 percent, 68 percent, and 66 percent of them respectively. The mainstream journals in which the panel members had not published were mostly specialist, applied, and interdisciplinary journals. Thus, none of the assessment panels covered all of mainstream economics as represented by the core mainstream journals.[12] Table 8.1 also reveals the near absence of publications in heterodox journals by members of all three panels (except Arestis), which implies that the panel members did not have the expertise or knowledge to judge the quality of heterodox economics submissions. This point is reinforced (except for Desai and Arestis) in Table 8.2, which is based on the references the 1989, 1992, and 1996 panel members made in their published articles. Finally, except for Desai and Arestis, none of the panel's heterodox references suggest that they were familiar with Marxian, Sraffian, or Institutionalist economics.

It is clear that not all the members of the 1989 and 1992 assessment panels for economics were selected because of their pre-eminence in economic research

Table 8.1 Assessment panels for economics, 1989–96

Panel Members in 1989	Number of Journal Publications[a]	Percentage of Journal Publications in Mainstream Journals	Percentage of Publications in Heterodox Journals	Percentage of Core Mainstream Journals in which Publications Occurred[b]
M. J. Desai	22	55	5	16
C. Feinstein	1	0	0	0
J. M. Flemming	17	100	0	16
J. Mirrlees	21	95	0	21
J. L. Nicholson	3	67	0	5
P. Sloane	14	57	14	14
L. A. Winters	15	80	7	16
Total	93	76	4	51

Panel Members in 1992	Number of Journal Publications[c]	Percentage of Journal Publications in Mainstream Journals	Percentage of Publications in Heterodox Journals	Percentage of Core Mainstream Journals in which Publications Occurred[d]
M. Artis	13	62	0	16
A. Atkinson	42	74	2	36
D. Hendry	39	82	3	30
J. Malcolmson	22	100	0	25
T. M. Podolski	0	0	0	0
P. Sloane	17	59	12	18
M. Steuer	2	50	0	2
L. A. Winter	27	70	4	20
Total	162	76	3	68

Panel Members in 1996	Number of Journal Publications[e]	Percentage of Journal Publications in Mainstream Journals	Percentage of Publications in Heterodox Journals	Percentage of Core Mainstream Journals in which Publications Occurred[f]
P. Arestis	27	26	59	7
J. Beath	4	75	0	5
A. Booth	15	0	0	0
K. D. George	9	89	0	11
C. Goodhart	26	69	8	25
D. Greenway	58	67	5	23
D. Henry	47	79	2	30
J. Malcolmson	28	100	0	30
P. Sloane	21	62	10	18
Total	235	65	10	66

Notes:

a As listed in the *SSCI: Source Index* for the period 1966–88.

b Excluding *International Journal of Industrial Organization, Empirical Economics, European Journal of Political Economy,* and *Recherches Economiques de Louvain.*

c As listed in the *SSCI: Source Index* for the period 1971–92.

d Excluding *Empirical Economics, European Journal of Political Economy,* and *Recherches Economiques de Louvain.*

e As listed in the *SSCI: Source Index* for the period 1971–94.

f Excluding *Empirical Economics, European Journal of Political Economy,* and *Recherches Economiques de Louvain.*

Table 8.2 1989, 1992, and 1996 economics panels' members references

Panel Members	Total Number of References*	Percentage of References to Core Mainstream Journals	Percentage of References to Core Heterodox and Other Non-Mainstream Journals
P. Arestis	697	25	36.4
M. Artis	230	27	0.4
A. Atkinson	915	39	0.3
J. Beath	43	60	2.3
A. Booth	417	2	0.5
M. J. Desai	265	45	10.0
C. Feinstein	50	14	0.0
J. M. Flemming	167	54	1.8
K. D. George	290	43	8.3
C. Goodhart	770	28	1.3
D. Greenway	1099	36	0.9
D. Hendry	2011	46	0.4
J. Malcolmson	466	67	0.4
J. Mirrlees	175	59	0.6
J. L. Nicholson	26	23	0.0
T. M. Podolski	0	0	0.0
P. Sloane	580	30	1.4
M. Steuer	25	4	0.0
L. A. Winter	424	30	1.7
Total	8650	36	4.2

Note:
* This includes journals, books, chapters in books, government publications, unpublished papers, archive material, and miscellaneous material.

at the time of the Exercises and they were not qualified to evaluate all areas of economic research. These clear violations of the central tenets of peer review undermine the legitimacy of the peer review process underlying RAE. Moreover, given the method of assessment used by the 1989 and 1992 economics panels, these faults had serious consequences for the assessing of the quality of heterodox research publications. That is, for the method of assessment used by the two panels to produce comparable ratings of publications and departments, it is necessary that each panel member be relatively familiar with the economic subject matter in each and all submissions. However, the panel members in either Exercise had not published in more than 36 percent of the core mainstream journals, had not in their references to their publications cited all of the core mainstream journals, and were, except for Desai, unfamiliar with the subject matter of heterodox economics. Therefore, one can only wonder how a panel member could have rated a publication in the *Cambridge Journal of Economics, Journal of Post Keynesian Economics,* or *Journal of Economic Issues* vis-à-vis a publication in *The Economic Journal, Review of Economic Studies, European Economic Review,* or *Kyklos*.[13] Similarly, one can only wonder how the members of both panels could believe that they reached a comparable rating for each department when the department submissions contained subject matter with which the panel members were not entirely familiar.

In one sense, the 1992 panel members realized that they failed on both accounts when they admitted that they ranked journals differently and dealt with interdisciplinary research unsatisfactorily. Moreover, by not explicitly taking steps to ensure that the assessing procedures were open to heterodox research, they could not help but be biased when rating them.[14] For example, a survey of the 1992 RAE publication submissions of five 5-rated, four 4-rated, thirteen 3-rated, and three 2-rated university economics departments revealed twenty-four publications in heterodox core journals. Four of those publications were in three 5-rated departments, none were in 4-rated departments, seven were in four 3-rated departments, and thirteen were in three 2-rated departments—see Appendix A.18. Thus it appears that if a department publication submission included a significant proportion of publications in core heterodox journals, it would most likely receive a two or three rating. Nevertheless, members of both panels stated that there were no profound disagreements with regard to rating individual publications or departments as a whole or that there was any discrimination against heterodox research (Minutes of the Conference of Heads of University Departments of Economics 4/11/89, 21/5/93; Flemming 1995; Feinstein 1995).

Peer review and vested interests

While such claims would startle knowledgeable researchers on peer review, it is only to be expected for economics.[15] As argued in Chapter 1, core mainstream journals form a close self-referencing system; hence mainstream economics has come to resemble a paradigm-bound normal science where the practitioners only converse with themselves. As a consequence, the community of mainstream economists has a vested interest in neoclassical theory and, by their very adherence to it, cannot see the evidence which would support an alternative view. It is not that new knowledge is not rewarded within mainstream economics. Indeed all academic labor processes by their very nature demand intellectual innovation and reward it in the reputations which are achieved by individuals amongst their peers. The knowledge which is produced, however, has to fit in with that which is already established. In paradigm-bound mainstream economics what is defined as knowledge has to conform with the neoclassical theoretic core, otherwise it is regarded at best as irrelevant, at worst as incompetent and unscientific. It is this kind of orthodoxy which has been achieved by mainstream economics and with it the attitude that those outside the mainstream are generally inferior economists whose research lacks any real academic value—see below.

The overriding propensity of mainstream economists to judge all economic research vis-à-vis the theoretic core of neoclassical theory (which reveals their preference for vested interests) meant that it was relatively easy for the members of the 1989 and 1992 economic panels to produce "comparable' ratings of publications and economics departments. That is, it was not important for the panel members to have detailed knowledge of all areas of economic research. Instead, all that they had to do when evaluating a research publication submission was to judge it solely on its congruence with the theoretic core of mainstream economics and ignore its other substantive content. Since the adherence to and/or understanding of the theoretic core was more or less the same for all panel members, as indicated by their journal publications (see Table 8.1: 1989 and 1992), they could independently arrive at the same evaluation of a research publication submission and of a department as a whole. Therefore, it is not surprising that they had no profound disagreements with regard to rating individual publications or departments. This also meant that panel members could evaluate heterodox publications of which they had no real understanding in a consistent manner—that of being incongruent with the core of mainstream economic theory and hence without question of lesser value than mainstream research.[16]

Impact of the RAE on heterodox economics after 1992

The combination of peer review and the RAE produced an institutional arrangement in the form of the economics panel which, because of its control over funding, had the power to affect the type of economic research carried out by British economists. Since the selection process promoted by the RES and carried out by CHUDE ensured that the members of the 1989 and 1992 economics panels were mainstream economists bar perhaps Desai, the message that the panels sent out with their evaluation of research and ranking of departments was that research in mainstream economics and publications in core mainstream journals was what was necessary for university economics departments to maintain or increase their research funding. Consequently, since the 1992 RAE economic departments, such as at the University of Manchester, took steps in the areas of recruitment policy and the direction of both departmental and individual work to emphasize mainstream research and de-emphasize and discriminate against heterodox research (Minutes of the Conference of Heads of University Departments of Economics 4/11/89; BBC, 1995).

To explore this impact of the RAE on British economics and especially heterodox economics, in the summer and autumn of 1994 a questionnaire was sent to over a 1000 British economists of which there were 382 useable responses from sixty-eight old and new universities.[17] The questionnaire was designed to explore the impact they felt the RAE was having on the recruitment and selection of heterodox economists generally and in their own institutions. Questions were also asked about the impact the RAE was having on both the work of their departments and on their own work. At every opportunity, respondents were given space to elaborate their answers and additional comments on the central hypothesis of the project were invited at the end.[18]

The impact of the RAE on British economics and particularly heterodox economics was carried by the economics departments themselves. That is, the departments as a unit first decided its "RAE policy," that is what kind of research and publications were relevant for a high RAE ranking. Once the RAE policy was established, staff was directed to pursue the appropriate research and publications; department recruitment policies were reinforced and/or changed to be consistent with the policy; and then finally the actual and recruitment and selection was conducted so that the research and publications of the staff hired were consistent with the department's RAE policy.

Department work

Responses to the questionnaire showed that British economics departments as a whole emphasized the need to publish in Diamond List journals or at least in mainstream journals—see Appendix A.18. More specifically, because of the RAE, respondents felt that there was more pressure to publish and specifically to publish mainstream material and publish in core mainstream journals—see Table 8.3:

> ... awareness of (supposed!) criteria for RAE permeates all research and publication activities.
>   ... there is a growing emphasis on publication in top X journals as the criterion of research performance ...
>   ... more pressure applied to everyone to be active in research and those that already are active to focus publication on kudos journals.
>   ... we got a 3. We need a 4+. The view is that not enough (mainstream) research is being done.

Table 8.3 Impact of the RAE on department work (Q. 6)

More Pressure to:	*Number*	*Per Cent*
Publish Diamond/core/mainstream	71	20.1
Target/research areas	62	17.7
Publish	50	14.2
Publish more (unspecified)	44	12.5
Do more technical/mainstream work	43	12.2
Publish in refereed journals	35	9.9
Greater division of labor	21	5.9
Neglect teaching	21	5.9
Other	6	1.7
Total	353	100.0

However, some respondents claimed that the RAE had little impact on their departments because they have always been mainstream, publishing driven, and driven to publishing in core mainstream journals. Thus, in combination, the result of the RAE was that publishing and publishing in core mainstream economic journals became an even more entrenched policy in a majority of British economics departments.

Directing research

One outcome of departments' RAE policy was that many individual economists, who did not already comply with it, actively or passively conformed to it—see Table 8.4:

> ... pressure to do the sort of work (publishing in core journals) which will assist the department in the ratings.
> ... I'm certainly considering status of the publication before proceeding with the article.
> ... felt it necessary to publish in a mainstream journal, which I have, but there has been an opportunity cost in some useful research I then did not have time for.

This acceptance of the policy of increasing neoclassical research and publishing in core neoclassical journals was justified in terms of supporting the department's quest for a better ranking and/or in terms of securing promotions:

> ... now set objective of publishing in the mainstream for benefit of departmental rating and my promotion prospects.
> All the department, mainstream and non-mainstream, acknowledge we must play the mainstream game. Did so at a special meeting.
> ... although one tries to resist, one has to consider the impact on the department and pressure from colleagues.
> ... my promotion has been directly linked to top journal publication.

Table 8.4 Ways in which own work affected by RAE (Q.7)

	Number	*Per Cent*
I am targeting core	46	20.2
I have gone more mainstream	44	19.3
I publish more	41	18.0
I have gone short-term	38	16.7
I target/do more research	30	13.1
I have switched to refereed journals	29	12.7
Total	228	100.0

On the other hand, heterodox economists whose research agenda and publishing were at odds with the RAE policy were asked and perhaps put under significant pressure to redirect their research and conform—see Appendix A.18. In fact, by not conforming, heterodox economists were placed at disadvantage within the department with regard to promotion and access to research and travel funds.[19] Moreover, because their work was considered devoid of any real value, they were treated almost as non-economists or even anti-economists as well as a department liability, and invited rather dismissive comments that verged on intellectual bullying:

> ... most non-mainstream aren't concerned with advancing knowledge in
> the subject but with either:(i) re-working old ideas which should have
> > been left for dead long ago
> > (ii) whining about how badly they've been treated
> > (iii) trying to find conspiracies against them.

Department recruitment policies

With the RAE policy in place, many respondents stated it had an impact on department recruitment policies by first placing more emphasis on publications and research and secondly by accentuating the importance of mainstream research and publishing in core journals—see Table 8.5:

> ... we only recruit those likely to get into core journals, not especially interested in teaching or admin, skills of applicants (or even English proficiency).
> ... research rating potential a prime consideration. Idea of looking for non-mainstream people now inconceivable.
> ... recently, main criterion seems to have been ability to publish in mainstream journals—in the past, judging from the composition of the department, things were different.
> ... the main change in our recruitment policy in recent years has been the emphasis on research and publication potential.

Table 8.5 Changes in recruitment policy in relation to economists in own institution (Q. 4)

	Number	*Per Cent*
More on publications	50	21.9
More on research	47	20.6
Change to mainstream explicit	36	15.8
Greater technical skills	28	12.3
Emphasis on core journals	23	10.1
Short-termism	9	2.6
Other	38	16.7
Total	228	100.0

Table 8.6 Recruitment policies always applied (Q.b4)

	Number	*Per Cent*
Always quality	49	27.2
Always research	40	22.2
Always mainstream/core	24	13.3
Always publications	19	10.6
Teaching/subject driven	41	22.8
Other	7	3.9
Total	180	100.0

However, other respondents stated that the RAE had no impact on their recruitment policies, largely because they were consistent with the requirements of the RAE in the first place—see Table 8.6:

> ... most promising in terms of publication in top journals. Always has been.
> ... the department's direction has not changed. We appoint people we think are "good." (Our notion of "goodness" no doubt favors the mainstream. That is what mainstream means of course.)

Thus, as a result of adopting RAE policies, the post-1992 recruitment policies of a majority of British economics departments became even more affirmative for the hiring of neoclassical economists.

Recruitment and selection

Given the RAE-influenced recruitment policy, the actual recruitment process and selection clearly favored the hiring of mainstream economists. As noted above, Manchester explicitly stated in its advertisements that it was seeking to hire specifically mainstream economists. Adverts for posts in other institutions similarly specify that applicants must be working within the mainstream and link this explicitly to either maintaining or improving their ranking in the assessment exercise:

> The college welcomes applications for Lectureships in Economics in any field of mainstream Economics. Successful candidates will have demonstrated outstanding potential in both research and teaching. Although candidates new to the profession need not have current publications, they must display the ability and intention to publish in leading international and UK journals. (Lectureships in Economics, Royal Holloway, University of London, 1995)
> The Department is seeking to build on its significant improvement at the last Research Assessment Exercise. The new appointments will be

expected to demonstrate the strong research commitment that results in significant publications. (Lectureships in Economics and/or Marketing/Corporate Strategy, University of Dundee, 1995)

The Department is particularly seeking to appoint someone with interests in a mainstream area of the subject to complement the research interests of the other Professors and to provide research leadership in the Department. (Chair in Economics, University of Kent at Canterbury, 1995)

The Department of Economics has expanded rapidly over recent years and is enjoying a growing reputation for its research. Bibliometric surveys have placed it among the leading UK universities in terms of the volume of its research output and it is successfully increasing the number of its publications in core journals. (Posts in Economics, University of Surrey, 1995)

Following from the recruitment policy and job advertisements, candidates, in the interviewing process, were quizzed on their research and in which core mainstream journal he or she planned to publish:

I personally have been interviewed at other universities where it has been clear that publishing in core journals is the criteria.

… in my inquiries regarding other posts at older universities I have been asked about research interests and the RAE and journals have been signalled. At a selection committee of a large older university I was recently asked directly which journals I aim to publish in over the coming 2 years.

Thus the actual appointment itself turned specifically on whether the department believed that the individual was a mainstream economist and would publish in core mainstream journals:[20]

… more emphasis on those working in core areas. Am partly responsible for this myself as we have to follow RAE signals. I don't set the rules. None of us like them. But was a chairman of the dept myself. No real options but to play by the rules.

… unwillingness to hire those who may not publish in core journals. …

Moreover, the respondents to the questionnaire revealed that at least twenty-four economics departments would pointedly not hire a heterodox economist—see Appendix A.18:

… in a recent chair appointment, a well-published and senior non-mainstream female economist was not shortlisted.

… we had senior member of staff who was a Marxist—but it would be unthinkable to replace him with a Marxist economist on retirement. Hence his course in Marxist political economy was dropped.

... we only employ competent economists who can teach macro and micro and do proper research. I regard "non-mainstream" economics as irrelevant to modern economics. When posts are limited it is important to fill them with people who can do research in central areas of the subject. There are no economics of scale in having unrelated non-mainstream people on one's staff.

... we are not interested in employing non-mainstream economists.

... we look for the best. Those outside the mainstream (as you put it) are generally inferior.

Consequently for the period 1992 to 1994 fifty-six of the ranked departments hired mainly neoclassical economists. Thus, of the approximately 285 economists hired by economic departments, 90 percent were mainstream economists and they were concentrated among those universities that positively discriminated against heterodox economists and affirmatively hired neoclassical economists. More significantly, while forty-three of the fifty-eight economic departments that entered the 1992 RAE had heterodox economists, only eleven departments hired heterodox economists—see Table 8.7. So, although heterodox economists constituted at least 20 percent of academic economists in British economic departments, of the 285 economists hired on temporary and permanent contracts by the fifty-six hiring economic departments, only 10 percent were heterodox economists. Finally, the disaggregated data on which Table 8.7 is based shows that three of the eleven departments hired 62 percent of the heterodox economists and that the eleven departments as a group have hired more mainstream than heterodox economists (32 vs. 31). Thus the impact of the RAE on hiring was to reduce the employment possibilities of heterodox economists in British university economics departments and to "pressure' those departments most open to heterodox economists to hire mainstream economists as well. As obvious as this outcome seems, some respondents were not even aware there was a biased selection going on:

Table 8.7 Hiring mainstream and heterodox economists, 1992–94

1992 RAE Rating	5	4	3	2	1
Economics Departments	10	13	22[a]	10	3[b]
Economics Departments Hiring Heterodox Economists in 1992–94	1	1	4	5	–
Mainstream Economists Hired 1992–94[c]	69	59	80	41	7
Heterodox Economists Hired 1992–94[c]	1	1	15	12	–

Notes:
a De Montfort University is included.
b Thames Valley University and Buckinghamshire College of Higher Education each received a one rating, but there were no responses from them to the questionnaire.
c These are subjective estimates of respondents; they include both permanent and temporary appointments (Questionnaire Survey 1994).

... the issue you have raised did not even occur to me, or for all I know, to anyone of my colleagues. There are many faults with the RAE, but this doesn't appear to be one of them at my institution.

I have seen no bias in the leading journals against non-mainstream economists.

Publishing rather poor stuff in specifically non-mainstream journals does not help diversity.

I do not believe there is a conspiracy against the non-mainstream, but by definition these represent approaches which most members of the profession believe are misguided. Nevertheless it does seem to me to be quite possible to get into the best journals with different ideas. Most mainstream journals take non-mainstream if it is good.

Future of heterodox economics

The UGC established the RAE as an institutional mechanism to provide it with a rationale for distributing research funds among university departments of a given subject area. Central to the Exercise was the assessment panel made up of pre-eminent peers who rate the research excellence of a department and thereby determine the amount of research monies it will get. Perhaps not initially intended to affect the areas of research carried out by British academics, the assessment panels in fact had that capability through its control of the allocation of research monies. Before the RAE, the dominance of mainstream economics in British economics departments and among British economists was due, in part, to the historical legacy (delineated in Chapter 6) that discriminated against Marxism, and, in part, since the 1970s to the leadership of the RES which maintained control over the "reputational' system that is central to the organization of academic work. The advent of the RAE and the economics panel, however, posed a potential threat to its leadership and hence to the continued dominance of mainstream economics. Therefore, the leadership of the Society acted quickly to capture the process by which assessors were appointed to the economics panel. In particular, the Society actively supported the establishment of CHUDE in 1987, whose most important activity was the selection of RES-acceptable candidates for the economics panels. Consequently, the assessors appointed to the 1989 and 1992 panels had the common characteristics of being mainstream economists and of holding a significant position within the RES, such as a member of the Council or Executive Committee, Treasurer, or President, being on the editorial board of *The Economic Journal*, and/or being a member of the CHUDE Standing Committee. With the capture of the economics panel, the RES obtained the power to cleanse economics departments of heterodox economists. That is, the RES ensured that mainstream, RES-connected economists dominated the 1989 and 1992 economics panels. Since the paradigm-bound view held that the quality of heterodox research was inferior to mainstream research was largely accepted by the assessors, the two panels financially rewarded departments who did mainstream research and published in core mainstream journals and generally damned those who did not. The real threat of financial sanction by the economics panel, in light of the declining financial support for universities and research, drove British economic departments to discriminate against heterodox research and the hiring of heterodox economists as well as to restrict if not eliminate the teaching of heterodox economics to students[21] (Minutes of the Conference of Heads of University Departments of Economics 5/11/88; Standing Committee 22/2/92; BBC 1995).

The cleansing process was not altered by the 1996 RAE. As noted above, the selection process was not open; there was behind-closed-doors selection of four panel members; not all panel members were pre-eminent in research; and the panel members were not qualified to evaluate all areas of economic research. Furthermore, the RES through CHUDE guided the selection of economists to the economics panel, with the outcome that all but one panel member held a leadership position in the Society, had help edit *The Economic Journal*, and/or was a member of the CHUDE Standing Committee. In addition, except for Arestis and Booth, the remaining panel members were part of the closed self-referencing group of mainstream economists who published in core mainstream journals; were influenced by articles, arguments and concerns contained within these core mainstream journals; and were not influenced by the arguments and concerns of economists who publish in the core heterodox journals. Finally, the assessment criteria delineated by the 1996 panel emphasized the members' subjective but professional judgment of the quality of journals and of published works, and publications in internationally reputed journals (Higher Education Funding Council for England 1995b).

The combination of panel members' intellectual allegiance to mainstream economics with the panel's assessment criteria made it improbable that the presence of one heterodox economist, Arestis, would be able to challenge the panel's historical tendency to reward mainstream and discourage heterodox research. As it turned out, the nineteen economic departments which improved their 1992 research ratings in the 1996 RAE deliberately hired almost exclusively mainstream economists (82 versus seven heterodox economists), with the most noted examples being Manchester, Manchester Metropolitan, Kent at Canterbury, London Guildhall, Portsmouth, St Andrews, and Nottingham who hired 48 mainstream and only two heterodox economists. On the other hand, the ten economics departments which did not improve upon their one to three ratings in the 1992 RAE hired 37 mainstream and 17 heterodox economists—see Appendix A.18. Thus, improvement in department rankings was explicitly linked to the near exclusive hiring of mainstream economists.

The outcome of the 1996 RAE made it more than likely that economics departments would attempt to improve their rating for the 2001 RAE by even more positive discrimination towards mainstream economists and mainstream economics, independent of any heterodox representation on the panel. Moreover, the 1996 results sanctioned the ongoing discrimination against heterodox economists and their research, which resulted in few young heterodox economists obtaining university teaching and research positions. As a consequence, the long-term outcome is that the number of heterodox economists in British university economics departments will decline significantly. Such a decline will result within a decade in the virtual disappearance of heterodox economists from the majority of British economic departments, with the remainder being increasingly invisible. The peer review-based RAE was established to provide a rationale for distributing research funds and not simply for evaluating the quality of research. Therefore, it is not simply the shortcomings of the panel members in terms of pre-eminence in research and subject coverage which has produced the current attack on heterodox economics, but the RAE itself in the context of a divided, paradigm-bound economics. For heterodox economics to have a chance of surviving in British economics departments, the ending of the RAE is necessary or, barring this, at least the elimination of the RES control over the selection of the economics panel and opening up the selection process so that the panel is accountable to all British economists. The extent to which this is possible is open to question; but without these changes the future of heterodox economics in Britain is problematical.

9 Research Assessment Exercise, the state, and the dominance of mainstream economics in British universities, 2000–2003

In the previous chapter, a discouraging set of conclusions and predictions were enumerated. Specifically, through the economics panelists reliance on Diamond List journals to rank departments, it was concluded that the Research Assessment Exercise (RAE) would continue to drive economic departments to positively discriminate in terms of their hiring, promotion, and research strategies towards mainstream economists and their research in order to maintain or improve their ranking (and hence their research funding). As a consequence, there would, in time, be no or only a token presence of heterodox economists in increasing number of departments. And, in turn, the near absence of heterodox economists in many economic departments would result in undergraduate, post-graduate, and research students only being taught mainstream economics and writing neoclassical doctoral dissertations. In a non-ergodic world with many different causal mechanisms and structures, these conclusions and predictions may not materialize. Whether they have or not provides the framework for this study on the dominance of mainstream vis-à-vis heterodox economics and economists in the United Kingdom at the dawn of the twenty-first century. The line of argument advanced in this chapter is that the conclusions and predictions continue to hold in that mainstream or neoclassical economic theory and discourse dominates British economic departments in terms of research, publications, undergraduate teaching, post-graduate teaching and research degrees; and a majority of departments have none or only a token heterodox economists on staff. And that these outcomes are in large part a result of the RAE and the emphasis placed on publishing in the Diamond List set of journals. To establish the argument, the first section will delineate the ranking-state of British economics circa 2001 relative to the 2001 RAE. In the next section, Quality Assurance Agency subject benchmark and content material is used to indicate a connection between the RAE and the dominance of mainstream vs. heterodox subject content of economic programs circa 2000–2002. This is followed in the third section by an examination of the impact of the RAE and the Diamond List on department hiring and promotion practices. Drawing on the previous material, the fourth section will address the dominance of mainstream economics in British universities.

The final section will address the role of state power in the fostering of intellectual uniformity in British economics.

2001 RAE, Diamond List journals, and economic departments

Out of the 94 British Universities and other institutions of higher education that offered undergraduate and post-graduate courses and degrees in economics circa 2000 (see Appendix A.19), only forty-one entered the 2001 RAE.[1] Concentrating on these forty-one economics departments, the impact of the Diamond List journals on their 2001 RAE ranking is examined in this section.[2] As noted in the previous chapter, British economists strongly believed that the so-called "Diamond List" of core mainstream economic journals was used by the panel assessors in the 1989 RAE to inform their judgment of the quality of research in economics departments. Although the Diamond List remained unofficial in the following years, the journals came to represent in the minds of British economists the "core" mainstream journals, which is not surprising since they dominate the journal-ranking studies of the past decade:[3] "[Diamond List journals] are the journals used in the now-regular university research assessment exercise as the principal criterion for international excellence. It is not easy to publish in these journals" (Oswald 1995: 6, Table 4). Thus, Diamond List journals are widely recognized by mainstream economists for their rigorous editorial and refereeing process and have a reputation for international excellence through their publication of articles that make substantive and/or original contributions to theory, methodology, policy and practice, and achieve technical excellence.[4] Hence, for mainstream economists in general as well as the members of the economics panel, they were (and are) in an almost commonsense way the "objective" measure of the quality of research and hence the principal determinant in ranking economic departments and other criteria, such as publications in less prominent journals and non-journal publications and the research culture, depth, vitality, and prospects of the department, mattered to a much lesser extent (Beath 2002; Backhouse 2002).

Evidence for this claim is threefold. As indicated in Table 9.1, the average number of Diamond List publications per department-rank increases dramatically with rank.[5] Moreover, when size of department is compensated for in terms of the percentage of Diamond List publications in total publications per rank and the number of Diamond List publications per active research staff, the initial results still hold. Second, these results are not altered when the Diamond List is expanded to include selected neoclassical and interdisciplinary journals—see Appendix A.19. It was hoped, when first proposed, that the expanded list would be accepted in place of the Diamond List as the indicator of research quality. However, as indicated in Table 9.2, this was not the case in the 2001 RAE. While the inclusion of the selected journals did not disturb the rankings (that is the values for rank 5 were still less than the values for rank 5*), the differences between the different ranks

Table 9.1 2001 RAE publication data by ranking: Diamond List journals

	5*	5	4	3
Total Active Research Staff	142.80	279.20	283.30	141.60
Total Diamond List Publications	238.00	323.00	246.00	64.00
Total RAE Publications	559.00	1107.00	1031.00	542.00
Publications in Diamond List Journals (Average per department)	59.50	35.90	4.50	5.80
Percentage of Diamond List Publications In Total RAE Publications	42.57	29.18	23.86	11.81
Diamond List publications Per Active Research Staff	1.67	1.16	0.87	0.45

Source: Derived from Appendix A.19.

Table 9.2 2001 RAE publication data by ranking: Diamond List and other selected mainstream and interdisciplinary journals

	5*	5	4	3
Total Active Research Staff	142.80	279.20	283.30	141.60
Total Diamond List and other Selected Journals Publications	263.00	418.00	379.00	159.00
Total RAE Publications	559.00	1107.00	1031.00	542.00
Publications in Diamond List and Selected Journals (Average per Department)	65.75	46.40	22.30	14.40
Percentage of Diamond List and Selected Journals in Total RAE Publications	47.03	37.76	36.76	29.33
Diamond List and Selected Journals Publications Per Active Research Staff	1.84	1.50	1.34	1.12

Source: Derived from Appendix A.19.

declined. In particular, the differences between the ranks of 5* and 3 as measured by the ratio 5*/3 declined for each measure. For example, 5* departments publish in Diamond List journals at a factor of 10 times greater than 3 departments whereas for the expanded Diamond List the factor difference drops to 4.5 (59.5/5.8 vs. 65.75/14.4). Moreover, the ratio of the percentage of Diamond List publications in total publications for 5* relative to 3 departments is 3.6 but the same ratio for the expanded Diamond List is 1.6 (42.57/11.81 vs. 47.03/29.33) which is not much of a difference at all. Finally, for the Diamond List publications per active research staff for 5* relative to 3 departments is 3.7 but the same ratio for the expanded Diamond List is 1.6 (1.67/0.45 vs. 1.84/1.12) which again is not much of a difference. Finally, the significance of the Diamond List is, through contrast with heterodox economic, history of economic thought, and methodology publications (H-HET-M), accentuated.[6] That is, as shown in Table 9.3, the lower the department ranking the greater the percentage of H-HET-M publications in total publications and the number of H-HET-M publications per active research staff.

Table 9.3 2001 RAE publication data by ranking: heterodox, history of economic thought, and methodology publications

	5*	5	4	3
Total Active Research Staff	142.80	279.20	283.30	141.60
Total H-HET-M Publications	10.00	30.00	49.00	37.00
Total RAE Publications	559.00	1107.00	1031.00	542.00
H-HET-M Publications (Average per department)	2.50	3.30	2.90	3.40
Percentage of H-HET-M Publications in Total Publications	1.79	2.71	4.75	6.83
H-HET-M Publications Per Active Research Staff	0.07	0.11	0.17	0.26

Source: Derived from Appendix A.19

Table 9.4 2001 RAE research groups in heterodox economics, history of economic thought, and methodology, by ranking

Department	Ranking	Research Group
Cambridge	5	Methodology and Political Science
Manchester	4	History of Thought, Methodology, and Heterodoxy
Stirling	4	Developments in Economic Thought
Aberdeen	3	Institutional Economics
East London	3	Post Keynesian Economics
Manchester Metropolitan	3	History of Thought/Political Economy

Moreover, the ratio of the percentage of H-HET-M publications in total publications for 5* relative to 3 departments is 0.26; and for H-HET-M publications per active research staff for 5* relative to 3 departments is 0.27. Thus, in general the research active staff in 3 departments produce 3.7–3.8 times as many H-HET-M publications as 5* department.

The above results strongly support the conclusion that the Diamond List journals and only them were taken by the 2001 RAE economics panel as the quantitative measure of research quality. Moreover, through its ranking decisions, the panel made it clear that the journals "added" to the Diamond List were distinctly inferior in representing research quality and hence publications in them did not contribute to a department's ranking any more than a publication in any other inferior mainstream journal. Thus, the attempt to broaden the Diamond List in the end severely hurt those departments that took the extended list seriously.[7] Finally, the panel made it clear that H-HET-M publications and faculty groups devoted to H-HET-M research had negative consequences for a department's ranking. Specifically, departments that had research groups in the areas of heterodox economics, history of economic thought, and methodology generally received a low ranking of 3 or 4 (see Table 9.4).

Thus, it is not just that H-HET-M publications represented *no* economic research but that they represented (to use a phrase that is becoming popular with mainstream economists) anti-economics[8] and being the enemy of economics such research and researchers should, it seems, be cleansed from the profession.[9]

Economics subject benchmark and the subject content of economic programs

The Quality Assurance Agency for Higher Education (QAA) is charged with reviewing the quality of higher education in the United Kingdom. Consequently it initiated a project to develop definite subject benchmark statements that would be used to evaluate the nature and characteristics of academic programs, which in our case would be the bachelor economics degree with honors.[10] In the benchmark statement, the stated aim of economics "is to analyse and understand the allocation, distribution and utilization of scarce resources" (Beath 2000: 1) and its methodology is deductive reasoning and the application of logical analysis applied to assumption-based models. This neoclassical-based aim and methodology is complemented with statements concerning subject knowledge and understanding associated with neoclassical teaching programs and with subject-specific skills and concepts, such as abstraction so to frame economic problems in terms of assumption-based mathematical models that can be quantified, opportunity costs, equilibrium, incentives, and the relevance of marginal considerations. The only recognition of the existence of heterodox economics and the importance of history of economic thought and methodology for economic students is the acknowledgement that as part of their knowledge of economics students should appreciate "the existence of different methodological approaches" and "the history and development of economic ideas and the differing methods of analysis that have been and are used by economists" (Beath 2000: 2). But these points are downplayed to the extent that they do not appear as part of the benchmark levels necessary for a graduate of an honors degree in economics. In short the economics benchmark statement enshrines neoclassical economic theory as the only economic theory to teach to undergraduate students and the only theory they are expected to know (Beath 2000; also see Backhouse (2002) and Simonetti (2007).

A second project of the QAA concerns subject reviews that are carried out in the terms of the aims and objectives established by the provider of undergraduate and taught post-graduate programs in the subject; and the aims and objectives in turn determine the content of the programs. Thus, the aims and objectives essentially define what the core knowledge of the subject students are expected to know. In the case of economics, economic departments qua their undergraduate and taught post-graduate degree programs are "free" to establish any aims and objectives on which to be evaluated. They could have included the aim/objective of "introducing students to mainstream and heterodox theories and their methodologies and to their historical origins and development," therefore making heterodox economics, history of thought and methodology part of the core subject knowledge that students are expected to know. However, given the antipathy mainstream economists have towards any economics that is not mainstream combined with the fact that the economic subject teams are generally dominated by such economists, departments may feel pressured to emphasis the components of the economic benchmark statement in their programs' aims and objectives; and at the same time de-emphasis or eliminate any heterodox material.[11] The QAA subject reviews in economics for England, Scotland, and Northern Ireland for the period 2000–2002[12] shows that the top economics departments did not include heterodox economics, history of economic thought, and methodology as part of the core economics students are expected to know (see Appendix A.20).[13] Hence, none of the departments ranked five-starred, five, or four included among their aims and objectives for their taught undergraduate and post-graduate courses statements regarding heterodox economics, history of thought and methodology. Rather their aims and objectives for the teaching of economics and the content of what is to be learned included the following phrases:

- providing students with theoretical and applied courses in *mainstream economics or the standard core of economic theory and method* (Essex, Birkbeck, Cambridge, Leicester, Manchester, Nottingham, Edinburgh, and Stirling);
- upon graduating students should have a sound understanding of the central ideas, concepts, tools, models and methods of *modern mainstream economic theory* (University College London, Warwick, Exeter, Cambridge, Leicester, Oxford, Bristol, Kent, Manchester, Newcastle, and Royal Holloway);
- students are exposed to leading-edge research, much of it originating within the Department (University College London, Birmingham, Nottingham, Southampton, Birkbeck, and Bristol);
- provide economic courses that are consistent with the benchmark statement in economics (Birmingham, Glasgow, Edinburgh, Stirling, Strathclyde, and St. Andrews); and
- students are to be familiar with mathematical methods and quantitative techniques and their application to economic problems (London School of Economics and Political Science, University College London, Essex, Bristol, Birmingham, Kent, Manchester, Stirling, St Andrews, Royal Holloway, East Anglia, Nottingham, Southampton, Liverpool, Sussex, Exeter, Cambridge, Leicester, and Oxford).

Given the exclusive emphasis on terms such as *modern-mainstream economics, core economic theory, the benchmark statement in economics*, and *mathematical methods and quantitative techniques*, the agenda of these departments is to only teach one view of economics to their students. Stating that what they teach is based on the up-to-date research carried out by the economics staff reinforces this. In light of the RAE emphasis on Diamond List publications, this means that the core subject matter students are expected to know is restricted to neoclassical economic theory. This does not mean that students in these departments are not exposed to heterodox economics or take classes in history of economic thought and methodology (see below). Rather these departments have decided that this material is extraneous to core subject knowledge students are expected to know. That is, heterodox economics, history of economic thought and methodology are considered by these departments unimportant, frivolous knowledge relative to the core mainstream economic theory and associate mathematical methods and quantitative techniques a student is expected to acquire.[14]

Because of the intellectual and academic prestige acquired by the 5-starred, 5- and 4-ranked departments through the RAE, they effectively set the benchmark for what is considered the appropriate economics to teach students. Therefore, it is not surprising to find that in 2000–2002 six of the eleven 3-ranked departments and eighteen of the twenty-nine subject-reviewed but non-ranked departments (that is departments or institutions that did not enter the RAE 2001 under economics) did not have required modules that included heterodox economics (see Appendix A.20).[15] These latter twenty-four departments justified their position by deferring to the elite departments in terms of wanting to "maintain the same academic standards." Consequently, they use the same language and phrases when delineating their aims and objectives for the teaching of economics and the content of what is to be learned:

- providing students with theoretical and applied courses in *mainstream economics or the standard core of economic theory and method* (Dundee, Hertfordshire, Hull, Liverpool John Moores, Queen's Belfast, Sheffield, and UWE Bristol);
- upon graduating students should have a sound understanding of the central ideas, concepts, tools, models and methods of *modern mainstream economic theory* (Loughborough, Manchester Metropolitan, Reading, Staffordshire, and Surrey);
- provide economic courses that are consistent with the *economics benchmark statement* (Aberdeen, Paisley, Sheffield, UCE Birmingham, and Ulster); and
- students are to be familiar with *mathematical methods and quantitative techniques* and their application to economic problems (Keele, London Guildhall [now London Metropolitan], Nottingham Trent, Portsmouth, Liverpool John Moores, Queen's Belfast, Staffordshire, and UWE Bristol).[16]

Rae, Diamond List, and department hiring and promotion practices

As indicated in the previous chapter, many departments prior to 1992 had hiring and promotion practices in place that emphasized publications or the capability of publishing in Diamond List (or more euphemistically core economic) journals. But since 1992 those departments that had such hiring and promotion practices followed them more closely while other departments quickly took them up. Consequently by 1994 all of the departments ranked five-starred, five, and four, and seven of the eleven 3-ranked departments in the 2001 RAE emphasized publications in the Diamond List journals and had restricted their hiring (and promotion) almost entirely to appropriately qualified neoclassical economists; and of these thirty-six departments, twenty-one would simply not hire a heterodox economist (see Appendix A.21, columns 2, 3, and 4).[17] These staffing practices were also explicitly delineated by Brunel, Exeter, Newcastle, and Queen Mary as part of their 2001 RAE submission; and implicitly suggested by departments, such as Nottingham, Oxford, Queen Mary, and Warwick, that sought to identify themselves as "top" departments and to establish that the quality of their research had improved in terms of publications in Diamond List journals.[18] Finally, the practices have remained in force to the present-day, with the apparent result that none of the 5-starred and 5-ranked departments and only one of the 4-ranked departments have hired heterodox economists over the period of 2000–2003 (derived from the 2003 Questionnaire—see Appendix A.23). Therefore it is unsurprising that the portion of Diamond List publications in a department's total RAE-submitted publications have generally increased from 1992 to 2001; and that the proportion of Diamond List publications in the total RAE-submitted publications has increased from approximately 17.34 percent in 1992 to 26.89 percent in 2001—see Table 9.5. Hence, it is fair to suggest that the top-ranked UK economics departments have become relatively more homogeneous and narrower in their research interests; or as one old university economist noted, the long-term (and perhaps the short-term) impact of the RAE is to make economic departments work with only one paradigm instead of engaging with a plurality of paradigms (Henkel 2000: 141).[19]

Mainstream economics in British universities

At the macro-institutional level, of the ninety-five UK universities and other higher education institutions that provided undergraduate and post-graduate degrees and instruction in economics in 2002–3, 57 (or 60 percent) had no heterodox economist on staff, 26 (or 27 percent) had one to three heterodox economists on staff, and only twelve (or 13 percent) had four or more heterodox economists on staff. Moreover, the fifty-seven, twenty-six, and twelve universities with none, one to three, and four or more heterodox economists on staff had 48 per cent, 32 per cent, and 20 per cent respectively of the total undergraduate and post-graduate student population of 29,223. Thus, in terms of staffing, mainstream economics was (and is) uncontested in 60 percent of the universities with 48 percent of the economic students and nearly so in another 27 percent of the universities with 32 percent of the students— see Table 9.6

Table 9.5 Proportion of Diamond List publications in RAE-submitted publications in 1992 and 2001, for selected departments and overall

Department	Rank 1992	Percentage of Diamond List Publications in Total RAE Publications 1992	Rank 1991	Percentage of Diamond List Publications in Total RAE Publications 2001
Birkbeck	5	33.33	5	38.55
City	3	15.38	3	10.71
Dundee	3	20.83	3	12.00
Durham	3	0.00	4	37.50
East London	2	0.00	3	15.38
Edinburgh	3	22.22	4	37.78
Essex	5	47.37	5*	53.98
Exeter	4	22.50	5	51.85
Glasgow	4	13.79	4	29.69
Leicester	3	28.95	5	33.87
London Guildhall	2	6.25	3	17.78
London School of Economics	5	26.72	5*	34.22
Newcastle	4	35.71	4	25.64
Queen Mary	4	15.15	5	39.24
St. Andrews	3	0.00	4	20.31
Surrey	3	8.33	3	17.46
Warwick	5	28.38	5*	41.18
York	5	20.00	5	26.62
Total		17.34		26.89

Source: Derived from Appendix A.18 and A.19.

Table 9.6 Department rank, heterodox economists, and student numbers for the period 2002–03

RAE Rank of Department	No. of Heterodox Economists in the Department (No. of Departments)			Total No. Students (Total No. Departments)
	None	1 to 3	4 or more	
5*	1605.5 (2)	1681.7 (2)	0.0 (0)	3287.2 (4)
5	3797.6 (6)	1387.3 (2)	820.0 (1)	6004.9 (9)
4	4398.9 (10)	1566.5 (6)	1651.0 (1)	7616.4 (17)
3	923.1 (3)	2470.6 (5)	912.8 (3)	3723.2 (11)
No Rank	2023.5 (13)	1813.9 (9)	2317.0 (17)	6737.7 (29)
No Rank/ No Subject Review	1377.9 (23)	476.0 (2)	0.0 (0)	1853.6 (25)
Total No. of Students (Total No. of Departments)	14126.2 (57)	9396.0 (26)	5700.8 (12)	29223.0 (95)

Source: Derived from Appendix A.20 and A.22.

Narrowing the analysis to the seventy universities covering 27,369.4 students for which there is information concerning the heterodox aims and objectives for the B.A. and post-graduate courses,[20] fifty-four departments with 88 percent of the students had no such aims and objectives, while sixteen departments with 12 percent of the students did—see Table 9.7A. Finally, combining staffing with aims and objectives, twenty-nine of the departments had no heterodox economists or heterodox aims and objectives for the B.A. and post-graduate courses, which implies a complete absence of heterodox economics in the education of their students. Hence 45 per cent of the 27,369.4 students inhabited an educational environment in which heterodox economic ideas were completely absence. Another eighteen departments with 27 percent of the students had one to three heterodox economists but no heterodox aims and objectives for their B.A. and post-graduate courses. Thus, these students get introduced to heterodox economics in some optional modules (derived from the 2003 Questionnaire—see Appendix A.23), but the overall presence of heterodox economics in their programs was weak, which strongly suggests that the students inhabited an education environment in which heterodox economic ideas had a weak presence at best. In total, some 72 percent of economic students inhabited an education environment in 47 (67 percent) economic departments in which the presence of heterodox economic ideas were weak if non-existent and the presence of heterodox economists ranges from very small to zero—see Table 9.7A.[21]

The seventy departments can be divided into three groups to further illustrate the dominance of mainstream economics in the teaching of undergraduate students and the training of post-graduate and research students—see Table 9.7B. The first group consists of forty-three departments in which the presence of a heterodox approach to economics was all but absence. The group consists of the twenty-nine departments that had no heterodox economists and did not include the presentation of heterodox economics in some degree among the aims and objectives of their undergraduate and postgraduate courses, five departments which had no heterodox economists but did have the presentation of heterodox economics in some degree among the aims and objectives of their undergraduate courses, and nine departments in which there was a single heterodox economist but did not include the presentation of heterodox economics in some degree among the aims and objectives of their undergraduate and post-graduate courses. With the course aims and objectives only narrowly focused on mainstream theory and too few heterodox economists providing "heterodox" electives, the undergraduate and post-graduate students in these departments (which is 60.1 percent of the undergraduates 77.2 percent of the post-graduates) had essentially no exposure to heterodox ideas and arguments in their required or elective courses so as to even have the opportunity to decide whether they were reasonable or not; and research students (which is 67.2 percent of the total) had no option but to do dissertations on mainstream topics—see Table 9.7B.[22] This dominance of the mainstream extended beyond the realm of instruction

Table 9.7 Departments, heterodox economists, heterodox course aims, and student numbers for the period 2000–03

(A)

No. of Departments with Heterodox Aims (No. of Students)	No. of Heterodox Economists in the Departments			Total No. of Departments (Total No. of Students)
	None	1 to 3	4 or more	
No	29 (12346.1)	18 (7450.4)	7 (4196.0)	54 (23992.5)
Yes	5 (402.5)	6 (1469.6)	5 (1504.8)	16 (3376.9)
Total No. of Departments (Total No. of Students)	34 (12748.6)	24 (8920.0)	11 (5700.8)	70 (27369.4)

(B)

	No. of B.A. Students 2002–03	No. of Post-Graduate Students 2002–03	No. of Research Students 2002–03	No. of Departments
Departments with no Heterodox Course Aims and One or None Heterodox Economist*	12837.5 (60.1%)	3174.1 (77.2%)	1270.3 (67.2%)	43 (61.4%)
Departments with no Heterodox Course Aims and Two or More Heterodox Economists	5961.8 (27.9%)	734.1 (17.9%)	417.2 (22.1%)	16 (22.9%)
Departments with Heterodox Course Aims and One or More Heterodox Economists	2570.4 (12.0%)	202.0 (4.9%)	202.0 (10.7%)	11 (15.7%)
Total	21369.7	4110.2	1889.5	70

Source: Derived from Appendix A.20 and A.22.

Note:
* Includes the five departments with heterodox course aims and objectives but have no heterodox economists–see note 21. The subject report for Swansea is not available, but the 1994 questionnaire results suggest no heterodox course aims.

and supervising dissertations. As noted above, it permeated the hiring and promotion decisions of these departments and established what were acceptable attitudes and topics. If for any reason an individual deviated from the acceptable, social, and institutional corrective pressure (which in some cases amounts to bullying) was forthcoming (derived from the responses to the 1994 and 2003 Questionnaires—see Appendixes A.21 and A.23). Thus, students in these departments were drilled with a single, uncontested view of economics, had virtually no opportunity to learn alternative economic theories (and were considered deviants if they displayed a curiosity and interest in them), and were taught by intellectually undifferentiated economists whose attitudes and topics are restrictedly and comfortably embedded in mainstream theory.

The situation was somewhat different at the sixteen departments that had two or more heterodox economists but did not include heterodox economics in the aims and objectives for their courses. Given their presence and in some case significant presence of heterodox economists, students would be at least exposed to material outside the mainstream in elective courses and perhaps unofficially in the required courses, while research students could do heterodox dissertations. Thus, the dominance of mainstream economics was less extreme in these departments as a whole that have 27.9 percent 17.9 percent, and 22.1 percent of the undergraduate, post-graduate, and research students respectfully. However, in the ranked departments the attitudes towards heterodox economists and economics were decisively negative with more than a hint of bullying: such as discrediting heterodox courses and preventing heterodox courses from being taught, pressuring heterodox economists to quit economics, or belligerently telling heterodox economists that they were not economists and what they do was not economics and hence deny them promotion on these grounds (derived from the responses to the 2003 Questionnaire—see Appendix A.23). Finally, the third and smaller group consists of eleven universities which had one or more heterodox economists and included the presentation of heterodox economics in some degree among the aims and objectives of their undergraduate and post-graduate courses. In these departments, which had 12 percent, 4.9 percent and 10.7 percent of the undergraduate, post-graduate, and research students respectfully, all students were made aware of mainstream and heterodox economics in the required and elective courses and encouraged to explore the different theories that make up the contested discipline, while research students are positively encouraged to do heterodox dissertations. Moreover, the work environment for heterodox economists was supportive in terms of research and teaching interests (derived from the responses to the 2003 Questionnaire—see Appendix A.23) (Henkel 2000).

The state, intellectual uniformity, and British economics

The foregoing discussion clearly suggests that the conclusions reached in Chapter 8 continue to hold and the predictions made in 1998 have materialized by 2003. That is, Diamond List journals continued to be the dominant factor in the RAE ranking of economic departments and hence have become the dominant factor in hiring and promotion decisions. This recursive combination resulted in more and more departments becoming dominated by neoclassical economists (while excluding heterodox economists) and directing their publication efforts towards Diamond List journals. As a result, by 2003 over 60 percent of British economic departments and 68 percent of the ranked departments had none or only a token heterodox economist on staff; and in contrast, less than 16 percent of the departments and 12 percent of the ranked departments had a sustained presence of four or more heterodox economists on staff. The contribution of the QAA with its subject benchmarks and subject reviews to the emerging dominance of mainstream economics was not included in the previous research (see Chapter 8). However, when accounted for in combination with the above results, we find that over 77 percent of the departments and 88 percent of the ranked departments included only mainstream economics in their course aims and objectives and that 63 percent of economic students and 76 percent of students in ranked departments reside in departments with none or one heterodox economists and which included only mainstream economics in their course aims and objectives. Again in contrast, 5 percent of economic students and 3 percent of students in ranked departments resided in departments with four or more heterodox economists and which included both heterodox and mainstream economics in their aims and objectives. These starkly contrasting figures fully support the conclusions and predictions made in the previous chapter.[23]

As suggested above, the RAE and the QAA combined with the anti-heterodox proclivities of mainstream economists produced the dominance of mainstream economics in British universities that is so visible today. But there is more to this story. The RAE is essentially driven by the pro-market ideology adopted by the Thatcher, Major, and Blair administrations since 1980 that universities are or should be like business enterprises, wealth creators as well as supporters of enterprise culture, and responsive to the needs of industry. However, for universities to fulfill this role their research agenda had to be altered and the RAE was designed in part to produce this transformation. Thus, the RAE was imposed upon the universities. But the universities also took on board the RAE and used its ranking system to differentiate and invidiously compare themselves; and such invidious comparisons were championed by disciplines qua departments, including economics.[24] Mainstream economists also manipulated the RAE to achieve a quite unintended outcome but one compatible with the Government's pro-market ideological agenda—that of making economics a uncontroversial market-supporting discipline by promoting only a single paradigmatic view and eliminating dissenting voices. Without the state-backed RAE supplemented by the QAA and its benchmarks and subject reviews, the rapid paradigmatic homogenization of economics that took place in the decade since 1992 would not have been possible. Still, this outcome is widely hailed in terms of increasing the quality of economic research and the appropriate concentration of research funding in the quality departments (which are all located in the old universities) (Henkel 2000; Morgan 2004; Harley 2002; Curran 2000; Moore 2002).

Quality of research, especially in disciplines with contested knowledge, is difficult to establish. Peer review, the method used in the RAE, is a problematical method of evaluating research quality, especially in economics where the evaluators are not selected by their peers and have an inadequate grasp of and ideological bias against heterodox economics. Moreover, the use of a select group of journals, such as the Diamond List journals, as a quantitative measure of research quality is not independent of a pre-determined view of what research is quality and what individuals and departments produce research quality. That is, if top journals are identified then top departments are simultaneously identified; and if a different set of top journals are identified then a different body of quality research and top departments are identified. Thus, in disciplines with contested knowledge, the power to select the top journals is also the power to determine what is or is not quality research and which departments are top and which are not (Lee 2006). In the RAE and QAA, this state-based and state-legitimizing power is controlled by mainstream economists and they have used it to champion particular neoclassical research over heterodox research and promote narrow neoclassical departments over more pluralistic ones. This state legitimizing process has resulted, not in increasing quality research (for the quality of research is not determined by who has the power to identify "quality" research), but in producing a paradigmatic homogenized discipline where dissenting and blasphemous views are suppressed. Thus the near-complete dominance of mainstream economics in British universities has emerged not because it is "right" or provides a better understanding of the provisioning process in market economies, but because it has access to state (and organizational) power and legitimacy to suppress competing heterodox explanations and subject heterodox economists to professional excommunication and other penalties. In this light, it is plausible to conclude that mainstream economics in the U.K. takes on the vestiges of a state church (see Chapter 1) and heterodox economics truly becomes blasphemous economics.[25]

In the end, a paradigmatic homogenized discipline is a harrowing outcome of the RAE and QAA. Intellectual diversity, free inquiry, and the principle that there is no humanly accessible truth that is not in principle open to challenge are indispensable to the achievement of the central purposes of a university. Hence an intellectual faction that has a monopoly on truths and wisdom and utilizes state and/or organizational power (such as control over research and teaching funding or university budgets) to maintain and enhance this monopoly, that rejects the unsettled character of all human knowledge, and that reject a diversity of approaches to unsettled questions is not compatible with the idea and nature of a university.[26] In this light, the anti-diversity and "we have the monopoly on truth" propensity of mainstream economists combined with a significant degree of the "operational" control of the state-backed RAE and QAA subject benchmark and subject reviews have worked together to violated the central mission of a university by creating a near-intellectually homogeneous environment in economics in British universities. Thus economics as it is now practiced by mainstream economists has the appearance of being a state church that is no more than a hire-hand for the government's pro-market propaganda.

Yet there is more. The implication that can also be drawn from this study of economics is that state-supported institutional mechanisms, such as the RAE and QAA, which engage in the allocation of resources to higher-education institutions can be captured by special interest groups. And once captured, the peer-review process can be utilized to legitimize the skewed distribution of resources. Clearly the peer-review process plays an important role in promoting and maintaining research and publication quality. However, when it becomes involved in determining qua legitimizing resource allocation decisions, it has the tendency to become manipulated; and when this happens criticisms are misdirected at peer-review (thus weakening its effectiveness in promoting research quality) instead of at its inappropriate role in allocating resources (Bence and Oppenheim 2004). Consequently, as a state-based resource allocation mechanism, the RAE is inherently flawed in that it cannot ensure that quality research is funded, but rather funds research that interest groups say is quality which is a good example of rent-acquiring behavior of an interest group vis-à-vis government.

Part III

Heterodox economics at the beginning of the twenty-first century

10 The emergence of heterodox economics, 1990–2006

As noted in Chapter 1, heterodox economic theory consists of a theoretical critique of neoclassical economic theory as well as a theoretical alternative to it. Moreover, it was pointed out that the theory was composed of a concatenated array of arguments drawn from different heterodox approaches. For this outcome to occur, engagement between the different approaches had to take place. Hence a heterodox "social movement"—that is the bringing together of different heterodox economists to exchange ideas and work together—was needed to produce the community of heterodox economists that in turn is working on developing a heterodox economic theory. The history of the "movement" or more accurately the emergence of the heterodox economics community from 1990 to 2006, primarily in the United States and the United Kingdom, is the focus of this chapter. The first part of the story concerns the adoption of heterodox economics as the "identifier" or name of a group of heterodox theories. With the name in place, the second strand of the story deals with of the emergence of the community of heterodox economists by focusing on professional integration across heterodox associations and journals in the second section, and on theoretical integration across heterodox approaches in the following section. The chapter concludes with an overview of heterodox economics in 2006 and a brief discussion on the future of heterodox economics in a contested landscape.

Emergence of heterodox economics as the identifier of a group of heterodox theories

Heterodox as an identifier of an economic theory and/or economist that stood in some form of dissent relative to neoclassical economics was used within the Institutionalist literature in the 1930s and 1940s. In particular, Institutionalists used it to identify their own dissent from the orthodox mainstream, but left the "heterodox" ambiguous as to whether it meant dissent within the orthodox but contributing to the development of a better mainstream theory or dissent qua complete rejection of the orthodox and the development of an blasphemous alternative economic theory.[1] This situation remained the state-of-affairs to the late 1960s when Joseph Dorfman (1970) used the phrase "heterodox economic thinking" to characterize the contributions of economists such as John A. Hobson, Thorstein Veblen, John R. Commons, and others. In this case, heterodox thinking meant dissenting in some way from orthodox, neoclassical economic thinking, but not necessarily rejecting neoclassical theory.[2] Dorfman's position was very similar to Allan Gruchy (1969) characterizing the neo-Institutionalist contributions of Clarence Ayres, J. K. Galbraith, Gunnar Myrdal, and others as dissenting from neoclassical theory, but at the same time presenting a constructive challenge to the orthodoxy. Then in 1972 Gruchy went further and imprecisely used heterodox economics as identifying an economic theory, in this case neo-Institutional theory, that stood in blasphemous contrast to mainstream theory; and finally in 1987 he explicitly used heterodox to identify Institutional as well as Marxian and Post Keynesian theories in this way. However, Gruchy and the Institutionalists were mostly alone in this usage of heterodox economics for the period 1970 to 1990,[3] although Post Keynesians (including Sraffians and Kaleckians), Marxists and many radical economists, and social economists considered their theoretical approaches to be in blasphemous opposition to mainstream theory.

By the 1990s, it became obvious to many "heterodox" that there were a number of theoretical approaches that stood in some degree in opposition to neoclassical theory. The approaches identified included Austrian economics, feminist economics, Institutional-evolutionary economics, Marxian-radical economics, Post Keynesian and Sraffian economics, social economics, and ecological economics; however, it was not possible to use any of the names of the various heterodox approaches to represent them collectively. Thus, terms, such as non-traditional, non-neoclassical, non-mainstream, were used to collectively represent them, but they did not have the right intellectual feel or a positive ring. Moreover, some thought that political economy (or heterodox political economy) could be used as the collective term, but its history of being another name for Marxian-radical economics made this untenable (see Chapter 3).[4] Therefore, to capture the blasphemous commonality of the various theoretical approaches in a positive light without prejudicially favoring any one approach, a descriptive term that had a pluralist "big-tent feel" combined with being unattached to a particular approach was needed. Moreover, "heterodox" itself became increasingly used in contexts where it implicitly and/or explicitly referred to a collective of alternative theories vis-à-vis neoclassical theory and to the economists that engaged with those theories. So in spite of its Institutionalist connection, heterodox economics fitted the bill and hence increasingly became the term of choice among Post Keynesians, Institutionalists, and similarly inclined economists.[5]

For example, heterodox economics, heterodox economists, and even just heterodox were used in 1992 to cover the diversity of non-neoclassical thought that characterized the economics department at the University of Tennessee as well as in correspondence on AFEEMAIL (starting in March 1994), on PEN-L (starting in January 1994), and on PKT (starting in January

1999).[6] More significantly was Eric Nilsson's establishment in 1995 of the short-lived *Review of Heterodox Economics* for the purpose of increasing the interchange of ideas between economists working within different heterodox approaches to economics which he identified as radical, Marxist, feminist, Post Keynesian, Institutionalist, Sraffian (neo-Ricardian), and others. The intent of the *Review* was to publish abstracts of working papers and dissertation projects that sought to make a contribution to heterodox economics. However, because of the high cost of processing the abstracts, the first issue in Summer 1995 listed only twelve working papers but did contain the contents of thirty-eight journals of interest to heterodox economists; while the second and last issue appeared in Winter 1996 and contained Anne Mayhew's critique of the *American Economics Review, Journal of Economic Literature,* and *Journal of Economic Perspectives,* the list of contents of forty-two journals, and notices of five books of interest to heterodox economists.[7] In addition, heterodox economics and heterodox economists began appearing with increasing frequency in articles and in titles and/or forwards of books, such as Samuels (1992), Jennings (1994), Moseley (1995), Foldvary (1996), Pressman (1996) and Prychitko (1998), that dealt with various heterodox theories including those mentioned above as well as Austrian, Georgist, and social economics.[8] Finally, it started to appear as a descriptor of conference topics: "The *Review of Political Economy* will sponsor a conference in a broad range of topics in heterodox economics, in Trier, German, from 28 to 31 July 1997" (*Review of Political Economy* 9(1) 1997: 103) (Lee 2002; Harley and Lee 1997; Lee and Harley 1998; Albelda, Gunn, and Waller 1987; Whalen 1996; Ramstad 1995; Davis 1997; Dow 1990, 2000; Toruno 2006; Moseley 1995, 2006; AFEEMAIL Archives, January, July, August, and September 1995; Mitchell 1996; Prychitko 2006; Schaniel 1992; Ropke 2005; Knoedler 2006).

The final stage in the general acceptance of heterodox economics as the "official" collective term for the various oppositional theories began circa 1999. First there was the publication of Phillip O'Hara's magnificent and comprehensive *Encyclopedia of Political Economy* (1999a), which explicitly brought together the various heterodox approaches:

> ... recently there has been some degree of convergence among the schools. This current work seeks to flesh out these commonalities, and thereby contribute towards some degree of unification of the traditions. We seek to cross bridges, showing interconnections where possible.
>
> (O'Hara 1999a: xv)

While O'Hara preferred the term "political economy" to collectively represent the various heterodox approaches, various entries in the *Encyclopedia*— such as exchange rates, exploitation, interest-rate–profit-rate link, journals of political economy, monetary theory of production, money, credit and finance: major contemporary themes, political economy: school, profit in

Sraffian political economy, and supply and demand: aggregate—included the terms heterodox economics, heterodox analysis, heterodox approaches, heterodox political economists, heterodox economists, heterodox journals, and heterodoxy. At the same time, in October 1998 I "formed on paper" the Association for Heterodox Economics (AHE) for the purpose of putting on a one-day fringe conference at the Royal Economic Society annual conference at the University of Nottingham in 1999—see below. The conference was opened to all heterodox economists in the United Kingdom and Ireland.[9] As it was quite successful, the AHE put on a two-day conference in London the following year. At this point, heterodox economics was clearly defined as a collective term that included Post Keynesian, Marxian-radical, Institutionalist, Feminist, Evolutionary, and Social economics; and by 2003 it included Austrian economics as well.[10] To publicize the conference and other activities of the AHE as well as heterodox activities around the world, I also developed from 1999 to the present an informal "newsletter" that eventually became (in September 2004) the *Heterodox Economics Newsletter*, which is sent to over 3500 economists worldwide.[11] Thus the combination of the publication of O'Hara's *Encyclopedia*, the formation and activities of the AHE, and the *Newsletter*, heterodox economics along with heterodox economists and heterodox itself became by 2006 the preferred terminology among heterodox economists.[12]

Emergence of the community of heterodox economists: professional integration

For the community of heterodox economists to exist, it must be grounded in a social system of work that produces economic knowledge that contributes to a heterodox understanding of the economy and the social provisioning process. Since a social system of work implies that participants are dependent on each other for the production of scientific knowledge, how strong or weak the community is, in part, a function of how dependent heterodox economists are on each other's research and on the extent to which they work on common research goals, and, in part, is dependent on the degree of integration of their social activities. Therefore, while a heterodox economist may find one particular heterodox approach, such as Post Keynesian economics, to his/her liking, he/she is also professionally and theoretically engages with economists who are perhaps partial to other heterodox approaches. Professional engagement includes attendance at heterodox conferences, membership in multiple heterodox associations, subscribing to and/ or serving on boards of multiple heterodox journals, and participating in cross-approach collective efforts to support and promote heterodox economics. Theoretical engagement (which is dealt with in the following section) extends from at least reading and teaching alternative heterodox approaches, to partaking in multi-approach theoretical discussions, and to actively synthesizing different heterodox approaches especially in collaboration with heterodox economists associated with the different approaches.

Professional integration

While it is sometimes claimed that the various heterodox approaches practiced strict professional segregation in the 1970s and up to almost the present day, there is in fact little support for it. There are three kinds of professional segregation to examine: legal, informal, and voluntary. First, "legal" segregation occurs when an association accepts or rejects applicants solely on the basis on their theoretical views and expels members if their theoretical views become questionable. This form of segregation has not been instituted by any heterodox (or mainstream) economics association past or present.[13] Moreover, since 1988 a number of new heterodox associations have formed, such as the European Association for Evolutionary Economics (1988), International Association for Feminist Economics (1992), Progressive Economics Forum (1998), Association for Heterodox Economics (1999), and Society of Heterodox Economists (2002), and have adopted explicit non-segregationist approaches towards their name, membership, and conference participation. Second, "informal" segregation exists when members of an association define its agenda in a manner that creates significant pressure on members not in favor of it to leave the association and on potential new members who are not in favor of the agenda not to join. This has occurred in two heterodox associations, URPE and CSE, in the mid-1970s. In the case of URPE, the attempt at informal segregation quickly failed and by the latter 1970s it openly embraced heterodox pluralism again, but the impact was long lasting in that a number of heterodox economists (particularly Institutionalist economists) left URPE and never returned. As noted in Chapter 7, the push for informal segregation within the CSE circa 1975 lead to the exodus of constructive Sraffians and other heterodox economists and this had a lasting impact on the heterodox community in the United Kingdom until the 1990s. However, by the mid-1990s the impact of these two incidents had dissipated and hence informal segregation has not been a disruptive factor within the heterodox community in either country for the past decade.

Professional integration across heterodox associations and journals

A third kind of segregation takes the form of a voluntary lack of professional engagement across heterodox approaches and associations. However, as noted in Chapter 4, American graduate programs with heterodox components had faculty with different heterodox approaches and hence their students received a heady heterodox mixture of theory. As a result, their graduates published in different heterodox journals that represented different theoretical traditions—see Appendix A.11. Moreover, as argued in Chapter 5, URPE, AFEE, and ASE contributed to the growth of Post Keynesian economics; and in addition, Post Keynesians were members of those heterodox associations—see Appendix A.12. In short, from the beginning in the 1970s, AFEE, ASE, and URPE open their conferences to Institutionalist, social economics, radical-Marxian, and Post Keynesian papers and sessions; appointed and/or elected heterodox economists to the editorial boards of their journals and to their governing bodies who also were members of other heterodox associations or engaged with Post Keynesian economics; and had members who held memberships in other heterodox associations, engaged with Post Keynesian economics, and subscribed to more than one heterodox economics journal. Therefore it is not surprising to find evidence of American heterodox economists engaging in professional integration across heterodox associations and journals circa 1990. That is, for the period 1987–95, approximately 1538 heterodox economists in the United States belonged to AFEE, ASE, AFIT, URPE, and/or subscribed to the *Journal of Post Keynesian Economics*—see Table 10.1. Each heterodox association and journal had from 8 percent to 88 percent of its members and subscribers belonging to a least one other heterodox association or subscribed to the JPKE and from 2.7 percent to 33.9 percent belonging to three or more. Overall 11 percent of the 1538 heterodox economists belonged to two or more associations or subscribed to the JPKE while 2.3 percent belonged to three or more—see Table 10.1. Moreover, the thirty-five economists that belonged to three or more associations or subscribed to the JPKE included Marxists (Burkett, Sherman), Institutionalists (Dugger, Mayhew), social economists (Elliott, Ulmer), and Post Keynesians (Minsky, Niggle)—see Appendix A.24, Table 1.

From circa 1990 to circa 2000, in spite of an apparent 51 percent decline in American membership, these four associations and the JPKE experienced significant growth in professional engagement, with an overall 19 percent of their members belonging to two or more and 5.3 percent belonging to three or more associations or subscribing to the JPKE—see Table 10.1. The forty American heterodox economists that belonged to the latter included those that clearly have the reputations of engaging across heterodox associations and heterodox journals—see Appendix A.24, Table 2. So by 2000 a community of heterodox economists that were professionally engaged had clearly emerged in the United States in the sense that a significant minority, if not majority, of the members of each association and the JPKE were engaged with one other and more than 5 percent and up to 28 percent were engaged with two or more associations. And in 2006, the overall degree of professional engagement remained about the same, even though American membership in the associations and subscriptions to the JPKE declined by 6 percent. More significantly, the percentage of the professional engagement of the membership of AFEE, ASE, and URPE increased. Consequently, an important characteristic of these associations is that a significant minority of their members is professionally engaged and becoming increasingly more so—see Table 10.1.

The above indicates that, even though individual heterodox associations and the JPKE continue to exist, heterodox economists in the United States coalesce into a professional community by 2000 and remained so. If we go beyond AFEE, ASE, AFIT, URPE, and the JPKE to include the International

Table 10.1 American heterodox economists membership in AFEE, ASE, AFIT, URPE, and/or subscription to the JPKE, 1987–2006

Association/Journal	Total Membership			Membership in Two or More			Membership in Three or More		
	1987–95	2000–01	2006	1987–95 (%)	2000–01 (%)	2006 (%)	1987–95 (%)	2000–01 (%)	2006 (%)
AFEE	608	306	239	25	44	50	5.5	12.7	13.8
ASE	416	142	128	25	38	41	7.2	19.0	18.8
JPKE	79	103	90	24	28	22	12.7	16.5	15.6
AFIT	59	101	120	88	78	63	33.9	27.7	20.8
URPE	585	294	312	8	16	17	2.7	6.5	7.1
Overall*	1538	750	707	11	19	19	2.3	5.3	5.1

Source: Derived from Appendix A.24, Tables 1 – 3.

Notes:

* Excludes double counting.

AFEE = Association for Evolutionary Economics; ASE = Association for Social Economics; JPKE = Journal of Post Keynesian Economics;
AFIT = Association for Institutional Thought; URPE = Union for Radical Political Economics

Association for Feminist Economics (IAFFE), the total number of American heterodox economists for 2000–2001 and 2006 increases, although the overall percentage of membership in two or more and three or more associations and the JPKE does not. However, for individual associations and the JPKE the percentages do increase for 2000–2001 and 2006—see Table 10.2. Hence, the core of American heterodox economists that were professionally engaged

Table 10.2 American heterodox economists membership in AFEE, ASE, AFIT, URPE, IAFFE, and/or subscription to the JPKE, 2000–06

Association/ Journal	Total Membership		Membership in Two or More		Total Membership in Three or More	
	2000	*2006*	*2000–01 (%)*	*2006 (%)*	*2000–01 (%)*	*2006–01 (%)*
AFEE	306	239	46	50	15.7	18.4
ASE	142	128	42	43	22.5	22.7
JPKE	103	89	31	22	19.4	15.7
AFIT	101	120	80	64	30.7	23.3
URPE	294	312	26	26	8.5	8.7
IAFFE	294	288	23	18	6.8	4.9
Overall*	975	944	20	18	5.3	5.1

Source: Derived from Appendix A.24, Tables 4–5

Notes:
* Excludes double counting.
IAFFE = International Association for Feminist Economics

Table 10.3 American heterodox economists membership in AFEE, ASE, AFIT, URPE, IAFFE, AHE, PEF, and/or OPE, subscription to the JPKE, and/ or receive HEN 2006

Association/ Journal	Total Membership	Membership in Two or More (%)	Membership in Three or More (%)
AFEE	239	55.6	28.0
ASE	128	52.3	29.7
JPKE	90	34.8	18.9
AFIT	120	69.2	33.3
URPE	312	42.9	18.6
IAFFE	288	23.3	9.4
AHE	20	85.0	50.0
HEN	223	78.0	32.8
PEF	12	33.3	25.0
OPE	26	61.5	34.6
Overall*	1020	28.7	9.6

Source: Derived from Appendix A.24, Table 6.

Notes:
* Excludes double counting.
AHE = Association for Heterodox Economics; HEN = *Heterodox Economics Newsletter*; PEF = Progressive Economic Forum; OPE = Outline on Political Economy List

increased their professional engagement, that is, the network that emerged between the professionally engaged economists became denser. This fact becomes even clearer when the number of heterodox associations is increased to include the Association for Heterodox Economics (AHE), Progressive Economics Forum (PEF), Outline on Political Economy (OPE), and *Heterodox Economics Newsletter* (HEN). In this case, for 2006 the number of heterodox economists in the United States increases to 1020, with 28.7 percent having membership in two or more associations, JPKE, OPE, and HEN and 9.6 percent in three or more—see Table 10.3. The point is that, as measured, nearly 30 percent of heterodox economists in the United States and professionally engaged with nearly 10 percent being significantly engaged. And these 10 percent or 96 heterodox economists represent those who's publications, intellectual arguments, and conference engagement have created a heterodox economics community and given it its personality and persona—see Appendix A.24, Table 6.[14]

Professional integration through the formation of heterodox associations: a case study of the Association for Heterodox Economics based on participant-observation[15]

As noted in Chapter 7, in the mid-1990s, the CSE, PKSG, and the Great Malvern conference were quite active. However, by 1998 the CSE no longer had an annual conference, the Great Malvern conferences had ceased, and the PKSG activities and attendance at its seminars had decline. Moreover, the Royal Economics Society (RES) accepted very few heterodox papers for its annual conference and generally created an environment that made many heterodox economists feel less than welcome. Thus, there existed no venue in the UK where heterodox economists could come together in a welcoming environment to give papers, debate, and socialize. This state of affairs changed rather quickly. At the 1998 RES Conference, I overheard Paul Dunne mention something about a fringe conference on peace and the economics of arms reductions he would like to put on at the 1999 RES Conference that was to be held at Nottingham University.[16] This got me thinking about putting on a heterodox fringe conference. My purpose for the fringe conference was to bring together as many of the British heterodox economists as possible to hear papers that interested them and to socialize and network. So in October 1998 I contacted the Nottingham University Conference Centre about hiring a room for a day-conference during the period of the RES Conference. When asked who I was representing, I came up with the Association for Heterodox Economics. Once the room and date (March 30, 1999) were agreed upon, I polled a number of colleagues to see if they thought the conference was a good idea and would support it. The feedback was very positive; so I put together a flyer calling for papers and sent it out to virtually all the heterodox economists I knew of in the UK (and elsewhere as well). The response to the flyer was better than I expected, which meant that the conference expanded from one to two rooms. To cover the expenses, a conference fee of £5.00 was charged and I was able to solicit support and contributions from the Open University, CSE, and EAEPE.

The conference was a success. There were eight sessions in which eighteen papers were given on such heterodox topics as financial fragility, whither Post Keynesianism, critical realism and econometrics, the regulation school, dialectics and method, and the non-neutrality of money. There was also a plenary session on the future of heterodox economics with presentations by Chick, Alan Freeman, and Luigi Pasinetti. Forty-four economists attended and their affiliations spanned the UK heterodox communities. At the conclusion of the conference, all the participants said that they would like to have another fringe conference at the RES 2000 Conference at St Andrews University, either as part of or outside of it. However, the RES rejected my proposal that the fringe conference be part its annual conference; and St Andrews refused to provide any rooms for the conference. Refusing to admit defeat and supported by many to hold a second fringe conference, I looked for an alternative conference site. Andrew Trigg came to my rescue and offered the Open University Conference Centre in London as the site for the conference (Association for Heterodox Economics 1999, 2000; Lee 1999b; Dasgupta 1999).

Establishing the AHE: the 2000 and 2001 London conferences

With the site for the second annual AHE fringe conference secured, Freeman, Trigg, and I began to organize it. Freeman came up with the conference title of The Other Economics Conference 2000 to signify that there was more to economics than what was to be found at the RES 2000 Conference. Next, when putting together the call for papers, we felt that we needed to be more specific about what we included under heterodox economics. Drawing upon our collective perspectives, we came up with Post Keynesian economics, Marxian economics, labor process theory, Institutionalist economics, feminist economics, evolutionary economics, history of economic thought, business history, social economics, input–output analysis, economic policy, interdisciplinary economics, Sraffian economics, and economic philosophy.[17] Thus, a call for papers via e-mail and post was sent to individuals in the UK, Ireland, and overseas. The call for papers resulted in over eighty submissions, about half being international. When selecting papers and organizing them into sessions, there was an initial tendency of grouping papers together representing a specific theoretical perspective, that is, for example, all Post Keynesian papers were grouped together separate from Marxist papers. However, Freeman objected to this intellectual segregation, especially since the purpose of the AHE was to bring heterodox economists together, not to divide them and put them into separate sessions. Hence all the conference sessions were identified by themes, such as "heterodox political economy: public finance."[18]

The conference was organized into three parallel sessions over two days in order to accommodate the sixty-one papers being presented on the many different facets of heterodox economics. In addition, there were also two plenary sessions at the conference. At the first session, Paul Omerod gave a lecture on "The Death of Economics Revisited" and at the second Chick and John Grahl debated whether the UK should join the European single currency. Finally, there was a conference dinner at which Bernard Corry gave the after-dinner speech.[19] Ninety-three conference participants came from the UK, Ireland, Europe, North America, and the Pacific Rim. During the conference, a meeting was held to discuss the future of the AHE and it was decided to form an open coordinating committee with Trigg as the coordinator.[20] It was charged with the mandate to put on an annual AHE conference and to engage in any other activities that would promote heterodox economics in the UK and Ireland.[21] There was also an extensive discussion at the meeting on whether the AHE should continue to hold fringe conferences at the RES conferences. However, the majority felt that this was being too confrontational and hence it was agreed to hold the AHE conference at a different time and place from the RES annual conference.

The third AHE conference, which was also held in London at the Open University Conference Centre, was even more of a success than the previous year, with eight-four papers being presented and three plenary sessions. One plenary session dealt with the concerns of the French movement for Post-Autistic Economics and the Cambridge students' proposal on the opening up economics, while a second session was on the future of heterodox economics. At the third plenary, Bob Coats gave a lecture on the history of heterodox economics, pointing out that ideas quickly switch in status from orthodox to heterodox and *vice versa*. Finally, at the conference dinner, John King, the after-dinner speaker, delighted his audience with spicy anecdotes and derisive tales of journal editors from hell. The success of the conference meant that the AHE was now an established association with a good financial base and a growing body of activists and participants (Association for Heterodox Economics 2000, 2001, 2002; Lee 2000b; Trigg 2001).

Building a community of heterodox economists

The purpose of the AHE and its annual conference was and is to bring all heterodox economists in the UK and Ireland together to hear papers that interest them, to socialize and network, and to build a community where pluralism, not division, existed. The themes of the first conferences promoted community with pluralism and the participants included heterodox economists from the CSE, PKSG, EAEPE, and the Cambridge Realist Workshop; the subsequent conferences Dublin (2002), Nottingham (2003), Leeds (2004) and London (2005, 2006) continued in the same vain. In addition, recognizing that the future of heterodox economics depends critically on the next generation of economists that emerge from academia, Wendy Olsen and

Alfredo Saad Filho obtained funding from the ESRC to organize an AHE advanced training workshop in heterodox research methodologies. The first AHE methodology workshop took place in November 2001 and covered causal explanations, modeling, grounded theory, statistical analysis, and qualitative research. There were twenty-six Ph.D. students in attendance from the UK, Ireland, Germany, Canada, and the US, many of which continued to participate in the AHE annual conference. The three subsequent workshops repeated the successes of the first one and hence promoted further professional engagement among Britain's heterodox economists. Finally, the AHE promoted professional engagement by representing all UK heterodox economists before governmental agencies, such as the Quality Assessment Agency regarding the revision of the subject benchmark statement for economics. Thus the AHE and its professional-engaging activities made a significant contribution to the building of a community of heterodox economists in the UK.[22]

Emergence of the community of heterodox economists: theoretical integration

Theoretical segregation involves the isolation of a particular theoretical approach and its adherents from all other approaches and their adherents; that is to say, theoretical segregation occurs when there is no engagement across different theoretical approaches. Again a popular view to articulate which elicits voluminous e-mails attesting to it but providing no supporting evidence. However, as will be shown below, it does not exist within heterodox economics currently and nor has it existed in the past among the various heterodox approaches. That is, in the first half of the twentieth century the development of Institutional economics did not occur independently of engagement with Marxism and the economics of Keynes; and Marxists were not adverse to drawing on Thorstein Veblen and also engaging with Keynes. Moreover, Marxism, and particularly Paul Sweezy and the monopoly capital school, drew upon the work of Michael Kalecki and Josef Steindl, who also contributed to the development of Post Keynesian economics. Finally, the development of Post Keynesian economics from the 1930s onwards engaged with Institutionalism and Marxism directly or indirectly through Gardiner Means, Kalecki, Steindl, and Piero Sraffa. This had as an outcome an alteration of the heterodox approaches—that is to say the various heterodox approaches were somewhat altered so as to be less distinct from each other and to be more conducive for integration with each other (Gruchy 1947, 1948; King 2002; Lee 1998; O'Hara 2000; Rosenof 1997; Sweezy 1958).

This general proclivity for pluralistic theoretical engagement continued unabated from the 1960s through the 1980s with various endeavors by heterodox economists to engage, integrate or synthesis Institutional, Post Keynesian, and Marxist-radical approaches (Becker 1963; Ward 1977), Institutional and Post Keynesian approaches (Brazelton 1981a; Wilber and Jameson

1983), Post Keynesian and Marxian-radical approaches (Levine 1975; Jarsulic 1988), Post Keynesian and Austrian (O'Driscoll and Rizzo 1985; Bohm 1989), Austrian and Institutionalists (Boettke 1989), Feminist and Marxist-radical approaches (Hartmann 1979; Mutari 2001), Institutional and Marxist-Radical Approaches (Stanfield 1995; Dugger 1989), Institutional and Social Economics (Schweitzer 1969; Hill 1978), ecological and Marxian-radical approaches (Gowdy 1988), and social and Marxian economics (Hunt 1979). Thus by 1990 many heterodox economists could no longer see distinct theoretical boundaries between the various approaches, an outcome that mirrors the professional integration already taking place.

From 1990 to the present day, heterodox economists continued the past integration efforts of engaging across the various heterodox approaches—see Table 10.4.[23] The theoretical engagement between Post Keynesian, Institutional, social, Marxian/radical, and feminist economics is unsurprising since, as delineated in the previous section, many heterodox economists are members of more than one heterodox association. In addition, we find that there are engagements between ecological and Marxian, social, and Institutional economics as well as between Austrians and Marxian/radical, Post Keynesian, Institutional, and feminist economics. Moreover, there are creative

Table 10.4 Theoretical work that engaged two (or more) heterodox approaches (representative sample for the period 1990–2006)

Post Keynesian Institutionalism	*Post Keynesian Feminism*	*Post Keynesian Marxism/Radical*	*Post Keynesian Austrian*
Lavoie (1992)	Levin (1995)	Dutt (1990)	Runde (1993)
Jennings (1994)	Danby (2004)	Crotty (1993)	Prychitko (1993)
Arestis (1996)	van Staveren (2006)	Lavoie (2006)	Mongiovi (1994)
Institutionalism Feminism	*Institutionalism Marxism/Radical*	*Institutionalism Social Economics*	*Feminism Marxism/Radical*
Peterson & Brown (1994)	Garnett (1999)	Stanfield (1994)	Matthaei (1996)
Waller (2005)	Mouhammed (2000)	Merrett (1997)	Gibson-Graham (1996)
	Dugger & Sherman (2000)	Niggle (2003)	Barker & Feiner (2004)
Feminism Social Economics	*Social Economics Ecological*	*Austrian Institutionalism*	*Austrian Marxism/Radical*
Emami (1993)	Gowdy (1994)	Horwitz (1998)	Adaman & Devine (1996)
Nelson (1993)	Ropke (2005)		Burczak et al. (1998)
			Prychitko (2002)
Ecological Institutionalism	*Ecological Marxism/Radical*	*Austrian Feminism*	*Other*
Soderbaum (2000)	Martinez-Alier (2003)	Horwitz (1995)	Kotz et al. (1994)
Vatn (2005)	Burkett (2006)		Levy (2002)
			Smelser & Swedberg (2005)

mixtures of heterodox approaches that are best described by their own names, such as the social structures of accumulation school, the French conventions school, and economic sociology. Finally to reinforce the theoretical integration obvious in Table 10.4, the informal but de facto editorial policies adopted by their editors resulted in papers being accepted for publication that engaged with the full range of heterodox approaches. Consequently, from 1993 to 2003 and from 2001 to 2007 the nine principal English-language generalist heterodox journals[24] cited each other so extensively that no single journal or sub-set of journals is isolated—see Appendix A.27. Hence they form a completely interdependent whole where all heterodox approaches have direct and indirect connections with each other.

It is clear that the heterodox community is not segregated along theoretical lines, but rather there is cross-approach engagement to such an extent that the boundaries of the various approaches do not simply overlap; they are, in some cases, not there at all. The ensuing theoretical messiness of cross-approach engagement is evidence to detractors of the theoretical incoherence of heterodox economics whereas to supporters of progress towards a more theoretically coherent heterodox economics—a glass half-empty of coherence vs. a glass half-full of coherence[25] (Nielsen 2002; Wrenn 2004; Lee 1998; O'Hara 1999a, 2000, 2007a, 2007b; King, 2002; Palermo 2005; Ropke 2004, 2005; Albelda, Gunn, and Waller 1987).

Heterodox economics in 2006

The absence of professional and theoretical segregation means that the heterodox community is a pluralistic integrative whole. Some heterodox economists hold distinct theoretical views while maintaining a broad professional engagement, while others hold broad theoretical views but maintain a narrower professional engagement. In any case, all heterodox economists have much in common that is positive (as opposed to holding only a critique of mainstream economics in common), which means they are all capable of producing scientific knowledge about the economy and the social provisioning process that is of direct and/or indirect interest to each other. This combination of professional and theoretical engagement has two important implications for heterodox economics. The first is that the community is distinct from the community of mainstream economists; and the second is that it generates the central value that underpins the community of heterodox economists: that is the value of pluralism—the right of different theoretical approaches to exist without qualification—and its corollary that engagement with the different approaches is a positive social value.[26]

So what does the community of heterodox economists look like in terms of its members, associations, publication outlets, work sites, conferences, and communications? First of all it is both a national and world-wide community. That is, it consists of at least twenty-seven heterodox associations, some of which were formed over thirty years ago while others were formed in the

Table 10.5 Heterodox economics associations, 2006*

Name	Date Formed	Country or Region of Primary Activity	Membership 2006 (if known)
Association d'Economie Politique (AEP)	1980	Canada	250
Association for Economics and Social Analysis (AESA)	Late 1970s	United States	
Association for Evolutionary Economics (AFEE)	1965	United States	360
Association for Heterodox Economics (AHE)	1999	United Kingdom and Ireland	167
Association for Institutionalist Thought (AFIT)	1979	United States	128
Association for Social Economics (ASE)	1970	United States	181
Association pour le Developpement Des Estudes Keynesiennes (ADEK)	2000	France	54
Association Recherche et Regulation	1994	France	
Belgian-Dutch Association for Institutional and Political Economy	1980	The Netherlands and Belgium	
Conference of Socialist Economists (CSE)	1970	United Kingdom	
European Association for Evolutionary Political Economy (EAEPE)	1988	Europe	
German Association of Political Economy		Germany	
German Keynes Society		Germany	100
International Association for Feminist Economics (IAFFE)	1992	World	624
International Confederation of Associations For Pluralism in Economics (ICAPE)	1993	United States/ World	
Japan Association for Evolutionary Economics (JAFEE)	1996	Japan	
Japan Society of Political Economy (JSPE)	1959	Japan	
The Japanese Society for Post Keynesian Economics (JSPKE)	1980	Japan	
Korean Social and Economic Studies Association (KSESA)	1987	Korea	179
Latin American Society for Political Economy and Critical Thinking (SEPLA)	2005	Latin America	
Progressive Economics Forum (PEF)	1998	Canada	188

Table continued on next page.

Table 10.5 (continued)

Name	Date Formed	Country or Region of Primary Activity	Membership 2006 (if known)
Society for the Advancement of Behavioral Economics (SABE)	1982	United States	
Society for the Advancement of Socio-Economics (SASE)	1989	World	
Society for the Development of Austrian Economics (SDAE)	1996	United States	
Society of Heterodox Economists (SHE)	2002	Australia	86
Sociedade Brasileira de Economia Politica (SEP)	1996	Brazil	
Union for Radical Political Economics (URPE)	1968	United States	363
US Society for Ecological Economics (USSEE)	2000	United States	

Note:
* This list of heterodox associations is not exhaustive.

last decade; and those identified are located in the United States, United Kingdom/Ireland, Japan, Brazil, Europe and seven other countries around the world—see Table 10.5. In addition, there are many heterodox economists not members of these associations but simply subscribe to heterodox journals, such as the JPKE, subscribe to heterodox newsletters such as HEN, or are members of particular heterodox e-mail lists such as OPE or MEX-V. Consequently, heterodox economists are found around the world—see Table 10.6 and Appendix A.25. Some associations and e-mail lists are specific to particular countries because of language (ADEK, KSESA, MEX-V) or particular focus (PEF), which means that the number of their members that belong to other associations may be low. However, other associations are not so constrained and hence 28 percent to 68 percent of their membership belong to two or more other heterodox organizations and from 15 percent to 34 percent belong to three or more—see Appendix A.26. Furthermore every heterodox organization has at least a few members that belong to four or more such organizations; and these fifty-five heterodox economists are well known for their professional engagement and leadership, with forty located in the United States, four in the United Kingdom, two each in Canada and Australia, and seven scatted around the world—see Table 10.6 and Appendix A.26.

The community also includes some thirty generalist heterodox journals, seventeen specialist journals, twenty-six interdisciplinary journals, and a whole host of popular journals. Some of the journals are national in orientation while others are international, particularly the *Post-Autistic Economics*

Table 10.6 Heterodox economists by country, 2006

Country	Number of Heterodox Economists	Membership/Subscription in Four or More Heterodox Organizations
United States	1026	40
United Kingdom	233	4
Canada	231	2
Korea	187	1
Mexico	113	
Australia	105	2
France	77	
Japan	58	1
Italy	44	1
Germany	39	
Brazil	35	
India	33	
The Netherlands	32	1
Austria	30	1
Turkey	25	
New Zealand	24	1
Spain	23	
Greece	21	
Rest of Europe	117	
Rest of World	106	1
Total	2559	55

Source: Derived from Appendix A.25 and A.26.

Review with its 9,410 subscribers from over 150 countries. Moreover, there are approximately fourteen heterodox book series and at least eight international publishers, including Ashgate, Cambridge University Press, Edward Elgar, Michigan University Press, Pluto, Routledge, M. E. Sharpe, and Verso, and a large number of national publishers that have a specific interest in publishing heterodox economics books. In addition, there are a large number of work sites, that is, academic departments in many different countries, where the production and teaching of heterodox economics takes place without prejudice. The number of departments around the world that offer post-graduate qualifications, such as a M.A. or Ph.D., in which heterodox economics is an important component is more than thirty; and it is the graduates of these post-graduate programs that will determine the character and personality of the heterodox community over the next two decades.[27] Finally, as a rough estimate there are at least thirty-five heterodox conferences a year around the world, including the annual conferences of many of the above heterodox associations, supplemented by AESA's and ICAPE's triennial conferences. The significance of the many conferences is that they promote and maintain social relationships between heterodox economists and hence help glue the community together. And when not attending conferences, heterodox economists, especially those in relatively isolated situations, rely on association newsletters or more generally the HEN to remain part of the community (Lee, Cohn, Schneider, and Quick 2005).

The response of mainstream economists to individual heterodox economists in recent years has not changed from the responses in earlier times. Such responses, while painful to individuals and threatens their continual membership in the community, do not necessarily affect the structural and relational components that maintain the community of heterodox economists. However, as noted in Chapters 2, 8, and 9, in the past decade the mainstream has threaten the actual structures of the community by attacking, through assessment exercises, subject benchmarking statements, and ranking departments and journals, the work site and production of doctoral students. Repulsing the attack requires, in part, that heterodox economics be taught to more students, that more doctoral students be produced, and that heterodox economists become more professionally and theoretically engaged through joining multiple heterodox associations, subscribing to multiple heterodox journals, attending multiple heterodox conferences, and engaging in open pluralistic theoretical dialogue with other heterodox economists. But what is really necessary to do is for heterodox economists challenge the research-assessment exercises, subject benchmark statements, and the mainstream ranking of journals and departments through, perhaps, developing their own methods of research assessments and ranking of journals and departments. All this will take is the will to act and in 2006 there are many members in the community of heterodox economists who have such capabilities.

11 Ranking heterodox economic journals and departments
Suggested methodologies

As noted in Chapters 1, 2, 8, and 9, the rankings of journals and their use to rank departments is used, in many cases, to attack heterodox economists and heterodox departments. In particular, the journal-ranking studies favor mainstream economic journals, while journal-based department-ranking studies do not include, in any meaningful way, heterodox economic journals resulting in mainstream departments being ranked higher than heterodox departments. Given the detrimental impact that ranking of journals and departments has on heterodox economists and the existence and prosperity of heterodox-pluralist departments, it is surprising that, aside from Geoff Hodgson's (1993) initial exploration, there have been no attempts from a heterodox perspective to rank heterodox journals or departments. Yet it is also not surprising, since the invidious comparisons generated by such rankings and the discriminatory purpose to which they have been put argue strongly for not embarking on a similar exercise albeit from a heterodox slant. So is it possible to develop a ranking of heterodox journals and departments and not, at the same time, invite invidious comparisons and promote intellectual bigotry and discrimination among heterodox economists? With the survival of heterodox economics at stake, an exploratory attempt is perhaps worthwhile. The purpose of this chapter is not actually to produce rankings, but explore whether it is possible to produce such rankings without the negative side effects. That is, the chapter is an exploration into the methodology of heterodox rankings rather than the construction of the rankings themselves.

The starting point of the exploration is asking the question "what should the rankings reveal in terms of the intellectual and social organization of heterodox economics?" To answer it necessitates a brief digression on the intellectual and social organization of heterodox economics as a social system of scientific activity which will then be employed to argue for a set of methodologies to be used to rank heterodox journals and departments. The second and third sections are devoted to experimenting with the methodologies on the ranking of heterodox journals and departments. In the case of heterodox journals, twenty have been selected as test subjects; and for departments, seventeen economics departments in the United Kingdom have been chosen for examination. The final section of the paper will evaluate the outcomes of the previous two sections and conclude that the suggested scoring-ranking methodologies for heterodox journals and departments would lead to a positive development of heterodox economics.

Organization of heterodox economics and the ranking of journals and departments

As argued in Chapter 1, for a community of heterodox economists to exist, it must be grounded in a social system of work that produces scientific or economic knowledge that contributes to the understanding of the economy and the social provisioning process. Moreover, its system of work is largely embedded in educational systems and their employment markets. A social system of work also implies that the participants are dependent on each other for the production of scientific knowledge. Thus, the criteria for a community of heterodox economists to exist is that individual heterodox economists must see themselves as supporting a differentiated body of theory that is an alternative to neoclassical economic theory and partake in social networks and institutions that are outside those which make up the community of neoclassical economists. How strong or weak the community is, in part, a function of how dependent heterodox economists are on each other's research and on the extent to which they work on common research goals. It is also a function of the department environment since that is the organizational locale for teaching students economics and training future heterodox economists and the site for the production of scientific knowledge that must be publishable in referred journals, books, and other reputable outlets.

Since the social system of work is the heart of the community of heterodox economists, it is essential that it enhance research dependency among heterodox economists and improve the department environment. This is partially achieved since heterodox economic theory is not hierarchically organized and hence not hierarchically valued. Thus any contribution to the development of theory, any exposition of the theory that assists students and the public to better understand the social provisioning process, and any utilization of the theory to improve the social provisioning process for society are equally valued. However, there is still the necessity of improving research dependency and departments and therefore a need to evaluate this progress. One way of improving the former is through the medium of peer-review publications, specifically peer-reviewed journals.[1] With non-hierarchical theory, equal-but-different value theory contributions, it is not possible to hierarchically rank heterodox journals according to their content (and therefore rank heterodox economic departments according to their journal publications).[2] But it is possible to evaluate and rank heterodox journals according to their promotion of research dependency. To improve departments, it is necessary to evaluate and rank them on multiple criteria: not just in terms of publications but also in terms of their contributions to promoting heterodox economics through providing a pluralistic undergraduate curriculum where students are invited to engage with heterodox as well as neoclassical economics, promoting graduate programs whose cores are heterodox economics, and encouraging the teaching staff to produce heterodox scientific knowledge and publish in heterodox economic journals and other publishing outlets.

Basis for evaluating and ranking heterodox economic journals

One purpose of heterodox economic journals is to publish peer-reviewed scientific knowledge, since it is through peer-reviewed and subsequent discussion by the heterodox community that scholarly quality of journal publications is maintained. Because peer-review is followed, it is assumed that articles published in heterodox journals are similar in overall scholarly quality in terms of being adequately researched and written, competent utilization of research methodologies and techniques, and addresses a topic of relevance at least to some heterodox economists. A second purpose is to build up the body of heterodox scientific knowledge. This is achieved in two ways, the first being to build up a body of specific knowledge associated with a particular heterodox approach, such as Institutionalism and the *Journal of Economic Issues*, a specific area or topic of research such as race and *Review of Black Political Economy*, or a general body of knowledge that is important to all heterodox economists, such as found in *Review of Political Economy*. Although they have the common goal of explaining the social provisioning process in its many aspects, heterodox economists have only gone part of the way of melding and synthesizing their different theoretical approaches and arguments. Hence not all heterodox scientific knowledge can be drawn upon by all heterodox economists. This makes for research and teaching uncertainty as well as hindering the overall development of heterodox economics. Therefore, the second way to build heterodox knowledge is to promote the development of an integrated heterodox economic theory through increasing the research dependency among heterodox economists. *It is the second purpose—building specific economic knowledge and integrated heterodox theory through research dependency—that is the basis for evaluating and ranking heterodox economic journals.*

The way to build a journal-specific body of scientific knowledge is for a journal to publish articles that draw upon scientific knowledge previously published in the journal. This *domestic production* of scientific knowledge is manifested in terms of journal *self-citations*. In the ranking literature, journal self-citations are often dismissed because they have little impact on the economics profession at large. This view, which is rejected here, is predicated on the assumption that the journal is not a location of a body of specialized knowledge. In particular, journals in specific research areas and journals associated with specific theoretical approaches and interests build an integrative body of knowledge that is represented in terms of self-citations. This is what makes the journal interesting and relevant to the authors and readers in the first place. Journals that do not build an identifiable body of knowledge become marginal to all researchers since there would not be any reason to take the time to examine its content.[3]

To promote the development of integrative theory through enhancing *research dependency* among heterodox economists, it is necessary to have them engage in their research with different heterodox approaches and draw upon different areas of research. This engagement is concretely manifested in terms of citations. Thus, a heterodox economist is building research dependency, hence integrative knowledge, when he/she cites articles from many different heterodox journals associated with different heterodox approaches and research areas. For a heterodox economist's research to contribute to research dependency it must also be utilized hence cited by other heterodox economists in their journal publications. Therefore the significance of an article for developing heterodox theory is the degree to which it contributes to research dependency through its drawing upon and utilizing in a wide range of heterodox research. Similarly, a journal is promoting research dependency when it publishes articles that cite journals associated with different heterodox approaches and research areas. In this case, the cited journals can be viewed as *imports* and increasing imports is a way to increase research dependency. Moreover, imported citations also represent *exported* citations from other heterodox journals; thus a journal's exported citations also contribute to research dependency. In short, the extent to which a heterodox journal import and export citations indicates the degree to which it promotes the development of heterodox economic theory through research dependency.[4]

A journal that is a significant builder of scientific knowledge through research dependency imports citations from and exports citations to most heterodox journals, has an overall balance of trade, and generates domestic production of citations equal to its imports equal exports. In contrast, a surplus trade balance indicates that a journal is not, relatively speaking, promoting research dependency because it is not drawing upon and engaging with other heterodox journals; a deficit trade balance implies that the journal's production of scientific knowledge is not readily useable by other journals and hence indicates a lack of contribution to research dependency; and a journal with significant domestic production relative to imports and exports is engaging in an inward production of scientific knowledge and not engaging in promoting the development of an integrative heterodox theory through research dependency and hence building a community of heterodox economists. *Therefore a journal's "score" and hence ranking is a summary evaluation of its contribution to building both specialized and integrative scientific knowledge.* The score or ranking itself depends on journal's domestic production of citations, the ratio of its imports and exports to its domestic production, its balance of trade, and the extent of its imports and exports. The overall intent of rankings qua evaluation is to indicate the extent that a journal needs to improve its building of specialized and/or integrative heterodox knowledge so that ultimately all heterodox journals can achieve the same highest score or ranking. So unlike any other ranking method, this novel and unique approach does not single out "core" journals that are more important than non-core journals; and does it not bias the rankings towards heterodox generalist journals and away from heterodox specialist and inter-disciplinary journals[5] (Eagly 1975; Stigler 1994; Stigler, Stigler, and Friedland 1995; Liner and Amin 2004).

Basis for evaluating and ranking heterodox economic departments

The basis for evaluating a heterodox economics department is its contribution to developing heterodox economic theory and policy, to training future heterodox researchers, and to enhancing the vitality of heterodox economics. One component of the contribution is the production, dissemination, and application of heterodox scientific knowledge by the teaching and research staff. In particular, the produced knowledge should be published in peer-reviewed heterodox journals and book series, in academic and commercial presses, in working papers, research reports, and policy evaluations, and in popular and other outlets; while its application involves promoting hetero-dox economic policies through publication in academic and popular presses and engagement with the public through various media outlets, government hearings, and other community engagements. A second component is the provision of an educational environment in which students can study the many varieties of heterodox economics in a non-threatening environment; for it is here that the direct dissemination of heterodox economic ideas, the training for future heterodox researchers, and the development of the infrastructure and academic/intellectual vitality of heterodox economics takes place. This involves providing a clearly delineated pluralistic undergraduate program where students are critically introduced to both heterodox and neoclassical economics; promoting M.A., M.Sc., or M.Phil. and Ph.D. programs that have clearly defined aims and objectives in which heterodox economics constitutes at least a portion, if not more, of the core instruction, that students are encouraged to pursue research and dissertation topics in all approaches in heterodox economics, and that have financial aid and scholarships available for students pursuing heterodox projects; and establishing and putting on seminars, conferences, research institutes, and other activities that engage with a variety of approaches in heterodox economics. The final component is the promotion of an active work and research culture that is cooperative and non-threatening to heterodox economists. This includes appointment, tenure, promotion, and research policies that are non-discriminatory towards and encourages heterodox research, publication, and teaching (RAE 2006).[6]

The three distinct components a heterodox economics department can be evaluated in terms of promoting heterodox economics are all important, since the existence of any one is dependent on the existence of the other two components and all three have to exist for there to be a heterodox department.

Therefore the method of ranking departments involves two steps. The first is to establish department sub-rankings of the three components and second to aggregate those scores to generate an overall department score hence ranking that is a *summary evaluation of its contribution to the building of heterodox knowledge, promoting the training of future heterodox researchers, and enhancing the vitality of heterodox economics.*[7] To ensure that the department rankings are used in a positive and constructive manner, a benchmark score for each component and overall is constructed so the components and overall rankings qua evaluation will indicate the extent that a department needs to improve its contribution to the development of heterodox economics and of the heterodox economics community as a whole.

Experiment in ranking heterodox economic journals

For the purpose here, a heterodox economic journal is defined as one in which more than 50 percent of the articles are heterodox in theory, discourse, and subject matter and/or contribute to the positive development of heterodox theory and discourse.[8] Given the definition, it is possible to identify eighty-eight heterodox journals, of which 31 are generalist, 17 are specialist, 26 are interdisciplinary, 14 are popular or not else classified—see Lee et al. (2005).[9] To explore the ranking of heterodox journals, twenty were selected from the list—thirteen generalist, two specialist, and five interdisciplinary—based entirely on journal accessibility—see Table 11.1. With the journals identified, a citation count was undertaken for the period 1993 through 2003 and is summarized in Appendix A.27. Using the evaluation categories—the total domestic production of citations, ratio of imports to domestic production, ratio of exports to domestic production, the balance of trade, and the extent of its imports and exports—the data for evaluation and ranking is derived and given in columns (2)—(7) in Table 11.1.[10]

To evaluate and rank heterodox journals in a way that does not lead to or promote invidious distinctions, the highest score hence ranking must be open to all journals simultaneously. This is possible when the evaluation qua ranking is relative to an independent goal and achievement of that goal does not necessitate a decline in ranking of a "competitor" and, moreover, is easier to obtain if all participants cooperate and work together. In terms of ranking heterodox economic journals, the goal is the *production of specialized and integrative scientific knowledge.* Hence the ranking methodology argued for here is specific to that goal. The benchmark to evaluate journals consists of the six citation categories given in Table 11.2 each of which has a minimum score of zero and a maximum score of one; and together they produce a maximum score of six which means that the journal is completely meeting the goal set for heterodox journals. A score of less than six indicates that the journal is not completely meeting the goal so there is room for improvement. The first category in Table 11.2 (column 2) is domestic production for which all journals score one except *Contributions to Political Economy,*

Table 11.1 Citations of twenty heterodox economic journals, 1993–2003

(1) Journal (Type of Journal)	(2) Domestic Production of Citations (DP)	(3) Ratio of Imports (I) to Domestic Production (I/DP)	(4) Ratio of Exports (E) to Domestic Production (E/DP)	(5) Balance of Citation Trade: Surplus, Deficit, Balance (amount), and Ratio of Exports to Imports (E/I)	(6) Extent of Imports (Ratio of the number of journals with 2 or more citations out of 19)	(7) Extent of Exports (Ratio of the number of journals with 2 or more citations out of 19)
Cambridge Journal of Economics (General)	551	1.27	1.74	S (256) 1.36	0.84	0.95
Capital and Class (General)	220	1.21	1.06	D (−34) 0.87	0.53	0.84
Capitalism, Nature, Socialism (Interdisciplinary)	204	0.41	0.27	D (−26) 0.97	0.37	0.32
Contributions to Political Economy (General)	30	2.37	2.30	D (−2) 0.97	0.37	0.37
Economy and Society (Interdisciplinary)	293	0.43	0.56	S (39) 1.31	0.42	0.78
Feminist Economics (General)	234	0.62	0.31	D (−72) 0.50	0.58	0.42
International Papers in Political Economy (General)	8	16.00	4.63	D (−91) 0.29	0.53	0.37
International Review of Applied Economics (General)	52	4.94	1.27	D (−191) 0.26	0.63	0.37
Journal of Economic Issues (General)	1631	0.32	0.38	S (97) 1.19	0.95	0.74
Journal of Post Keynesian Economics (General)	826	0.56	0.93	S (302) 1.64	0.53	0.79
Metroeconomica (General)	72	3.15	1.69	D (−105) 0.54	0.37	0.53

Table continued on next page.

Table 11.1 (continued)

(1) Journal (Type of Journal)	(2) Domestic Production of Citations (DP)	(3) Ratio of Imports (I) to Domestic Production (I/DP)	(4) Ratio of Exports (E) to Domestic Production (E/DP)	(5) Balance of Citation Trade: Surplus, Deficit, Balance (amount), and Ratio of Exports to Imports (E/I)	(6) Extent of Imports (Ratio of the number of journals with 2 or more citations out of 19)	(7) Extent of Exports (Ratio of the number of journals with 2 or more citations out of 19)
New Left Review (Interdisciplinary)	338	0.11	1.93	S (616) 17.21	0.37	0.79
Research in Political Economy (General)	35	7.20	1.71	D (–192) 0.24	0.68	0.32
Rethinking Marxism (Interdisciplinary)	248	1.19	0.29	D (–224) 0.25	0.74	0.47
Review of African Political Economy (Specialist)	262	0.21	0.08	D (–36) 0.36	0.21	0.26
Review of Black Political Economy (Specialist)	126	0.22	0.29	S (8) 1.29	0.21	0.26
Review of Political Economy (General)	146	3.73	2.09	D (–240) 0.56	0.84	0.74
Review of Radical Political Economics (General)	383	1.15	1.61	S (174) 1.39	0.95	0.95
Review of Social Economy (General)	204	1.91	0.71	D (–245) 0.37	0.74	0.47
Science and Society (Interdisciplinary)	247	1.11	0.60	D (–126) 0.54	0.53	0.58
Total	6087	0.86	0.86	B (0) 1.00	1.00	1.00

Source: Derived from Appendix A.27; and Lee, Cohn, Schneider, and Quick 2005]

Table 11.2 Ranking heterodox economic journals

(1) Journal/Building (Type of Journal)	(2) DP Score	(3) I/DP Score	(4) E/DP Score	(5) E/I Score	(6) Extent of Imports Score	(7) Extent of Exports Score	(8) Overall Score for Specialized and Integrative Heterodox Knowledge
Capital and Class (General)	1.00	0.79	0.94	0.87	0.53	0.84	4.97
Review of Radical Political Economics (General)	1.00	0.85	0.39	0.61	0.95	0.95	4.75
Cambridge Journal of Economics (General)	1.00	0.73	0.26	0.64	0.84	0.95	4.42
Journal of Economic Issues (General)	1.00	0.32	0.38	0.81	0.95	0.74	4.20
Journal of Post Keynesian Economics (General)	1.00	0.56	0.93	0.35	0.53	0.79	4.16
Science and Society (Interdisciplinary)	1.00	0.89	0.60	0.54	0.53	0.58	4.14
Economy and Society (Interdisciplinary)	1.00	0.43	0.56	0.69	0.42	0.79	3.89
Rethinking Marxism (Interdisciplinary)	1.00	0.81	0.29	0.24	0.74	0.47	3.63
Feminist Economics (General)	1.00	0.62	0.31	0.50	0.58	0.42	3.43
Review of Social Economy (General)	1.00	0.09	0.71	0.37	0.74	0.47	3.38

Table continued on next page.

Table 11.2 (continued)

(1) Journal/Building (Type of Journal)	(2) DP Score	(3) I/DP Score	(4) E/DP Score	(5) E/I Score	(6) Extent of Imports Score	(7) Extent of Exports Score	(8) Overall Score for Specialized and Integrative Heterodox Knowledge
Review of Political Economy (General)	1.00	0.00	0.00	0.56	0.84	0.74	3.14
Capitalism, Nature, Socialism (Interdisciplinary)	1.00	0.40	0.27	0.68	0.37	0.32	3.04
Review of Black Political Economy (Specialist)	1.00	0.22	0.29	0.71	0.21	0.26	2.69
New Left Review (Interdisciplinary)	1.00	0.11	0.007	0.00	0.37	0.79	2.34
Metroeconomica (General)	0.50	0.00	0.31	0.54	0.37	0.53	2.25
Contributions to Political Economy (General)	0.50	0.00	0.00	0.97	0.37	0.37	2.21
Review of African Political Economy (Specialist)	1.00	0.21	0.08	0.36	0.21	0.26	2.12
International Review of Applied Economics (General)	0.00	0.00	0.73	0.26	0.63	0.37	1.99
Research in Political Economy (General)	0.00	0.00	0.29	0.24	0.68	0.32	1.53
International Papers in Political Economy (General)	0.00	0.00	0.00	0.29	0.53	0.37	1.19

Metroeconomica, International Papers in Political Economy, International Review of Applied Economics, and *Research in Political Economy* which score 0.5, 0.5, 0.0, 0.0, and 0.0 respectively.[11] The other five categories consist (columns 3–7) of the five ratios. The scores for columns (3), (4), and (5) are derived from columns (2), (3), and (4) in Table 11.1 and are based on minimizing their distance from one, where one represents "balance," except for those ratios whose distance from one are greater than one so their score is zero. The scores for columns (6) and (7) in Table 11.2 are taken from columns (6) and (7) in Table 11.1 and are a ratio that varies between zero and one where approaching one means that the journal is increasingly "engaged" with more and more other heterodox journals. Thus the closer the scores are to one the more effective the journal is in promoting the development of an integrative heterodox theory through research dependency. The scores and rankings of the journals are given in Table 11.2.

What is evident from the scores is that most journals are building specific scientific knowledge, but there is a shortfall in developing an integrative theory among all the journals. The lower the overall score of the journal, the lower the number of journals it cites as imports and the number of journals that cite it as an export, more out of balance the balance of trade citations are, and the lower of the ratio of imports to domestic production of citations is. More specifically, a score of five indicates that the journal contributes to the building of specific and integrative heterodox scientific knowledge that is spread across virtually all of heterodox economics. A lower score, such as four, three, or two indicates a declining contribution to developing an integrative heterodox economic theory, while a score approaching one indicates that the journal contributes very little to the building of heterodox knowledge at all.

In some cases, journals can improve their scores through generating more domestic production of citations relative to their import citations, while others can improve their score by increasing import citations and from a broader number of journals.[12] More generally, both integrative and specialized knowledge production, hence scores, can be significantly improved for all journals if the surplus journals would increase their import citations and the number of journals from which they import the citations; and if many of the deficit journals—such as the *Review of Social Economy, Review of Political Economy, Metroeconomica, Rethinking Marxism,* and *International Review of Applied Economics*—made some effort to engage in import-substitution through promoting domestic production.[13] As for the rankings themselves, the top five heterodox journals include most but not all of the approaches in heterodox economics; radical and Marxian journals are the closest to making an outstanding contribution to the building of heterodox economic knowledge than generally thought (comprising five of the top ten journals), while the three interdisciplinary journals make a significant contribution to building of heterodox knowledge (ranking sixth, seventh, and eighth).[14]

Experiment in ranking heterodox economic departments

To illustrate the methodology of ranking heterodox economic departments, seventeen British economic departments are selected because of the availability of the necessary information to carry out the experiment. Each of the departments had for the period 1996 to 2000, two to fifteen heterodox economists and had B.A. programs in economics—see Appendix A.22. In addition, in the period 2002–3, eleven had taught post-graduate (M.A., M.Sc., or M.Phil.) programs in economics and thirteen had doctoral students—see Appendix A.27. Finally, the 2001 RAE provides information on publications, the Quality Assurance Agency and the Higher Education Statistics Agency provides information on undergraduate and graduate programs for the period 2000–2003, and a 2003–4 questionnaire completed by British heterodox economists provides information on the teaching and work environment for each department.[15]

Publications

The first of the three components that generate the rankings of heterodox economic departments is the production of heterodox scientific knowledge, as represented by the publications of their heterodox economists, which contribute to the understanding of the economy and the social provisioning process. Utilizing the submissions to the 2001 RAE and since the 2001 RAE allowed the submission of only four publications per economist drawn from the period 1997 to 2000, the maximum number of publications for a heterodox economist is expected to be four. Thus, the maximum total publication score for a department is the number of heterodox economists times four. Since this measure is dominated by the number of heterodox economists in the department, a relatively larger department may produce more scientific knowledge in an "absolute sense" than a smaller department while the productivity of the heterodox economists in the smaller department may be greater. To account for this, a productivity measure is introduced; thus the productivity of a department is measured by the number of publications per heterodox economist and the score can range from a maximum of four down to less than one. Finally, a measure is needed to capture the extent that a department's publications promote the building of specialized and integrative heterodox knowledge. The proxy for this measure is the summation of the overall journal scores in Table 11.2 for each journal publication divided by the number of journal publications in which the department published, with the range of possible scores being zero to 4.97; and given its importance, it is weighed three times more than the other measures.[16] The results of the sub-categories and the overall score for publications are given in Table 11.3.

As expected, the larger the department in terms of the number of heterodox economists, generally the greater the number of total publications and the higher the ranking—size does matter. However, the productivity of departments

Table 11.3 Heterodox departments ranked according to their publications

Department	Number of Heterodox Economists	Total Publications	Publications per Heterodox Economist	Building Heterodox Knowledge	Overall Score for Publications
SOAS	10	35.0	3.50	9.99	48.49
Cambridge	15	28.0	1.87	12.78	42.65
Staffordshire	5	20.0	4.00	11.31	35.31
East London	8	22.0	2.75	10.20	34.95
Manchester Met.	8	22.0	2.75	9.84	34.59
Open	6	18.0	3.00	11.97	32.97
Manchester	4	16.0	4.00	11.10	31.10
Leeds	4	15.0	3.75	11.82	30.57
Bath	3	12.0	4.00	12.60	28.60
Aberdeen	3	12.0	4.00	10.14	26.14
Stirling	2	8.0	4.00	12.99	24.99
Nottingham Trent	2	5.0	2.50	10.89	18.39
Sheffield	2	8.0	4.00	5.97	17.97
Strathclyde	2	7.0	3.50	6.63	17.13
Leeds Metropolitan	2	1.0	0.50	15.75	14.25
East Anglia	4	6.0	1.50	0.00	7.50
Middlesex	5	4.0	0.80	0.00	4.80

Source: Higher Education and Research Opportunities in the United Kingdom, RAE 2001, http://www.hero.ac.uk/rae/

varies significantly with eleven departments falling short of the expected four publications per heterodox economist. Finally, the building heterodox knowledge score varies among the departments. The overall publication score represents a department's capabilities of contributing to the production of heterodox knowledge and the positive development of heterodox theory and discourse, with SOAS, Cambridge, Staffordshire, East London, and Manchester Metropolitan being the five departments with the best capabilities to contribute. But are their capabilities significant? For a department to have the capabilities of making a publication contribution to heterodox economics, a minimum overall score of 34 or better is required—which would be a department of five heterodox economists each with four publications that mostly appeared in heterodox journals with scores of three or better. For a department to have the capabilities to make substantive publication contribution to heterodox economics, a minimum overall score of 53 or better is required—which would be a department of nine economists each with four publications that mostly appeared in heterodox journals with scores of four or better.[17] With such benchmarks, it is clear that in this "experiment" the top five departments in Table 11.3 have the capabilities to make a contribution to heterodox economics. However, it is possible for all departments to improve their contribution capabilities by adopting strategies of hiring more heterodox economists, of improving department productivity, and/or of targeting particular heterodox journals. Thus, there is nothing in the ranking process that prevents a department from achieving the capabilities of making a contribution or even a substantial contribution; and it is the improving of these department capabilities in the production of scientific knowledge that helps contributes to the development of heterodox economics and the community of heterodox economists.

Teaching

A second component in the ranking of a heterodox department is the teaching of heterodox economics since this is the basis for the training of future heterodox researchers (RAE 2006). All undergraduate programs should ensure that students are critically introduced to neoclassical economics. The seventeen departments in Table 11.3 do meet this criterion, but to what extent do they ensure that their undergraduates are equally well exposed to heterodox economics? This can be evaluated in terms of whether the aims and objectives of department's B.A. economics program mentions heterodox economics (three points if they do and zero points if they do not); whether the B.A. program has required courses that include the teaching of heterodox economics (two points if they do and zero points if not); and whether it has optional courses with heterodox content (one point if they do and zero points if not).[18] In addition to teaching undergraduates, the development of heterodox economics and the community of heterodox economists require advanced training of economists in heterodox economics. Thus, the seventeen departments can also be evaluated in terms of their promotion of heterodox economics in their taught post-graduate economic programs relative to aims and objectives (3,0), required courses (2,0), and optional courses (1,0); and in their support of doctoral students doing dissertations with heterodox content (two points if there is support and zero points if not). The impact a department's teaching has on the promotion and development of heterodox economics is dependent on student numbers. Hence, the teaching scores are weighted by program size so that the significance of teaching is increased through the number of students being taught and supervised. The points for size are shown in Table 11.4

Therefore the overall score on teaching is derived by the following algorithm: $size_u \times [aims + required + optional]_u + size_{p-g} \times [aims + required + optional]_{p-g} + size_d \times support_d$, with the maximum score being fifty-six and the minimum being zero. The detailed results are given in Appendix A.27 and the summary results in Table 11.5 below.

The overall score represents the department's teaching commitment to heterodox economics with SOAS, Manchester Metropolitan, Manchester, and Leeds being the departments with the greatest overall commitment. Yet, by any account the majority of overall scores are low, and this is due to some

Table 11.4 Program-size weights

Undergraduates		Post-Graduates		Doctoral	
No. of Students	Points	No. of Students	Points	No. of Students	Points
1–150	1	1–25	1	1–25	1
151–300	2	26–50	2	26–50	2
301–450	3	51–75	3	51–75	3
451–	4	76–	4	76–	4

Table 11.5 Teaching commitment to heterodox economics

Department	BA Score	Post-Graduate Score	Doctoral Score	Overall Score for Teaching
SOAS	12	18	6	36
Manchester Met.	24	0	2	26
Manchester	4	12	4	20
Leeds	9	6	4	19
Aberdeen	12	0	2	14
East London	12	0	2	14
Open	12	0	2	14
Bath	12	0	0	12
Leeds Metropolitan	12	0	0	12
Nottingham Trent	9	0	2	11
Cambridge	0	2	8	10
Staffordshire	1	6	2	9
Middlesex	6	1	0	7
Sheffield	3	0	2	5
Strathclyde	1	0	2	3
East Anglia	0	0	2	2
Stirling	2	0	0	2

degree to the small size of the economic programs. But the main reason for the low scores is the partial teaching commitment by department to heterodox economics.[19] In particular, heterodox economics was not included in the aims and objectives of eleven or in the required courses of eight B.A. programs. Moreover, six departments did not have post-graduate programs and of the remaining eleven departments, only one had heterodox economics in its aims and objectives, while only three had it in the required courses. Finally, only one department (SOAS) had a complete teaching commitment to heterodox economics across all the programs. For a department to make a substantive teaching contribution to heterodox economics, it should have, like SOAS, a complete teaching commitment and a minimum program size of 2 for each program, which produces an overall score of 28. With such a benchmark, it is clear that (excluding SOAS), nine departments have the possibility of making a substantive teaching contribution. On the other hand, if a department wants to make a teaching contribution to heterodox economics only in the area of undergraduate education, it should have an overall score of 12 or higher. In this case, five departments have this capability, with two others having the possibility. However, it is possible for all departments to improve their teaching commitment by adopting teaching strategies of rewriting aims and objectives to include heterodox economics and including heterodox economics in some way in required courses; and by (if the resources are available and is compatible with the educational aims of the college or university) starting a post-graduate program in which heterodox economics is a significant component.

Work environment

The final component in the ranking of a heterodox department concerns the work environment since it has an impact on the training of future heterodox researchers and on the vitality of heterodox economics (RAE 2006). While it is becoming increasingly the norm that bullying, sexual, religious, and ethnic harassment, and threatening behavior is unacceptable in the workplace, the subtle and not so subtle academic equivalents of these actions are commonplace in many departments where heterodox economists teach and engage in research. Because the department is the site of the social production of scientific knowledge and the transmission of this knowledge to students, the more intellectually open, non-bullying, non-threatening the work environment is for heterodox economists, the more likely will be the production of heterodox scientific knowledge and the introduction of heterodox economics to students. How non-discriminatory and supportive a department's work environment is towards heterodox economists can be evaluated in terms of its attitude or view of heterodox publications, heterodox research, teaching heterodox economics, hiring and/or promoting heterodox economists, and heterodox economics in general with five points for a positive attitude, 2.5 points for a 'somewhat' positive attitude, and zero points for an anti-heterodox attitude.[20] The result of the sub-categories and the overall score for the work environment are given in Table 11.6. What is clear is that the majority of the departments provide a good work environment (a score of 20 and above) for heterodox economists. On the other hand, five departments (with scores less than 12.5) provide an unsupportive if not an outright hostile environment. The most striking, if obvious, evidence from Table 11.6 is the connection between a department's attitude towards heterodox publications and research and the hiring of heterodox economists—the more negative the attitude towards the former the less likely heterodox economists will be hired. However, to improve the work environment is quite difficult if the majority of the faculty in the department have such a negative attitude. Perhaps the best strategy for departments with good working environments is to continue promoting pluralism in both research/publications and in hiring. But for heterodox economists in departments with a poor work

Table 11.6 Work environment for heterodox economists

Department	Publications	Research	Teaching	Hiring/ Promotion	Department Attitude	Overall Score for Work Environment
East London	5.0	5.0	5.0	5.0	5.0	25.0
Leeds Metropolitan	5.0	5.0	5.0	5.0	5.0	25.0
Manchester Met.	5.0	5.0	5.0	5.0	5.0	25.0
Middlesex	5.0	5.0	5.0	5.0	5.0	25.0
SOAS	5.0	5.0	5.0	5.0	5.0	25.0
Staffordshire	5.0	5.0	5.0	5.0	5.0	25.0
Leeds	2.5	2.5	5.0	5.0	5.0	20.0
Nottingham Trent	2.5	2.5	5.0	5.0	5.0	20.0
Open	2.5	5.0	5.0	2.5	5.0	20.0
Stirling	2.5	5.0	5.0	2.5	5.0	20.0
Strathclyde	0.0	5.0	5.0	0.0	5.0	15.0
East Anglia	2.5	2.5	2.5	2.5	2.5	12.5
Manchester	0.0	2.5	5.0	0.0	0.0	7.5
Aberdeen	2.5	2.5	0.0	0.0	0.0	5.0
Bath	0.0	0.0	5.0	0.0	0.0	5.0
Sheffield	0.0	0.0	5.0	0.0	0.0	5.0
Cambridge	0.0	2.5	0.0	0.0	0.0	2.5

Source: 2003 Questionnaire on the Impact of the Research Assessment Exercise on Heterodox Economics; also see Appendix A.23

environment, the best strategy is perhaps to create institutes or other orga-nizational-based centers of scholarly excellence and expertise as a way to develop in the short-term a more supportive work environment but with the long-term agenda of gradually altering the department's overall work envir-onment thereby increasing its work environment score. In both cases, main-taining and/or improving the work environment for heterodox economists requires continuous efforts.

Ranking departments

The overall "contribution" profile of a department is represented by a com-posite of the three component scores. Because of the importance of knowl-edge building, the publication score has a weight of 70 percent while the teaching and work environment scores have a weight of 30 percent.[21] There-fore, given the component scores, the overall score for a department can be derived—see Table 11.7. As noted above, the overall score represents the degree that the department, as a place of research, teaching, and work environment, contributes to the production of heterodox scientific knowl-edge, to its impartation to future generations of students and training of future heterodox researchers, and to enhancing the vitality of heterodox economics. Thus, in terms of scores qua ranking, SOAS makes the most substantial contribution, followed by three distinct clusters of seven, five, and four departments whose contributions in terms of research, training, and vitality are less than the previous cluster.

While the comparative differences reflected in the scores qua rankings could promote invidious comparisons among the departments that would be a misinterpretation of their significance. The point of the scores is to indicate to departments how they might improve their contribution to developing heterodox economics. This is done by comparing the benchmark score to the department's score. That is, for a department wanting to make a substantial contribution in research, in teaching at the undergraduate, post-graduate and doctoral level, and in the work environment, it needs to achieve at least the benchmark score of 51.50—see benchmark$_{u-pg-d}$ in Table 11.7. Thus, we see that while SOAS exceeds the overall minimal score for making a substantial contribution, its publication score could be increased. More importantly, SOAS could make more of a substantial contribution if it increases the number of heterodox economists and publications and increases student numbers at all levels. On the other hand, if Open University wants to make a substantial contribution to heterodox economics, it would have to increase its publication score through hiring more heterodox economists, increase its publication productivity, place more publications in heterodox journals with scores of four and above, and develop a post-graduate program. However, if a small department seeks to provide an excellent undergraduate education in heterodox economics coupled with good publications and work environment, then it needs to achieve at least the benchmark score of 33.40—see benchmark$_{u}$

Table 11.6 Ranking Heterodox Economic Departments

Department	Number of Heterodox Economists	Publications Score	Teaching Score	Work Environment Score	Overall Score
SOAS	10	48.49	36	25.0	52.24
Manchester Met.	8	34.59	26	25.0	39.51
East London	8	34.95	14	25.0	36.17
Staffordshire	5	35.31	9	25.0	34.92
Cambridge	15	42.65	10	2.5	33.61
Open	6	32.97	14	20.0	33.28
Leeds	4	30.57	19	20.0	33.10
Manchester	4	31.10	20	7.5	30.02
Aberdeen	3	26.14	14	5.0	25.53
Bath	3	28.60	12	5.0	25.12
Stirling	2	24.99	2	20.0	24.09
Leeds Metropolitan	2	15.75	12	25.0	22.13
Nottingham Trent	2	18.39	11	20.0	22.13
Strathclyde	2	17.13	3	15.0	17.39
Sheffield	2	17.97	5	5.0	15.58
Middlesex	5	4.80	7	25.0	12.96
East Anglia	4	7.50	2	12.5	10.50
Benchmark$_{u\text{-}pg\text{-}d}$	9	53.00	28	20.0	51.50
Benchmark$_u$	5	34.00	12	20.0	33.40

Notes:
Overall Score = (.7) (Publication Score) + (.3) (Teaching Score + Work Environment Score)

in Table 11.7. So, for example, if Leeds Metropolitan wants to make this kind of contribution to heterodox economics, it would need to hire more heterodox economists and increase publication productivity. All three of these cases indicate that it is not the department score that is significant *per se* but relative to the benchmark score. The point of the overall score hence ranking is to help departments develop strategies to make more of a contribution to the production of scientific knowledge and the development of heterodox economics.

A possible way forward

The methodology for ranking journals and departments developed in this chapter has a single core component—the promotion of the development of heterodox economics and the community of heterodox economists which is the prize. The scoring hence ranking of heterodox journals is methodologically designed to encourage journal editors to develop strategies for their journal and in conjunction with other heterodox journal editors to promote the building of specialized and integrative heterodox knowledge. The desired outcome of the strategies is that all heterodox journals will eventually make equal contributions so that it is not possible to claim that one heterodox journal is "better" than another. The methodology of scoring and ranking of departments is also designed to encourage department chairs and faculty to develop ways of making the site of the social production and dissemination of heterodox scientific knowledge more research productive, engaged in training future heterodox economists, and conducive to heterodox economics. That is, a department can utilize the methodology in this chapter to develop its own strategies to improve its contribution to the prize. In the end it is not the score or the ranking that is significant but the effort to contribute to producing scientific heterodox scientific knowledge and developing heterodox economics and its community of economists. It is the eye on the prize that is central to the methodology.

Whether the methodology developed in this chapter for scoring hence ranking heterodox journals and departments can promote the development of heterodox economics and the community of heterodox economists will only be known after discussion by heterodox economists. However, if the methodology is deemed at least adequate, then heterodox economists will be able to present an alternative measure of the quality of their journals and departments. In a world where heterodox economists and their journals and departments are always on the defensive, advocating an alternative measure is not just a radical and emotionally needed step forward, but also a proclamation that heterodox economists are not second-class or invisible economists but are equal to but different from neoclassical economists. To do nothing is not an option.

Appendix

The Appendix can be obtained from the author and found at the following website: www.heterodoxnews.com/APPENDIX

A.1   Microeconomic textbooks used in Table 1.1
A.2   Production of doctorates in economics in United States universities, 1920–2003
A.3   Diamond List journals
A.4   Top 25 economic departments in the United States with PhD programs, 1959–2003
A.5   Ranking of heterodox economics journals derived from the ranking literature, 1972–2003
A.6   Rankings of United States economics PhD programs with a major or minor heterodox component, 1959–2000
A.7   American academic radical-Marxian economists, 1930–60
A.8   American radical-Marxian economists not located in United States university economics departments, 1930–60
A.9   American radical-Marxian economists, 1961–70
A.10 Data on the cross-citation of selected mainstream and heterodox economics journals, 1993–2003
A.11 Heterodox economics PhD programs and publications by graduates, 1976–95
A.12 Social network of American Post Keynesian economists, 1978–95
A.13 Data on Workers' Educational Association tutorial classes in economics, 1909–54
A.14 Data on independent working class education movement, 1910–40
A.15 Data on Conference of Socialist Economists, 1970–75
A.16 Social network of Marxist-heterodox economists participating in Conference of Socialist Economists activities, 1970–75
A.17 Social network of economists participating in Post Keynesian-heterodox activities, 1970–96
A.18 Data on the Research Assessment Exercise, 1989–96
A.19 Data on the 2001 Research Assessment Exercise

Notes

1 Introduction

1 This suggests that the thesis implicitly supports a quite crude form of 'Whig' history of economics.

2 The texts examined included Mas-Colell, Whinston, and Green (1995), Varian (1992), and Kreps (1990); and they are assigned in the graduate microeconomic theory courses at Massachusetts Institute of Technology, Harvard University, Princeton University, Yale University, University of Wisconsin-Madison, University of California-Los Angeles, University of Chicago, and Duke University, all of which are top-ranked doctoral programs—see Table 2.4 on page 46. (See the Departments websites and Tower 1995.)

3 There is an ongoing controversy whether over the past decade neoclassical and 'mainstream' economics mean the same thing; and hence whether neoclassical and mainstream microeconomics are the same. However, for this chapter and throughout the book, the two terms are considered the same and used interchangeably, primarily because the starting date of the controversy—the 1990s—occurs at the end of the time period covered in the book (Colander et al. 2004; Davis 2006; Lawson 2006).

4 Wit and ridicule are recognized by both the blasphemer and the devoted as powerful rhetorical devices that clearly illuminate the salient points of the reasoned arguments. Reasoned arguments, however brilliant, have little impact if dully expressed. Hence the guardians of the church frequently attempt to get the state to suppress blasphemous wit and ridicule, while leaving untouched blasphemous reasoned arguments delivered in a sober and genteel, that is, dull, fashion (Lund 1995b).

5 In particular, if the devotee is so distraught by the way the blasphemous material is presented so as to lead him/her to a breach of the peace in some manner, then the blasphemer can be subject to judicial penalties, even if he/she did not think the presentation to be disturbing, as in the Gay News case in 1977 (Nash 1999; Levy 1993).

6 For a similar demarcation without the religious analogy see Backhouse (2000, 2004) where he uses mainstream/orthodox, dissent, and heterodoxy; also see Desai (1991).

7 For example, see the essays in Holt and Pressman (1998) on Barbara Bergmann, James Buchanan, John R. Commons, Milton Friedman, Frank Knight, and Thomas Schelling.

8 Heterodox economics is not yet a settle body of non-neoclassical theory and nor have all current heterodox economists shorn their minds of neoclassical concepts. But whatever faults, contradictions, and omissions there may be, the direction of development for both is towards a complete separation from neoclassical economics.

9 This methodological position is subject to an extensive ongoing debate within heterodox economics.

10 This does not imply that somehow scientists and science—and certainly not economists and economics–are in a self-enclosed field separate from society and its influences.

11 Thus it is possible to have the production of "legitimate" scientific knowledge that is not an explanation of a real-world phenomenon but is accepted and promoted by the state for other purposes. That is, science does not necessarily get at unique 'truths' of real world phenomena.

12 Some economists deny that a clear distinction can be made between neoclassical and heterodox economics, but the material presented in the subsequent chapters make it clear that mainstream economists clearly perceive a difference and deliberately penalize heterodox economists for holding the wrong theory.

13 The data in Appendix A.10 pertains only to those selected Diamond List core mainstream journals. However, further examination of the *SSCI: Citation Reports* reveals that the other Diamond List journals as well as all the lesser mainstream journals do not cite heterodox economic journals.

14 From this it is evident that heterodox economists are aware of what is going on in mainstream economics, which is in direct contrast to the view held by many mainstream economists that heterodox economists are depressingly ignorant about mainstream theory.

15 The theoretical core is not written in stone—there are developments. Particular concepts may be created, developed, and/or modified, such as rationality and bounded rationality. But what is not possible is for any of the core concepts, such as rationality (and any modifications) to be ejected from the core. If this occurred, then all the previous scientific knowledge of neoclassical economics would be called into question. Consequently, the theoretical core may (and in fact does) contain concepts that are contradictory.

16 Backhouse's criteria for the existence of a community of heterodox economists are similar: self-identification, core theoretical assumptions being anti-neoclassical, and a set of institutions outside of similar neoclassical institutions (Backhouse 2000, 2004).

17 The importance of recollections, interviews, oral histories, and other forms of life histories is that they help uncover the hidden, revealing the previously unknown existence of social relationships, characterizing the bonds that unite members of heterodox groups, and providing accounts of the workplace which illuminate the role of power in the hiring, firing, and the profession's management of blasphemous dissent (Mata and Lee 2007).

18 The material included in the Appendix is so extensive that it cannot be included with the book. However, it can be obtained from the author and found at the following website: http://www.heterodoxnews.com/APPENDIX–formatted.pdf.

2 The contested landscape and dominance in American economics in the twentieth century

1 Commonly used texts circa 1870–80 included F. Wayland, *Elements of Political Economy*, J. S. Mill, *Principles of Political Economy*, H. Fawcett, *Manual of Political Economy*, J. E. T. Rodgers, *Manual for Political Economy for Schools and Colleges*, and J. E. Cairnes, *Leading Principles of Political Economy* (Barber 1988b, 1988c; Jones 1988; Mason 1982; Cross 1967; Snavely 1967; Brazer 1982).

2 For a discussion of American exceptionalism and its impact on American social science, including economics, and American history, see Ross (1991) and Novick (1988).

3 For example, Benjamin Andrews noted at the same time of the Haymarket incident that:

... men like Walker, Jevons, Hearn, and Marshall ... have set out to ascertain whether [*laisser-faire*] is really so fatal to wage-workers as it is commonly made to appear. A new theory of wages and of profits has been constructed, according to which equitable distribution occurs through the workings ... of natural economic laws, all apart from control by government. ... profits do not prey upon wages.

(Andrews 1886: 141)

And in retrospect, Jacob Hollander noted that " ... when socialistic writing had challenged the right of capital to any share in distribution, did the orthodox political economy make any serious attempt to ascertain the service of capital in production" (Hollander 1903: 268). One source of support and encouragement for this line of thinking was from the capitalists and their pundits as a way to dele-gitimize workers' claims on profits in the form of higher wages coupled with falling prices—see Livingston (1987).

4 The synthesis also required the construction of a Whig view of the history of economic theory in terms of the continuity thesis. The thesis states that Smith's, Ricardo's, Mill's, and Marshall's theory of prices are part of the same supply and demand theoretic tradition. Hence there was no disjunction between classical political economy and neoclassical price theory. The claim that only a single the-oretical tradition existed in economics was a blatant effort to marginalize and then rid economics of heterodox theories.

5 Those historically oriented economists who could not reconcile their historicist vision and particularistic canon of historians eventually drifted into economic history (Ross 1991).

6 For example, see the case studies of Brown University, Harvard, University of Michigan, Yale, Columbia, University of Pennsylvania, University of California, Stanford, University of Virginia, and Wisconsin. The studies reveal that well-known neoclassical economists, such as F. Taussig, T. Carver, C. Bullock, F. Taylor, A. Hadley, I. Fisher, J. B. Clark, E. R. A. Seligman, and R. Mayo-Smith taught the basic and advanced theory courses; and they assigned their own or other neoclassical texts, such as Marshall's *Principles of Economics*, and prepared lectures based on the works of W. S. Jevons, Marshall, J. B. Clark, and E. Bohm-Bawerk. From 1890 to 1910, 4181 copies of Marshall's *Principles* were sold in the United States. Moreover, if their professors dismissed "marginal utility econom-ics," economic graduate students, such as at Johns Hopkins, held semi-clandestine meetings to study it. Finally, of the sixty-two economists with the major respon-sibility for teaching economics in twenty-eight leading colleges and universities from 1870 to 1900, only four—*Thorstein Veblen, Lindley Keasby, Edward Bremis*, and *Edward Ross*—could be viewed as critical of neoclassical price theory; and if the future Institutionalists, *John Commons* and *Wesley Mitchell*, are included, the number comes to six. With less than 10 percent of economic professors critical of neoclassical price theory cira 1900, it is reasonable to conclude that neoclassical price theory dominated the lectures in the university classroom at the dawn of the twentieth century (Mason 1982; Brazer 1982; the case studies in Barber 1988a; Macmillan 1942; Gettleman 1987; Snavely 1967; and Parrish 1967).

7 See Steedman (1989b, 1995, and 2004) and Howard and King (1989).

8 From 1885 to 1900 there were numerous cases involving economics, economists and academic freedom. For example, *Benjamin Andrews*, President of Brown University, was attacked by members of the Brown Corporation for supporting bimetallism because it was a view not held by the friends of the University, espe-cially those inclined to give gifts and legacies. Other examples include *Henry C. Adams* being denied promotion at the University of Michigan for promoting free trade because it conflicted with the regents' protectionist position; Cornell not

renewing *Adams's* contract because he denounced the behavior of the nation's industrialists during the aftermath of the Haymarket incident; *Richard Ely* being attacked by colleagues or the Board of Regents for supporting labor and the role of the state in the economy, thus in one case undermining his tenuous position at Johns Hopkins and nearly doing the same at Wisconsin in a second case; *J. Allen Smith* being dismissed by Marietta College for apparently voting for William Jennings Bryan in the 1896 elections (financial issues were also a factor) and *I. A. Hourwich* being bullied into resigning from the University of Chicago by J. Laurence Laughlin for participating in a Populist convention in 1894; *Bemis* being attacked by his senior colleague, Laughlin, for holding progressive/radical political opinions, and cautioned and then dismissed by his employer, the University of Chicago, for making "pro-labor" comments in the context of the 1894 Pullman strike because they hurt the University's chances of getting much needed Rockefeller money; *Ross* being shifted from economics to sociology and eventually dismissed by Stanford University for making speeches that promoted economic reforms and others that promoted racism (which may have been the direct cause of his dismissal) that upset Mrs. Stanford; *Thomas E. Will* and *Bemis* being dismissed from Kansas State Agricultural College (now University) in 1899 for being associated with Populism and teaching economics that was relevant for the producing classes; and *Commons* having his academic positions undermine at the University of Indiana and Syracuse University for praising George and Marx and for supporting populist causes and the playing of baseball on Sunday. [Barber 1988b, 1988d, 1988e; Donnan 1952; Brazer 1982; Cookingham 1988; Henderson 1988; Bergquist 1972; Mohr 1970; Goldman 1944; Will 1901; Furner 1975; Schlabach 1963–64; Coats 1968; Ross 1991; Beauregard 1988]

9 At the formation of the American Economic Association in 1886, some economists believed that one of its purposes was to promote equally any and all economic research that fell within the tradition of Smith, Ricardo, Malthus, and Mill, whether it be "heterodox" or "orthodox." However, because the Association also promoted and supported the professionalization of American economists, it quickly ended up simply promoting "orthodox" neoclassical theory over Marxism and Georgism and later in the twentieth century Institutionalism and other heterodox approaches. Hence the Association reinforced the orthodoxy vs. heterodox distinction and thereby made and continues to this day to make a significant contribution to the neoclassical homogenization of American economists (Ely 1887; Furner 1975; Haskell 2000).

10 The statistics on the number of doctorates in economics for the period 1904 to 1940 are incomplete at best. First of all, there are no aggregate statistics for the period 1904 to 1919. Secondly, the yearly aggregate statistics for the period 1920 to 1940 put out by the National Academy of Sciences/National Research Council (see Appendix A.2) does not include doctorates from all institutions, such as The Brookings Institution that produced 40 of them. The best guess for the number of doctorates given in economics for the period of 1920 to 1940 is in excess of 2100. However there is no reason to assume that the percentages given above would change appreciably with this larger number of doctorates.

11 This accounts, in part, for the large sales of neoclassical textbooks by Ely, Taussig, and Henry Seager (see Dorfman 1959: 211). In addition, 18,428 copies of Marshall's *Principles* were sold from 1911 to 1940 (Macmillan 1942).

12 One example of this was *Columbia University* in the inter-war period. Prior to 1920, the Department was clearly neoclassical in orientation. However, the combination of a general environment supportive of Institutionalism and the hiring of Wesley Mitchell in 1922 and subsequent Institutionalists in the 1920s transformed its character to an Institutionalist one. Consequently while neoclassical price theory was taught, it was not given the emphasis and accolades that it would

receive at Harvard, Yale, or Princeton. Graduate students of the 1930s felt this neglect and agitated for additional courses in neoclassical price theory. The Department slowly responded to these concerns, first by hiring Harold Hotelling in 1931 and establishing a theory seminar in 1932. Later in 1938 a course titled "The Structure of Neo-Classical Economics" was offered to graduate students and taught by Milton Friedman. The outcome of this was that graduate students generally ceased to closely identify with Institutionalism. The question of theory and its lack of prominence were addressed in 1946 when George Stigler and William Vickrey were hired to teach neoclassical price theory. Although it took over fifteen years after 1946 for the pre-war Institutionalists generation to retire and be replaced by neoclassical economists, the Department's tone became increasingly neoclassical and graduate students interested in Institutional economics dwindled to the vanishing point by the mid-1950s, helped along by the fact that Stigler bullied graduate students who were interested in Institutional economics. Another example was the transformation of *Chicago's Department of Political Economy* after 1915 from being diverse and pluralistic (but not including Marxian or radical economists) to one emphasizing neoclassical price theory. The focus of the hiring from 1916 to 1940 was increasingly on neoclassical theorists such as Jacob Viner, Frank Knight, Henry Schultz, Paul Douglas, Lloyd Mints, and Oskar Lange. Neoclassical price theory with competitive markets increasingly became the core for economic theorizing, with the inevitable consequence of increasing criticisms directed at Institutional economics. The hiring of Milton Friedman in 1946 continued the general dominance of neoclassical price theory that had been established over the previous two decades, but its particular theoretical orientation changed to that of the "Chicago School." Similarly, after the Scott Nearing debacle in 1915 and the retirement of Simon Patten in 1917, *economics at Pennsylvania* had to rebuild itself. Raymond Bye, who was partial to Marshall, maintained the neoclassical heritage started by Patten through the inter-war period and into the post-war period as well (Rutherford 2001, 2003b, 2004; Hammond 2000; Ginzberg 1990; Dorfman 1955; Fusfeld 1997; Emmett 1998; Reder 1982; Sass 1982).

13 For example, Friedman taught neoclassical price theory at Columbia in 1938–39 and at Chicago in 1946 and taught virtually the same course. In addition, while at Columbia Stigler and Friedman maintained a close working correspondence regarding aspects of neoclassical price theory. Thus, graduate students at both universities were taught the same price theory. The outcome of this common training in neoclassical price theory was that newly minted Ph.D.s were differentiable in terms of research interests only. This perhaps accounts for why economists trained at Institutionalist-oriented economics departments, such as Wisconsin, were not generally discriminated against (Hammond 2000; Hammond and Hammond 2000; Biddle 1998).

14 Besides excluding Marxism and Georgism, American economists and the American Economic Association were unreceptive to sociologists and effectively excluded feminist concerns and ideas. If the pre-1970 evolution of the economics department at the University of Manitoba is indicative of developments at other Canadian universities, a very similar story could also be told about economics at Canadian universities (Bernstein 2001; Pentland 1977; Baragar 2004; Horn 1999).

15 For example, there was the International School of Social Economy in Girard, Kansas, the Karl Marx School in Boston, the Work People's College in Duluth, Minnesota, the Brookwood Labor College in Katonah, New York, the Commonwealth College near Mena, Arkansas, and the Rand School of Social Science, Jewish Workers University, and the New York Workers School all in New York City. In addition, the Communist Party established branches of the Workers Schools in twelve other cities including San Francisco, Boston and Chicago. The

yearly attendance at these schools ranged from a couple of hundred to 5,000 for the Rand School (in 1918) and to 10,000 for the Workers School (1934–35).

16 For example, the Rand School offered courses on the economics of socialism, on wealth and income, and on economic problems, while the New York Workers School offered courses on political economy and advanced political economy, on American applied economics, and on modern economic theories. In addition, there were courses on the history of the labor movement, trade-union problems, American history, and the history of the class struggle.

17 For example, the Henry George School of Social Science in New York City was established in 1930 and continues to operate today. Branches of the school were established in other cities including Chicago, St. Louis, Philadelphia, San Francisco, and Los Angeles.

18 The president of Bryn Mawr College expressed great dissatisfaction with *Lindley Keasbey's* "socialistic" discourse in the classroom and eventually forced him out in 1905. Keasbey went to the University of Texas where his unorthodox economic ideas resulted in his removal from teaching economic courses in 1909. Moreover, the President of University of California-Berkeley thought that *Ira Cross* was a socialist simply because he gave some lectures circa 1914 on the philosophy of socialism and radical political movements. In addition, *Emily Balch*, who taught economics at Wellesley College (1896–1918), advanced slowly up the academic ladder because of her socialist and reformist extracurricular activities; *George Cox* was dismissed by Dartmouth College in 1915 for expressing pro-socialist sympathies; and the regents of the University of Washington refused to hire *Charles McKinley* because of his alleged radicalism. Finally, 1914–15 *Scott Nearing*, an economist at the University of Pennsylvania, championed the Progressive cause of abolishing child labor and lectured on it in the classroom. And for this, the University's trustees attempted to muzzle him, denied him promotion, and then fired him. The trustees then went on to encourage a general exodus of Progressive economists; and with the retirement of Patten in 1917, their task was complete. It should be noted that the American Economic Association refused to support Nearing and was applauded by some members for doing so because, they alleged, Nearing was weak on the elementary principles of economic theory.

19 For example, *Patten* was "forced" to retire in 1917 by the University of Pennsylvania ostensibly because he reached mandatory retirement age, but really because of his unorthodox economic and social views and because the University trustees were offended by his "defense of German values" and the fact he introduced a pacifist at a public meeting. In addition, *Nearing* was dismissed from Toledo University in 1917 for his anti-war position and prevented from speaking at Clark University in 1922 because of his radical-Veblenian critique of higher education; *Allen Eaton* was dismissed by the trustees of the University of Oregon for attending a meeting of the People's Council for Democracy and Peace and then writing a letter about it to an Oregon paper while *Arthur Calhoun, A. Morse*, and *G. Arner* were dismissed from Maryville College, Marietta College, and Dartmouth College respectively for their "socialistic teaching or sentiments"; and in1919 and 1921 Valparaiso University and Albany College respectfully expelled students because of their socialistic political opinions. Moreover, in 1918, *Balch's* academic appointment was not renewed by the Wellesley College trustees because of her pacifist and peace activities during World War I. However, the academic careers of economists such as Ely or three economics professors at the University of Nebraska, who were extremely vocal and clearly"non-scientific" in their anti-German pronouncements, including the recommended firing of anti-war economic professors, did not suffer. It should be noted that Balch received the 1946 Nobel Peace Prize, the first and only American economist to receive a Nobel prize (Nearing 2000; Saltmarsh 1991; Solomon 1980; Sinclair 1923; Bernstein 2001; Baranik 1990; Gruber 1975; Cohen 1993).

20 For example, *Louis Levine* (who later changed his name to Lewis L. Lorwin), who taught economics at University of Montana, was in 1919 suspended by the chancellor for having privately published a monograph on mine taxation that upset mining interests in the state and hence alienate friends of the University in the state legislature and therefore adversely affect state appropriations. He was reinstated two months later. In addition, in 1920 *James Stevens* was dismissed from Middlebury College (after being identified as a pacifist, socialist, or Bolshevist), in part, for his attitude and belief on social questions; in 1922, *Arthur White* was dismissed from Muskingham College for the way he taught economics; and because of his talk to coal miners in a workers' education class during the bitter 1928 coal strike, the Southern Coal Operators Association got Ohio University to suggest to *Cornelius Fink* that he seek employment elsewhere. The business class routinely accused *Theresa McMahon* of being an anarchist because of her support of working people and the minimum wage and pressured (unsuccessfully because of her support from organized labor) the University of Washington to dismiss her (Deibler 1919, 1921; Trachtenberg 1920; Sinclair 1923; McMahon 1989; Gutfeld 1970; Beauregard 1988).

21 It should be noted that many years after their demise, two of the clubs, Karl Marx Society of Brooklyn College and Marxist Study Club of the City College of New York, were listed as subversive organizations by the U.S. government. College administrators also directed their conservative attitudes towards campus-based activities that, however, did not include their students, as with the case of the Bryn Mawr Summer School for Women Workers. The combination of having instructors who held progressive or leftist political views and could teach about Marxism and socialism and did present critical views of American capitalism and of working women wanting to study Marxism, read proletarian novels, and observing ongoing strikes resulted in conservative members of the college's Board of Trustees in the 1930s branding the summer school as a leftist labor school. As a result, the summer school was eventually evicted from the Bryn Mawr campus in 1935. The offending economic instructors included *Colston Warne* (who resigned from the University of Pittsburg in 1930 in response to the university trustees attempt to dismiss him for giving a speech on the living conditions in the local coal fields; a year earlier the University dissolved its Liberal Club and expelled two students in part for having a meeting on the Mooney–Billings case and Warne was an advisor for the Club), *Broadus Mitchell*, *Theresa Wolfson* (who help organize a chapter of the Intercollegiate Socialist Society, was a socialist, worked for trade unions, and taught labor history and economics), and *Leo Huberman* (a communist and later help found the *Monthly Review*). The first three were identified as dangerous radicals by the forerunners to McCarthyism (Greer 2001; Heller 1984, 1986; Kessler-Harris 1980; Dilling 1935; Sabine and Wittke 1929; Committee on Un-American Activities 1957).

22 Radical and politically active professors in Canada in the 1930s (and 1920s) were also subject to inquisitions, dismissal, or not being hired (Horn 1999, 2000; Baragar 2004).

23 For example, *Robert Brady* (University of California-Berkeley) had to testify before the House Un-American Activities Committee in 1938 and was branded a "prematurely anti-fascist." Not to be outdone, New School for Social Research (1940), the University of California (1942), and Stanford (1940s) put policies in place disqualifying communists or fellow travelers for faculty appointments. In addition, Columbia University and Bradford Community College dismissed *Donald Henderson* and *Horace Davis* respectively in part for their political activities—another factor in Henderson's dismissal was his failure to complete his Ph. D. dissertation; while *Myron Hoch* and *Kenneth May* (a graduate student in mathematics who wrote his Ph.D. dissertation "On the Mathematical Theory of

Employment") were dismissed from the College of the City of New York and University of California-Berkeley respectively for being identified as members of the Communist Party and therefore holding political beliefs that were incompatible with their faculty position. Moreover, at Harvard, decisions to retain economic instructors in the 1930s seem to disproportionately not include those, such as *Raymond Walsh, Alan Sweezy,* and *John K. Galbraith,* who were involved in union activities or involved with the New Deal; while Johns Hopkins University's Academic Council censured *Broadus Mitchell* for using inappropriate language when denouncing in class the Supreme Court for over turning New Deal legislation, which resulted in Mitchell resigning from the University. Furthermore, in the late 1930s members of the Texas legislature tried to fire *Robert Montgomery* from the University of Texas for advocating socialism, that is public ownership or at least rate regulation of public utilities; while Texas businessmen wanted the University to fire *Montgomery, Clarence Ayres, Edward Hale,* and *Clarence Wiley* because they did not like what they were teaching. In 1942, *Fagg Foster, Wendell Gordon,* and *Nelson Peach,* junior members of the University of Texas economics department, were dismissed or explicitly denied rehiring at the end of their one-year contract by the Board of Regents for negative comments made about a public meeting in which the Wage and Hour Law of 1938 was attacked. Finally, beginning in the late 1930s the FBI initiated a reoccurring surveillance and investigation of Galbraith that lasted forty years.

24 The post-1945 red scare was in fact a continuation of the inter-war red scare, as epitomized by Elizabeth Dilling's identification of the "red network" in the United States (Goldstein 1978; Fischer 2006). She identified a number of red economists including *Balch, Paul Brissenden, Calhoun, Commons, Davis, Robert Dunn, Henderson, John Ise, Frank Knight, William Leiserson, Broadus Mitchell, Wesley Mitchell, Jessica Peixotto, David Saposs, Rexford Tugwell, Warne, Wolfson,* and *Leo Wolman.* While quite inaccurate as a list of "red economists," there is some overlap with the list I have constructed—see Appendix A.7, columns A and B—of twenty academic economists who were interested in or utilized Marxian ideas. Some utilized Marxian economic theory in their published writings, while others actually presented Marxian ideas in class. There were even a few who taught Marxian economic theory. Sweezy's course on the economics of socialism at Harvard is a well-known example, but there were also radical economics instructors at the University of Southern California and at the University of Louisville who taught Marxian economic theory in their classes. Finally, there were also cases of professors, such as *Addison Cutler* and *Henderson* at Columbia University, and students assembling in small informal and perhaps secret groups to discuss Marxian and other radical theory.

25 When the possibility presented itself, such as at Harvard, it was explicitly rejected by the neoclassical economists; or when a broader economics program was established, such as by *Patten* at the University of Pennsylvania, it was not maintained over time. Finally, when individual economists pursued this line of research, such as *Carleton Parker* at the University of California, they received little if any intellectual support from their colleagues.

26 The research program was concerned with the institutional context and social control of economic activity, the use of scientific methods, the social-psychological foundations of economic theory, the behavior of business enterprises and the functioning of product and labor markets, and the business cycle (Rutherford 2000a).

27 There were also attempts to provide institutional support for the network, such as Hamilton and Amherst College and the Brookings Graduate School, Mitchell and Maurice Clark and Columbia University, and the group of Institutionalists at Washington Square College of New York University; however, they were often

short-lived and certainly did not extend past 1940. In the case of the Brookings Graduate School, a financial crisis, the fact that the training received by the students seem inappropriate for careers in public service, and its non-neoclassical ethos (which to an outsider made the School appear hopelessly weak) brought Hamilton down and eliminated the School—perhaps to the approval of neoclassical departments at other universities. The new Brookings Institution was put in the hands of a moderately conservative Institutionist economist, Harold Moulton (Rutherford 2000b, 2003a, 2004; Critchlow 1985).

28 An example of this intolerance was the founding of the Econometric Society as a defense organization against Institutionalism (Myrdal 1972).

29 For example, because Frederic Mills's 1927 empirical work on prices was not based on neoclassical price theory, neoclassical economists saw it as flawed. However, when Mills began using neoclassical terminology in his 1930s work on price and technological change it was seen as a contribution. The change in terminology was, in part, brought about by professional pressure (Woirol 1999).

30 Marxist economists, such as Addison Cutler who was taught by Hamilton at Amherst and graduated from Brookings, also noted this declined of Institutionalism, but with some regret because they felt that it could contribute to Marxian economic theory and that it did contribute to understanding of capitalism (Mount 1936; Cutler 1938, 1939; Rutherford 2004).

31 Neoclassical economists faced other heretical and blasphemous controversies in the 1930s, one being constant marginal costs and L-shaped or continuously declining average total cost curves. Since the perverse behavior of costs were based on constant (as opposed to declining) marginal products and the rejection of decreasing returns to scale, neoclassical economists in the post-war period expended considerable energy to suppress these ideas (Lee 1984; Marcuzzo 1996; Aslanbeigui and Naples 1997b).

32 Economist *Emily Huntington* (University of California-Berkeley) refused to sign the California oath of allegiance until she was on the verge of being fired. Two other economists, *Walter Fisher* (University of California-Berkeley) and *Stephen Enke* (University of California-Los Angeles) were fired for not signing the oath or resigned before being fired; the former took a position at Kansas State University and the latter a position with the Rand Corporation. Finally, the negative impact of the oaths on collegiality contributed to *William Fellner's* (University of California-Berkeley) decision to move to Yale University (Huntington 1971; Cookingham 1987; Marshall 1992).

33 For example, University of California-Berkeley faculty voted 78 percent in approval of the statement that Communist Party members were unfit for university appointments solely on the grounds of their political affiliation (Innis 1992). In addition, the Dean of the Graduate School at Michigan made sure that no graduate student who was a vocal antagonist of McCarthyism, such as *Edward Shaffer* and *Myron E. Sharpe*, would get a degree (Samuels 2004).

34 This argument was not extended to academics who became ideologically committed professional witnesses for HUAC, including *Louis Budenz* (who taught economics at Notre Dame and Fordham University).

35 Economists dismissed or denied appointments for one or more of these were *Peach* (Syracuse University), *Daniel Thorner* (University of Pennsylvania), *Davis* (University of Kansas City and Benedict College), *Laurent R. LaVallee* (Oregon State College and Dickinson College), *Vera Shlakman* (Queens College), *Otto Nathan* (New York University), *W. Lou Tandy* (Kansas State Teachers College at Emporia), *Shaffer* (colleges in Kansas and Tennessee), *Tucker P. Smith* (Olivet College), and *Karl Niebyl* (Boston University). Moreover, the Texas state legislature tried to get *Ayres* fired in part because he opposed the requirement of a loyalty oath at the University of Texas. In addition, *Harold Vatter* was threatened

with the denial of tenure (Oregon State College at Corvallis and Carleton College); and *Niebyl* was asked about his connection with the Communist Party (New School for Social Research). Finally, Louisiana State University in Baton Rouge would not permit *Warne* (Consumer Union and Amherst College) to speak on campus. It is commendable of Amherst College to stand by *Warne* even though he was identified as a top ten academic collaborator with communist fronts and enterprises in 1953.

36 This is not surprising since a mark of a good university or college president was to make sure their institutions were free of radicals (McVey and Hughes 1952: 54).

37 Universities also collaborated with the FBI on the use of student informants to spy on progressive/radical students (Shaffer 2004).

38 It should be noted that the AEA was not neutral when evaluating economic theories or economists—it clearly disapproved of Marxism and Marxist economists and essentially collaborated "with the anti-communist witch hunters in Washington" (Coats 1998: 143); and its editors of the *American Economic Review* were inclined not to publish Marxist-oriented articles. Moreover, at the height of McCarthyism, the editor published a review of Klein's book *The Keynesian Revolution* (Klein 1947), in which the reviewer irrelevantly linked Klein to Marxism. Damning leftists in public was, the editor claimed, an appropriate editorial decision. Finally, the AEA did not defend left-feminist economists—*Dorothy Douglas, Mary Keyserling*, and *Caroline Ware*—and the consumer movement of which they were apart when attacked by HUAC (Bernstein 1999, 2001; Wright 1948; Storrs 2003, 2006).

39 This acquiescence was evident among economists (and philosophers) and their professional associations—see Davis (1965) and McCumber (2001).

40 The blacklisting affected *Davis* and *Thorner* when they tried to get an academic position in the middle and late 1950s. The blacklisting operated in part through letters of recommendation. For example, Gardner Ackley, the chairman of the Economics Department at the University of Michigan in 1954, said that he would use the letter of recommendation to warn prospective university employers not to hire two graduate students, *Shaffer* and *Sharpe*, who had been called before the House Un-American Activities Committee but defied it. It should be noted that Ackley did resist significant administrative pressure to force Shaffer and Sharpe to withdraw from the program. However, because of his HUAC appearance, Shaffer was unable to obtain work in Ann Arbor. Moreover, Ackley's antipathy towards him prevented him from getting a University loan. Thus Shaffer was forced to withdraw from the graduate program. He later obtained his economics Ph.D. from Columbia and became an economics professor at the University of Alberta. Because of his Marxist reputation, Sharpe was having trouble with his dissertation advisor before being called before HUAC. For political reasons, his advisor blocked the completion of the dissertation, so Sharpe also left the economics graduate program. After leaving, he established the publishing enterprise, International Arts and Sciences Press, Inc. and later changed its name to M. E. Sharpe Inc., and published heterodox economic books and journals—see Chapter 5. Ackley also stated that when hiring economists in his department, impressions of character, political beliefs and religious views were considered. However, this process of blacklisting was not foolproof if other factors intervened, as was the case with *Douglas Dowd*. When applying for a position at Cornell University in 1953, the University of California-Berkeley sent a reference letter that described Dowd as a radical. However, because the economists at Cornell felt that they had too many Jews in the department, they rejected a talented Jew from Yale University and took the radical whom they (mistakenly) assumed was not Jewish. In any case, blacklisting ensured that there was no alternative academic employment in the public or private sector for purged economists. Suggesting that employment

in the private sector was the way out of McCarthyite repression, as Milton Friedman (1962: 20) argued, is an Orwellian rewriting of history, since the business community actively promoted McCarthyism (Schrecker 1986; Horn 1954a, 1954b; McGrath 1954b; Shaffer 1998a, 1998b; Sharpe 2002; Dowd 1997).

41 Returning from his wartime service in 1945, *Paul Sweezy* still had two years left on his contract with Harvard. However, the economics department made it quite clear that it would not grant tenure to a Marxist. So Sweezy resigned his position and left. This had the consequence that the economics of socialism course he team-taught with Edward Mason would not be taught again. When taught in the 1930s, it did persuade some Harvard students to adopt a radical view of American society. Later in 1949, the Harvard Economics department denied tenure to *Richard Goodwin* largely because of his left-wing political beliefs. Consequently he left the United States for Cambridge, England. To escape red-baiting harassment (perhaps originating from being identified as a top academic communist collaborator), *Dorothy Douglas* resigned from Smith College in 1955. In that same year, *Lawrence Klein* left the University of Michigan for the University of Oxford largely because of harassment by some members of the department for previous involvement in the Communist Party (and anti-Semitism may have also been a factor). It is of interest to note that Ackley characterized Klein's communist involvement as due to a lack of maturity, balance, and judgment. *Thorner* picked up teaching at Delhi University and later in France. On the other hand, those who stayed and remained in university employment, such as *Paul Baran* (Stanford University), were given heavier teaching loads, had their salary frozen, were harassed by government agents, and were denied passports and hence foreign travel for research purposes. After he was dismissed from New York University, *Nathan* attempted to go to Europe to pursue work as an economist. The State Department rejected his passport application and in the ensuing activities of trying to get the decision overturned, he was charged with contempt of Congress for refusing to answer questions about his political activities (Brazer 1982; Sweezy 1965; Tonak and Savran 1987; Arestis and Sawyer 2000; Foley 1989; Schrecker 1986; Hall 1989; Matthews 1953; Beck 1959).

42 In 1948 *Robert Eisner* had contemplated doing a doctoral dissertation on "Karl Marx and the Accumulation of Capital." However, he was urged that, in the climate of the times, it was an unwise topic for one looking to a promising career in government or academia. As a result, Eisner did his dissertation on "Growth, Investment and Business Cycles: A Critique and Development of Some Recent Theories." In 1946 *May* completed his dissertation "On the Mathematical Theory of Employment" in which he examined aggregation problems in one- and two-sector models, Keynes's equation of effective demand, and the optimum problem in a collective economy. Drawing on his dissertation and his interest in Marxism, he wrote, from 1946 to 1950 a series of articles on aggregation problems and the labor theory of value. However, in the context of McCarthyism and being a former member of the Communist Party, the prospect of being called before HUAC was frightfully real and it did happen in 1954. Thus, he seems to have gradually shifted his research interests to the safer area of social choice theory, although continuing to write book reviews for *Science and Society* and *Econometrica* that dealt with mathematical economics, labor theory of value and socialism up until 1958 (Eisner 1978; Jones, Enros, and Tropp 1984; Enros 1984).

43 The California oath controversy and the stress rising from it probably was one of the factors responsible for *Brady's* suicide attempt in 1951; and Harvard's forced dismissal of *Ray Ginger* in 1954 lead to his alcoholism and eventual death in 1975 from cirrhosis of the liver (Dowd 1994; Ginger and Christiano 1987).

44 An example was the Department of Economics at the University of Michigan putting social pressure on *Kenneth Boulding* not to issue a statement opposing

military conscription and urging students to refuse to be conscripted during the Korean War. Boulding bowed to the pressure (Brazer 1982). It should also be noted that a similar red-scare campaign, the snuffing out of criticisms, and the suppression of the heterodox Canadian political economy approach also took place at Canadian universities (Horn, 1999, 2000).

45 Not content with attacking radical academics, the universities (and state legislatures) were unhappy with students forming small Marxian study societies or even attending meetings of progressive student groups; so they had spies report on the meetings. In many cases, they made sure that students were not exposed to progressive or radical ideas by disbanding or not recognizing progressive-communist-based student organizations such as American Youth for Democracy (which was also identified as a subversive organization by the United States government), preventing progressive-left speakers from appearing on campus, and dismissing students who made positive comments about communism. One minor example at the personal level involved Ackley. When lecturing to his undergraduate macro-economics class on the business cycle and Keynesian fiscal policy in 1948, he refused to let a student (Edward Shaffer) present an alternative Marxist-radical explanation for economic downturns and the ineffectualness of Keynesian fiscal policy. A more significant example concerned *Sweezy*. When he gave a lecture to students at the University of New Hampshire, the State's Attorney General descended upon the University requesting that the students give him the notes they took at the lecture. In addition, students and administrators fed information on "left-wing" student activities to the FBI. With such a discouraging and repressive academic and campus environment, it is not surprising that some students were scared to put books on Marxism on the shelves in their dorm rooms while others were unaware of Marxist contributions to their majors and particularly unaware of Marxist alternatives to neoclassical economics and that, by the mid-1950s, the progressive-left student organizations and radical politics had nearly disappeared from American campuses (Shaffer 2002, 2004; Schrecker 1986, 1998; Diamond 1992; Lowen 1997; Sorenson 1980; Henrickson 1981; Billingsley 1999; Selcraig 1982; Price 2004; and *Newsletter on Intellectual Freedom* June 1957: 8 and September 1957: 9).

46 Passed in 1952, the McCarran–Walter Act was used in, for example, in 1969 to prevent the Marxist economist Ernest Mandel from entering the country.

47 For example, General Motors attacked the Worker Education Service of the University of Michigan because one of its classes had a anti-management bias and promoted Marxist ideas. Evidence for this was the use of a Congress of Industrial Organization pamphlet that attributed inflation to profits. This eventually led to its demise. Business groups also attacked fairly mainstream economists as well if they attacked their vested interests. In some cases, universities sided with the business groups and used their institutional power to force retractions by the economists and revisions in their research publications. Perhaps the most notable case in this regard was the Iowa Margarine Incident at Iowa State College in 1943. There are other such incidents, especially in the area of agricultural economics where agricultural, business, and state and national political interests easily combined to attack the academic freedom of economists. Moreover, there was the decade-long attack on Harvard's economics department by conservative alumni for promoting Keynesian-socialist (?) economics and branding Alvin Hansen, Seymour Harris, Joseph Schumpeter, and Galbraith as Fabian socialists or worse; in particular, they held up the tenure appointment for Galbraith for nearly a year (1948–49) because of his commitment to New Deal policies and Keynesianism. Finally, there was the long-term interaction between the business community and conservative economists at Chicago that created in the post-war period the Chicago School of economics whose agenda was not simply

to make the world safe for corporations, but also to make economics politically conservative (Selcraig 1982; Hardin 1976; Lipset 1975; Dobbs 1962; Pasour 1988; Parker 2005; Van Horn and Mirowski 2005).

48 Attempts to limit the market of textbooks whose content and/or political leanings of the author did not agree with the conservative political sensibilities of the day was not limited to Tarshis or Samuelson; it also affected other lesser-known economists, such as *Bye*, whose fairly traditional textbook *Principles of Economics* was attacked because of his socialist leanings (Davidson 2002).

49 In keeping with the McCarthyite tenor of the period, the president of the University used the FBI, State Department, and the military establishment to make sure that there were no communist professors. Still, this did not prevent the FBI from listing Modigliani as a subversive (Diamond 1992). There were also other critics of Keynesianism. In 1950 the economics department at the University of Chicago advised a young Keynesian graduate student, who had just passed his Ph.D. comprehensive exams at the tender age of twenty-one, *Andre Gunder Frank*, to leave because he was unsuited for the graduate program (Frank 1997). And thirteen years later, Jesse Helms equated Keynesianism with unacceptable radical liberalism that supported the unacceptable, racial integration (Billingsley 1999).

50 In the 1960s local Miami businessmen and the Young Americans for Freedom criticized *Warren Samuels* for the content of his government and business course he was teaching at the University of Miami, while the steel and car manufacturers tried to pressure Michigan State into dismissing *Walter Adams* because of his criticisms of their bigness and mode of operation. In both cases, the universities stood by their professors.

51 For example, to relieve it of its financial crisis, in 1962 a businessman offered to donate more than ten million dollars to the University of Kansas City, subject to a number of conditions including that the Economics Department be completely re-oriented in its political and social philosophy. The University trustees, however, declined the offer.

52 To make room for these changes, history of economic thought and economic history were frequently dropped as required core courses and some times dropped altogether from the course offerings. The new economic historians that emerged in the 1960s aided and abetted these changes by rejecting the view that economic history was fundamental to economic analysis and reposition it as an applied field of economics (Barber 1997a; Aslanbeigui and Naples 1997a; Lazonick 1991).

53 Because of McCarthyism and its after affects, the newly-trained, high-powered neoclassical theorists and econometricians were mostly politically neutral, that is they supported the status quo. Hence they did not support politically sensitive projects such as research on poverty; and nor did they support areas, such as social economics, that resisted the use of mathematics. Thus, they discouraged graduate students from taking courses in those areas.

54 American mainstream male economists were not just satisfied with discriminating against heterodox economists; they also discriminated against women economists. Prior to 1940 women economists found it very difficult to get academic positions outside of women's colleges. And in the post-war period 1945–60, women economists found it difficult to get positions even at women's colleges. Moreover, women graduate students were ignored, set apart from male graduate students, or simply thought less of. So it appears that the discriminatory proclivity is a substantive and defining characteristic of mainstream mostly male economists and their associate institutions (Albelda 1997).

55 Ironically, apparently Moore himself was denied tenure at Houston because he did not publish in the good journals that appeared on his list (Lower 2004).

56 The top fifteen departments include Chicago, Columbia, Harvard, Michigan, Minnesota, MIT, Northwestern, Pennsylvania, Princeton, Rochester, Stanford, UC-

Berkeley, UC-Los Angles, Wisconsin, and Yale. The next nine departments include Brown, Carnegie-Mellon, Cornell, Duke, Maryland, New York, UC-San Diego, Virginia, and Washington. See Appendix A.4—last column.

57 Explicitly excluding unimportant journals (from a mainstream perspective) from ranking studies frequently occurred. For example, Lovell (1973: 39–40) and Brauninger and Haucap (2003) excluded history of economic thought journals from their studies of the quality, reputation, and relevance of economic journals.

58 The eight departments were American University, Colorado State at Fort Collins, University of California at Riverside, University of Massachusetts at Amherst, University of New Hampshire, New School University, University of Notre Dame, and the University of Utah—see Chapter 4.

59 When ranked by opinion, the departments fare better but still remained within the bottom 40 percent (with the exception of the University of Massachusetts at Amherst).

60 The thirteen departments were Columbia University, University of Connecticut, University of California-Berkeley, University of Maryland, University of Michigan, University of Nebraska, University of Oklahoma, Rutgers University, Stanford University, Temple University, University of Tennessee, University of Texas, and Yale University—see Chapters 4 and 5.

61 Moreover, this explicit bias against doctoral "heterodox" departments was also replicated in the ranking of economics departments at elite liberal arts colleges. Bodenhorn (2003) ranked the economic departments of fifty elite liberal arts colleges us quality-rated journals. His list of journals included six heterodox journals but excluded at least six others, including *Review of Radical Political Economics*, *Capital and Class*, *Feminist Economics*, and *Review of Political Economy*. Ignoring these journals biased the ranking towards mainstream dominated departments relative to those with some kind of heterodox presence—such as Bucknell, Connecticut College, Franklin and Marshall, and Dickinson (all ranked from 37 to 44) out of fifty elite colleges.

62 The impact of journal and departments rankings on heterodox economics in the United Kingdom has been the cleansing and restructuring of formerly pluralist-heterodox economic departments at the University of Manchester and the University of Cambridge in the last decade, and the general cleansing of heterodox economics from British economic departments—see Chapters 8 and 9.

63 There were also several *ad hominem* arguments that were advanced for reorganizing the department, such as the heterodox faculty did not show proper respect to neoclassical economists and their knowledge claims, they were extremely closed-minded, and the department was one-dimensional. Only irony can be used to characterize such arguments.

64 To put it another way, the Commission simply assumed that all economists spoke the same language, that is, were intellectually-theoretically the same—a conclusion that clearly emerges from the work of Klamer and Colander (1990).

65 Economics was not the only academic discipline whose future was shaped by McCarthyism; anthropology and philosophy were also affected. In general, political repression in the United States has been consciously used to eliminate dissent and promote acceptable activities for Americans (McCumber 2001; Price 2004; and Schultz and Schultz 2001).

3 Radical economics in post-war America, 1945–70

1 Georgism continued in the post-war period, albeit even more marginalized and invisible. As a result, it ceased to contribute to American radical economics.

2 The schools included the School for Jewish Studies (New York City), Jefferson School for Social Science (New York City), Abraham Lincoln School (Chicago),

Samuel Adams School (Boston), Boston School for Marxist Studies, Tom Paine School of Social Sciences (Philadelphia), Walt Whitman School of Social Sciences (Newark), Joseph Weydemeyer School of Social Sciences (St. Louis), Ohio School of Social Sciences (Cleveland), Michigan School of Social Sciences (Detroit), Seattle/Pacific Northwest Labor School (Seattle), and the Tom Mooney/California Labor School (San Francisco).

3 Texts used in the course included *Wage-Labor and Capital, Value, Price and Profit*, and *Capital* by Marx as well as *Nature of Capitalism* by Anna Rochester and *Political Economy* by Lev Leontiev.

4 The Jefferson and California Labor Schools were at least somewhat serious about exposing their students to neoclassical economics, as evident by their libraries' subscriptions to the *American Economic Review*.

5 The Attorney General subversive list also contained twelve bookstores located in Washington, D.C., Boston, and throughout California that participants in the schools might visit. This is not as strange as it may seem since in 1951 the Supreme Court made just the possession of *The Communist Manifesto* and *State and Revolution* a crime (this was overturned in a 1957 Supreme Court decision). The John Birch Society went further in 1965 and made threats against a bookstore owner for stocking *Capital*. A precursor to this was the Oklahoma City police raid in 1940 of the Progressive Book Store and the arrest of the communists who managed it. The "crime" was the selling of radical books, which included *Capital* and literature and if the prosecution had won, then the city and the state of Oklahoma would have presided over a public book burning (Wiegand and Wiegand 2007; Karolides 2006).

6 The trained economists included *Davis* who gave a course on the American economy in the twentieth century; *Valadimir Kazakevich* who gave courses on the history of economic thought and the economics of socialism; and *Victor Perlo* who gave courses on imperialism and Marxian economic theory. The core instructors who were not trained as economists included Elizabeth Lawson, Albert Prago, and Meyer Weise who gave seminars on *Capital* for nearly a decade, George Squier, Sidney Gluck, David Goldway, and Doxey Wilkerson (who was a professor of education and later in 1960 got fired by his college for supporting the black student sit-in movement). In addition, it should be noted that *Niebyl* taught at the Abraham Lincoln School (1943), that *Sweezy* taught at the Samuel Adams School, and that *Klein* was involved with the Abraham Lincoln and the Samuel Adams Schools where he taught courses in macroeconomics tilted a bit towards public policy. Because Klein was teaching, in a diluted form, material that eventually appeared in his book *The Keynesian Revolution*, he was criticized by the Communist Party for not putting enough Marxism in his courses or in his talks to college CP groups. Finally, *Howard Sherman* attended one of these schools as a student and took a course on Marxist economics, but he was not impressed with the teacher or with the dogmatic presentation of the material.

7 One area missing from the above discussion is the use of economists and Marxian theory by the left political parties. One example of this was Max Shachtman adoption of the argument developed by Edward Sard, an economist who obtained an MA from Columbia University (1936) and wrote his dissertation on the history of the labor theory of value, that post-war capitalism depended on a "permanent arms economy." Another omission is the absence of discussion of the Party's view of educational activities, while additional research is also needed to determine whether the courses offered by the schools that attacked Keynes for example actually drove away perspective students (Drucker 1994; Murphy 2007).

8 Of the twelve economists, eleven were academic economists and all had a significant interest in Marxism. The eleven academic economists represented 52 percent of the (identified) radical-Marxist economists in academia—see Appendix, A.7,

columns A and B. Maurice Dobb was the one foreign economist associated with *Science and Society*.

9 Utilizing Marxian arguments, John Darrell (1937) wrote an extraordinary insightful review of *The General Theory*. Edward Mount (1936) wrote an equally insightful evaluation that appeared in the more popular *New Masses*.

10 Subscribers also felt the political heat and asked to be taken off the subscription lists.

11 *Science and Society* was listed as a subversive publication by the US government. The FBI first investigated the journal in December 1942 and continued to do so until the early 1960s. It is not clear that the surveillance had a negative impact, but since the FBI also monitored advertisers and distributors, pressure could have brought upon them to disassociate themselves from the journal (Price 2004–5).

12 There was, for example, in 1952 an article on the structure of a capitalist war economy that utilized a Marxian two-sector model in its analysis; and there was also an article on socialist planning. Later in 1959 there were two articles by Dobb on Marxism and social laws and the emergence of capitalism.

13 At the height of McCarthyism, 1949 to 1954 *Baran* published in the *Monthly Review* under a pen-name; and he was well protected relative to other academic Marxist economists. Moreover, in 1954 *Sweezy* was jailed by the State of New Hampshire for refusing to answer questions regarding the membership and activities of the Progressive Party, the contents of a lecture given at the University of New Hampshire, and whether he believed in communism. In 1957 the United States Supreme Court overturned the verdict (Sweezy 1965; Goldstein 1978; Foster 1987).

14 What this section and A.7 and A.8 in the Appendix make clear is that academic and non-academic Marxists existed in the 1950s. Thus Baran was not the only academic Marxist in the United States; and he may have not been the best academic Marxist. As noted in the previous chapter (note 42) May did first-class work on the labor theory of value and thus was Baran's equal if not better.

15 See Appendix, A.7, column F and A.8 column E. For example, *Dissent* published numerous articles by the non-academic economist *Ben B. Seligman*, who took a progressive-radical attitude towards the issue of monopolies and mergers, Marxian economics, and socialism. He also suggested, contra to the position held by many Marxists, that Keynesian theory as articulated by Keynes, Joan Robinson, and others and Marxian theory were not that different or incompatible with each other (Seligman 1955, 1956, 1958, 1959). In addition, *James O'Connor* argued that there was no Marxian theory of monopoly (O'Connor 1960).

16 Speaker bans at most colleges and universities were ignored, lifted or done away with by the mid-1960s, partly because of court rulings. Yet in 1963 only sixteen major universities had clearly stated policies allowing communists-radicals to speak on campus. Thus there was still considerable opposition both inside and outside academe to communists and Marxists speaking on campus. For example, considering the rebellious students who supported racial integration as the new communist threat, the North Carolina state legislature enacted such a ban in 1963 which stated that any state college or university that permitted a member of the Communist Party, or a person who advocated the overthrow of the United States government, or a person who used the Fifth Amendment to refuse to answer any questions regarding communism would lose its state funding. The administrators at the University of North Carolina acquiesced to the ban, collaborated with the State Bureau of Investigation and HUAC to enforce the ban, and used the ban to prevent any controversial speaker from appearing on campus. The Supreme Court struck down the act in 1968 (*Newsletter on Intellectual Freedom*, September 1963: 58, July 1964: 45, September 1965: 66, March 1966: 19, 22, May 1968: 37; Hamm 1997; Wynkoop 2002; Billingsley 1999).

17 This is clearly captured by the following ditty sung to the tune of "God Bless America" by a University of Texas economics graduate student:

> God bless free enterprise
> System divine,
> Stand beside her
> And guide her
> Just so long as the profits are mine,
> God bless Wall Street,
> May she flourish,
> Corporations,
> May they grow,
> God bless free enterprise,
> The sta-tus quo.

(Rossinow 1998: 132–33)

18 For example, see Carney (1967), Nell (1967a), and Gordon (1967).

19 Sponsors and supporters of the REP included *Douglas Dowd, Huberman, Seymour Melman,* and *Victor Perlo,* all active radical economists prior to 1960—see Appendix, A.7, A.8, and A.9. In addition, *Sweezy, David Bazelon, Robert Heilbroner,* and *Seligman* were identified as possible REP sponsors.

20 For example, at Michigan State University the SDSers met informally to discuss Marxism, imperialism and political theory. Independent of the REP, SDSers got together to study Marxism or in some cases to attend classes in Marxism at "free universities" that were established after 1965 as counter-institutions to the unfree, anti-radical conservative universities. In Boston in 1966 a group of SDSers got together to read and discuss Marx, focusing mostly on his earlier philosophical writings, but also on the economics for which they used Sweezy's *The Theory of Capitalist Development* as a guide. Again in 1967, the Harvard SDS in conjunction with The American Institute for Marxist Studies sponsored a series of lectures on Marxism and contemporary problems; one of the lectures was on monopoly capital, presented by *Sharpe* and commented on by *David Wheeler* and *David Levey* (Gordon 1966; Rossinow 1998; Sale 1974; *New Left Notes,* March 6, 1967; *AIMS Newsletter,* IV.2, March–April, 1967).

21 Interest in Marxism was also fueled by the emergence and growth of factional Marxist groups, such as the Progressive Labor Party; but their knowledge of Marxist economic theory was doctrinaire, simple, and minimal.

22 Part of the material in the preceding and following paragraphs comes from the Wilcox Collection of Contemporary Political Movements, which is part of the Kansas Collection located in the Kenneth Spencer Research Library at the University of Kansas. The specific material used came from the Radical Education Project (call number: RH WL Eph 2095), New University Conference (call numbers: RH WL D197, RH WL D206), Center for Marxist Education folder (call number: RH WL Eph 921), Center for Marxist Research folder (call number: RH WL Eph 922), American Institute for Marxist Studies folder (call number: RH WL Eph 165), and the Socialist Scholars Conference folder (call number: RH WL P42).

23 Evenitsky also planned to produce annotated bibliographies on Marxism and economics for the *AIMS Newsletter* but died before doing so.

24 Other more politically oriented journals emerged at the same time. One such journal was *New University Thought.* Established in 1960, its purpose was to publish articles that would be radical in their mode of analysis. Although few economic articles appeared in its pages, it did carry Don Villarejo's important article on stock ownership and the control of corporations and Melman's

article on the economics of armament and disarmament (Villarejo 1961, 1962; Melman 1962).

25 Like *Monthly Review*, *Dissent* also continued to publish popular economic articles for the intellectuals and activists in the 1960s, but with a progressive-radical attitude. Topics covered included economic policy, the impact of the military and the Vietnam War on the economy, the modern corporation, automation and unions, poverty, and the economic development of underdeveloped countries (Brand 1962; Seligman 1964, 1965, 1966; Beller 1967).

26 For the five years it was in existence, the SSC attracted not only socialist scholars but also many other people—unions members, white-collar workers, college students, and political and community activists. Thus, the attendance at the Conferences was large by any account: 1965—1000, 1966—over 2000, 1967— early 3000, 1968—600, 1969—800, and 1970—600. However, this mixed audience and participants meant the academics that lead it had difficulty dealing with discussion that dealt with political commitment. This conflict, which affected the SDS and the New Left in general, between socialist scholarship and the working towards new theories of social change and activism that was pushing semi-pragmatically toward change now, eventually resulted in its demise in 1970. In the early 1980s, the Socialist Scholars Conference was re-established—see http://www.socialistscholars.org/ (accessed June 19, 2007) (Buhle 1967; Fischer, et al. 1971).

27 The papers were published in Fischer (1971).

28 The *AIMS Newsletter* began with less than 200 subscribers in 1964 and had over 3000 by 1970.

29 The course description was the following:

> A close study of U.S. monopoly capitalism from its early through present forms. Modern methods of monopoly: price fixing, built-in inflation, increased exploitation, super-profits from discrimination. Who owns America, how giant corporations are controlled, role of stock market. Monopoly control of government: the tax system as indirect exploitation, subsidies to monopolies. Militarization of the economy. Anti-monopoly struggle: failure of trust-busters; tactical battles against racism, poverty, unemployment, etc. Concept of anti-monopoly coalition. Transfer of ownership and control to working class. Strategic goal of socialism.
>
> (Center for Marxist Education, Fall Term 1969, Schedule of Classes, Wilcox Collection, see footnote 19)

30 Members of the Party attempted to replicate AIMS and the Center for Marxist Education elsewhere in the country. For example, *Niebyl* set up the Center for Marxist Research in San Jose, California in 1974 along the lines of AIMS. Its purpose was to "fill a badly felt gap in the analytical and theoretical equipment of those who, having painfully become aware of the worldwide crisis of the capitalist economies and the resulting confusion and misorientation, want to understand the meaning and causes of these disastrous conditions in order to sanely and positively react to them." Hence it provided Marxist scholars with a well-equipped library, seminars, and a newsletter.

31 An example of an individual operating within this community of radical scholars is *Michael Lebowitz*. He became acquainted with *Science and Society* as an undergraduate at New York University's School of Commerce in the late 1950s. He then became an editor of *Studies on the Left* in the 1960s in which he also published. Finally, he participated in the Socialist Scholars Conferences (Parry et al. 1986; Appendix, A.9).

32 The figures are derived from A.9 in the Appendix. A core radical-Marxist economist has two or more entries in columns A—G, while a fellow traveler has only a single entry.

33 Shortly after the July 1967 conference, a number of radical academics in the humanities, social sciences, and physical sciences at the University of Michigan thought of setting up a radical scholars group, but nothing came of their efforts.

34 The objective of the NUC was to assist radicals who work in and around institutions of higher education in their efforts to create a new American form of socialism and a complementary non-repressive educational system. As part of its activities, it established a speakers' bureau. Although URPE members, Arthur MacEwan and Ted Behr, were involved in the NUC and MacEwan a listed speaker, URPE as an organization had little official contact with it. The NUC was disbanded in 1974.

35 Although not clearly perceived and articulated, New Left economists also felt that neoclassical theory promoted a war mentality, as exhibited in the guns and butter production possibilities curve example found in textbooks. Rejecting war, they responded with a marijuana and butter production possibilities curve. As noted in the previous chapter, World War II and the Cold War contributed significantly to post-war legitimation and support of neoclassical theory (Bernstein 2001).

36 Participants in at least one of the meetings included Jim Bass, John Bishop, Barry Bluestone, John Edgren, William Fleischman, Sol Jacobson, Sandy Kelman, Craig Morgan, Dean Sanders, Larry Sawers, Howard Wachtel, Michael Zweig, and Lane Vanderslice (Wachtel and Vanderslice 1973).

37 The participants also identified issues that were either ignored in neoclassical economics or were treated in an inadequate fashion, including imperialism and foreign economic policy of the United States, American national planning, contemporary political economy, and centralization versus decentralization in economic and political affairs (Wachtel and Vanderslice 1973).

38 The issue of pursuing traditional academic roles versus working for the movement was discussed as well, but with no resolution.

39 Independent of the activity at Michigan, a group of graduate students and young professors at Harvard in 1968, including Samuel Bowles, Arthur MacEwan, Thomas Weisskopf, Richard Edwards, Michael Reich, Stephen Marglin, Herbert Gintis, Stephan Michelson, and Patricia Quick, were engaged in seminars and conversations to develop an approach to economics that, unlike neoclassical economics, could illuminate rather than ignore or obfuscate their political concerns with racism, sexism, imperialism, injustice, and the alienation of labor. They tried out their ideas in a collectively taught course on "The Capitalist Economy: Conflict and Power." They subsequently joined and became extremely active in URPE (Arestis and Sawyer 2000; Edwards et al. 1970).

40 A short digression on the use of the words in the name is appropriate here. First, "Union" was preferred over "Association" since it reflected the basic objective of the group to unite liked-minded radicals. Second, as noted above, the activists in the 1960s preferred the label "Radical" because of its inclusiveness. Hence a radical economist could be a Marxist economist as well as an economist who used Marxian theory and Institutionalist theory and even neoclassical theory. The common feature of all radical economists was their critical view of American capitalism and the need for economic theory to address important economic-social problems. As for "Economics" as opposed to economy, the answer is twofold. First "political economy" was at that time just another way of saying Marxism and the founders did not want to restrict their Union to just Marxists. The second reason is that the founders saw themselves as economists who did economics and more specifically as political economists, as opposed to the usual dry, technocratic, apolitical mainstream economist, who did political economics. Lastly, it was felt that URPE should be a union "for Radical Political Economists"

and not a union "of Radical Political Economists" since the founders wanted to welcome and include activist oriented individuals with an interest in economics. Thus the Union for Radical Political Economics is simply a self-description of the founders and what they organized (Mata 2005: 67).

41 Topics covered at the conference included (1) neo-capitalism, (2) Cuba as a model for economic development, (3) the political development of under-development, (4) decentralized socialism, (5) the relevance of Marxist, neo-classical, and Institutionalist economic analysis to current problems, (6) what is wrong with the way economics is being taught and applied, and (7) what can academic economists do for the Movement (*New Left Notes* November 11, 1968).

42 Ten papers were presented at the Conference on the American economy and contemporary economics, poverty in the domestic economy, economic development and the international economy, and organizational activity. The reason the conference was held in Philadelphia was its organizers decided to piggy-back on the AEA job market that was being held. And the latter was being held in Philadelphia because many of the job market candidates would not go to the Chicago ASSA meetings in protest of the Chicago's police attack upon demonstrators during the August Democratic National Convention. Not wanting their students not to get jobs, professors from the University of Michigan and other institutions got the AEA to agree to have the Philadelphia job market.

43 At the 1968 meetings there were sessions on income distribution, economics of empire, urban political economy, development of a radical theory, relations between rich and poor countries, economic contradictions in historical perspective, political economy of inequality, and comparative economic development in socialist countries; and in the two panel sessions were on teaching and the political economy of women's liberation. At the 1969 meetings, there was a report on the status of blacks and women in the economics profession, a session on teaching, and workshops on economic theory, development-international-imperialism, urban-poverty-racism, and monopoly capital.

44 For example, the first issue of the *Newsletter* announced a "neat new graduate program in economics" at SUNY Stony Brook in which there were opportunities to study imperialism, class relations, property, and domestic colonialism in the ghetto. In the following summer 1969 issue the *Newsletter* announced that the economics department at American University hired URPE members Larry Sawers and Howard Wachtel; while the winter 1970 issue announced that American University added an option on the political economy of social change to the Ph.D. economics program. It is of interest to note that the political economy graduate program at New School for Social Research was not introduced until Fall 1971.

45 The *Newsletter* carried course outlines on economic development, American capitalism and social alternatives, urban economics, studies in labor insurgency, and ideology and social change.

46 URPE also published the papers given at the 1968 conference (Wachtel and Bluestone 1969) as well as three occasional papers. In addition to the *Review* there were other often short-lived radical journals that published economic articles by URPE members. One such journal was *Ripsaw*, a journal of radical criticism and analysis published by Columbia University graduate students. It published articles by Edel, Zweig, and Surkin, all members of URPE (see Appendix, A.9).

47 For example, see Wachtel and Bluestone (1969), Michelson (1969b), Weaver (1969), Sclar (1969), Behr (1969a), Herman (1969), McKelvey (1969), Hinckley (1969), Brooks (1970), Sawers and Weaver (1970), Anonymous (1970).

48 In these formative years, URPE had an ambivalent attitude about the usefulness of neoclassical economic theory:

> For some of us [members of URPE], although the tools of formal economics appear to have their uses, the basic questions of neoclassical economics appear wrong, in that they take for given in their parameters the very institutions of society, and the attitudes imposed on the individual by society, which we are challenging. The American celebration implicit in the notion of a grand Neoclassical Synthesis seems to us a cruel sham. Some members of URPE consider furthermore that traditional economics is not merely more limited in its uses than most curricula imply: it may be a distinct social evil, in that it trains students to avoid the larger questions relating to capitalist institutions and modes of decision making, and inhibits the challenging of these institutions and their operations.
>
> (*URPE Newsletter*, vol. 1.4: 12–13; also see the interchange between Zweig (1969 and 1971) and Weeks (1969) as well as Salmans (1970))

In contrast, the Bay Area Collective of Socialist Economists issued a manifesto in August 1969 in which it rejected neoclassical economic theory and argued that Marxism should replace it:

> Dissent within economics which aspires to become a revolutionary ideology must fight and win its battles in economic theory before it can become a real threat to the corporate ruling class. Success or failure on the economic battlefield marks the difference between a revolutionary theory and merely a cultural protest. It is no accident that the Marxist tradition, which offers the only revolutionary potential, has been first and foremost grounded in political economy. It follows that any attempt to revive, rejuvenate, and reassert Marxism as a revolutionary theory must prove itself on this battlefield.
>
> (Fuchs et al. 1969: 17; also see Weaver 1970)

49 The tension between academics and activists did not ceased—see for example Dowd (1982).
50 A similar process took place in the United Kingdom—see Chapter 6.
51 Western or European Marxism was only beginning to affect the thinking of American radical and Marxist economists at the end of the 1960s. Thus, its influence on the pluralistic tendency in URPE and its formation was minimal. However, this was not the case after 1970.
52 The previous generation of radical-Marxist economists that became involved in URPE included Dowd, Magdoff, Melman, O'Connor, Perlo, Howard Sherman, and Sweezy (see Appendix, A.9).

4 The contested landscape of American economics, 1965–80

1 Indicative of this prior to 1970 is, as argued in Chapter 2, the near total absence of Ph.D. granting economic departments that offered fields in social economics, Institutional economics, or political economy (that is radical-Marxist economics) or that incorporated heterodox economic theory directly into their core theory courses, with the University of Texas perhaps being the exception.
2 This was and is also the attitude of neoclassical economists towards feminist economics and feminist economists; that is, for example, "A feminist economist will be a bad economist" (Albelda 1997: 100). Consequently, like the other heterodox approaches, feminist economists have had a negligible impact on neoclassical theory.
3 Harry Johnson made a similar statement to Joan Robinson when rejecting her submission on the capital controversy to the *Journal of Political Economy*. In the

letter to Robinson, Johnson stated that the Cambridge England school deliberately or unwitting did not understand the neoclassical model of general equilibrium. He further claimed that their critique of neoclassical general equilibrium theory and proposed replacement with Sraffa's "production of commodities by means of commodities" help perpetuate the myth that Marxism was a scientific subject and not an emotional religious movement. Finally he proposed that Robinson should submit her paper to a journal for the amateur intellectual or to an obscure journal whose readers would not have heard of the Cambridge controversies. And this attitude was not restricted to academe as indicated by the Board of Education in Roselle, New Jersey proudly banning the purchase of *The Affluent Society* by Galbraith and *The Age of Keynes* by R. Lekachman because they supported "permissive liberalism" (Johnson 1971b; *Newsletter for Intellectual Freedom*, September 1972: 147; Karolides 2006).

4 A well-known case of harassment of radical graduate students occurred at Columbia in 1970 when an uninvited Harold Barger attended a course taught by *Lawrence Tharp*. In addition, while teaching at MIT as an assistant professor, circa 1970, *Duncan Foley* mentioned to a senior colleague that Pareto criterion was irrelevant to real political debate; and his colleague's response was that if Foley really believed that he should get out of economics. Then there were also the not-so-well-known cases of Bard College firing *Laurence Shute* in 1966 for his radicalism, Occidental College not renewing *Shaffer*'s contract and Washington University not renewing *Judith Shapiro*'s and *Jeff Morris*'s contracts because of their opposition to the Vietnam War and/or the kind of economics they taught, and of the University of Connecticut economics department attempt to dismiss *William Tabb* in 1969 because of his political writings (even though he had a significant number of economic publications) and anti-war activism. Finally, there are the unknown number of cases in which a department refuses to continue an appointment of an "all but dissertation" instructor on the grounds of not completing his/her dissertation, but was also heavily influenced by the instructor's unacceptable involvement in the New Left/anti-war movement and in Marxian-heterodox economics, such as the case of *David Levey* at Yale in 1969. It should be noted that neoclassical economists often deny that these events took place in the 1960s and early 1970s. However, in the disciplines of history, political science, and sociology the old-guard acted precisely the same way towards their radicals, calling them amateurs and intellectually ill-prepared and unfit to be teaching in a university. Hence they were denied tenured and/or outright fired. In short, economics was not an isolated case; rather the attitudes and behavior of neoclassical economists was no different from their conservative-mainstream colleagues in other disciplines or from conservative-minded administrators who attempted to fire communist academics or academics involved in the anti-Vietnam War movement. Finally, it should be noted that the FBI responded to the rise of radicalism and Marxism in the academic community by investigating the radical academic caucuses and cooperating with universities (such as MIT) in matters of faculty appointments and promotions through providing information on the subversive-radical nature of the candidates (Tharp 1970; Arestis and Sawyer 2000; Foley 1999; Wolfe 1971; Nicolaus 1973; Wiener 1989; Shute 2002; Keen 1999; Novick 1988; *Newsletter for Intellectual Freedom*, November 1969: 93, January 1970: 6, November 1971: 128, March 1973: 37, July 1975: 111; Shaffer 2002, 2004; Levey 2004; Stein 1973; Shapiro 2005; Tabb 2004; Diamond 1992).

5 For example, for seven of the leading economic departments—Chicago, Columbia, Harvard, Michigan, Stanford, UC-Berkeley, and Wisconsin (see Table 2.2)—relatively few of the full, associate, and even assistant professors took a positive stance against the Vietnam War; but it was somewhat otherwise for the graduate students. Moreover, relative to other social sciences and humanities disciplines

(except for Political Science), economists were more conservative with respect to radical student activities and racism. Apparently 80 percent of economists did not believe that "white racism was the cause of black riots," while 58 percent of economists did not believe that most colleges and universities were racists. It was this same discipline where in the 1950s over 50 percent of its members believed that a communist was not fit to be a teacher and should be dismissed from academia (McCaughey 1976; Ladd and Lipset 1975). Of course there were exceptions, such as the economists listed in the Appendix, A.9.

6 Such an attitude was also the response in the 1990s to undergraduates who were ardent feminists and wanted to pursue economics at the graduate level (Albelda 1997).

7 The case of *Clinton Jencks* is of interest in this respect. He obtained a B.A. in economics in 1939 from the University of Colorado. After the war, he became a labor organizer for the left-wing International Union of Mine, Mill and Smelter Workers. As part of his activities, Jencks held steward's training sessions where he introduced the attendees to the basics of Marxian economic theory. McCarthyism and especially the Federal government throughout the 1950s persecuted Jencks; as a result he became blacklisted and politically unemployable. Consequently he went back to graduate school and obtained a Ph.D. in economics from the University of California-Berkeley in 1964, but not before being harassed again for his left-wing activities by the government. He obtained a position at San Diego State College where he received tenure in 1967, but not before having to explain his run-in with the government to the college president. Apparently to avoid controversial issues, Jencks did his dissertation on the "Impact of Nationalization on Working Conditions of British Coal Miners" and his initial publications were in this area. Towards the end of the 1960s with the somewhat leftward shift in the political environment, he began research on the history of his former union. However, it does not appear that he joined the Union for Radical Political Economics or other heterodox activities. As a result his left-wing leanings were effectively squashed when it came to economics, although he remained an active union organizer (Williamson 1970; Schrecker 1998; Fariello 1995: 380–90; Baker 2007).

8 For example, circa 1965 after universities received his reference letters, *Lebowitz* did not get second interviews because one of them stated that he was a non-conformist in attire and politics (Lebowitz 2002).

9 One poignant example is found in a letter *E. Kay Hunt* sent to Joan Robinson:

> My leftist views and my strong capital controversy have created strong opposition to my tenure. One senior professor in our department (Carl Uhr) has publicly made the statement that anyone "who takes the Robinson-Sraffa view on the capital controversy deserves tenure only in the state mental hospital."
>
> (Hunt 1972)

Hunt did, however, receive tenure. This attitude was not restricted to economics, as in the well-known case of the University of California versus Angela Davis (circa 1970) and in the lesser-known case at the University of Texas of the non-renewal of a contract of a philosopher who had made some revolutionary statements, or to American universities. Moreover, women economists were in general discriminated against; and the discrimination became twice as severe (so to speak) if the woman economist was also a feminist economist. In addition, when considered for tenure, the decision could have easily included sexual fantasies about her body, as did occur in other disciplines. Finally, heterodox female economists had a greater chance of being denied tenure than heterodox male economists, even in departments where the latter were present. For example, while the scarcity of tenured heterodox feminist economists in mainstream economic departments is not surprising, the fact that there were no tenured female economists (heterodox feminist or otherwise) at University of Massachusetts-Amherst circa 1980 is (Meranto, Meranto, and Lippman 1985; Rossinow 1998; Horn 1999; Albelda 1997; Stimpson 2000; Shackelford 2002 and personal conversation).

10 The immediate response to the decision was complaints by undergraduate and graduate students of the absence of courses taught from a radical or Marxist perspective. Although the Department listened to them, it essentially refused to act on the complaint. But some senior members of the department did not like the decision and steps were taken to get *Herbert Gintis* an untenured associate professor position in the department (which was unpopular among some of the faculty, such as Alexander Gerschenkron who was absolutely contemptuous of radical students who questioned the status quo, Harvard University, and the Vietnam War). However, Gintis left in 1974 to take a tenure position at the University of Massachusetts-Amherst and join in the building of the program of political economy and Marxism (and *Tom Weisskopf*, also a radical economist, left in 1972 to take a tenure position at the University of Michigan). The only radical economist who remained in the department by 1975 was *Stephen Marglin* who obtained tenure before getting interested in and identified with radical economics. Yet some of the senior faculty still felt that it was important to have a Marxist-radical economist on staff; thus William Lazonick was hired in 1975 followed by Julie Schor in 1985. When she left in the early 1990s, the position was not filled, leaving Marglin as the only radical economist at Harvard (Lazonick 2004; Lipset 1975).

11 In 1974, the AEA established a Committee on Political Discrimination. It examined the Quick case and found that political grounds were not the basis for not renewing her contract but rather it was the poor quality of her Harvard dissertation. It also examined the San Jose 3 case and found that they were victims of university politics not "political discrimination. "In general, the Committee acquiesced to political discrimination because it was supposedly too difficult to prove but more accurately due to the fact that radical-heterodox economists had violated professional-scholarship norms which made it impossible for the economists on the Committee to view the victims as bona fide economists. Consequently the harassment, discrimination, and exclusion directed at Marxists, radicals-progressives, and heterodox economists did not stop in 1975, as the cases of Herbert Aptheker (1976) and Bertell Ollman (1978) clearly indicated as well as the fact that David Landes did not obtain a full-time tenure track position again until 2001. Charges of corny theory and inadequate research, rejection for being a radical-socialist, a climate of fear and suppression, and the denial of tenure or non-renewal of contract of radical-heterodox voices also continued unabated through the 1970s and on into the 1980s and 1990s, as indicated by the cases of *Gunnar Tomasson* (Harvard University), *David Levine* (Yale University), and *Rob Wright* (Napa Valley Community College) (Blecker 2002; Tomasson 2001; Richardson 1982; MARHO 1978; Schrecker 1979; Meranto, Meranto, and Lippman 1985; Coyle 2002; Parenti 1995).

12 Such harassment was also caused by groups outside the university, as in the case of the John Birch Society threatening *W. Robert Brazelton*, a heterodox economist, at the University of Missouri-Kansas City for teaching about the USSR in his comparative-systems course. The threat was credible enough for police protection to be supplied.

13 As for labor economics, starting in the 1950s successful efforts were made to marginalize contributions from Institutional economists and the imperfect

competition/non-market-clearing paradigm of John Dunlop, Clark Kerr, Richard Lester, Lloyd Reynolds and the Cambridge Group. In their place was substituted a neoclassical perfect competition market clearing approach that turned labor economics into a branch of applied neoclassical microeconomics. For example, the transformation of labor economics at Wisconsin from an Institutionalist to a neoclassical approach between 1957 and 1970 resulted in the complete cleansing of the former and the complete hegemony of the latter (Kaufman 2001, 2004; Boyer and Smith 2000; Cain 1993).

14 The intention of such and similar discriminatory requirements was to destroy the heterodox field and/or to prevent graduate students from specializing in heterodox economic theory—as did occur at Yale and Rutgers.

15 An interesting example of this was the Cornell economics department efforts to prevent graduate students from participating in the special field called the "Program in Participation, and Labor Managed Systems." When initially started, the Program was fairly mainstream in terms of method and theory; but by the end of the 1970s it had become interdisciplinary, eclectic, and pluralistic-heterodox in method and theory as well as critical of neoclassical theory. This was due in part to solidaristic-oriented graduate students becoming involved in the program. To curb this eclectic-heterodox interest of its graduate students, the economics department used its power of the allocation of assistantships (with tuition waiver and support) back by a Chicago-style qualifying exam process to determine eligibility for the assistantships and carried out a negative campaign against the Program to ensure that no assistantship was given to a graduate student interested in the Program. Given such discriminatory and vehement opposition to the Program, it is not surprising that the department eventually eliminated it. However, its ethos continues in the International Association for the Economics of Participation (Rock 2002).

16 Some well-established academic economists, such as Wassily Leontief, objected to the methods used by economic departments to maintain intellectual orthodoxy, but they were ignored (Leontief 1982; Du Boff 2002; Golden 1975).

17 For example, there was the experience of Richard Lester at the hands of acting *American Economic Review* editor Fritz Machlup in 1946 (however, his paper was published by Paul Homan, who replaced Machlup as editor). This was repeated in 1964, when the editor of the *Journal of Political Economy* refused to publish a paper by Gardiner Means attacking the findings of DePodwin and Seldon (1963). And it was repeated again in 1974 when the editor of the *Review* rejected a paper by Means responding to criticisms by George Stigler and James Kindahl (1973) (Lee 1984, 1999a).

18 In his 1980 report as the managing editor of the *Review*, Borts noted that not many heterodox papers were submitted to the journal over the previous decade and most of those were rejected because they were not of high quality (which he claimed *a priori* to be the case in 1972) and because his referees, who did not approve of heterodox economics, did not want to allocate journal space to heterodox articles—which in fact violated the editorial policy Borts put forth in 1972. A case in point was the rejection of *Anwar Shaikh*'s 1973 paper on the transformation problem on the grounds that it was unsuitable for the *Review*. His solution to the issue was that heterodox economists should just publish in their own journals (Borts 1972, 1981; Shaikh 1973; Mata 2005).

19 In the 1950s several of the Presidents-elect, such as Calvin Hoover, Edwin Witte, Morris Copeland, and George Stocking, were pre-war Institutionalists and hence sympathetic to heterodox views and put on heterodox sessions at the annual conference. But the 1960s saw a succession of Presidents-elect, such as Paul Samuelson, Gottfried Haberler, George Stigler, Fritz Machlup, and Milton Friedman, who had little or no interest in heterodox economics, with the consequence

that there were fewer and fewer heterodox sessions and heterodox economists as participants.

20 This concerted campaign against the very existence of heterodox economics and heterodox economists appears as institutionalized pathological behavior since the number of Ph.D. programs in the 1970s with a heterodox component of any discernable sort number less than twenty-five out of the 120 that existed and with a major heterodox component number less than ten—see Tables 4.1 and 4.2. Moreover, since the total number Ph.D.s in economics awarded by the "major" and "minor" heterodox programs was less than 5 percent and 15 percent respectively of the 8502 Ph.D.s in economics and econometrics awarded from 1971 to 1980 (see Appendix, A.2) and since not all graduates of these programs were heterodox economists, it is quite likely that the total number Ph.D.s awarded to heterodox economists was no more than 5 percent. With such small numbers, why would neoclassical economists care—except that the ideological agenda accepted in 1900, which is now so deeply institutionalized, makes them care and hence makes them intolerant and anti-pluralistic.

21 There are a number of short articles covering the histories of AFEE, URPE, and ASE since 1970 and the formation of AFIT in 1979—see Bush (1991), Davis (1999), Fleck (1999), O'Hara (1995, 1999b), Sturgeon (1981), Mata (2005).

22 An example of an unsuccessful effort is the University of Houston. Efforts to make Institutionalism a major component of the doctoral program started in 1967 when E. E. Liebhafsky became chair of the department, followed by Milton Lower and Tom DeGregori. However, the situation never stabilized for a number of reasons, including the complete opposition to anything Institutionalist by a group of orthodox true believers. They gained control of the department in 1973 and that was the end of Institutionalism in the doctoral program. In the first three years of the experiment, several of the Institutionalist graduate students were active in SDS which suggests that this Institutionalist experiment was abetted and supported by student activism (Ciscel 2004; DeGregori 2004).

23 Similar efforts were made in Canadian universities, such as the nearly twenty-year effort, 1962 to 1980, by heterodox economists at the University of Manitoba to build a cohort of professors, establish heterodox courses, and to establish an explicit department policy embracing methodological pluralism (Pentland 1977; Baragar 2004).

24 Texas was ranked as a distinguished economics department in 1934, but declined to adequate plus in the 1960s—see Table 2.4 and Appendix A.6.

25 In the late 1960s, the economic history course (which was a required course) took a Marxist and Institutionalist approach, the history of economic thought course (which was also required) was influenced by Marx, Veblen, and other heterodox economists, and the economic development course was influenced by Marx, Baran, Sweezy, and Magdoff.

26 In the early 1980s, UC-Riverside's faculty included Howard Sherman, Victor Lippit, Robert Pollin, Frederic Lee, and Nai-Pew Ong which produced a Marxist-Institutionalist-Post Keynesian continuum of heterodox courses.

27 The interest of the graduate students in heterodox economics at these programs is in part indicated by the existence of URPE chapters (which comprised mostly graduate students) at five of the universities.

28 The Institutionalist economists at Nebraska, Greg Hayden, Wallace Peterson, and Jerry Petr, established a field in Institutional Economics, but the history of this effort is unknown (Fullwiler 2002).

29 Apparently, the initial groups of student radicals gave James Tobin a hard time in his theory course by asking questions such as "what is capital?" that he refused to teach it again for a number of years.

30 In early 1971, Yale invited Sweezy to give a seminar in Marxian economics, but he declined saying that the department should hire a young Marxist economist to give it.
31 Because existing faculty and graduate student interest were essential for establishing and maintaining the heterodox minor component in the Ph.D. programs of the thirteen departments, retirement and denial of tenure combined with non-replacement, the drop in graduate student interest by the late 1980s, and pressure from mainstream faculty to limit the field meant that the Institutionalist component of the graduate programs at Oklahoma, Maryland, and Tennessee disappeared in the 1980s and the 1990s while the heterodox fields at Michigan, Stanford, Berkeley, and Yale were abolished by the mid-1990s (Blecker 2002; Weisskopf 2002; Bernstein 2002).
32 In addition, Dan Kanel and the Wisconsin department of agricultural economics supported Institutional perspectives. In 2004 a section in Institutional and Behavioral Economics was established within the American Agricultural Economics Association.
33 See Schmid (2004) for a more substantive delineation of Institutionalism at Michigan State.
34 Because of the absence of information regarding the efforts of heterodox economists at the level of solely M.A. programs, it is not possible to say if this list is complete or not.
35 Of the remaining four departments, Nebraska and Tennessee appeared to have eliminated heterodoxy out of spite, while there is no evidence on why heterodoxy disappeared at Oklahoma and Temple.

5 The history of Post Keynesian economics in America, 1971–95

1 Although not discussed here, it is clear that the Cambridge capital controversy of the 1960s contributed significantly to the construction of the Post Keynesian identity and hence contributed to the making of a Post Keynesian community in the United States (and in Britain)—see Mata (2005).
2 To illustrate this, Howard Sherman remembers that an Institutionalist sitting next to Joan Robinson had said:

> "We all agree that there should be vast changes in Economics. The most important thing is to get rid of all of this abstract theory and begin with institutional description." Of course, the first sentence was true. The second sentence was silly, especially sitting next to one of the greatest abstract theorists. It does illustrate the gap I felt between the institutionalists and all of the rest.
>
> (Sherman 1994)

Davidson also noted that:

> I was disappointed with the results of our meeting ... I believe we need some famous economist, who is highly visible, to champion the cause of opening up our profession. Unfortunately no one at our meeting, who met my visibility requirement, was willing to make the necessary effort.
>
> (Davidson 1972a)

Whether Eichner was naive in his expectations is debatable. It is possible that his optimism helped convinced heterodox economists to participate in the emerging social network of Post Keynesian economists.

3 Despite Galbraith's sympathy, Eichner's attempt to get the AER opened to heterodox articles was completely unsuccessful. He also tried to get the AEA annual
conference open to sessions on Post Keynesian economics and was similarly
unsuccessful. Rebuffed by the AEA and faced with increasing number of cases of
discriminatory and exclusionary actions by neoclassical economists and mainstream
journals, Eichner became more and more inclined to take positive and independent
steps towards establishing Post Keynesian economics (Lee 2000a).

4 For example, Davidson (1965) used the term to refer to literature on monetary
theory published after 1945.

5 The neoclassical connotation of post-Keynesian definition declined in use in the
1970s and by 1980 it had died.

6 In his 1969–70 correspondence with Robinson, Eichner also used neo-Keynesian
and Anglo-Italian interchangeably with post-Keynesian (Lee 2000a).

7 In October 1972, Eichner referred to it as the anti-neoclassical group. Two months
later the group adopted the name Political Economy Club (Lee 2000a).

8 Due perhaps to her growing disenchantment with the Cambridge–Kalecki–Pasinetti
line of theorizing, Robinson by the late 1970s became bothered with Eichner's
relatively narrow view as what constituted Post Keynesian economics. Davidson
agreed with Robinson's assessment:

> I know what you mean regarding Al Eichner's attempt to straight jacket
> what Post-Keynesians School means. If you will note Al always uses a hypen
> between the Post and the Keynesian and we at the journal have specifically
> removed the hypen. It is a subtle way to suggest that Post Keynesian in our
> view of the JPKE is much broader than Post Keynesian in the view of Al
> Eichner.
>
> (Davidson 1979; Robinson 1979)

9 The newsletter, which lasted for twenty-seven months and was sent out in January
1972, April 1972, September 1972, February 1973, November 1973, and March
1974, was warmly received and Eichner was commended for his efforts (Lee
2000a; Wachtel 1973).

10 Nell conceived of the textbook at the New Orleans meeting. It was eventually
published in 1980 as *Growth, Profits, and Property: essays in the revival of political
economy*.

11 Eichner gave a paper on "Outline for a New Paradigm in Economics," and
Minsky on "An Alternative to the Neo-Classical Paradigm: one view" (Lee
2000a).

12 The first meeting was held at New School but only Eichner, Nell, Frank Roosevelt, and one other showed up. The purpose of the meeting was to discuss what
was the best way forward in terms of developing an alternative paradigm and to
open up the economics profession to dissident viewpoints. Perhaps this was due to
the lack of interest of URPE members in Post Keynesian economics. It was at this
time that Anwar Shaikh was expelled from the URPE-New York chapter for his
sympathies with Sraffa and the Cantabrigians. This was the same period that he
was working on his "infamous" humbug production function paper (Mata 2005;
Lee 2000a; Roosevelt 1975; Shaikh 1974).

13 At the session Nell gave a paper on "The Implications of the Sraffa Model" and
Eichner spoke on "Development and Pricing in the Megacorp" (Lee 2000a).

14 Howard Sherman chaired the session and Roosevelt gave his well-known paper
"Marxian vs. Cantabrigian Economics: a critique of Piero Sraffa, Joan Robinson
and company" (URPE 1974c).

15 Examples of papers on or related to Post Keynesian topics given at URPE sessions
from 1975 to 1983:

Title	Year	Author
Neoclassical, Neo-Ricardians, and Marx	1975	A. Medio
Classical Theories of the Allocation of Surplus Output vs. Neoclassical Theories of the Allocation of Given Resources	1976	V. Walsh and H. Graham
Neoclassical Economics and the Origins of Modern Political Economy	1977	J. Clifton
Keynes and Equilibrium Economics	1977	N. Shapiro
Reading General Equilibrium Theory: a critique of the Arrow–Debru approach	1977	J. Eatwell
Production, Reproduction, Gifts and Commodities	1979	J. Eatwell
Monopoly, Inflation and Economic Crisis	1980	D. Kotz
Marx's Theory of Credit	1980	C. Niggle
Inflation: the Keynesian contribution to the crisis in accumulation	1981	M. Zweig
Credit Expansion and the Reproduction of Crisis in the U.S.	1981	B. Pollin

Sources: URPE 1975b, 1977a, 1977b, 1979, 1980b, 1981.

16 As Howard Sherman notes " ... one of the few pleasures of going to national conventions over many years was meeting Eichner. We never arranged anything, but we often bumped into each other and had some good talks" (Sherman 1994).
17 For the fascinating story about the textbook, see King and Millmow (2003).
18 Other participants in the seminar included Anwar Shaikh, Nell, Roy Rotheim, Eileen Applebaum, Kregel, Stephen Rousseas, Ingrid Rima, and nineteen other economists. Of the thirty-two participants, only fourteen came from universities and colleges located in New York City.
19 In recent years, some Post Keynesians have argued that the contributions of Sraffa and the Sraffians and Kalecki and the Kaleckians are not part of Post Keynesian economics. That position was not entertained by virtually all economists that contributed to the building of Post Keynesian economics from 1971 to 1995. Moreover, the development of Post Keynesian microeconomics was influenced by Kalecki and Sraffa. (Lee 1998; Davidson 2003–4, 2005; Lavoie 2005, 2006; King 2002, 2005a; Tymoigne and Lee 2003–4).
20 Illustrative of the theme of the conference was the paper presented by Kregel, entitled "Sraffa's Theory of Prices and the Post-Keynesian Theory of Price Change and Inflation."
21 The heresy was, in Weintraub's view, the original ideas of Keynes and their extension in the area of theory and their application to economic policy (Davidson 1998).
22 Kenneth Boulding was a little unhappy with the name of the journal and was concerned that it might compete with the *Journal of Economic Issues* which, he felt, might prove fatal to both journals (Boulding 1977).
23 As noted in Chapter 2, Sharpe was an economic graduate student at Michigan who was a victim of McCarthyism—see note 40.
24 Those who contributed the seed money became the initial board of editors.
25 Michele Naples was also hired in 1978 by Douglass College. Other heterodox economists at Rutgers in this period included James Street (University), Bruce Steinberg (Livingston), Lourdes Beneria (Livingston), Patricia Linton (Douglass), and Margret Andrews (Cook). The total number of mainstream economists numbered more than seventy.
26 The tangible outcome of CEAR was its nineteen working papers, of which five were co-authored by graduate students, six given at conferences, and six published.

27 Davidson also applied for NSF grants and was rejected for the same reason (Davidson in King 1995a).
28 The book reviews included Kregel's *The Reconstruction of Political Economy*, Ian Steedman's *Marx After Sraffa*, John Cornwall's *Modern Capitalism*, Weintraub's *Capitalism, Inflation, and Unemployment*, Alessandro Roncaglia's *Sraffa and the Theory of Prices*, and Harris's *Capital Accumulation and Income Distribution* (Malizia 1975; Mumy 1979; Barkin 1980; Keenan 1980; Steinberg 1981; Michl 1982).
29 Brazelton presented earlier versions of the paper at the 1979 and 1980 annual meetings of the Association for Institutional Thought (AFIT): "Keynesian Economic Theory, the Post-Keynesian Neoclassical Synthesis and Recent Critical Analysis" (1979) and "The Foundations of Post-Keynesian Economics" (1980). In the latter paper, he identified Davidson, Eichner, Minsky, and Weintraub and argued that "the essential point of post Keynesian analysis is that the economy is a more complex, institutionalized, indeterminate and 'spirited' animal than the prevailing, orthodox, 'Keynesian,' analysis (which misinterprets Keynes) assumes" (Brazelton 1981b: 86). Moreover, in 1979 and 1980, AFIT sponsored sessions specifically oriented to Post Keynesian economics: "Post-Keynesian Economics: creative synthesis or anachronistic creation," and "Keynes and Economic Policy." Interest in Post Keynesian economics was also evident at the 1983 meetings where there was a session on "Institutional Economics and the Economics of Keynes" and Peter Lichtenstein gave a paper on "Post-Keynesian Economics: future prospects" where he boldly stated that Post Keynesian economics was a unique blend of Keynesian, Institutional, and Marxian economic theory (AFIT 1979, 1980, 1983; Lichtenstein 1986).
30 Papers on or related to Post Keynesian topics give at AFEE sessions for 1979, 1980, 1982, and 1983:

Title	Year	Author
A Monetary Theory of Production: Keynes and the Institutionalists	1979	D. Dillard
Modern Capitalism and the Trend toward Deindustrialization	1979	J. Cornwall
Capitalist Financial Processes and the Instability of Capitalism	1979	H. Minsky
Elements of Post Keynesian Analyses: an institutional connection?	1980	R. Brazelton
Why Economics is not yet a Science	1982	A. Eichner
Institutionalism, Post Keynesianism, and Neo-Marxism: an evaluation	1983	A. Gruchy

Sources: AFEE 1979, 1980, 1982, 1983.

31 Solidarists are Catholic economists who promote an alternative socio-economic organization where emphasis is placed on the dignity of the individual, cooperation in the workplace, and solidarity in the decision-making apparatus directed to the common good of the whole society (Waters 1988; Thanawala 1996).
32 The two papers presented by Post Keynesians were "The Micro Foundations of the Corporate Economy" by Eichner and "Kalecki and Power" by Miles Groves (ASE 1983).
33 Grant taught a course with the title "Contemporary Political Economy: Problems of Advanced Capitalism as Viewed by post-Keynesians and Marxists" (Grant 1977a).

34 Grant died in 1983 and his position at Roosevelt University was filled the following year by Frederic Lee.

35 Others in the group include Johan Deprez, Esther Gesick, Radhika Balakrishnan, Fritz Efaw, Fiona MacLachlan, Mary Merva, William Gaynor, and Steven Gabel. It should be noted that some were well acquainted with Marx but had not heard of Post Keynesian economics; but they were delighted when they discovered it.

36 For example, Lee wrote class papers on "Normal Cost Pricing and the Capital Controversy" and "Market Prices and Cost of Production Prices." In addition, in early 1981 a seminar was set up by Lee and other graduate students where professors and graduate students were invited to give talks critically evaluating particular aspects of neoclassical economics. Speakers and topics included Toshio Ogata on the "notion of competition in Marshall and Cournot," James Street on "neoclassical, Institutional, and structural approaches to economic development," Davidson on "money and neoclassical economics," and Eichner on "theory of aggregate distribution in neoclassical economics" (Lee 1981a, 1981b; Ogata 1981).

37 For example, see Lee (1981d), Carvalho (1984–85), Deprez (1985–86), and Terzi (1986).

38 It is of interest to note that as a group the heterodox economists at Rutgers out published the neoclassical economists as a group. Thus virtually unpublished neoclassical economists got tenure while published heterodox economists did not.

39 Davidson conceived of the Post Keynesian Workshop as a continuation of the Trieste Summer School (which ran from 1981 to 1990).

6 The contested landscape of British economics, 1900–70

1 To inhibit this acquisition, the British government outlawed in 1799 and again in 1819 unauthorized lectures, debates, and reading rooms open to the public.

2 Mechanics' Institutes in the north of England and mutual improvement associations that continued to operate into the last twenty years of the nineteenth century also provided the same sort of educational services and many of their working class members developed an alternative Social Darwinism form of socialism based on organicism and co-operation from evolutionary science (Laurent 1984; Rose 2002).

3 Illustrative of this were the educational activities of the Leicester Secular Society. In January 1884, H. M. Hyndman gave a lecture on "Constructive Socialism," followed by William Morris's first presentation of "Art and Socialism." Subsequently, in 1889 the Society held a series of lectures billed as individualism vs. socialism where the stalwarts of the Fabian Society gave lectures based on their essays that were published that same year in *Fabian Essays in Socialism*. Finally, in the 1890s, the Society had Tom Mann speak on "The Standard of Life and How to Raise It" and Eleanor Marx Aveling speak on "Christianity, Secularism, Socialism." The Society also started a library for its members in 1881 and in 1885 opened it to the public. Included among its 700 to 1000 volumes were Adam Smith's *Wealth of Nations*, David Ricardo's *Principles of Political Economy*, John Stuart Mills's *Political Economy*, and John E. Cairnes's *Essays in Political Economy*. Thus there was a significant interest in economics among the Leicester secularists (Nash 1992; Gould 1900; and the archives of the Leicester Secular Society located at the Leicestershire Records Office, Leicester, United Kingdom).

4 The book and pamphlet literature included *England for All* (1881) by H. M. Hyndman; *Wage, Labour and Capital* (1885), *Value, Price and Profit* (1898), and *Capital* vol. I (1887) by Karl Marx; *The Socialist Catechism* (1886) by J. L. Joynes; and *Merrie England* (1894) by Robert Blatchford. In addition there were weekly newspapers, such as *Justice* (1884), *Commonweal* (1885), *Freedom* (1886), and the *Clarion* (1891).

5 The critiques of the labor theory of value were actually little more than asserting that Marx was wrong, confusing use-value and utility, and asserting that the "marginal utility theory of exchange" was correct. Thus, the critiques were a ideological legitimization process to cleanse Marxism from acceptable social and scientific discourse.

6 In this context, there was discrimination against hiring and retaining lecturers either at universities or in the university extension movement that questioned fundamental components of economic theory. Such lecturers, such as *John A. Hobson* and *Peter Kropotkin*, were declared unfit to lecture to students because of their ignorance of theory and the possibility of using the lecture room for disseminating dangerous opinions.

7 The Oxford extension lecturers were influenced by the methodology of the historical school and hence adopted an historical and empirical approach to the study of past and current economic and social issues in a policy-oriented manner. Thus they did not reject Marshallian theory *per se* but made it historically contingent. On the other hand, at Cambridge, Mary Paley [Marshall] was asked to write an introductory text on economics for students enrolled in the Cambridge extension classes. The result was *Economics of Industry* (1879), co-authored with her husband, which patronized and denigrated workers, accepted the status quo of markets and suggested that markets have almost always existed, presented an embryonic neoclassical economic theory to legitimize capitalism, argued that workers wages and associated living conditions were more or less appropriate for their laboring skills and hence contributions to production, and promoted class harmony. Alfred Marshall maintained this position throughout his life and embued his students, such as Walter T. Layton and David H. MacGregor, with it (Marshall and Marshall 1890; Whitaker 1975; Groenewegen, 1995, 2007).

8 Because industrialists, Tory newspaper editors, and "respectable people" rose to complain whenever lectures became too progressive, too open to discussions of Marxism and Georgism, the content of courses were generally restricted to what was acceptable.

9 Courses in economics made up less than five per cent of all courses given (Jepson 1973: 153).

10 Arnold Toynbee gave a lecture to such an unruly, hostile audience in 1883 and as a result suffered a mental and physical collapse.

11 Indicative of this interest was the formation in circa 1904 of groups of Welsh miners to study Marxian economics. In one case when the miners asked the county council education committee if they could use a school classroom for their meeting to study Marxian economics, they were refused because the economics being studied was not orthodox.

12 On the other hand, if a political-economic course was given, such as "Political and Social Problems," perhaps only fifty students would enroll, which was too few to cover costs while the discussion class would consist of fifty students all wanting to speak thus making the class impossible.

13 For example, in 1911–13, the 27 (or 29) tutorial classes in economics were all taught by tutors with university degrees, including Henry Clay (BA Oxford), H. M. Hallsworth (MA University of Manchester, student of W. S. Jevons), Arthur Greenwood (MA Victoria University), H. O. Meredith (MA Cambridge, student of Marshall), Layton (BA Cambridge, student of Marshall), MacGregor (BA Cambridge, student of Marshall), and R. V. Lennard (BA Oxford). With the exception of Clay, the rest were tutors, fellows, and/or professors at Armstrong College, Leeds, Cambridge, and Queen's College Belfast. London was an exception because tutorial class lecturers were not allowed to teach for the University of London—see Appendix A.13.

14 Being located in extra-mural departments, the full-time tutorial lecturers were not members of subject-specific departments. Hence extra-mural departments could not be the organizational location of subject-specific academic activities—its remit was adult education not, for example, economics.

15 Clay developed the book from the lectures he gave at WEA tutorial classes in economics. Thus, the book consisted of a theoretical core that was Marshall's theory of supply and demand suitably rendered for WEA students surrounded by a description of the organization of industry in Britain, discussion of money, banking and the trade cycle, and an analysis of the state, wealth, and welfare. The latter discussion was approached from the perspective of a radical liberal moving towards the Labour Party in that the drawbacks of capitalism could be addressed through thoughtful social-economic policy carried out by the state. All of this was obvious to the Marxist tutors and students of the IWCE movement. The economics lectures given by Layton to his WEA tutorial classes also exclusively drew upon Marshall's theory, as evident by his 1914 book *The Relations of Capital and Labour* (see Groenewegen 2007).

16 By the 1920s numerous fundamental criticisms of Marshall's theory had emerged. The critiques were directed at the very notion of utility-driven decision making, at the existence of land as a non-produced scarce factor input, at the existence of the individual and market supply curve and demand curve, and at the existence of supply and demand determined prices (Veblen 1919; Hamilton 1919; McCormick 2002; Lee 1990, 1998; Sraffa 1925, 1926; Panico 1991; Aslanbeigui and Naples 1997b). Consequently, by the late 1930s the culmination of the attacks had promoted visions of developing a theory of prices that was altogether different from Marshall/neoclassical price theory. But these criticisms and alternative vision were not part of the economics presented to WEA students.

17 One of the main arguments for the dismissal of Marx's labor theory of value centered on heterogeneous labor skills and their reduction to unskilled labor skills (Steedman 2004). That Marx's arguments are less than convincing is well-known. But Marshall also engaged in the same game with his representative firm and "individual peculiarities provisionally neglected" or "average or representative" consumer. These theoretical entities (which eliminated the theoretical relevance of heterogeneity) were accepted without question while Marx's approach was not, which suggests that the critique of Marx's labor theory of value was motivated and driven by political concerns. It is also possible that more extended critiques of Marxian theory were given in the tutorial classes. One apparently popular critique was that it was nearly devoid of a Marshallian micro foundation that included consumers, preferences, enterprises, and a theory of prices (Smith 1993).

18 For example, the Cambridge tutorial classes in economics in the 1930s as well as views from the classroom fit this description. Moreover, by the late 1930s it was possible to find neoclassical socialists teaching tutorial classes, such as the case of H. D. Dickinson and perhaps Percy Ford. Thus students would get Marx but without the labor theory of value and in its place would be Marshallian price theory (King 2004a; Dickinson 1936–37; Ford 1935–36; M.R. 1936–37; Michaels 1937–38; Fieldhouse 1983).

19 In particular, many in the WEA championed courses in philosophy, literature, and other humanities classes because they tended to make workers believe in the harmony of the social classes and hence accept the social status quo.

20 The WEA constantly rejected Marxian economic theory because of its acceptance of class conflict; and argued that having Marxian theory as the central theory to be taught with Marshall's theory criticized and rejected, such as in the labor colleges (see below), was to engage in propaganda instead of objective teaching and genuine education. That is, the WEA argued that the labor colleges taught students what to think, whereas it taught students how to think: " ... [WEA] is

aiming rather at making people think and reason for themselves than at imparting a definite body of knowledge" (Cole 1932: 131). Yet, the WEA openly advocated the revitalization or the establishment of branches in areas where Marxian economics was taught so to direct workers away from it. Moreover, by making Marshall's theory scientifically superior in the way it did, WEA in fact indirectly told students what to think. But this probably had no impact on many WEA students since they had no interest in questioning the status quo (Rose 2002: 279).

21 In the 1920s, the Board of Education believed that the funding of the WEA was a sound political investment against extremism. This judgment had, perhaps, a good foundation in that of the twenty-four WEA classes held in Edinburgh in 1924–25, the lecturer in only one class was a suspected Labour Party supporter while eighteen lecturers were known or suspected Conservatives or Liberals (Phillips and Putnam 1980). Moreover, economic lecturers associated with universities were preferred over unattached lecturers because the former were less dogmatic. Thus, the WEA was seen as a more benign approach to working-class education compared with the approach of the Marxist-oriented labor colleges.

22 The best example of this was in 1925 when the WEA provisionally entered into a scheme with the Trades Union Congress where its purpose was to equip workers with knowledge to secure social and industrial emancipation. The WEA quickly came under pressure from central and local government to withdraw from it. Although the scheme was never implemented, conditions were placed upon the WEA for receiving grant aid, such as having to abandon its traditional identification with the working class.

23 From 1909 to 1940, there were over 500 three-year tutorial classes in economics. Assuming that each class had thirty students, at least 15,000 adults were to some degree inoculated against Marxism (extrapolated from the data in Appendix A.13).

24 The rationale for concentrating on supply and demand analysis for some students was that it would enable them to hold their own against capitalists who were supposedly well-versed in it.

25 Beginning in 1903, Lees-Smith exposition of economic theory in his lectures to Ruskin students became more and more Marshallian, less and less tolerant of relief given to the unemployed or to minimum wages (since it would increase unemployment), and increasingly contemptuous of Marxian economics (Seed 1910; also see Craik 1964: 43–44). During this time, he also gave lectures in 1904–5 on the "Outlines of Economic Theory" to candidates for the Oxford Diploma in economics. The evolution of his lectures mirrored his publications in the *Economic Journal*—see Lees-Smith (1905, 1906, 1907; also see Leonard 2000). Thus, from the students' perspective, Lees-Smith's neoclassical analysis of the impact of the minimum wage on employment was not impartial and without political agenda, but simply capitalist propaganda parading as objective science.

26 Consequently, informal classes on Marxism were set up and a Marxian society established.

27 As noted above, the insistence of making Marshallian theory the central focus of the economic theory lectures was not an impartial decision, but one that the Ruskin students saw as favoring capitalism.

28 For the early years, 1910 to 1914, the comparability between the Diploma and the economics taught at Ruskin was at least partially assured since Furniss offered informal instruction for Diploma candidates in economic theory, public finance, and money and credit as well as gave lectures on foreign trade and trade unionism. Thus, in the first five years 1910 to 1914, 55 Ruskin students sat for the Diploma, with fifty being successful and twenty-six obtaining distinctions. The economics of the Diploma was also not materially different from the economics taught by the WEA. For example, compare the 1903 and the 1913 Diploma

requirements to the description of the suggested economics tutorial course that emerged from the Oxford Joint Conference on Education of Workpeople. Thus, the economics of the WEA, Ruskin College, and the Diploma were the same— Marshall's price theory and its transformation over time to 1940 (*The Oxford Diploma in Economics* 1903, Oxford University Archives, 26334e.31; Harrop 1987; Holland, Price, and Adams 1913).

29 Ford was educated at the London School of Economics; Coleman read history and economics at Newnham College, Cambridge, 1914–16; Plummer had a M.Sc. in economics from the London School of Economics and a B.Litt from Oxford; and Smith obtain a first in Philosophy, Politics, and Economics at Oxford in 1932 and a B.Litt in economics in 1934 from Oxford. Smith in particular argued that Marx did not develop a coherent theory of prices, wages or profits and hence rejected as almost incomprehensible, the labor theory of value and surplus value. However, he did note that Marx had something useful to say about the trade cycle, but that was not predicated on the labor theory of value (Smith 1937, 1939; also see Ford 1935–36; Dickinson 1936–37).

30 This outcome was first voiced by students during the 1909 strike; but in any case by the 1930s it seems that the students themselves had little interest in studying Marxism, which is not surprising since many of them were former WEA students.

31 Because pro-Plebs ex-Ruskin students were active in disseminating the message and organizing classes, the establishment of Plebs League branches occurred very quickly—Oxford (December 1908), South Wales (January 1909), Wigan (April 1909) and London (November 1909). In September 1909 the Rochdale and District Labour College was established and held classes in Marxian economics and industrial history. In addition, Plebs- and CLC-affiliated classes were formed in South Wales, Northumberland, Merseyside, Brighton, and London. By 1913, the provincial classes had approximately 1000 students and were taking place in north-east Lancashire, Rochdale area, Brighton, Manchester, the Rhondda Valley in Wales, Birmingham, and Edinburgh. Finally, from 1909 to 1915 fifty different provincial locations offered CLC-affiliated classes.

32 The qualifications to be a NCLC organizer were knowledge of Marxian economics, past service to the labor movement, and practice in speaking. Since many organizers were graduates of the CLC, their knowledge of Marxism was assured—see Appendix A.14.

33 Without CLC educated tutors, the NCLC had a problem of recruiting competent tutors. This was remedied somewhat by taking on tutors who had attended labor colleges and/or taken postal courses, but this was clearly second-best to CLC-educated tutors. Moreover, during the 1930s and beyond, ex-CLCers who could be tutors at labor colleges became occupied with trade union, political party, and Co-operative Society work. The lack of well-trained Marxist economists thus contributed to the decline of the IWCE movement—without teachers no Movement was possible.

34 For the period 1909 to 1916, the political economy course was not always offered. This disappointed students, since many came to the CLC with already reading and studying the first volume of *Capital*. Moreover, some students demanded an almost exclusive emphasis on Marxism, a position that the CLC refused to accept, in part, because to understand Marxian economics knowledge of classical political economy and of the historical school was necessary (Atkins 1981).

35 In response to the WEA's liberal approach to education and the supposedly impartiality of its economics tutors, the promoters of labor colleges exclaimed:

> Many people are horrified to hear it said that the working class standpoint in Economics is bound to be different from that of the capitalists. These tender beings dream of a certain "impartial" social science bringing about the

reconciliation of the hostile classes, as if it were possible to avoid taking sides on economic questions in a society in which the interests of the workers are sharply opposed to those of the employers, the needs of the tenants conflict with those of the houseowners, and so on. True! the professors of political economy in the Universities claim to be impartial men of science. But nobody believes them: their attitude is recognized as a necessary, professional pose. Their teaching has become a mere system of apologetics, by means of which they reveal the moral reasons that justify the plundering of the working class.

(Maclean 1916: 9)

36 An example of the high level of understanding of Marxian economics that lecturers acquired is Thomas's (1922) delineation of the economic doctrines of Karl Marx.

37 For example, see Brumaire (1910), Ablett's *Easy Outlines of Economics*, McLaine (1923), and Colyer (1932).

38 For example, in the post-war period of the CLC some students found the emphasis on Marxian economics dated and wanted more discussion of Marshallian economics because it was 'modern' and more material on the rise of big business in the economy. The students' complaints were dismissed by the College because it found the lectures satisfactory. Interesting, McLaine (1923) argued that students should also draw upon contributions made by Marshallian economists. This indicates that McLaine did not really understand Marxian and Marshallian economics theory as well as the weakening of Marxian economics at the beginning of the interwar period (Macintyre 1980; Lewis 1984).

39 As noted in note 15, Marshall/neoclassical price theory was theoretically questionable if not incoherent. Furthermore, through a series of very abstract and unrealistic assumptions, it was removed from any contact with the real world, and was taught by using abstract and meaningless examples. Hence Marshallian theory provided even less an understanding of capitalism than did the flawed Marxian theory. Thus Stuart Macintyre's (1980) critique of the Marxism taught and engaged with in the IWCE movement in Britain in the 1920s is incorrect and, moreover, reveals an ignorance of Marshallian theory and how it was taught to students. In addition, the complaints that this cadre of Marxist economists did not take the transformation problem seriously and that labor colleges had low standards, if true, was not any different from the Marshallian economists who refused to seriously consider the implications of Sraffa's critique of the supply curve and dismissal of Marshallian theory, Keynes's theory of effective demand, and full-cost pricing and the low standards of Oxford, Cambridge, and London who permitted students to graduate without really understanding the theoretical shortcomings of Marshallian economics. In this light, it is problematical to argue that CLC and NCLC tutors were less qualified in terms of knowledge of the relevant subject matter than WEA tutors.

40 The economic decline of the South Wales coalfields had a particular devastating impact on the miners' institute libraries, which up to the 1920s were community focal points for reading and studying Marxism. With the loss of their 'mining' income, the libraries ceased buying books of any kind. Thus, when the State started offering and providing support for the libraries, many reluctantly accepted it. However, the State support was in part a strategy to divert unemployed miners from radical activities and studying Marxism by providing them with a comfortable place to carry out inert activity of reading largely non-radical literature, a favorite among miners in any case (Francis 1976; Rose 2002; Baggs 2001, 2004).

41 As part of the attempt, various syllabuses on the British labor movement, finance, economic history, and economic geography were published as well as one by Maurice Dobb (n.d. but circa 1925) on "The Development of Capitalism."

42 The political economy study course covered Marxist theory of value, capital and surplus value, wages and the accumulation of capital, the distribution of surplus value, economic crisis, and imperialism. Readings for value theory were the same as the CLC and NCLC had for their classes on Marxian economics. However, by the time the student got to the part on economic crisis, the degree of academic difficulty was that of an advanced Cambridge undergraduate or post-graduate student. Clearly this was beyond the teaching level of the CLC and the labor colleges, and the breadth and depth of what was included in the study guide was beyond the training and intellectual horizon of the cadre of the working class CLC and NCLC lecturers and tutors. Thus the guides were probably done by Dobb the only Marxist capable of this and had the working conditions to do it (Wolfram 1976).

43 The readings included in the syllabuses were not significantly different than what were found in CLC and NCLC courses on Marxian economics. They included Marx's *Wage-Labour and Capital*, *Value, Price and Profit*, and *Capital* as well as Engels's *Anti-Duhring*, Lev Leontiev's *Political Economy*, and Lenin's *Imperialism*.

44 The Marx's School in London also encouraged an attempt to establish a similar school in South Wales in 1934, but nothing came of it (Lewis 1993).

45 According to MacGregor, at Cambridge circa 1905, *Principles* was the only economics to read and Marxism was not taught at all and the historical school much discouraged (MacGregor 1942).

46 The course at Nottingham had the following structure and components:

> *Synopsis*—Scope and method of economics; economic laws. *Demand*—Law of diminishing utility, marginal and total utility; law of demand; elasticity of demand; consumers' rent. *Supply*—Factors of production and their remuneration; laws of diminishing and increasing return. *Equilibrium of Supply and Demand*—Market price; normal price; stock and produce exchanges. *Distribution*—Effect of competition; trade unions; legislation; co-operation; monopolies; socialism
>
> (University College of Nottingham, *Prospectus of 1915–1916*: 110)

47 Illustrative of this neoclassical exclusiveness is the 1935 unofficial bibliography for students in the Honour School of Philosophy, Politics, and Economics. The economic theory, economic organization, currency and credit, public finance and statistical method reading were entirely restricted to current neoclassical theory and their forerunners and to non-Marxist descriptions and analysis. Marx showed up only once under the history of economic thought and the readings for labor moments included some books on socialism (Hargreaves et al.1935).

48 While most universities had student socialist societies of one form or another, they were mostly interested in political issues and in many cases rejected Marx and revolutionary socialism. The best know of them was the Cole Group at Oxford, but none of the students who later became economists—Colin Clark, Evan Durbin, Hugh Gaitskell, Arthur Grant, and James Meade—were Marxist economists; rather they were all neoclassical economists of one perspective or another.

49 The Scottish Economic Society did the same for Scotland.

50 During the 1930s, the *Economics Journal* and the *Review of Economic Studies* did publish articles and reviews that dealt with Marxism, especially in relation to Keynes. However, they had little impact on the long run content of both journals or on the scholarship and research interests of British academic economists, perhaps with Joan Robinson being the exception (Howard and King 1992).

51 While the statement is apt to be denied by economists, it should be noted that Marxist economic historians suffered from the discriminatory practices of their "neutralist" colleagues. Eric Hobsbawm suggests that blacklisting of Marxist

historians started in 1948, with the result that there was virtually no hiring of Marxist historians for nearly a decade; and those that had academic positions were denied promotion. In addition, between 1945 and 1950 the Labour government purged the Civil Service and the BBC of communists. Moreover, as noted above, the WEA dismissed or made life very difficult for members of the CP, including Marxist economists such as Ronald Bellamy. Finally, university appointment boards asked candidates whether they were communists. Thus, it is not clear why economists insist that conditions were different in economics by claiming there was no discrimination against Marxist or other radical economists (Coleman 1987; Hobsbawm 1978; Hobsbawm in Abelove et al. 1983; Childs 1997; Lewis 1950; Burton 1954; Fieldhouse, 1985).

52 This point needs further exploration with regard to economists such as Henry Phelps Brown as well as economists whose research areas were not yet impregnated with neoclassical theory such as economic development, labor economics, and industrial economics.

53 Another heterodox or at least dissenting economist was George Shackle, but his work had no discernible impact on British economics between 1951 and 1969 when he held the Brunner Chair of Economic Science at the University of Liverpool.

54 The purpose of the Communist Party Historians' Group was to challenge the perspectives of non-Marxian bourgeois historians. Formed in 1946 by a number of Marxist historians, including Dobb, the group met regularly for discussion and members produced over thirty books and one hundred articles and chapters in books. It also raised its own income to finance its activities; held conferences, weekend schools, and public lectures; established the journal *Past and Present* for the purpose of publishing Marxian and non-Marxian radical historical material; produced a bulletin promoting local history; and somewhat successfully established regional branches. To achieve its purpose, the Group consistently attempted to build bridges between Marxists and non-Marxists with whom they shared some common interests and sympathies. The achievements of the Group included contributing to the emergence of the field of social history and labor history, transforming the study of the English Revolution, and influencing the general teaching of history through the publication of popular general textbooks (Hobsbawm 1978; Schwarz 1982; Kaye 1995).

55 Bodington graduated from Oxford with a degree in Classics in 1930. After witnessing the hunger marches in the 1930s, he became interested in Marxian economics. From 1930 to 1960 he taught, worked in Civil Service, and was a director for a trading company. He later became involved with the Conference of Socialist Economists—see Chapter 7. The group of Marxist economists probably belonged to the Communist Party Economists' Group (or sub-committee). The Group in the 1950s consisted of some thirty to forty Marxists, mostly workers and political activists but also Dobb, Meek, and Bellamy. Up until the 1970s it devoted much of its activities to supporting communists in the trade union movement, offering advice on applied and policy issues. For example, in the period 1957 to 1960, the Group organized lectures and summer schools to reassess developments in the world economy and the theory of crisis. It only started to deal with theoretical issues after the Party attracted some young academic economists in the 1970s, such as Dave Purdy, Pat Devine, Bob Rowthorn, David Currie, John Grahl, and Bill Warren. The period 1977 to 1979 was one of intense debate with the Party leadership over wage struggles, income policies, and the causes of inflation. Still, not much is know about the Group's overall activities (Bellamy 1986–87; Andrews 1995; Grahl 2000).

56 It is difficult to know how much Marxian economics was taught in the first postwar decade. What is known is that in 1955 Meek gave 30 Glasgow lectures on

"theories of value, distribution and welfare" of which two were on Marx's theory of value and distribution.

57 Within the CP there continued to be research utilizing Marxian economics—see Aaronovitch (1955, 1961, 1964).

58 For the period of 1945 to the early 1950s, the British economists associated with left-wing Keynesianism included Joan Robinson, Richard Kahn, Nicholas Kaldor, G.D.N. Worswick, Josef Steindl, and Fritz Burchardt.

59 Marxists had two addition problems with the left-wing Keynesian arguments. The first is that the problem with capitalism seemed to be based on monopoly, so if the state regulated and controlled monopolies then the exploitation of workers would cease. Second, was that given a rigid degree of monopoly, an increase in money wages would have no impact on real wages, implying that trade unions could not increase workers real wages.

60 In addition, in the revised edition of *Political Economy*, Eaton (Bodington) acknowledged Sraffa's contribution to the theoretical problem of the measurement of the organic composition of capital.

61 However, concern about offering appointments to radicals still existed. For example, in the early 1970s attempts were made when hiring new staff at universities to distinguish between applicants who were radicals and those who were not (Griffith 1972).

62 Harry Johnson sought to blame the crisis on the suffocating dominance of Oxbridge and the wholly inadequate and Cambridge bias training of British economists (Johnson 1968, 1973, 1974).

63 The perception of crisis jointly with the turning to monetarism contributed to Keynes's declining influence among economists (Hodson 1973).

64 For example, Meek (1959b, 1959c) suggested that some developments within neoclassical oligopoly theory might be usefully incorporated into Marxian economic theory. In addition, Dickinson argued, as he did in the 1930s, that Marxists should not reject marginal utility theory or the abstinence theory of interest and profits and claimed that "one day the barrier between the orthodox bourgeois economists and the orthodox Marxian economists will be broken down, and a new synthesis will emerge – the economics of a truly human society" (Dickinson 1963: 35).

65 The use of such critiques reflected the influence the Communist Party Historians' Group had upon the New Left. There was also opposition to utilizing such non-Marxist critiques of capitalism, although the reasons given were insubstantial, generally revealing a lack of understanding of the critiques. See Blackburn (1969, note 11: 170).

66 *The New Reasoner* carried only three articles on economics, all written by Meek (1959a, 1959b, 1959c) in which he re-examined the strengths and weaknesses of Marxian and neoclassical economics and of a Marx–Keynes synthesis or left-wing Keynesianism. As for *University and Left Review* it carried articles on full-employment, nationalisation, Labour's economic policy, managerial organization of industry and banking, and the analysis of capitalism as a social and economic system. For the entire run of both journals, see http://www.amielandmelburn.org. uk/home_index.htm.

67 In 1964 John Saville and Ralph Miliband founded the annual *Socialist Register*, which also provided a publishing outlet for papers on Marxian economics.

68 This change of content and emphasis coincided with the change of editorship of the NLR that began a programme to introduce to the British left the many currents and individuals of European Marxism (Chun 1993; Widgery 1976; Rustin 1980).

7 Heterodox economics in Britain, 1970–96

1 It also appears that the Communist Party and its Economic Committee contributed to the formation of the CSE, but behind the scenes, which would account

for Aaronovitch's involvement at this early date. However, additional research is needed on this conjecture (Devine 2007).

2 Barratt Brown chaired the conference. Dobb gave a paper "Some Reflections on the Sraffa System and the Critique of the so-called Neoclassical Theory of Value" which was discussed by Mario Nuti; Phil Leeson gave a paper on "The Present State of Development Theory" which was discussed by Bob Sutcliffe; and Murray gave a paper on "The Internationalization of Capital" which was discussed by Rowthorn. While all papers elicited comments by the participants, the last paper received the most intense discussion. Geoff Harcourt's 1969 *Journal of Economic Literature* article was also circulated as background reading for Dobb's session (Aaronovitch, Murray, and Radice 1969; Nuti 1970a; Radice 1973c).

3 The CSE was and is not a job-academic-based organization like the Association of University Teachers in Economics or the Association of Polytechnic Teachers in Economics. Hence, as an organization, it was/is equivalent to the Royal Economic Society (RES), but the opposite of it. Perhaps this is why the RES completely ignored the CSE and its activities in the 1970s and up to the present-day (Minutes of the Council of the Royal Economics Society 1970–80; Royal Economic Society Papers, British Library of Political and Economic Science, London School of Economics).

4 About eighty people attended the conference which opened with a paper by Bellamy (1971), followed by sessions on "British Crisis and Tory Policy," "Concentration and Centralisation of Capital in Western Europe," "Internationalisation of Capital and the State in Western Europe," "Labour in Western Europe," and "Western Europe and Neo-colonialism" ("Fourth Socialist Economists' Conference" 1971; Glyn 1971; Radice and Picciotto 1971; Radice 1972b).

5 The *Bulletin* lasted until 1976 when it was superseded by *Capital and Class*. Another popular publishing outlet for Marxian-Post Keynesian-heterodox UK economists from 1971 to 1980 was the *Australian Economic Papers* edited by Harcourt (and others)—see Steedman (1971), Steedman and Metcalfe (1973), Llewellyn and Tarling (1974), Mainwaring (1976), Broome (1977), Hodgson and Steedman (1977), and Chick (1978c).

6 The CSE membership flyers of this period contained the following statement:

> Broadly speaking, our work lies within a Marxist perspective, but the organization does not exclude any political tendency on the left, believing that such an approach is essential if our work is to be worthwhile (Conference of Socialist Economists 1972a, 1973, 1974b).

7 The CP also carried on similar and but not always supporting activities, as there was much sectarianism at this time. In any case, for example, it had a conference in 1971 on "The Opposing Trends in Imperialism: unity versus contradiction" which Dobb chaired and Bellamy spoke. In addition, the Marx Memorial Library held classes on "Elementary Marxist Economics" and "Marxist Political Economy v. Bourgeois" (*Marx Memorial Library Bulletin*, no. 60, October–December, 1971).

8 The conference attracted nearly 200 participants, including a large number of students. Although the numbers dwindled in successive sessions, there was an atmosphere of sustained interest and debate. Papers given at the conference included David Yaffe's "The Marxian Theory of Crisis, Capital and the State," Jan Kregel's "Post-Keynesian Economic Theory and the Theory of Capitalist Crisis," Les Fishman's "Inflation," and Barratt Brown's "Capitalism in the Second Half of the 20th Century" (CSE *Newsletter*, February 1973; Conference of Socialist Economists 1972b).

9 The papers given included "The Post-Keynesian (Radical) Approach to Monetary Theory" by Kregel (1974), "A Critique of Radical Keynesianism" by Adrian

Winnett, "Elements of Marxist Monetary Theory" by Rowthorn, "Inflation and Marxist Theory" by Pat Devine, "Inflation and Unemployment" by Meghnad Desai, and "Inflation as an International Phenomenon" by George Zis. Kregel's and Winnett's papers prompted an extended discussion which included the argument that Kalecki and Robinson were real radical Keynesians. However, apparently many conference participants were not familiar with the emerging Post Keynesian monetary theory and dismissed it as simply "bourgeois monetary theory" (Radice 1973c; Winnett 1973; Devine 1973; Zis 1973).

10 Papers given at the conference included D. Fishman's and H. Ergas's "Marx's Theory of Money," Photis Lysandrou's "International Monetary Theory," and Yaffe's "Inflation and World Crisis" (CSE *Newsletter*, January 1975).

11 In its first year of existence, the CSE had approximately 140 U.K./Ireland participants, of which 134 (or 96 percent) were university-based and 98 (or 70 percent) were economists or quite interested in Marxian economic theory and economic issues in general. The figures were compiled from participant and subscribers records for 1970 as well as a list of Marxist economists held by Radice (and copies held by the authors). Of the 140 individuals identified, only those who had obvious non-university addresses were classified as not university-based; all others were classified as university-based. The 42 individuals who were not classified as economists were either associated with other disciplines or could not be associated with any discipline.

12 To illustrate, the London CSE group put on a series of political economy seminars John Harrison, Jesse Schwartz, P. Sloan, Alfredo Medio, Ben Fine, and Andrew Glyn speaking on productive and unproductive labor in Marxian political economy, Marx's theory of capital reproduction and accumulation, Marx and monopoly capital, Italian economic development since World War II, Marx's circuit of capital, and the real crisis of British capitalism (CSE *Newsletter*, October 1973 and February 1974; Fine in Arestis and Sawyer, 2000). A further illustration can be found in the speaker's list that was formed 1973:

Speaker	Topic
Andrew Glyn	The Current Crisis, The Irrelevance of Bourgeois Economics, Basic Elements of Marxist Theory
John Harrison	Political Economy of Housework, Productive and Unproductive Labour, Introduction to Marxist Economic Theory
Robin Murray	Modern Capitalism
Hugo Radice	International Firms
Jesse Schwartz	The Theory of Value in Smith and Ricardo, Marx's Labour Theory of Value, The Meaning of the Capital Theory Controversy
David Yaffe	Crisis, Capital and the State

Source: CSE *Newsletter*, May 1973 and July 1973.

13 At the 1972 CSE conference, Jean Gardiner and Maureen Mackintosh held a meeting for women economists to discuss their work, including work on women's issues. This led to the holding of seminars and the establishment of the Political Economy of Women study group the following March 1973. The seminar brought together people working in related areas. Topics of discussion included housework and productive labor, political economy of the family, reproduction of labor power, family and industrialization, the state in relation to women, and feminism and socialism. The Political Economy of Housing study group began with a work-in-progress meeting in November 1973 which was designed to bring socialist economists working in the area together. However, it quickly expanded to include

planners, sociologists, geographers, social administrators, and community-studies people. Topics of discussion included tenants' struggles, land nationalization, property development, housing-market models, construction of high-rise flats since 1945, housing associations, gentrification, and solicitors and the housing market. In 1975 it published a collection of papers under the title of *Political Economy and the Housing Question* (Conference of Socialist Economists 1972b; CSE *Newsletter*, May 1973, July 1973, October 1973, February 1974, May 1974, November 1974, July 1975, November 1975).

14 Attending the CSE conference was Theo van der Klundert, a Dutch economist associated with *De Economist*. After Dobb and Nuti delivered their papers he got their permission to have them published in *De Economist*. Except for changes in the title, Dobb's and Nuti's papers were published pretty much as is. [Dobb 1970a, 1970b; Nuti 1970a, 1970b]

15 *Steedman* introduced himself to Sraffa's book and attended Dobb's lectures while an undergraduate at Cambridge (1961–64). He continued his close examination of the book and its implications for Marxian economic theory for the rest of the decade. Moreover, he spent a year in Italy (1970–71) where he gained first-hand knowledge of the use of Sraffa's system for examining Marx. The first fruit of his research with regard to Marx was a 1970 paper "Marx on the Falling Rate of Profit" (which he corresponded with Dobb about), a version of which was published in the *Bulletin* 1972. The significant of the article was that Steedman used Sraffa's system to examine Marx arguments on the rate of profit and showing their shortcomings (MacLennan 1969b; CSE *Newsletter*, April 29, 1970; Steedman 1972b, 1976; Arestis and Sawyer 2000).

16 The capital theory controversy was a popular topic at Cambridge and elsewhere. In 1972–73, Harcourt gave lectures on it at Cambridge as well as seminars all over the UK and Europe.

17 His talk was later published—see Steedman (1972a).

18 His talk was later published as Rowthorn (1972, 1973, 1974).

19 Although already in use in Italy, the term neo-Ricardian first appears in English in Medio's 1972 paper "Profits and Surplus-Value: Appearance and Reality in Capitalist Production." The paper was published in *A Critique of Economic Theory* (1972), a draft of which was available at the day school. Later Rowthorn used neo-Ricardian in his article, "Marxism and the Capital Theory Controversy," which appeared in the Autumn 1972 issue of the *Bulletin*. Shortly, thereafter Radice used it to characterize Steedman's Sraffian critique of neo-classical capital theory his December 1972 report on CSE activities for the past year—see Radice (1972b). In the Spring issue of the *Bulletin*, Rowthorn used the term in his article "Vulgar Economy (Part II)." Finally, Medio, who was present at the 1972 capital theory seminar, wrote a paper titled "Neoclassicals, Neo-Ricardians, and Marx" which circulated privately in Cambridge in the winter of 1973–74—see Medio (1977). After this, the term became widely used to denote both the Sraffian critique of neoclassical capital theory as well as the use of Sraffa to positively reconstruct economic theory—called the constructivist Sraffian approach—emerging at Cambridge (Harcourt 1979).

20 *Hogdson* was Steedman's student in 1972–74. Steedman taught him history of economic thought in 1972–73 and 1973–74. Hodgson wrote a Sraffian-style M.A. thesis on joint production under Steedman's supervision.

21 Papers were distributed before the conference and included Geoff Pilling's "Law of Value in Ricardo and Marx," Geoff Hodgson's "Marxist Epistemology and the Transformation Problem," John Harrison's "Productive and Unproductive Labour in Marx's Political Economy," Stan Broadridge's "A Comment on the Transformation Problem," and Patrick Goode's "The Concept of Law in Marx." The latter four were later published in the *Bulletin* ("Law of Value Conference" 1973).

22 Hodgson argued

> ... that it is necessary to accept the *formal* results of the Sraffa school. ... At the same time it is necessary to develop theories of value, fetishism, exploitation, and capitalist development that are compatible with Sraffa's formal results. Sraffa can serve to liberate us from illogicalities, but he does not provide us with a conceptual system. This task of theoretical development may involve a substantial revision of *Capital*, but there is no doubt that we shall still find that work far more useful than [sic] Sraffa's *Production of Commodities by Means of Commodities*.
>
> (Hodgson 1975: 112)

23 An example of this view is the following:

> ... we criticise neo-Ricardians ... deriving propositions directly from technical relations while ignoring the existence of values as an essential intermediate step. ... We criticise [the neo-Ricardians] because their method prevents them from being able to treat such matters in any way which corresponds to Marx's view of the science of society.
>
> (Fine and Harris 1977: 120)

24 There was also a political dimension to this controversy which is not addressed here: the Marxists drawing on Sraffa, at least in Britain, tended to see wages as driving inflation and hence were inclined to accept incomes policy as a way to control inflation whereas the Marxists drawing on Gramsci traced inflation to excessive capital accumulation and hence were not in favor of incomes policies. The complexity of the controversy and its impact on CSE and the development of heterodox economics need further research. In addition, there was an acrimonious debate among the CP economists on whether they should engage in political or academic (theoretical) activities—that is whether to attempt to influence the policies of the Labour government or to develop an economic theory qua doctrine that is agreed upon by all before engaging with politics. This also had a negative impact on CSE which needs to be explored (Grahl 2000; Devine 2007; Toporowski 2007).

25 The irony of the debate was that the two "grand old" Marxists (or Meekist as the case may be), Dobb and Meek, supported the engagement between Sraffa and Marx and felt that the divisiveness weakened the possibility of a Marx–Sraffa–Post Keynesian synthesis that would replace neoclassical economics. The younger Marxist economists essentially dismissed them as almost neoclassical economists (Dobb 1975–76a, 1975–76b; Meek 1977, 1978; Atley and McFarlane 2001; Howard and King 2004; Fine, 1986).

26 In 1980–81, approximately 36 percent of CSE members were associated with economics, while 16 percent, 31 percent, and 17 percent were associated with politics, sociology/anthropology, and other (Conference of Socialist Economists 1981).

27 For example, by 1976 both Hodgson and Steedman had left the CSE because they felt that economic discussion was becoming increasingly dominated by Marxists who insisted on developing Marxian theory without taking into account the Sraffian critiques or the possible contributions of other heterodox economic traditions.

28 There existed political organizations, such as the CP, that heterodox economists could join and utilize their expertise; but most of these were "connected" in some manner to the CSE. In particular, a number of CSE economists were engaged in CP activities in the 1970s—see Appendix A.16, column G.

29 For example, *Victoria Chick*, working from first principles and mostly on her own, moved over a decade from mainstream economics in 1963 to Post Keynesian economics in 1973. As a consequence of her intellectual journey, she had difficulty publishing her critiques of neoclassical macroeconomics as well as her work on the *General Theory* until the late 1970s when Harcourt published in the *Australian Economic Papers* her critique of Robert Clower's understanding of the Keynesian revolution—also see below (Chick in Arestis and Sawyer 2000; Chick 1978c).

30 Before being appointed as the Head of the Economics Division at Thames Polytechnic in 1974, *Skouras* taught at Middlesex Polytechnic (now Middlesex University) where he came into contact with Nuti, Eatwell, and Joan Robinson who had given a series of lectures there. Because he was skeptical of neoclassical economic theory and a pluralist, this contact led him to become interested in Cambridge-based Post Keynesian economic theory (Daniel 1999; Driver 1999; Skouras 1999).

31 A second purpose of *Thames Papers* was to generate economic discussion within the Economics Division at Thames Polytechnic and to build up its reputation and make it better known among economists (Skouras 1999).

32 Generally, the papers were invited either as a result of talks with the author(s) or having heard them giving papers on the subject. In fact, one duty of the members of the editorial board was, in part, to bring interesting papers and economists to the attention of Skouras.

33 In 1978 Skouras became the Head of the Department of Applied Economics at North-East London Polytechnic and Philip Arestis succeeded him as Head of the Economics Division at Thames. At the same time the editorial board was expanded to include individuals from other London-based polytechnics (Skouras 1999).

34 Arestis first became aware of Eichner's work on macroeconomic modeling in the late 1970s. In May 1982 he put on a conference on Post Keynesian economics and invited Eichner to be the keynote speaker. Thus a conversation was struck up between them concerning short-period Post Keynesian macro-econometric modeling that lasted until the latter's death in February 1988 (Street et al. 1988; Arestis in King 1995a; Arestis in Lee 2000a: 70–71).

35 Harcourt's paper was the second survey of Post Keynesian economics after the Eichner and Kregel (1975) well-known article on Post Keynesian theory.

36 This increasing emphasis on Post Keynesian economics was also reflected in changes in the composition of the members of the editorial board which now included Eichner (1987–88), Ciaran Driver (1987–89), George Blazyca (1988–89), and Frank Skuse (1988–89).

37 From 1977 to 1988, there were twenty-three issues of the *Review* and fifteen publications by Post Keynesian-heterodox economists as well as another thirteen articles of interest to them.

38 Papers presented at the conference included K. Laski, "Kalecki's Theory of the Business Cycle," Wlodzimierz Brus, "Kalecki and Socialist Development," Bob Rowthorn, "Kalecki, Keynes and Income Distribution," and Eprime Eshag, "The Political Economy of Michal Kalecki" (CSE *Newsletter*, November 1978).

39 Post Keynesian-heterodox economists that attended the seminar in the 1980s included Bernard Corry, Harcourt, Kaldor, Kahn, Sheila Dow, Chick, John Brothwell, Stephen Frowen, Tony Lawson, Tony Thirlwall, Joan Robinson, Peter Kriesler, and Terry O'Shaughnessy.

40 There was also a Social Science Research Council/Economics and Social Research Council funded Political Economy Study Group that was established in the early 1980s by Francis Green and Steve Rankin. The themes of its seminars included Marxian and neo-Marxian political economy, Eastern Europe and the economics of transition, and the history and methodology of economics. In 1992 and 1993, the Group's applications to the Economics and Social Research Council for renewed study group funding were unsuccessful with the result that it folded.

41 For example, *Krishna Bharadwaj* arrived in Cambridge in 1967 to work on elaborating the Sraffian critique of mainstream theory as well as how Sraffa's approach differed from mainstream theory. While there, she engaged with Sraffa, Joan Robinson, Dobb, Luigi Pasinetti, and Kaldor and met a number of younger economists interested in the revival of classical and Marxian theory. *John Eatwell*, on the other hand, was a 1960s Cambridge undergraduate and became a teaching fellow at Trinity College in 1970. Throughout the 1970s he worked on developing a Keynes-Sraffa synthesis as a replacement for neoclassical economics (Bharadwaj, Eatwell, and Nuti in Arestis and Sawyer 2000; Harcourt 1993–94).

42 For the start-up financing of the journal, Eatwell and colleagues intended to ask Joan Robinson, Kaldor, Dobb, Sraffa, and Richard Kahn for contributions. However, when approached, Kahn suggested that Academic Press would be interested in such a project. The Press was and agreed to provide the start-up financing.

43 The CPES economists that were also in the CSE and identified as socialist economists included Eatwell, Nuti, Paine, Rowthorn, and Singh; and the other CPES economists included Mahmoud Abdel-Fadil, Francis Cripps, Roger Tarling, John Wells, and Frank Wilkinson.

44 The CPES also published, in conjunction with the Higgins Labor Research Center at the University of Notre Dame, the *International Contributions to Labour Studies*. The annual journal was published from 1991 to 1997.

45 About two hundred or more persons attended the conference, which by all accounts was a lively affair. Steedman and Hodgson made a number of interventions which seemed to carry the day, but still for some convinced against their will were of the same opinion still. Papers from the conference and subsequent discussion were published in Steedman et al. (1981).

46 The activities of the Cambridge Policy Group, which existed in the 1970s, also contributed to the development of Post Keynesian-heterodox economics at Cambridge, but its history, hence contributions, have not been written up. In general the social and organizational history of economics at Cambridge is undeveloped, especially for the post-1945 years. Consequently, while the eventual demise of Post Keynesian-heterodox economics at Cambridge was seen as early as 1974, the actual process by which it occurred has not yet been told (Lawson 2000; Mongiovi 2001; Millmow 2003).

47 Institutional and social economics did not really exist in Britain, that is, as a body of collectively recognized economists engaged in research that is clearly associated with arguments published in, for example, the *Journal of Economic Issues* or the *Review of Social Economics*. In 1987–88, there were only three British economists that belonged to the Association for Social Economics and only seven who belonged to the Association for Evolutionary Economics.

48 For example, in 1979 *Peter Reynolds* completed his dissertation on "Macroeconomic Theories of Distribution and their Relationship with Economic Dynamics" which dealt with Kalecki's theory of distribution. Then in 1980 he produced a paper on "Kalecki and the Post-Keynesians: a reinterpretation;" and in 1987 he published *Political Economy: a synthesis of Kaleckian and Post Keynesian economics*. Although *Malcolm Sawyer* received Eichner's newsletter in 1973 (see Chapter 5 and Lee 2000a: 165), he did not really become engaged with the Post Keynesian approach until the early 1980s when he attended Arestis's 1982 conference and re-established contact with Eichner and Arestis (who was a fellow M.Sc. student at the LSE in 1966–68). In 1979–80 he became, through Aaronovitch, interested in the work of Kalecki which resulted in two books in the 1980s on macroeconomics and Kalecki (Sawyer 1982, 1985) and finally an edited volume on Post Keynesian economics (1988) (Reynolds and Sawyer in King 1995a; Toporowski 2007).

49 Some of his other Cambridge students included David Dequech, Mario Garcia, Peter Kriesler and Rod O'Donnell.
50 In 1982, Eatwell became editor of the book series "Studies in Political Economy," first published by Academic Press and then by Macmillan. The aim of the series was to publish books that furthered the constructivist Sraffian agenda of reconstructing economic theory in light of Sraffa's *Production of Commodities* and then applying the theory to problems in international trade, development economics, fiscal and monetary policy and other economic problems. One of the first books in the series was Milgate's *Capital and Employment: A Study of Keynes's Economics* (1982); and others of particular interest include *Interest and Profit in the Theories of Value and Distribution* (Panico 1988) and *An Essay on Money and Distribution* (Pivetti 1991) (Eatwell in Arestis and Sawyer 2000; Eatwell 1982).
51 This emergence can be charted in John King's annotated bibliography of Post Keynesian economics (1995b). Starting in 1970, King identified five British economists publishing Post Keynesian material, four of whom were at Cambridge. By 1975, fourteen such economists were identified with eight located at Cambridge; then in 1983, twenty-five economists were publishing Post Keynesian material with less than half from Cambridge; and finally in 1987, twenty-two British economists were publishing Post Keynesian material with eight from Cambridge.
52 In addition, in the early 1980s, Aaronvitch established a "Radical Economics" book series published by Macmillan. The aim of the series was to see if radical economic theory could interpret the world better than mainstream theory and if it could show how to change it as well. Eleven books were published in the series including four by economists partook in the CSE and Post-Keynesian-heterodox activities: Keith Cowling's *Monopoly Capitalism* (1982), Michael Bleaney's *The Rise and Fall of Keynesian Economics* (1985), Paul Hare's *Planning the British Economy* (1985), and Sawyer's *The Economics of Michal Kalecki* (1985).
53 Part of the material in this section is found in the Economic and Social Research Council records of the Study Group and part is drawn from the *PKSG Newsletter*, Issues 1–7, January 1995 to December 1997, copies of which are in the possession of the author and can be accessed at *http://www.heterodoxnews.com/htnf/htn43/ PSSGNews1.pdf* and *http://www.heterodoxnews.com/htnf/htn43/PKSGNews2.pdf* (both accessed on 28 May 2008). The hyphen in Post-Keynesian was inserted for grammatical correctness and hence was an official part of the Group's name.
54 The 'E' was omitted because Arestis and Check felt that PKSEG was too clumsy.
55 This perception or view of Post Keynesian economics was also articulated by Dow (1991), but she downplays the Sraffian contribution, a trend that continued throughout the 1990s—see Arestis (1996) and Arestis and Dow in King (1995a).
56 The significance of this is that Post Keynesian economics becomes widely viewed by British heterodox economists as an approach that warrants particular attention. One acknowledgement was the 11th Keynes Seminar whose theme was "Keynes and the Post-Keynesians" and was supported by the PKSG. The program included papers by Chick on "Contributions of Post Keynesian Economics," Desai on "A Critique of Post-Keynesian Economics," Kregel on "A Post-Keynesian Explanation of the Current Slump," and Arestis on "An Independent European Central Bank: a Post-Keynesian perspective." Discussants and attendees included Steedman, Sawyer, John McCombie, Fred Lee, Reynolds, Corry, Dow, Douglas Mair, Frowen, and Frank Brouwer, all of whom were involved in the activities of the PKSG.
57 The themes of the conferences were "Finance and Economic Development" (1991), "Money and Finance in the Economic Restructuring of Europe, East and West" (1992), "Keynes, Knowledge and Uncertainty" (1993), "Symposium on the Theory of the Firm" (1994), "The Relevance of Post-Keynesian Economic Policies Today" (1995), and "Second International Conference on Keynes, Knowledge and Uncertainty" (1996).

58 A *PKSG Bulletin* was planned to replace the *PKSG Newsletter* starting in 1998, but it never materialized.
59 See Lee (1995, 1996), A. Dow (1995), Halevi (1995), Riach (1995), Smithin (1996), Downward (1996), and Kriesler (1996).
60 The grant covered expenses such as travel and subsistence for speakers and participants, secretarial costs, and stationary, photocopying, telephone, and postage costs. Over time when funds were limited, post-graduate students were given preference for reimbursement of travel costs.
61 It was published in 1995—see Arestis and Chick (1995). Edward Elgar also published other books that contained papers given at the PKSG, including Arestis and Chick (1992), and Dow and Hillard (1995, 2002a, 2002b). In addition, Macmillan/St. Martin's published a book containing papers given at the PKSG (Arestis and Sawyer 1997).
62 There were seminars at Cambridge (1996, 1997), Glasgow Caledonian University (1998), University of the West of England (1999), and Manchester Metropolitan University (2000). From 1998 to 2000, the PKSG had six seminars with fifteen papers presented and an average of twenty-two participants. In addition, Arestis and Sawyer in conjunction with the PKSG organized a series conferences from 1996 to 2000 that including honoring Paul Davidson (1996, 1998) and Geoff Harcourt (1997), political economy of central banking (1997), and economics of the third way (2000).
63 The first Post-Graduate Conference took place at Leeds in November 1996 with six papers presented, a round table discussion on post-graduate research and Post Keynesian economics, and forty-one participants. The subsequent conferences also took place at Leeds (1997 with 13 papers and 63 participants; 1998 with 22 papers; 1999 with 12 papers; and 2000 with 11 papers); and the last one took place at School of Oriental and African Studies (2001 with eight papers). The Leeds post-graduate students involved in this include Karl Petrick (Western New England College), Giuseppe Fontana (University of Leeds), Gary Slater (Bradford University).
64 This included the Stirling conference in honor of Brian Loasby (1997) and the Association for Heterodox Economics 1999 and 2000 conferences.
65 The conference papers were published in Pheby (1989).
66 Pheby's rationale for establishing ROPE, which initially was called *The Review of Post Keynesian Economics*, was that the JPKE was North American-centric which meant that Post Keynesian in the UK, Europe, Scandinavia, and Australia have felt excluded and the more adventurous and innovative work of some Post Keynesians seemed to be rejected by the JPKE, hence it was becoming intellectually stale. Thus the aim of the journal was to develop linkages between Post Keynesians and other groupings of economists, such as Institutionalists, subjectivists, and behavioralist economists and to emphasis the more positive and progressive aspects of Post Keynesian economics. Pheby and his editorial board subsequently realized that the journal's was too narrow given its projected contributors and readership; thus the name was changed to ROPE (Eichner 1987; Lawson 2000).
67 Successive Malvern conferences also produced papers for further issues of ROPE as well as an opportunity for the meeting of the editorial board.
68 For its first five years, ROPE included a "newsletter" with each issue which carried notes about the PKSG (as noted above), the Malvern conferences, and Edward Elgar's interest in publishing books in the areas of Post Keynesian and radical economics.
69 Also published in the series was Marc Lavoie's well-known book *Foundations of Post-Keynesian Economics* (1992).
70 Also published in the series were five exceptional books by Goodwin and Punzo (1987), Asimakopulos (1988), Jarsulic (1988), Torr (1988), and Kurz (1990) that examined the theoretical core of Post Keynesian-heterodox economics.

71 Some of the individuals included Alan Freeman, Francis Green, Sawyer, Peter Nolan, Jerry Coakley, Massimo De Angelis, Man-Seop Park, Downward, Lee, Singh, Paul Auerbach, David Harvie, and Hillard. Moreover a number of Leeds post-graduate students who also attended the PKSG meetings attended the 1996 CSE conference: Andrew Brown, Chris Forde, Harvie, Slater, and David Spencer.

72 After Harcourt retired, the seminar was taken over by Mark Roberts and it is now incorporated into the Queens' College, Cambridge, seminar series.

73 In 1988, the European Association for Evolutionary Political Economy (EAEPE) was established. It quickly started a newsletter (first issue was January 1989), made informal links with ROPE, and began carrying ads about the PKSG (as noted above). It later carried ads about the Malvern conference, CJE, and the CSE conference. Initially EAEPE started with fifty-one British members and by 1996 it had increased to one hundred and twelve, with an overlap with the Post Keynesian-heterodox community of at least thirty individuals. However, in spite of EAEPE's penetration into the Post Keynesian-heterodox community, it had relatively little impact on it (*EAEPE Newsletter*, January 1989, July 1989, January 1991, January 1992, and January 1995; European Association for Evolutionary Political Economy 1996).

74 The activities are given at the end of Table 7.3.

8 Research Assessment Exercise and its impact on heterodox economics, 1989–96

1 The 1986 RAE consisted of the UGC asking British universities to complete a four-part questionnaire covering various aspects of their research income and expenditure, research planning, priorities, and output. The responses received were considered by the UGC's subject subcommittees and were rated against a variety of scales and standards (Phillimore 1989).

2 The history of the unofficial modified list is an example of mainstream economists attitude towards heterodox economists and their research and journals. In particular, in the process of making the modified list a number of heterodox journals, such as the *Cambridge Journal of Economics*, *Journal of Post Keynesian Economics*, and *Capital and Class*, were deliberately rejected because they were heterodox (Lee and Harley 1998).

3 A further advertisement in the *Guardian* (June 14, 1994) noted that the appointee to the Chair in Economic Theory must be an active researcher, contributing at the leading edge of *mainstream economic theory*; and in another advertisement in the November 8, 1994 the *Guardian* stated that the appointee must be an active researcher, contributing at the leading edge of mainstream macroeconomics, either theoretical or applied.

4 In 1994–95 some twenty job specifications were obtained by sending for details of posts advertised in the educational press. Out of these, only three did not specify an area of interest within mainstream economics or make reference to ranking in the 1992 RAE.

5 In old and new British universities heads of economics departments are largely appointed by the administration rather than being elected by the members of the department. Hence department heads do not necessarily represent the interests and views of the members of the department.

6 The UFC requirement that each panel must include one representative from the non-UFC sectors of the Higher Education system. Podolski, the representative of the ex-polytechnics on the panel, was one of five economists nominated for the spot by The Standing Conference of Heads of Economics in Polytechnics.

7 Steuer was chosen for the panel because Atkinson, Hendry, and Ulph thought that he would be an appropriate generalist (Standing Committee 19/9/92).

8 This claim made at the November 4, 1989 meeting of CHUDE is at variance with the comment made in personal correspondence by one panel member who said

that he based his provisional assessment on the documentation and bibliographies and did not read the published research at all systematically.

9 For the purpose of the exercise, the core mainstream journals consisted of the Diamond core plus the "additional" mainstream journals; and the "core" heterodox journals consisted of those listed in the *SSCI*—see Appendix A.18.

10 The *SSCI: Source Index* does not carry all the journal publications of the panel members because it does not cover all economic journals. Therefore, the number of journal publications given for each panel member in Table 8.1 does not represent the total number of their publications. In addition, most panel members had journal publications which did not appear in the core mainstream or heterodox journals; thus columns two and three in Table 8.1 generally do not sum to 100 percent.

11 In addition, the panel members published and/or edited over fifty books between them.

12 This point is further reinforced by scanning the references of the articles published by the panel members. The 1989,1992, and 1996 panel members referenced over 80 percent of the mainstream journals; however, most of the references were restricted to the smaller set of journals in which their own work appeared. The little referenced and un-referenced journals were the specialists, applied, and interdisciplinary journals. The ignored journals included the *Journal of Development Economics, Journal of Financial Economics, International Journal of Industrial Organization, Public Finance, Regional Studies, Urban Studies*, and *Journal of Transport Economics and Policy.*

13 Since the panel members were also unfamiliar with the subject matter of history of economic thought, comparative economic systems, regional economics, and transport economics, one can only guess how they rated publications in *Journal of Asian and African Studies, History of Political Economy, Regional Studies*, and *Journal of Transport Economics and Policy* vis-à-vis publications in *The Economic Journal* for instance. This point is important since John Hey, as managing editor of *The Economic Journal*, stated that he rejected submissions in history of economic thought when he *believed* that the emphasis was on the history as opposed to the economics (Hey 1995,1996a, 1996b).

14 The Advisory Board for the Research Councils made this point in their review of peer review (Advisory Board for the Research Councils 1990: 31).

15 Lack of consensus when rating the value of a piece of research, bias against individual researchers and particular subjects, bias against researchers at low-status institutions, cronyism, discrimination against certain types of research (such as applied research and non-orthodox research), making major errors of assessment, and making assessments which lack scientific rigor have long been noted as possible problems with peer review; and no peer-review system can be said to have completely escaped them. Furthermore, peer review presupposes that *everybody* in the research "community" shares the same value scale as to what is good and bad research which is reasonably unique. Such consensus has never existed in any research community and certainly does not exist in a divided research community such as economics. Finally, it has been widely acknowledged that peer review can be a mechanism used by those who support the ruling paradigm to reinforce their hegemony (Peters and Ceci 1982; Roy 1982, 1984; Lock 1985; Smith 1988b; Leslie 1990; McCutchen 1991).

16 The outcome of this socially-constructed congruence between what panel members thought to be research excellence and what top-ranked departments (such as Essex which received a five in the 1992 RAE) thought to be research excellence are the slogans: "what the department values the RAE values" or "the RAE matches our standards" (derived from the 1994 questionnaire survey—see below).

17 However, only 374 could be attached to a specific institution of higher education—see Appendix A.18.

18 The details and methodology of the questionnaire are found in Harley and Lee (1997). For the questionnaire and a summary of the results, see Appendix A.18.
19 In describing the support that the economics department gave to scholarship and research, one institution from which details were received of advertised posts offered full costs to staff attending mainstream conferences but only 50 percent of costs to those who wished to attend heterodox or other non-mainstream conferences.
20 Heterodox candidates know this and therefore submerge their heterodox research interests and take up mainstream research interests:

> ... I am a Marxist, but since I am on probation until Jan. I have been forced to do mostly mainstream research or else I know I wouldn't be made permanent.
> ... on advice from a present colleague, when I applied for my current post, I stressed my ability to teach mainstream micro. I also told them that my research interest was general equilibrium. Subsequently I "came out" and pointed out my research as Marxist equilibrium. I doubt I would have got my present post had I not pursued this little deception.

21 Evidence from the questionnaire survey suggested that many departments did not make an effort to retain Marxian economics courses when their enrolments decline or to offer M.A. and M.Phil. programs that contained heterodox modules.

9 Research Assessment Exercise, the state, and the dominance of mainstream economics in British universities, 2000–2003

1 To account in part for the fifty-three non-submissions, the Royal Economic Society asserted that weaker economic departments submitted to the Management and Business Studies unit of assessment (Royal Economic Society n.d.). However, no argument or evidence was offered to support the assertion. On the other hand, the RAE panelists of Business and Management Studies felt that "the quality of the research submitted was high on the whole, with a substantial portion of at least national standing and a significant fraction of international standing" (Bessant et al. 2003: 54). The main difference between the submissions to the Economics and Business-Management panels was that the research submitted to the latter tended to be more empirical than theoretical. Moreover, they felt that economics could make significant contributions to research and the research culture in business schools.
2 For a listing of the Diamond List journals and for the number of 2001 RAE publications for each journal, see Appendix A.19.
3 The Diamond List journals are generally referred to as the core or blue-ribbon or top research mainstream neoclassical journals because of their frequent appearance as top journals in studies on rankings of economic journals. That is, from eight to twenty-two Diamond List journals are included in each of the twelve journal-ranking studies covering the period 1994 to 2003 listed in Appendix A.19. In addition, twenty-five of the journals appeared in at least one of the studies while fifteen appeared in half or more of the studies. The basis for such stability arises from the stability of beliefs concerning core journals and from the comparative stability in terms of journals' citation impact (Burton and Phimister 1995; Sutter and Kocher 2001; Lee 2006).
4 See "Section III: Panels' Criteria and Working Methods—3.30 Economics and Econometrics, UOA 38," at http://www.hero.ac.uk/rae/Pubs/5_99/ByUoA/crit38.htm (accessed June 4, 2008).
5 The RAE ranking system for 2001 (and 1996) is as follows:

Rating	Description
5*	Level of international excellence in more than half of the research activity submitted and attainable levels of national excellence in the remainder.
5	Levels of international excellence in up to half of the research activity submitted and attainable levels of national excellence in virtually all of the remainder.
4	Levels of national excellence in virtually all of the research activity submitted, showing some evidence of international excellence.
3a	Levels of national excellence in over two-thirds of the research activity submitted, possibly showing evidence of international excellence.
3b	Levels of national excellence in more than half of the research activity submitted.
2	Levels of national excellence in up to half of the research activity submitted.
1	Levels of national excellence in virtually none of the research activity submitted.

6 The list of heterodox economic journals is derived from the RAE submissions and contains most of the top international heterodox journals—see Appendix A.19. This list is a sub-set of the heterodox list used in the previous chapter as well as the more comprehensive list found in Lee et al. (2005). The list of history of economic thought and methodology journals used is also derived from the RAE submissions. They include all the top international journals—see Appendix A.19.

7 At the new universities, economists were encouraged or even told to publish in the extended list if they could not do so in the Diamond List. Hence, this is possible evidence for the frequently heard charge that the economics panel shifted the goal posts in favor of a small pre-selected group of departments whose members have the restricted capability of publishing in Diamond List journals.

8 The title of William Coleman's rather interesting book as well as its many comments against heterodox economists neatly captures this attitude: *Economics and its Enemies: two centuries of anti-economics* (2002).

9 The negative impact of the history of economic thought on department rankings has been evident since the 1992 RAE when nine of the twelve departments that submitted such publications (see Appendix A.18, "1992 RAE Diamond List," column 5 less Hull and Nottingham Trent) received a ranking of 3 or 2. Perhaps it was the well-founded belief by departments that the RAE economics panel reacts quite negatively towards any H-HET-M publications which led thirty-one universities to place a total of 145 such publications (which is more than was submitted to the economics panel) in units of assessment outside of economics. This may explain why four of the top six heterodox departments, including SOAS, Leeds, Open University, and Staffordshire (see Chapter 11), opted to place twenty-three heterodox economists with fifty-three H-HET-M publications in non-economic units of assessment (Appendix A.19 and A.22, column 1996–2000).

10 The 2000 benchmark statement in economics was developed by nineteen economists drawn from 5- to 3-starred to not-ranked departments and included three members of the RAE 2001 economics panel. Subsequently, in 2006 the statement was reviewed, revised, and published in 2007. The review group contained no heterodox economists and the revised benchmark statement does not differ significantly from the 2000 statement (Beath 2007).

11 The economic subject teams for the 2000–2001 that visited sixty universities and university colleges in England and Northern Ireland drew from fifty-three subject specialists of which eleven can be identified as heterodox economists—Arestis, Ayres, Hadjimatheou, Paliginis, Reynolds, Riach, Sawyer, Skuse, Vint, Walters,

and Wynarczyk—see Appendix A.17. Being 80 percent of the subject specialists does suggest that mainstream economists dominated the subject teams. See "Subject Overview Report" at http://www.qaa.ac.uk/reviews/reports/subjReports.asp?subjID=1 (accessed June 4, 2008).

12 For the period 2000–2002, there were no economics subject reports for Wales.

13 The results are not surprising since in 1994 only two (Cambridge and Leicester) of the twenty-nine 5-starred, 5- and 4-ranked programs had required classes that included heterodox economics (see Appendix A.21).

14 Backhouse (2002) has documented this attitude as it relates specifically to the history of economic thought.

15 These results are not surprising since in 1994 six of the eleven 3-ranked departments in 2001 did not have required modules that included heterodox economics with the only change being that London Guildhall (now London Metropolitan) eliminated the heterodox content in its required classes in order to make their courses more mainstream while Aberdeen introduced heterodox economics into its required courses. In addition in 1994 thirteen of the 23 non-ranked departments in 2001 did not have required modules that included heterodox economics; and by 2000–2002 there was a net increase to sixteen of the 23 departments. Finally, of the thirty-five non-ranked departments or institutions surveyed in 1994, twenty-three did not have required modules that included heterodox economics. In short, of the seventy-six department or institutions covered in the 1994 questionnaire plus De Montfort University, fifty-six or 74 percent did not have modules that included heterodox economics (see Appendices A.20 and A.21).

16 The Quality Assurance Agency for Higher Education, Review Reports, Subject Level, Economics, http://www.qaa.ac.uk/reviews/reports/subjReports.asp?subjID=1 (accessed June 4, 2008).

17 Some of the reasons given for never hiring a heterodox economist includes the following: (1) not likely to get publications in Diamond List journals (Birkbeck, Newcastle, and St Andrews); (2) research is of low quality and devoid of any real academic value (Exeter, Oxford, and York); and (3) would not support/enhance the department's academic reputation (Aberdeen).

18 See "RA5a: Structure, environment and staffing policy" of the named universities that are part of their 2001 RAE submissions which can be found at http://www.hero.ac.uk/rae/index.htm (accessed June 4, 2008).

19 This conclusion was also voiced by many of the respondents to the 1994 and 2003 Questionnaires.

20 These seventy departments had 94 percent of the 29,223 students taking economics. Of the twenty-five excluded departments, nineteen had thirty students or less and no heterodox economists. Of the remaining six departments whose student numbers ranged from 142 to 453, four had no heterodox economists and two had one to three heterodox economists—see Appendices A.20 and A.22.

21 In addition, there were five departments that had heterodox aims and objectives for their B.A. courses but no heterodox economists on staff. Except for De Montfort (whose aims and objectives reflected an earlier time when the department was dominated by heterodox economists), this admittedly strange coincidence suggests a weak presence of heterodox economics. In fact, one of the departments, Salford, ended its heterodox component in 2002. If the 399.5 students from these departments (excluding De Montfort) are included with the above, then the number of students increases to 76.9 percent and the number of departments increases to 74 percent.

22 At four of the universities with a single heterodox economist, elective courses at the undergraduate and post-graduate level were offered as well as an option of doing a "heterodox" doctoral dissertation.

23 It is sometimes argued that heterodox economists and heterodox economics can flourish outside of economic departments and particular reference is made to business schools. While the adversarial environment characteristic of mainstream departments are absent and heterodox economists have greater freedom in teaching and pursuing their research interests in the non-economic academic units, they can still feel pressure to conform to the RAE interests of the academic unit in which they are located. In particular, the group of journals that are considered most significant for RAE ranking purposes in Business and Management Studies do not include heterodox economic journals but do include, depending upon the study consulted, various Diamond List journals. Moreover, heterodox journal submissions were generally found in business school that received a lower ranking than business schools with Diamond List submissions. Finally, in some cases, business school submissions that included economic (as opposed to business and management studies) publications lacked to some extent internal coherence which resulted in a lower ranking. Thus, for these reasons, over time it is reasonable to expect that heterodox economists will be subject to pressure to publish in mainstream journals and/or engage in research that can be published in the top-tier business and management-studies journals. In addition, the teaching of heterodox economic theory and supervising research students interested in heterodox economics are somewhat limited. Thus, it is problematical whether heterodox economists and heterodox economics can flourish outside of economic departments in the long term (derived from the responses to the 2003 Questionnaire—see Appendix A.23; Geary et al. 2004; Baden-Fuller et al. 2000; Podsakoff et al. 2005; Harzing 2005; Cooper and Otley 1998; Bessant et al. 2003).

24 For example, see the economic department websites of East Anglia, London School of Economics, Nottingham, University College London, Warwick, Queen Mary, and others.

25 An interesting but ultimately failed example of using organizational power to suppress heterodox economics was the attempt to form the Scottish Research Institute for Economics. The proposed institute would have centralized much of the economic research in Scotland and directed it to three research areas. The "leading or core economic journals" were the targeted publishing outlets for the research. Since such journals are all mainstream journals (and this was the point of selecting them) that do not publish heterodox research, the institute would have effectively suppressed heterodox research in Scotland. This would have the intended additional impact of promoting the teaching of mainstream economics and making all Scottish departments alike in this regard. Thus, mainstream research and teaching would have come to dominant Scotland because of organizational power ("The Scottish Institute for Research in Economics,' April 5, 2004; "The Scottish Institute for Research in Economics (SIRE)—a Proposal," 30 September 2004).

26 The wording is derived from an "academic bill of rights": 108th Congress 1st Session, House Concurrent Resolution 318—"Expressing the sense of the Congress that American colleges and universities should adopt an Academic Bill of Rights to secure the intellectual independence of faculty members and students and to protect the principle of intellectual diversity." Advocates of the bill are extremely conservative. For more information, see http://studentsforacademicfreedom.org (accessed June 4, 2008) and Aby (2007).

10 The emergence of heterodox economics, 1990–2006

1 See Commons (1932, 1936), Ayres (1936), and Gruchy (1947, 1948).

2 This view remains popular among economists who are generally not engaged with heterodox economics—for example, see Hirsch (1988), Kern (1997), and the

essays in Holt and Pressman (1998) on James Buchanan, Milton Friedman, Frank Knight, and Thomas Schnelling.

3 See, for example, Street (1983), Petr (1984), Dopfer (1986), and Tool (1989).

4 This issue still exists today in that some find heterodox economics too uninspiring and would like heterodox political economy, political and social economy, or Institutional-evolutionary political economy instead—see O'Hara (2000, 2002a, 2005, 2007a).

5 Illustrative of this transition was the use of heterodox political economy, heterodox perspectives, and heterodox economics at Hobart and William Smith College over the period from the late 1980s to the early 1990s to collectively refer to the various heterodox approaches. For example, in 1993 Charles Whalen taught a course on political economy that included a survey of heterodox economics which covered Austrian, Marxian, Sraffian, Institutional, Feminist, and Post Keynesian economics (course outline is in the possession of the author) (Albelda, Gunn, and Waller 1987; Jennings 1994, 2006).

6 AFEEMAIL is the discussion list for the Association for Evolutionary Economics and its archive can be found at Heterodox Economics Web: http://www.orgs. bucknell.edu/afee/HetDisc.htm (accessed 6 June 2008); PEN-L is the discussion list for the Progressive Economists Network and its archive can be found at http:// archives.econ.utah.edu/archives/pen-l/index.htm (accessed June 6, 2008); and PKT is the discussion list for Post Keynesian Thought and its archive can be found at http://archives.econ.utah.edu/archives/pkt/index.htm (accessed June 6, 2008). For the period 1994 to 1999 there were over 300 messages that included the term "heterodox" and of these approximately 150 had the terms "heterodox economics" and/or "heterodox economists." It needs to be noted that while the PKT discussion list started in 1993, it is only possible to search it for "heterodox" for the period 1999 to 2004 when it was discontinued.

7 The two issues of the *Review* can be found at http://www.heterodoxnews.com/ *Heterodox Economics Newsletter* issue 41 (21 March 2007) (accessed June 6, 2008). Nilsson stopped publishing the *Review* because it was too costly to produce; however, he did post on the web one outcome of the *Review*, information on twenty-eight journals of interest to heterodox economists. This list of heterodox journals was first put on the web in 1994 and last updated in September 1995 but has a long web life being cited and/or referred to as late as 2004 (Nilsson 1995, 2006). The most recent version of a list of heterodox economic journals is found in Lee et al. (2005).

8 In 1995 Prychitko established a "heterodox" book series with the State University of New York Press on "Diversity in Contemporary Economics." The aim of the series was to publish scholarly manuscripts that explored methodological and/or theoretical alternatives to (not just criticisms of) mainstream neoclassical economics. And the series was not bound to any one ideology or school of thought, but welcome contributions from Austrians, Feminists, Institutionalists, Post Keynesians, radicals, Sraffians, and others. Unfortunately, the book series was shortlived with Prychitko's book as the only publication (Prychitko 2006, AFEEMAIL July 9, 1995).

9 Concretely, this meant Marxist, radical, Post Keynesian, and evolutionary economists.

10 While many heterodox economists welcome Austrian economists into the heterodox community, many Austrian economists seem to have little interest in being part of it, perhaps because of the former's questioning perspective about free markets.

11 The *Heterodox Economics Newsletter*, which comes out every two to three weeks, can be found at http://www.heterodoxnews.com (accessed June 6, 2008).

12 Evidence for this is their widespread usage on the Capital and Class, Feminist Economists Discussion Group, International Association for Feminist Economics, Online on Political Economy, AFEEMAIL, PEN-L, and PKT discussion lists

from 2000 to 2006 (perhaps on the order of 3 to 5 times greater than for the period of 1994 to 1999).

13 However, some "local" actions have occurred, such as when the local New York City chapter of URPE expelled Anwar Shaikh in 1975 because he engaged with Sraffian-Post Keynesians (Mata 2005).

14 To provide a comparison with the mainstream, there are approximately 14,775 members of the American Economic Association located in the United States; or there are about fourteen AEA mainstream economists for every heterodox economist.

15 For a more detailed history of the formation of the AHE, see Lee (2002).

16 The fringe conference that Dunne proposed was never held.

17 This encompassing view of heterodox economics was retained for the 2001 AHE Conference; but for the 2002 and subsequent AHE Conferences it was reduced to a more general statement: All economists are encouraged to come together and hear a diversity of papers on topics not well represented in mainstream economics. Papers from a plurality of perspectives and topics are encouraged.

18 This approach has generally been retained for the subsequent AHE conferences. The only exception was the two sessions on Austrian economics at the 2001 AHE Conference. The exception was made in order to get Austrian economists involved in the AHE. The drawback to the approach is that schools of thought or branches of economics are disguised and this has prompted some heterodox economists who are only familiar with a ghettoized heterodox economics to argue that the AHE appears to be closed when it is not.

19 This conference format has been retained for the subsequence AHE conferences.

20 Subsequent coordinators include Gary Slater, Andrew Mearman, and currently Alan Freeman.

21 Prior to the Conference, few heterodox economists from Ireland participated in heterodox activities in the UK However, given the interest of the two that attended the Conference combined with the AHE's intention to include all "local" heterodox economists, its mandate was extended to include Ireland as well.

22 In 1996–2000 and in 2002–3 there were approximately 174 and 166 heterodox economists in the UK—see Appendix A.22. In 2006, there were approximately 233 heterodox economists, in spite of the impact of the RAE—see Chapters 8 and 9. Of the 233, ninety-five belonged to two or more heterodox associations while twenty-three belonged to three or more. Moreover, the AHE had seventy UK members in 2006, of which twenty belonged to other heterodox associations or subscribed to the JPKE—see Appendix A.25.

23 The 1990s also witness the publication of "encyclopedias" on various heterodox approaches, where Post Keynesians refer to Institutionalism and Austrianism (King 2003), Institutionalism refers to feminism and Post Keynesianism (Hodgson, Samuels, and Tool 1994), and feminist economics refers to Institutionalism, Marxism, and Post Keynesian economics (Peterson and Lewis 1999).

24 The journals include *Cambridge Journal of Economics, Capital and Class, Feminist Economics, Journal of Economic Issues, Journal of Post Keynesian Economics, Metroeconomica, Review of Political Economy, Review of Radical Political Economics,* and *Review of Social Economy.*

25 Consequently, allegations that heterodox economists maintain a "strict" allegiance to a particular approach that is the *truth* as well as the phrases "rigidity of heterodoxy" and "staleness of work" lose meaning and substance.

26 Heterodox economists also extend the value of pluralism and its corollary to mainstream economics, but the mainstream economists generally do not reciprocate.

27 It should be noted that every one of the post-graduate programs take a pluralistic-integrative approach to teaching heterodox economics.

11   Ranking heterodox economic journals and departments

1 Other ways of improving research dependency includes heterodox departments exchanging scholars and hiring each other doctoral students and heterodox economists attending common heterodox conferences, engaging in joint research projects, and publishing in heterodox book series and other heterodox publishing outlets.

2 Consequently, while it is possible to categorize heterodox economic journals as generalist, specialists, interdisciplinary, and popular, it is not possible to hierarchically rank the categories in terms of importance and quality.

3 It is important to note that all subject specialist journals, such as labor, industrial, health, and financial economics, require the building up of self-citations to be successful.

4 The import and export measures used to "measure" research dependency do not deal in enough detail with the issue of concentration. A Herfindahl concentration index or a Gini coefficient would help illuminate whether the import/export citations are concentrated in a few heterodox journals with a long tail or more evenly distributed. The latter could indicate an increased degree of research dependency. On the other hand, some degree of concentration may reflect the use of specialized knowledge from specific heterodox journals. These issues cannot be currently addressed with the citation data constructed for this chapter. But it is certainly a topic for future exploration (Stigler 1994).

5 While there is a tendency to think of the "score" and the ensuing ranking as objective or natural, it is in fact incorrect to do so. Both the score and the ranking are socially constructed to advance the argued for goal of promoting the community of heterodox economists through enhancing research dependency. Thus the score is not an ad-hoc creation but a reasoned, argued for outcome, which like all other constructed knowledge, can be contested.

6 A fourth possible component for evaluating a heterodox economics department are national and international peer esteem indicators, such as honors and awards from professional societies, keynote addresses at major conferences, editorships, prestigious fellowships, learned society involvement, and others. However, the lack of data prevents it from being utilized in this chapter.

7 This method is quite similar to the method to be used to rank economic departments in the 2008 Research Assessment Exercise in the United Kingdom.

8 The definition enables specialist journals (such as history of economic thought journals) and interdisciplinary journals to be included as heterodox journals. It also means that heterodox journals that publish articles critical of neoclassical economic theory for the purpose of clearing at least some of the ground for developing heterodox theory do not cease to be heterodox journals.

9 While the definition argues for what constitutes a heterodox journal, a majority of the eighty-eight journals (and their editors and readers) see themselves as heterodox journals. The definition is not ad-hoc, although it is open to change; and the list can always be altered.

10 The impact of the size of a journal measured in terms of the number of articles published on its score hence ranking is neutralized by the use of ratios based on self-citations.

11 The received scores for this category are based on my evaluation of the effort the journals make towards building a body of scientific knowledge associated with it.

12 This may be easier said than done for specialist journals because their demands for specific knowledge may limit the number of different heterodox journals from which it imports citations and may limit the number of heterodox journals to which it can export citations. Only by examining a number of heterodox specialist journals (as opposed to two in this experiment) can this supposition be resolved.

13 A possible implication of a journal's low domestic production is that the economists who publish in it do not consider it very important for the research they want to publish in it; hence they treat the journal opportunistically. And a possible reason for this is that the journal lacks a sense of direction or vision qua contribution to heterodox economics.

14 A network analysis of the citations provides a slightly different picture. The *Journal of Economic Issues, Cambridge Journal of Economics,* and the *Journal of Post Keynesian Economics* are the central journals in the network of heterodox journals, while the *Review of Social Economics, Review of Political Economy,* and *Review of Radical Political Economics* are less so. On the other hand, the *Review of Radical Political Economics* is best at linking different journals in the network while the *Cambridge Journal of Economics* and *Journal of Economic Issues* are also good at linking journals, but are dependent on the journals they link with. For a more detailed discussion, see Appendix A.27.

15 Ideally the information should cover the same time period, but this was not possible for the experiment, which is why it is an illustration of the methodology rather than a ranking per se. There is also a problem concerning the selectivity of publications. It is possible because of department qua RAE pressure, some heterodox economists submitted mainstream publications in place of heterodox publications. However, the examination of the submitted publications by heterodox economists suggests that the possible selectivity bias is quite small.

16 Weighing the building knowledge measure more than the other measures is an example of the use of professional judgment, which is widely accepted in all assessment-ranking exercises. And professional judgment can also be contested, and that is also accepted, at least to some degree.

17 The benchmarks are derived from British department staffing and publishing characteristics and their RAE rankings, from the ranking criteria for the 2008 RAE (RAE 2006), from American department staffing and publishing characteristics and their ranking (Goldberger et al. 1995), and from professional judgment based on participant-observation in American and British economic departments.

18 The weightings are derived from the importance the Quality Assurance Agency gives to aims and objectives, required courses, and elective courses: see the Quality Assurance Agency for Higher Education, Review Reports, Subject Level, Economics, http://www.qaa.ac.uk/reviews/reports/subjReports.asp?subjID=1 (accessed June 5, 2008).

19 This outcome may be related to the percentage of heterodox economists in the department. However, data on department size for 1996–2000 is not easily available for all departments in the experiment. Moreover, in departments with a small percentage of heterodox economists, the overall teaching score is susceptible to a sudden and drastic decline if the mainstream economists take concerted action against the heterodox content.

20 Another aspect of a good work environment, which however is not considered here due to the lack of information, is equity in teaching load across all staff, not just males.

21 This weighting is being used by the Economics and Econometrics sub-panel for the 2008 RAE (RAE 2006). If the weightings are altered to 50 percent for each component, the rankings do alter, but not very dramatically—the correlation between the two rankings is 0.92.

Bibliography

Aaronovitch, S. (1955) *Monopoly: a study of British monopoly capitalism*, London: Lawrence and Wishart.

—— (1961) *The Ruling Class: a study of British finance capital*, London: Lawrence and Wishart.

—— (1964) *Economics for Trade Unionists: the wage system*, London: Lawrence and Wishart.

Aaronovitch, S., Murray, R., and Radice, H. (1969) General Letter, 10 November, CSE Records.

AAUP (1941) "Academic freedom and tenure," *Bulletin of the American Association of University Professors*, 27(1): 40–46.

Abelove, H. et al. (eds.) (1983) *Visions of History*, New York: Pantheon Books.

Aby, S. H. (ed.) (2007) *The Academic Bill of Rights Debate: a handbook*, Westport: Praeger Publishers.

Ackerman, F. and Nadal, A. (2004) *The Flawed Foundations of General Equilibrium: critical essays on economic theory*, London: Routledge.

Adams, J. (1994) "Maryland School of Institutional Economics," in G. M. Hodgson, W. J. Samuels, and M. R. Tool (eds.) *The Elgar Companion of Institutional and Evolutionary Economics*, 378–82, Aldershot: Edward Elgar.

Adaman, F. and Devine, P. (1996) "The Economic Calculation Debate: lessons for socialists," *Cambridge Journal of Economics*, 20(5): 523–37.

Adelman, I. (1990) "My Life Philosophy," *The American Economist*, 34(2): 3–13.

Adelstein, R. P. (1988) "Mind and Hand: Economics and Engineering at Massachusetts Institute of Technology," in Barber (1988a): 290–317.

Advisory Board for the Research Councils (1990) *Peer Review*, London: Advisory Board for the Research Councils.

AFEE (1965–95) Program for the Annual Meeting.

AFIT (1979–94), Program for the Annual Meeting.

Albelda, R. (1997) *Economics and Feminism: Disturbances in the Field*, New York: Twayne Publishers.

Albelda, R., Gunn, C., and Waller, W. (eds.) (1987) *Alternatives to Economic Orthodoxy*, Armonk: M. E. Sharpe, inc.

Allen, J. S. (1986) "The Marxist Scholar and Political Activism," *Science and Society*, 50(3): 336–40.

Altenbaugh, R. J. (1990) *Education for Struggle: The American Labor Colleges of the 1920s and 1930s*, Philadelphia: Temple University Press.

American Economic Association (1938) "Who's Who in the American Economic Association, 1938," *American Economic Review Supplement-Handbook*, 28(3): 1–104.
—— (1949) "The 1948 Directory of the American Economic Association," *American Economic Review*, 39(1): 1–343.
— 1957 "The 1956 Handbook of the American Economic Association," *American Economic Review*, 46(4): 1–522.
—— (1964) "The 1964 Handbook of the American Economic Association," *American Economic Review*, 54(1): 1–472.
Andrews, E. B. 1886. "Political Economy, Old and New," *The Andover Review*, 6: 130–48.
Andrews, G. (1995) "Young Turks and Old Guard: intellectuals and the Communist Party leadership in the 70s," in G. Andrews, N. Fishman, and K. Morgan (eds.) *Opening the Books: essays on the social and cultural history of British communism*, 195–209, London: Pluto Press.
Anderson, P. (1969) "Components of the National Culture," in A. Cockburn and R. Blackburn (eds.) *Student Power: problems, diagnosis, action*, 214–84, Harmondsworth: Penguin Books.
Anonymous. (1969) "Radicals Try to Rewrite the Book: New Left economists seek to put a theoretical base under their attack on capitalism," *Business Week*, 2091: 78–82.
—— (1970) "West Coast Conference," *URPE Newsletter*, 2(2): 3.
Anon. (1973) "Maynard's Boys and Girls," *New Statesman*, (June 15): 870–72.
Arestis, P. (1992) *The Post-Keynesian Approach to Economics*. Aldershot: Edward Elgar.
—— (1996) "Post-Keynesian Economics: Towards Coherence," *Cambridge Journal of Economics*, 20(1): 111–35.
Arestis, P. and Chick, V. (eds.) (1992) *Recent Developments in Post Keynesian Economics*, Aldershot: Edward Elgar.
—— (eds.) (1995) *Finance, Development, and Structural Change*, Aldershot: Edward Elgar.
Arestis, P. and Driver, C. (1984) "The Macrodynamics of the U.S. and U.K. Economies through two Post-Keynesian Models," *Thames Papers in Political Economy* (Summer).
Arestis, P. and Riley, J. (1980) "Monetarism: The Principal Issues and Areas of Disagreement," *British Review of Economic Issues*, 2(6): 51–69.
Arestis, P. and Sawyer, M. (1990) Personal communication. December 5.
—— (1996) "The Tobin Financial Transaction Tax: its potential and feasibility," *International Papers in Political Economy*, 3(3): 1–37.
—— (eds.) (1997) *The Relevance of Keynesian Economic Policies Today*, New York: St. Martin's Press.
—— (eds.) (2000) *A Biographical Dictionary of Dissenting Economists*, 2nd edn, Cheltenham: Edward Elgar.
Arestis, P. and Skouras, T. (eds.) (1985) *Post-Keynesian Economic Theory: a challenge to neo-classical economics*, Sussex: Wheatsheaf Books.
Arnot, R. P. (1942) *An Introduction to Political Economy*, London: Lawrence and Wishart Ltd.
Ashley, M. P. and Saunders, C. T. (1930) *Red Oxford*, Oxford: The Holywell Press, Limited.
Asimakopulos, A. (1988) *Investment, Employment, and Income Distribution*, Boulder: Westview Press.

Aslanbeigui, N. and Choi, Y. B. (1997) "Dan Fusfeld: Teacher and Mentor," in N. Aslanbeigui and Y. B. Choi (eds.) *Borderlands of Economics: essays in honor of Daniel R. Fusfeld*, 25–31, London: Routledge.

Aslanbeigui, N. and Naples, M. I. (1997a) "The Changing Status of the History of Thought in Economics Curricula," in N. Aslanbeigui and Y. B. Choi (eds.) *Borderlands of Economics: essays in honor of Daniel R. Fusfeld*, 131–50, London: Routledge.

—— 1997b. "Scissors or Horizon: neoclassical debates about returns to scale, costs, and long-run supply, 1926–1942," *Southern Economic Journal*, 64(2): 517–30.

ASE (1970–95) Program for the Annual Meeting.

ASSA (1984–95) *Allied Social Science Associations Program*.

Association for Heterodox Economics (1999) Programme and Abstracts.

—— (2000) Programme.

—— (2001) Programme.

—— (2002) Programme.

Atkins, J. (1981) *Neither Crumbs nor Condescension: the Central Labour College, 1905–1915*, Aberdeen: Aberdeen People's Press.

Atley, T. and McFarlane, B. (2001) "Maurice Dobb, Historical Materialism, and Economic Thought," in S. G. Medema and W. J. Samuels (eds.) *Historians of Economic Thought*, 63–92, London: Routledge.

Attewell, P. A. (1984) *Radical Political Economy Since the Sixties: a sociology of knowledge analysis*, New Brunswick: Rutgers University Press.

Ayres, C. E. (1936) "Fifty Years'Development in Ideas of Human Nature and Motivation," *American Economic Review*, 26(1): 224–36.

Bach, G. L. (1972) "Comment," in A. Lindbeck (ed.) *The Political Economy of the New Left*, 2nd edn, 103–18, New York: Harper and Row.

Backhouse, R. E. (1998) "The Transformation of U.S. Economics, 1920–60: viewed through a survey of journal articles," in M. S. Morgan and M. Rutherford (eds.) *From Interwar Pluralism to Postwar Neoclassicism*, 85–107, Durham: Duke University Press.

—— (2000) "Progress in Heterodox Economics," *Journal of the History of Economic Thought*, 22(2): 149–55.

—— (2002) "The Future of the History of Economic Thought in Britain," in E. R. Weintraub (ed.) *Future of the History of Economics*, 79–97, Durham: Duke University Press.

—— (2004) "A Suggestion for Clarifying the Study of Dissent in Economics," *Journal of the History of Economic Thought*, 26(2): 261–71.

Baden-Fuller, C., Ravazzolo, F., and Schweizer, T. (2000) "Making and Measuring Reputations: the research ranking of European business schools," *Long Range Planning*, 33(5): 621–50.

Baggs, C. (2001) "How Well Read was my Valley? Reading, popular fiction, and miners of South Wales, 1875–1939," *Book History*, 4: 277–301.

—— (2004) "The Whole Tragedy of Leisure on Penury: the South Wales Miners' Institute Libraries during the Great Depression," *Libraries and Culture*, 39(2): 115–36.

Bagnall, N. and Cox, E. (1973) "The Youthful Rebels," *Encounter*, 40.3: 49–55.

Baker, E. R. (2007) *On Strike and on Film: Mexican American families and blacklisted filmmakers in cold war America*, Chapel Hill: University of North Carolina Press.

Baragar, F. (2004) "Heterodox Economics at the University of Manitoba," in W. J. Samuels (ed.) *Research in the History of Economic Thought and Methodology*, Vol. 22-C, *Wisconsin "Government and Business" and the History of Heterodox Economic Thought*, 169–94, Amsterdam: Elsevier.

Baran, P. A. (1957) *The Political Economy of Growth*, New York: Monthly Review Press.

Baran, P. A. and Sweezy, P. M. (1966) *Monopoly Capital*, New York: Monthly Review Press.

Baranik, R. (1990) "Bimba, Anthony (1894–1982)," in M. J. Buhle, P. Buhle, and D. Georgakes (eds.) *Encyclopedia of the American Left*, 86–87, New York: Garland Publishing, inc.

Barber, W. J. (1988a) *Breaking the Academic Mould: economists and American higher learning in the nineteenth century*, Middletown: Wesleyan University Press.

—— (1988b) "Political Economy from the Top Down: Brown University," in Barber (1988a), 72–94.

—— (1988c) "The Fortunes of Political Economy in an Environment of Academic Conservatism: Yale University," in Barber (1988a), 132–68.

—— (1988d) "Political Economy in the Flagship of Postgraduate Studies: The Johns Hopkins University," in Barber (1988a), 203–24.

—— 1988e. "Political Economy in an Atmosphere of Academic Entrepreneurship: the University of Chicago," in Barber (1988a), 241–165.

—— (1997a) "Reconfigurations in American Academic Economics: A General Practitioner's Perspective," *Daedalus*, 126(1): 87–103.

—— (1997b) "Postwar Changes in American Graduate Education in Economics," in A. W. Coats (ed.) *The Post-1945 Internationalization of Economics*, 12–30, Durham: Duke University Press.

Barkan, J. (1997) "A Blast from the Past: Paul A. Baran and Paul M. Sweezy's *Monopoly Capital*," *Dissent*, 44: 95–101.

Barker, D. K. and Feiner, S. F. (2004) *Liberating Economics: feminist perspective on families, work, andgGlobalization*, Ann Arbor: The University of Michigan Press.

Barkin, D. (1980) "Review of *Modern Capitalism: It's Growth and Transformation* by J. Cornwall," *Review of Radical Political Economics*, 12(1): 73–74.

Barrow, C. W. (1990) *Universities and the Capitalist State: corporate liberalism and the reconstruction of American higher education, 1894–1928*, Madison: The University of Wisconsin Press.

BBC. (1995) Radio 4: *File on 4*—Research Assessment Exercise, 28 November.

Beale, H. K. (1936) *Are American Teachers Free?*, New York: Charles Scribner's Sons.

Beath, J. A. (2000) "Economics," Gloucester: Quality Assurance Agency for Higher Education. http://www.qaa.ac.uk/academicinfrastructure/benchmark/honours/economics.pdf (accessed 10 June 2008).

—— (2002) "Comments on RAE Rankings and Top Journals," *Royal Economic Society Newsletter*, 119: 6. http://www.res.org.uk/society/pdfs/newsletter/oct02.pdf (accessed 12 June 2008).

—— (2007) "Economics," Gloucester: Quality Assurance Agency for Higher Education. http://www.qaa.ac.uk/academicinfrastructure/benchmark/statements/Economics.pdf (accessed 12 June 2008).

Beauregard, E. E. (1988) *History of Academic Freedom in Ohio: case studies in higher education 1808–1976*, New York: Peter Lang.

Beck, C. (1959) *Contempt of Congress: a study of the prosecutions initiated by the Committee on Un-American Activities, 1945–1957*, New Orleans: The Phauser Press.

Becker, J. F. (1963) "Economic integration and the Administration of Values," *Studies on the Left*, 3(4): 49–77.

—— (1966) "Prosperity in Crisis," *Studies on the Left*, 6(4): 84–93.

Beckerman, W. (1976) "Crisis: in the Economy or Economics?" *New Statesman* (January 23): 90- 91.

Beed, C. and Beed, C. (1996) "Measuring the Quality of Academic Journals: the case of economics," *Journal of Post Keynesian Economics* 18.3: 369–96.

Behr, T. (1969a) "The Politics of URPE: An Editorial," *URPE Newsletter*, 1(2): 1, 3.

—— (1969b) "National Secretary's Report," *URPE. Newsletter*, 1(2): 20–21.

Bellamy, R. (1955) "British Monopoly Capitalism," *The Marxist Quarterly*, 2(4): 251–53.

—— (1956) "The Basic Economic Laws of Monopoly Capitalism," *The Marxist Quarterly*, 3(1): 14–24.

—— (1957) "Mr. Strachey's Guide to Contemporary Capitalism," *The Marxist Quarterly*, 4(1): 21–30.

—— (1970) "State Monopoly Capitalism," CSE Records.

—— (1971) "Prospects for the European Economic Community," *Bulletin of the Conference of Socialist Economists*, 1: 7–20.

—— (1981) Letter to F. Lee, in F. Lee (ed.) *Oxford Economics and Oxford Economists, 1922–1971: recollections of students and economists*, 185–91, Oxford: Bodleian Library, (1993).

—— (1986–87) "Maurice Dobb," *Bulletin of the Marx Memorial Library* 108: 38–46.

Beller, I. (1967) "American Behemoth: the concentration of U.S. corporate power," *Dissent*, 14.6: 742–56.

Bence, V. and Oppenheim, C. (2004) "The influence of Peer Review on the Research Assessment Exercise," *Journal of Information Science*, 30(4): 347–68.

Bender, T. (1993) *Intellect and Public Life*, Baltimore: The Johns Hopkins University Press.

Bergquist, H. E. (1972) "The Edward W. Bemis Controversy at the University of Chicago," *AAUP Bulletin*, 58(4): 384–93.

Bernard, P. R. (1990) "The Making of the Marginal Mind: academic economic thought in the United States, 1860–1910," Ph.D. dissertation, University of Michigan.

Bernstein, M. A. (1990) "American Economic Expertise from the Great War to the Cold War: some initial observations," *Journal of Economic History*, 50: 407–16.

—— (1995) "American Economics and the National Security State, 1941–53," *Radical History Review*, 63: 9–26.

—— (1999) "Economic Knowledge, Professional Authority, and the State: the case of American economics during and after World War II," in R. F. Garnett, Jr. (ed.) *What Do Economists Know? New Economics of Knowledge*, 103–23, London: Routledge.

—— (2001) *A Perilous Progress: economists and public purpose in twentieth-century America*, Princeton: Princeton University Press.

—— (2002) Personal communication, 11 February.

Bessant, J. et al. (2003) "The State of the Field in UK Management Research: reflections of the research assessment exercise (RAE) panel," *British Journal of Management*, 14: 51–68.

Betz, H. K. (1988) "How Does the German Historical School Fit," *History of Political Economy*, 20(3): 409–30.

Biddle, J. (1998) "Institutional Economics: a case of reprodutive failure?" in M. S. Morgan and M. Rutherford (eds.) *From Interwar Pluralism to Postwar Neoclassicism*, 108–33, Durham: Duke University Press.

Billingsley, W. J. (1999) *Communists on Campus: race, politics and the public university in sixties North Carolina*, Athens: The University of Georgia Press.

Blackburn, R. (1966) "The New Capitalism," in P. Anderson and R. Blackburn *Towards Socialism*, 114–45, London: Collins.

—— (1969) "A Brief Guide to Bourgeois Ideology," in A. Cockburn and R. Blackburn *Student Power: problems, diagnosis, action*, 163–213, Harmondsworth: Penguin Books.

Blackman, J. H. (1971) "The Outlook for Economics," *The Southern Economic Journal*, 37(4): 385–95

Blaug, M. (1999) "The Formalist Revolution or What Happened to Orthodox Economics after World War II?" in R. E. Backhouse and J. Creedy (eds.) *From Classical Economics to the Theory of the Firm: essays in honour of D. P. O'Brien*, 257–80, Cheltenham: Edward Elgar.

Bleaney, M. (1985) *The Rise and Fall of Keynesian Economics*, London: Macmillan.

—— (1996) "An Overview of Emerging Theory," in D. Greenway, M. Bleaney, and I. Stewart *A Guide to Modern Economics*, 3–18, London: Routledge.

Blecker, R. A. (2002) Personal communication, 11 February.

Bloland, H. G and Bloland, S. M. (1974) *American Learned Societies in Transition: the impact of dissent and recession*, New York: McGraw-Hill Book Company.

Bluestone, B. (1969) "Report of the Secretariat," *URPE Newsletter*, 1(1): 5–7.

Blyth, J. A. (1983) *English University Adult Education, 1908–1958*, Manchester: Manchester University Press.

Bodenhorn, Howard, 2003, "Economic Scholarship at Elite Liberal Arts Colleges: a citation. analysis with rankings," *Journal of Economic Education* 34(4): 341–59.

Boettke, P. J. (1989) "Evolution and Economics: Austrians as Institutionalists," *Research in the History of Economic Thought and Methodology*, 6: 73–90.

Bogdanoff, A. (1925) *A Short Course of Economic Science*, revised edn, London: The Labour Publishing Company Limited.

Bohm, S. (1989) "Subjectivism and Post-Keynesianism: towards a better understanding," in J. Pheby (ed.) *New Directions in Post-Keynesian Economics*, 59–93, Aldershot: Edward Elgar.

Booth, H. (1968) "Chicago Conferences: what role for professionals?" *Radicals in the Professions Newsletter*, 1(4): 2–4.

Bortis, H. (1997) *Institutions, Behaviour and Economic Theory*, Cambridge: Cambridge University Press.

Borts, G. H. (1972) "Statement of Editorial Policy," *American Economic Review*, 62(4): 764.

—— (1981) "Report of the Managing Editor, *American Economic Review*," *American Economic Review*, 71(2): 452–64.

Boulding, K. (1977) Letter to Paul Davidson, 27 September, S. Weintraub Papers, Box 9, folder 2.

Bowen, H. R. (1953) "Graduate Education in Economics," *American Economic Review*, 43 (4-Part 2): 1–223.

Boyer, G. and Smith, R. (2000) "The Development of the Neoclassical Tradition in Modern Labor Economics," *Industrial and Labor Relations*, 54(2): 199–233.

Brand, H. (1962) "Disarmament and the Prospects of American Capitalism," *Dissent*, 9(3): 236–51.

Brauninger, M. and Haucap, J. (2003) "Reputation and Relevance of Economics Journals," *Kyklos*, 56(2): 175–98.

Braverman, H. (1974) *Labor and Monopoly Capital*, New York: Monthly Review Press.

Braxton, J. M. (1986) "The Normative Structure of Science: social control in the academic profession," in J. C. Smart (ed.) *Higher Education: handbook on theory and research*, vol. 2: 309–57, New York: Agathon Press, inc.

Brazelton, W. R. (1981a) "Post Keynesian Economics: an Institutional compatibility?" *Journal of Economic Issues*, 15(2): 531–42.

—— (1981b) "The Foundations of Post Keynesian Economics," *Review of Institutional Thought*, 1: 85–86.

—— (1998) Personal communication, 14 August.

—— (2004) "The Oklahoma "Institutionalist" School," in W. J. Samuels (ed.) *Research in the History of Economic Thought and Methodology*, vol. 22-C, *Wisconsin "Government and Business" and the History of Heterodox Economic Thought*, 245–60, Amsterdam: Elsevier.

Brazer, M. (1982) "The Economics Department of the University of Michigan: a centennial retrospective," in S. H. Hyman (ed.) *Economics and the World Around It*, 133–275, Ann Arbor: The University of Michigan Press.

Breit, W. and Culbertson, Jr., W. P. (1976) "Clarence Edwin Ayres: An intellectual's Portrait," in W. Breit and W. P. Culbertson (eds.) *Science and Ceremony: The Institutional Economics of C. E. Ayres*, 3–22, Austin: University of Texas Press.

Bronfenbrenner, M. (1964) "Marxian Economics in the United States," *American Economic Review*, 54.6: 1019–26.

—— (1970a) "Radical Economics in America: a 1970 survey," *The Journal of Economic Literature*, 8(3): 747–66.

—— (1970b) "The Vicissitudes of Marxian Economics," *History of Political Economy*, 2(2): 205–24.

—— (1973) "A Skeptical View of Radical Economics," *The American Economist*, 17(3): 4–8.

—— (1993) "Wisconsin 1947–1957: reflections and confessions de mortuis nil nisi bolognam," in R. Lampman (ed.) *Economists at Wisconsin, 1892–1992*, 130–38, Madison: The Board of Regents of the University of Wisconsin System.

Brooks, D. (1970) "More on the Politics of URPE," *URPE Newsletter*, 1(4): 17.

Broome, J. (1977) "Sraffa's Standard Commodity," *Australian Economic Papers*, 16 (29): 231–36.

Brown, C. (1968) "Sociology: insurgency at the ASA Convention," *Radicals in the Professions Newsletter* 1(9): 17.

Brown, E. (1981) "The Neoclassical and Post-Keynesian Research Programs: the methodological issues," *Review of Social Economy*, 39(2): 111–32.

Brumaire, L. (1910) "Economics or – What?" *The Plebs Magazine*, 2.10: 245–48.

Buhle, M. J, Buhle, P., and Georgakas, D. (eds.) (1990) *Encyclopedia of the American Left*, New York: Garland Publishing, inc.

Buhle, P. (1967) "American Radical History: A Progress Report," *New Left Notes*, 2(2): 2.

—— (ed.) (1990) *History and the New Left: Madison, Wisconsin, 1950–1970*, Philadelphia: Temple University Press.

Bunting, D. (2002) Personal communication, 11 February.

Burczak, T., Cullenberg, S., Prychitko, D., and Boettke, P. (1998) "Socialism, Capitalism, and the Labor Theory of Property: a Marxian-Austrian dialogue," *Rethinking Marxism*, 10(2): 65–105.

Burgum, E. B., et al. (1941) "Editorial," *Science and Society*, 5(1): 1.

Burkett, P. (2006) *Marxism and Ecological Economics: toward a red and green political economy*, Boston: Brill.

Burrows, J. H. (1978) "The Teaching of Economics in the Early Days of the University Extension Movement in London, 1876–1902," *History of Economic Thought Newsletter*, 20: 8–14.

Burton, E. (1954) "Academic Freedom and the Communists," *The Marxist Quarterly*, 1(2): 104–16.

Burton, M. P. and Phimister, E. (1995) "Core Journals: a reappraisal of the Diamond List," *Economic Journal*, 105(1): 361–73.

Bush, P. D. (1991) "Reflections on the Twenty-Fifth Anniversary of AFEE: philosophical and methodological issues in Institutional economics," *Journal of Economic Issues*, 25(2): 321–46.

Cain, G. G. (1993) "Labor Economics," in R. Lampman (ed.) *Economists at Wisconsin, 1892–1992*, 234–46, Madison: The Board of Regents of the University of Wisconsin System.

Campbell, A. (2002) Personal communication, 13 February.

Carlson, V. (1968) "The Education of an Economist Before the Great Depression: Harvard's economics department in the 1920's," *The American Journal of Economics and Sociology*, 27: 101–12.

Carnegie Commission on Higher Education. (1973a) *The Purposes and the Performance of Higher Education in the United States: approaching the year 2000*, New York City: McGraw-Hill Book Company.

—— (1973b) *Priorities for Action: final report of the Carnegie Commission on Higher Education*, New York City: McGraw-Hill Book Company.

—— (1973c) *Governance of Higher Education: six priority problems*, New York City: McGraw-Hill Book Company.

Carney, L. S. (1967) "The Economics of International Capitalism," *New Left Notes*, 2(13): 4–6.

Cartter, A. M. (1966) *An Assessment of Quality in Graduate Education*, Washington, D.C.: American Council on Education.

Carvalho, F. (1984–85) "Alternative Analysis of Short and Long Run in Post Keynesian Economics," *Journal of Post Keynesian Economics*, 7: 214–34.

—— (1998) Personal communication, 26 October.

Christiansen, J. (1974) "Could Karl Marx Teach Economics in America?" *Newsletter of the Union for Radical Political Economics*, 6(3): 32–33.

Chester, N. (1986) *Economics, Politics and Social Studies in Oxford, 1900–85*, London: The Macmillan Press Ltd.

Cheyney, E. P. (1940) *History of the University of Pennsylvania, 1740–1940*, Philadelphia: University of Pennsylvania Press.

Chick, V. (1978a) "Keynesians, Monetarists and Keynes: the end of the debate – or a beginning?" *Thames Papers in Political Economy*, (Spring).

—— (1978b) "Keynes" Theory, Keynesian Policy and the Post-War inflation," *British Review of Economic Issues*, 1(3): 1–24.

—— (1978c) "The Nature of the Keynesian Revolution: a reassessment," *Australian Economic Papers*, 17.30: 1–20.

Childs, D. (1997) *Britain Since 1945: a political history*, 4th edn, London: Routledge.

Chun, L. (1993) *The British New Left*, Edinburgh: Edinburgh University Press.

Church, R. L. (1974) "Economists as Experts: the rise of an academic profession in the United States, 1870–1920," in L. Stone *The University in Society*, volume 1, *Europe, Scotland, and the United States from the 16th to the 20th Century*, 571–609, Princeton: Princeton University Press.

Ciscel, D. (2004) Personal communication, 21 September.

Clancy, R. (1952) *A Seed was Sown*, New York City: Henry George School of Social Science.

Clecak, P. (1968) "Monthly Review: an assessment," *Monthly Review*, 20(6): 1–17.

Coats, A. W. (1963) "John Elliotson Symes, Henry George and Academic Freedom in Nottingham during the 1880s," *Renaissance and Modern Studies*, 7: 110–38.

—— (1967) "Sociological Aspects of British Economic Thought (ca. 1880–1930)," *The Journal of Political Economy*, 75: 706–29.

—— (1968) "Henry Carter Adams: a case study in the emergence of the social sciences in the United States, 1850–1910," *Journal of American Studies*, 2: 177–97.

—— (1971) "The Role of Scholarly Journals in the History of Economics: an essay," *Journal of Economic Literature*, 9(1): 29–44.

—— (1998) "Economists, the Economics Profession, and Academic Freedom in the United States," in W. L. Hansen (ed.) *Academic Freedom on Trial*, 124–54, Madison: University of Wisconsin.

Coats, A. W. and Booth, A. E. (1978) "The Market for Economists in Britain, 1945–75: a preliminary survey," *Economic Journal*, 88(3): 436–54.

Cohen, J. B. (1990) "Jewish Workers University," in M. J. Buhle, P. Buhle, and D. Georgakas (eds.) *Encyclopedia of the American Left*, 393–94, New York: Garland Publishing, inc.

Cohen, M. (1990a) "The Labour College Movement Between the Wars: national and north-west developments," in Simon (1990a), 105–36.

—— (1990b) "Revolutionary Education Revived; the communist challenge to the Labour Colleges, 1933–45," in Simon (1990a), 137–52.

Cohen, R. (1993) *When the Old Left was Young: student radicals and America's first mass student movement, 1929–1941*, New York: Oxford University Press.

Colander, D. (2001) "An Interview with Paul Davidson," *Eastern Economic Journal*, 27(1): 85–114.

Colander, D., Holt, R. P. F., and Rosser, J. B. (2004) "The Changing Face of Mainstream Economics," *Review of Political Economy*, 16(4): 485–99.

Colander, D. and Landreth, H. (1998) "Political Influence on the Textbook Keynesian Revolution: God, man and Lorie Tarshis at Yale," in O. F. Hamouda and B. B. Price (eds.) *Keynesianism and the Keynesian Revolution in America: a memorial volume in honour of Lorie Tarshis*, 59–72, Cheltenham: Edward Elgar.

Cole, G. D. H. (1932) "The Tutorial Class in British Working-Class Education," *The International Quarterly of Adult Education*, 1(3): 127–48.

Cole, G. D. H. et al. (1918) *The W.E.A. Education Year Book*, London: The Workers' Educational Association.

Coleman, D. C. (1987) *History and the Economic Past: an account of the rise and decline of economic history in Britain*, Oxford: Clarendon Press.

Coleman, W.O. (2002) *Economics and Its Enemies: two centuries of anti-economics*, New York: Palgrave Macmillan.

Colfax, J. D. (1973) "Repression and Academic Radicalism," *New Politics*, 10: 14–27.

Collard, D. A. (1990) "Cambridge After Marshall," in J. K. Whitaker (ed.) *Centenary Essays on Alfred Marshall*, 164–92, Cambridge: Cambridge University Press.

Collier, C. F. (1979) "Clark and Patten: exemplars of the new American professionalism," in R. V. Andelson (ed.) *Critics of Henry George: a century appraisal of their strictures on Progress and Poverty*, 261–72, Rutherford: Fairleigh Dickinson University Press.

Collins, R. (1998) *The Sociology of Philosophies: a global theory of intellectual change*, Cambridge: Belknap Press.

Colyer, W. T. (1932) *An Outline of Economics*, Revised, London: N.C.L.C. Publishing Society, Ltd

Committee on Un-American Activities. (1957) *Guide to Subversive Organizations and Publications (and Appendix)*, Washington, D.C.: Government Printing Office.

Commons, J. R. (1932) "Institutional Economics: comment," *American Economic Review*, 22(2): 264–68.

—— (1936) "Institutional Economics," *American Economic Review*, 26(1): 237–49.

Conference of Heads of University Departments of Economics. (1989–94) Minutes, Royal Economic Society.

Conference of Socialist Economists. (1970–82) *Newsletter*, CSE Records.

—— (1972a) "Introduction to the Conference of Socialist Economists (CSE)," CSE Records.

—— (1972b) "1972 Conference: The Nature of Capitalist Crisis," CSE Records.

—— (1973) "Conference of Socialist Economists (CSE)," CSE Records.

—— (1974a) "Conference on Imperialism," CSE Records.

—— (1974b) "Conference of Socialist Economists (CSE)," H. Radice Personal Files.

—— (1975) "C.S.E. Activities 1974/75," CSE Records.

—— (1981) "CSE Membership Handbook, 1980–81," CSE Records.

—— (1988–96) CSE Conference, CSE Records.

Conroy, M. E. and Dusasky, R. (1995) "The Productivity of Economics Departments in the U.S.: publications in the core journals," *Journal of Economic Literature*, 33 (4): 1966–71.

Cooke, A. (2006) *From Popular Enlightenment to Lifelong Learning: a history of adult education in Scotland, 1707–2005*, Leicester: National institute of Adult Continuing Education.

Cookingham, M. E. (1987) "Social Economists and Reform: Berkeley, 1906–61," *History of Political Economy*, 19(1): 47–65.

—— (1988) "Political Economy in the Far West: the University of California and Stanford University," in Barber (1988a), 266–89.

Coolidge, C. (1921) "Enemies of the Republic: are the "Reds" stalking our college women?" *The Delineator* (June): 4–5, 66–67.

Cooper, C. and Otley, D. (1998) "The 1996 Research Assessment Exercise for Business and Management," *British Journal of Management*, 9(2): 73–89.

Cornell, F. (1976) "A History of the Rand School of Social Science—1906 to 1956," Ph.D. dissertation, Columbia University.

Cowling, K. (1982) *Monopoly Capitalism*, London: The Macmillan Press Ltd.

Coyle, E. (2002) Personal communication, 23 February.

Crane, D. (1965) "Scientists at Major and Minor Universities: a study of productivity and recognition," *American Sociological Review*, 30(4): 699–714.

Craik, W. W. 1912. "The Central Labour College Provincial Classes," *The Plebs Magazine*, 4.9: 201–2.

—— (1964) *The Central Labor College, 1909–29*, London: Lawrence and Wishart.

Critchlow, D. T. (1985) *The Brookings Institution, 1916–1952: expertise and the public interest in a democratic society*, DeKalb: Northern Illinois University Press.

Cross, I. B. (1967) *Portrait of an Economics Professor*, Berkeley: University of California, Bancroft Library, Regional Oral History Office.

Crotty, J. R. (1993) "Rethinking Marxian Investment Theory: Keynes-Minsky instability, competitive regime shifts, and coerced investment," *Review of Radical Political Economics*, 25(1): 1–26.

Curran, P. J. (2000) "Competition in UK Higher Education: competitive advantage in the Research Assessment Exercise and Porter's Diamond model," *Higher Education Quarterly*, 54(4): 386–410.

Cutler, A. T. (1938) "The Ebb of Institutional Economics," *Science and Society*, 2(4): 448–70.

—— (1939) "On Institutional Economics: Professor Cutler replies," *Science and Society*, 3(4): 514–18.

Dabysing, S. and Jones, D. (1983) "A Simplified Post-Keynesian Model of Inflation for Teaching Purposes," *British Review of Economic Issues*, 5.13: 87–106.

Dahrendorf, R. (1995) *LSE: a history of the London School of Economics and Political Science, 1895–1995*, Oxford: Oxford University Press.

Danby, C. (2004) "Toward a Gendered Post Keynesianism: subjectivity and time in a nonmodernist framework," *Feminist Economics*, 10(3): 55–75.

Daniel, S. (1999) Personal communication, 23 July.

Danner, P. L. (1991) "The Anniversary Issue," *Review of Social Economy*, 49(4): 439–43.

Darrell, J. (1937) "The Economic Consequences of Mr. Keynes," *Science and Society*, 1(2): 194–211.

Dasgupta, P. (1999) Personal communication, 7 May.

Davidson, P. (1965) "Keynes's Finance Motive," *Oxford Economic Papers*, 17: 46–65.

—— (1968) "Money, Portfolio Balance, Capital Accumulation and Economic Growth," *Econometrica*, 36: 291–321.

—— (1969a) Letter to Joan Robinson, 14 November, Joan Robinson Papers, vii/114/80.

—— (1969b) Letter to Joan Robinson, 15 December, Joan Robinson Papers, vii/114/84–88.

—— (1970a) Letter to Joan Robinson, 2 March, Joan Robinson Papers, vii/114/90–91.

—— (1970b) Letter to Joan Robinson, September, Joan Robinson Papers, vii/114/102.

—— (1970c) Letter to Sidney Weintraub, 21 October, S. Weintraub Papers, Box 2, folder 1.

—— (1972a) Letter to Alfred S. Eichner, 18 January, Paul Davidson Papers, Box 2, folder-Alfred Eichner.

—— (1972b) *Money and the Real World*, New York: John Wiley and Sons.

—— (1972c) Letter to A. Eichner, 5 October, P.Davidson Papers, Box 2, folder Alfred Eichner.

—— (1977) Letter to S. Weintraub, 29 July, S. Weintraub Papers, Box 9, folder 2.

—— (1978) Letter to S. Weintraub, 29 March, S. Weintraub Papers, Box 4, folder 3.

—— (1979) Letter to Joan Robinson, 3 May, Joan Robinson Papers, vii/114/173–74.

—— (1980a) Letter to J. K. Galbraith, 3 June, S. Weintraub Papers, Box 11, folder 4.

—— (1980b) Letter to Stuart Speiser, 3 June, S. Weintraub Papers, Box 11, folder 4

—— (1980c) "Post Keynesian Economics," *The Public Interest*, (Special Issue): 151–73.

—— (1981) Letter to Eric Roll, 12 February, S. Weintraub Papers, Box 11, folder 4.

—— (1986) "A Post Keynesian View of Theories and Causes for High Real Interest Rates," *Thames Papers in Political Economy* (Spring).

—— (1998) "Twenty Years Old and Growing Stronger Every Day," *Journal of Post Keynesian Economics*, 21(1): 3–10.

—— (2002) Personal communication, 15 January.

—— (2003) Personal communication to M. Forstater, 25 January.

—— (2003–4) "Setting the Record Straight on *A History of Post Keynesian Economics*," *Journal of Post Keynesian Economics*, 26(2): 245–72.

—— (2005) "Response to Lavoie, King, and Dow on what Post Keynesian is and who is a Post Keynesian," *Journal of Post Keynesian Economics*, 27(3): 393–408.

Davidson, P. and Weintraub, S. (1977a) "Proposal for the *Quarterly Journal of Post-Keynesian Economics*," S. Weintraub Papers, Box 9, folder 1.

—— (1977b) "Keynesian Economic Journal," S. Weintraub Papers, Box 9, folder 1.

—— (1977c), "*The Journal of Post-Keynesian Economics*," S. Weintraub Papers, Box 9, folder 1.

Davis, H. B. (1961) "The Unproductive Nature of "Productive" Labor," *Science and Society*, 25(1): 20–25.

—— (1962) "Imperialism and Labor: analysis of Marxian views," *Science and Society*, 26(1): 26–45.

—— (1965) "Notes on Marxian Economics in the United States: reply," *American Economic Review*, 55: 861–63.

Davis, J. B. (1997) "Comment," in A. Salanti and E. Screpanti (eds.) *Pluralism in Economics: new perspectives in history and methodology*, 207–11, Cheltenham: Edward Elgar.

—— (1999) "Social Economics: Organizations," in P. A. O'Hara (ed.) *Encyclopedia of Political Economy*, 1038–40, London: Routledge.

—— (2006) "The Turn in Economics: neoclassical dominance to mainstream pluralism?" *Journal of Institutional Economics* 2(1): 1–20.

Dawidoff, N. (2002) *The Fly Swatter: how my grandfather made his way in the world*, New York: Pantheon Books.

DeGregori, T. R. (1987) "Resources Are Not; they become: an Institutional theory," *Journal of Economic Issues*, 21(3): 1241–63.

—— (2004) Personal communication, 20 September.

Deibler, F. S. (1919) "Statement on the Case of Professor Louis Levine of the University of Montana," *Bulletin of the American Association of University Professors*, 5(5): 13–25.

—— (1921) "Report of the Sub-Committee of Inquiry for Middlebury College," *Bulletin of the American Association of University Professors*, 7(5): 28–37.

De Leon, S. and Fine, N. (eds.) (1927) *The American Labor Year Book, 1927*, New York: Vanguard Press.

DePodwin, H. J. and Seldon, R. T. (1963) "Business Pricing Policies and Inflation," *Journal of Political Economy*, 71: 116–27.

Deprez, J. (1985–86) "Time in a Multi-Industry, Fixed-Capital World," *Journal of Post Keynesian Economics*, 8(2): 249–65.

Desai, M. (1991) "The Underworld of Economics: heresy and heterodoxy in economic thought," in G. K. Shaw (ed.) *Economics, Culture and Education: essays in honour of Mark Blaug*, 53–63, Aldershot: Edward Elgar.

Devine, P. (1973) "Inflation and Marxist Theory," CSE Records.

—— (2007) Personal communication, 7 May.

Diamond, A. (1989) "The Core Journals in Economics," *Current Contents*, 21: 4–11.

Diamond, S. (1992) *Compromised Campus: the collaboration of universities with the intelligence community, 1945–1955*, New York: Oxford University Press.

Dickinson, H. D. (1936–37) "A Comparison of Marxian and Bourgeois Economics," *The Highway*, 29: 82–85.

—— (1963) "Contemporary Marxist Economics," *The New Left Review*, 21: 30–35.

Dilling, E. (1935) *The Red Network: a who's who and handbook of radicalism for patriots*, Chicago.

Divine, T. F. (1991) "The Origin and the Challenge of the Future," *Review of Social Economy*, 49(4): 542–45.

Dobb, M. H. (1922) "Marx and Marshall," *The Plebs*, 14(4): 106–9.

—— (1943) *Economics of Capitalism: an introductory outline*, London: Lawrence and Wishart, Ltd.

—— (1949) "A Critical Review of Recent Tendencies in Bourgeois Economic Thought," Maurice Dobb Papers, Lectures DD127.

—— (1950) "Full Employment and Capitalism," *The Modern Quarterly*, 5(2): 125–35.

—— (1952) "The Accumulation of Capital," *The Modern Quarterly*, 7(2): 95–100.

—— (1955) "Recent Trends in Economic Theory in Britain and America," Maurice Dobb Papers, Publications DA22.

—— (1969) "Theories of Distribution From Ricardo to Sraffa," 22 October, Maurice Dobb Papers, DD216.1–23.

—— (1970a) Letter to P. Sraffa. 6 August, Maurice Dobb Papers, CB27(3).1–2.

—— (1970b) "The Sraffa System and Critique of the Neo-Classical Theory of Distribution," *De Economist*, 118: 347–62.

—— (1975–76a) "The Crisis in Economic Theory: some random comments on the debate," Maurice Dobb Papers, Publications DA 111.

—— (1975–76b) "A Note on the Ricardo–Marx–Sraffa Discussion," *Science and Society*, 39(4): 468–70.

—— (n.d.) *The Development of Capitalism: an outline course for classes and study circles*, London: Labour Research Department.

Dobbs, Z. (1962) *Keynes at Harvard: economic deception as a political credo*, revised edn, New York City: Veritas Foundation.

Donnan, E. (1952) "A Nineteenth-Century Academic Cause Celebre," *The New England Quarterly*, 25: 23–46.

Donnelly, M. S. (1985) "Academic Freedom and the Cold War: the case of Dr. Horace Davis," University of Missouri-Kansas City Archives, Arts and Sciences Department of Economics, Horace Davis, KC: 3/11/4, Box 1.16.

Donovan, G. (2004) "Economics Split Divides Notre Dame," *National Catholic Reporter*, 9 April, Http://www.natcath.com/NCR_Online/archives2/2004b/040904/040904c.php (accessed 19 June 2008).

Dopfer, K. (1986) "Causality and Consciousness in Economics: concepts of change in orthodox and heterodox economics," *Journal of Economic Issues*, 20(2): 509–23.

Dorfman, J. (1949) *The Economic Mind in American Civilization, 1865–1918*, vol. 3, New York: The Viking Press.

—— (1955) "Department of Economics," in *A History of The Faculty of Political Science, Columbia University*, 161–206. New York: Columbia University Press.

—— (1959) *The Economic Mind in American Civilization, 1918–1933*, vol. 4, New York: The Viking Press.

—— (1970) "Heterodox Economic Thinking and Public Policy," *Journal of Economic Issues*, 4(1): 1–22.

Dow, A. (1995) "The Future of Post Keynesianism," *PKSG Newsletter*, Issue 2: 1–2.

Dow, S. C. (1990) "Beyond Dualism," *Cambridge Journal of Economics*, 14(2): 143–57.

—— (1991) "The Post-Keynesian School," in D. Mair and A. G. Miller (eds.) *A Modern Guide to Economic Thought*, 176–206, Aldershot: Edward Elgar.

—— (2000) "Prospects for the Progress of Heterodox Economics," *Journal of the History of Economic Thought* 22(2): 157–70.

Dow, S. C. and Hillard, J. (eds.) (1995) *Keynes, Knowledge and Uncertainty*, Aldershot: Edward Elgar.

—— (eds.) (2002a) *Post Keynesian Econometrics, Microeconomics and the Theory of the Firm*, Aldershot: Edward Elgar.

—— (eds.) (2002b) *Keynes, Uncertainty and the Global Economy*, Aldershot: Edward Elgar.

Dowd, D. (1974) Letter to Joan Robinson, 22 May, Joan Robinson Papers, vii/124/1.

—— (1982) "Marxism for the Few, or Let 'em Eat Theory," *Monthly Review*, 33.11: 14–28.

—— (1994) "Against Decadence: the work of Robert A. Brady (1901–63)," *Journal of Economic Issues*, 28(4): 1031–61.

—— (1997) *Blues for America: a critique, a lament, and some memories*, New York: Monthly Review Press.

—— (1998) Personal communication, 1 January.

—— (2002) Personal communication, 12 February.

Downing, L. A. and Salomone, J. J. (1969) "Professors of the Silent Generation: how the Cold War affected political commitments of professors," *Trans-action*, 6(8): 43–45.

Downward, P. (1994) "A Reappraisal of Case Study Evidence on Business Pricing: neoclassical and Post Keynesian perspectives," *British Review of Economic Issues*, 16: 23–43.

—— (1996) "The Future of the Post Keynesian Economics Study Group," *PKSG Newsletter*, Issue 4: 6–8.

Drews, W. and Fieldhouse, R. (1996) "Residential Colleges and Non-Residential Settlements and Centres," in Fieldhouse and Associates (1996), 239–63.

Driver, C. (1999) Personal communication, June.

Drucker, P. (1994) *Max Shachtman and His Left*, Atlantic Highlands: Humanities Press.

Du Boff, R. B. (2002) Personal communication, 24 February.

Dugger, R. (1974) *Our Invaded Universities: form, reform and new starts*, New York: W. W. Norton and Company, Inc.

Dugger, W. M. (1977) "Social Economics: one perspective," *Review of Social Economy*, 35: 299–310.

—— (1979) "The "Long Run" and its Significance to Social Economy," *Review of Social Economy*, 37: 199–210.

—— (ed.) (1989) *Radical Institutionalism: contemporary voices*, New York: Greenwood Press.

—— (1993) "Challenges Facing Social Economists in the Twenty-First Century: an Institutionalist erspective," *Review of Social Economy*, 51: 490–503.

Dugger, W. M. and Sherman, H. J. (2000) *Reclaiming Evolution: a dialogue between Marxism and Institutionalism on social change*, New York: Routledge.

Duncan, R. (1992) "Independent Working Class Education and the Formation of the Labour College Movement in Glasgow and the West of Scotland, 1915–22," in R. Duncan and A. McIvor (eds.) *Militant Workers: labour and class conflict on the Clyde, 1900–1950*, 106–28, Edinburgh: John Donald Publishers Ltd.

—— (2003) "Ideology and Provision: the WEA and the politics of workers' education in early twentieth-century Scotland," in S. K. Roberts (ed.) *A Ministry of Enthusianism*, 176–97, London: Pluto Press.

Dunne, P. (ed.) (1991) *Quantitative Marxism*, Cambridge: Basil Blackwell.

Dusansky, R. and Vernon, C. J. (1998) "Rankings of U.S. Economics Departments," *Journal of Economic Perspectives*, 12(1): 157–70.

Dutt, A. K. (1990) *Growth, Distribution, and Uneven Development*, Cambridge: Cambridge University Press.

Eagly, R. V. (1974) "Contemporary Profile of Conventional Economists," *History of Political Economy*, 6(1): 76–91.

—— (1975) "Economics Journals as a Communications Network," *Journal of Economic Literature*, 13(3): 878–88.

Earnest, E. (1953) *Academic Procession*, Indianapolis: The Bobbs-Merrill Company, Inc.

Eaton, J. (1949) *Political Economy: a Marxist textbook*, London: Lawrence and Wishart Ltd.

—— (1951) *Marx Against Keynes*, London: Lawrence and Wishart Ltd.

—— (1966) *Political Economy*, revised edn, New York: International Publishers.

Eatwell, J. 1982. "Series Editor's Preface," in M. Milgate *Capital and Employment*, v–vii, London: Academic Press.

Eatwell, J. and Milgate, M. (eds.) (1983) *Keynes's Economics and the Theory of Value and Distribution*, London: Duckworth.

Edwards, R. C. et al. (1970) "A Radical Approach to Economics: basis for a new curriculum," *American Economic Review* 60: 352–63.

Efaw, F. (1998) Personal communication, 27 October.

Eichner, A. S. (1976a) Letter to P. Davidson, 16 June, P. Davidson Papers, Box 2, folder Alfred Eichner.

—— (1976b) Letter to Colleague, 1 October, P. Davidson Papers, Box 2, folder Alfred Eichner.

—— (1977) Letter to Sidney Weintraub, 17 January, S. Weintraub Papers, Box 4, folder 1.

—— (ed.) (1979) *A Guide to Post-Keynesian Economics*, White Plains: M. E. Sharpe, Inc.

—— (1983) "The Post-Keynesian Paradigm and Macrodynamic Modelling," *Thames Papers in Political Economy* (Spring).

—— (1987) Letter to P. Davidson, P. Davidson Papers, Box 2, folder Alfred Eichner.

—— (1991) *The Macrodynamics of Advanced Market Economies*, Armonk, New York: M. E. Sharpe.

Eichner, A. S. and Kregel, J. A. (1975) "An Essay on Post-Keynesian Theory: a new paradigm in economics," *Journal of Economic Literature*, 13: 1293–1314.

Eisner, R. (1978) "Machlup on Academic Freedom," in J. S. Dreyer (ed.) *Breath and Depth in Economics: Fritz Machlup – the man and his ideas*, 3–12, Lexington: D. C. Heath and Company.

Elliott, J. E. and Cownie, J. (eds.) (1975) *Competing Philosophies in American Political Economics*, Pacific Palisades: Goodyear Publishing Company.

Elmslie, B. (2004) Personal communication, 21 September.

Ely, R. T. 1887. "Political Economy in America," *North American Review*, 146: 113–19.

Emami, Z. (1993) "Challenges Facing Social Economics in the Twenty-First Century: a feminist perspective," *Review of Social Economy*, 51(4): 416–25.

Emmett, R. B. (1998) "Entrenching Disciplinary Competence: the role of general education and graduate study in Chicago economics," in M. S. Morgan and

M. Rutherford (eds.) *From interwar Pluralism to Postwar Neoclassicism*, 134–50, Durham: Duke University Press.

Enros, P. (1984) "Kenneth O. May – Bibliography," *Historia Mathematica* 11: 380–93.

Ericson, E. E. (1975) *Radicals in the University*, Stanford: Hoover Institution Press.

European Association for Evolutionary Political Economy. (1996) *1996 Handbook*, Cambridge: Victoire Press.

Evenitsky, A. (1960) "Monopoly Capitalism and Marx's Economic Doctrines," *Science and Society*, 22(2): 134–49.

—— (1963) "Marx's Model of Expanded Reproduction," *Science and Society*, 27(2): 159–75.

Fariello, G. (1995) *Red Scare: memories of the American inquisition, an oral history*, New York: W. W. Norton and Company.

Fazzari, S. (2002) Personal communication, 11 February.

Feinstein, C. (1995) Personal communication, 25 September.

Feis, H. (1920) "Economics in the British Workers' Educational Association," *Quarterly Journal of Economics*, 34(2): 366–72.

Fels, R. (1975) "Economics and Bias," *New York Times*, March 29: 28.

Fieldhouse, R. (1977) *The Workers' Educational Association: aims and achievements, 1903–1977*, Syracuse: Syracuse University.

—— (1983) "The Ideology of English Adult Education Teaching, 1925–50," *Studies in Adult Education*, 15: 11–35.

—— (1985) *Adult Education and the Cold War*, Leeds: Leeds Studies in Adult and Continuing Education.

—— (1990) "Bouts of Suspicion: political controversies in adult education, 1925–44," in Simon (1990a), 153–72.

—— (1996a) "The Nineteenth Century," in Fieldhouse and Associates (1996), 10–45.

—— (1996b) "An Overview of British Adult Education in the Twentieth Century," in Fieldhouse and Associates (1996), 46–76.

—— (1996c) "The Workers' Educational Association," in Fieldhouse and Associates (1996), 166–98.

—— (1996d) "University Adult Education," in Fieldhouse and Associates (1996), 199–238.

Fieldhouse, R. and Associates. (1996) *A History of Modern British Adult Education*, Leicester: National Institute of Adult Continuing Education.

Fine, B. (1986) *The Value Dimension: Marx versus Ricardo and Sraffa*, London: Routledge and Kegan Paul.

Fine, B. and Harris, L. (1976) "Controversial Issues in Marxist Economic Theory," in R. Miliband and J. Saville (eds.) *The Social Register 1976*, 141–78, London: The Merlin Press.

—— (1977) "Surveying the Foundations," in R. Miliband and J. Saville (eds.) *The Socialist Register, 1977*, 106–20, London: The Merlin Press.

Fine, N. (ed.) (1930) *The American Labor Year Book, 1930*, New York: Rand School of Social Science.

Fischer, G. (ed.) (1971) *The Revival of American Socialism: selected papers of the Socialist Scholars Conference*, New York: Oxford University Press.

Fischer, G, et al. (1971) "Preface," in G. Fischer (ed.) *The Revival of American Socialism*, v–xiv, New York: Oxford University Press.

Fischer, N. (2006) "The Founders of American Anti-Communism," *American Communist History*, 5(1): 67–101.

Fisher, P. (2002) Personal communication, 11 February.

Fleck, S. (1999) "Union for Radical Political Economics," in P. A. O'Hara (ed.) *Encyclopedia of Political Economy*, 1200–203, London: Routledge.

Flemming, J. (1991) "The Use of Assessments of British University Teaching, and Especially Research, for the Allocation of Resources: a personal view," *European Economic Review*, 35: 612–18.

—— (1995) Personal communication, 18 September.

Foldvary, F. E. (ed.) (1996) *Beyond Neoclassical Economics: heterodox approaches to economic theory*, Cheltenham: Edward Elgar Publishing, Ltd.

Foley, D. K. (1989) "An Interview with Wassily Leontief," *Macroeconomic Dynamics* 2: 116–40.

—— (1999) "The Ins and Outs of Late Twentieth-Century Economics," in A. Heertje (ed.) *The Makers of Modern Economics*, vol. 4, 70–118, Cheltenham: Edward Elgar.

Fones-Wolf, E. A. (1994) *Selling Free Enterprise: the business assault on labor and liberalism, 1945–60*, Urbana: University of Illinois Press.

Ford, P. (1935–36) "What is Living and What is Dead in Marx," *The Highway*, 29 82–85.

Fosmoe, M. (2003a) "The Great Divide," *South Bend Tribune*, 3 March.

—— (2003b) "Views on Economics Split Polarize ND Faculty," *South Bend Tribune*, 4 March.

Foster, J. B. (1987) "Sweezy, Paul Malor," in J. Eatwell, M. Milgate, and P. Newman (eds.) *The New Palgrave Dictionary of Economics*, vol. 4, 580–82, London: The Macmillan Press Ltd.

Foster, J. F. (1967) Interview, August, Oral History Collection, University of North Texas.

"Fourth Socialist Economists' Conference," (1971) CSE Records.

Francis, H. (1976) "Workers' Libraries: the origins of the South Wales Miners' Library," *History Workshop*, 2: 183–205.

Francis, G. E. (1972) "The Doctrines of the Union for Radical Political Economics: departure or distraction from the American Institutional tradition?" Ph.D. dissertation, University of Colorado.

Frank, A. G. (1997) "The Cold War and Me," *Bulletin of Concerned Asian Scholars*, 29(3): 79–84.

Franklin, R. S. and Tabb, W. K. (1974) "The Challenge of Radical Political Economics," *Journal of Economic Issues,* 8(1): 127–50.

Friedman, M. (1962) *Capitalism and Freedom*, Chicago: The University of Chicago Press.

Froman, L. A. (1930) "Graduate Students in Economics, 1904–28," *American Economic Review*, 20(2): 235–47.

—— (1942) "Graduate Students in Economics, 1904–40," *American Economic Review*, 32(4): 817–26.

—— (1952) "Graduate Students in Economics," *American Economic Review*, 42(4): 602–8.

Frow, E. and Frow, R. (1990) "The Spark of Independent Working-Class Education: Lancashire, 1909–30," in Simon (1990a), 71–104.

Fuchs, S. et al. (1969) "Collective of Socialist Economists Manifesto," *Something Else!*, 2 (August): 15–18.

Fullwiler, S. T. (2002) Personal communication, 11 February.

Furner, M. O. (1975) *Advocacy and Objectivity: a crisis in the professionalization of American social science, 1865–1905*, Lexington: The University Press of Kentucky.

Furniss, H. S. (1931) *Memories of Sixty Years*, London: Methuen and Co. Ltd.

Fusfeld, D. R. (1972) "Post-Post-Keynes: the shattered synthesis," *Saturday Review*, (January 22): 36–39.

Fusfeld, D. R. (1997) "An Intellectual Journey," in N. Aslanbeigui and Y. B. Choi (eds.) *Borderlands of Economics: essays in honor of Daniel R. Fusfeld*, 3–24, Routledge: London.

Gaffney, M. and Harrison, F. (1994) *The Corruption of Economics*, London: Shepheard-Walwyn (Publishers) Ltd.

Galbraith, J. K. (1977a) Letter to Sidney Weintraub, 23 May, S. Weintraub Papers, Box 9, folder 1.

—— (1977b) Letter to Paul Davidson, 17 August, S. Weintraub Papers, Box 9, folder 2.

Gannon, F. X. (1969–73) *Biographical Dictionary of the Left*, vols. 1–4, Boston: Western Islands.

Garnett, R. F. (1999) "Postmodernism and Theories of Value: new grounds for Institutionalist/Marxist dialogue?" *Journal of Economic Issues* 33(4): 817–34.

Geary, J., Marriott, L., and Rowlinson, M. (2004) "Journal Rankings in Business and Management and the 2001 Research Assessment Exercise in the UK," *British Journal of Management*, 15: 94–141.

Gettleman, M. 1982. "Rehearsal for McCarthyism: the New York State Rapp-Coudert Committee and academic freedom, 1940–41," unpublished.

—— (1987) "Introduction: the themes of seminary scholarship," in M. Gettleman (ed.) *The Johns Hopkins University Seminary of History and Politics: the records of an American educational institution, 1877–1912*, 1–82, New York: Garland Publishing, Inc.

—— (1990) "Jefferson School of Social Science," in M. J. Buhle, P. Buhle, and D. Georgakas (eds.) *Encyclopedia of the American Left*, 389–90, New York: Garland Publishing, Inc.

—— (1993) "The New York Workers School, 1923–44: communist education in American society," in M. E. Brown et al. (eds.) *New Studies in the Politics and Culture of U.S. Communism*, 91–122, New York: Monthly Review Press.

—— (2001) "Lost World of U.S. Labor Education: curricula at east and west coast communist schools, 1944–57," unpublished.

Gibson-Graham, J. K. (1996) *The End of Capitalism (as we knew it): a feminist critique of political economy*. Cambridge: Blackwell Publishers.

Gilbert, J. (1968) "Images of the Socialist Scholars Conference," *Radical America*, 2(5): 62–64.

Ginger, A. F. and Christiano, D. (eds.) (1987) *The Cold War Against Labor*, vols. 1 and 2, Berkeley: Meiklejohn Civil Liberties institute.

Ginzberg, E. (1990) "Economics at Columbia: recollections of the early 1930's," *The American Economist* 34: 14–17.

Glyn, A. (1971) "The British Crisis and Entry into the EEC," *Bulletin of the Conference of Socialist Economists*, 1 (Winter): 21–31.

Goldberger, M. Maher, B. A., and Flattau, P. E. (eds.) (1995) *Research-Doctorate Programs in the United States: continuity and change*, Washington, D.C.: National Academy Press.

Golden, S. (1975) "Radical Economics Under Fire," *The New York Times* (February 2, Section 3): 1–2.

Goldman, E. F. (1944) "J. Allen Smith: the reformer and his dilemma," *Pacific Northwest Quarterly*, 35: 195–214.

Goldman, L. (1995) *Dons and Workers: Oxford and adult education since 1850*, Oxford: Clarendon Press.

Goldstein, R. J. (1978) *Political Repression in Modern America: 1870 to the present*, Cambridge: Schenkman Publishing Co., Inc.

Goldway, D. (1986) "Fifty Years of *Science & Society*," *Science and Society*, 50(3): 260–79.

Goodwin, C. D. W. (1973) "Marginalism Moves to the New World," in R. D. C. Black, A. W. Coats, and C. D. W. Goodwin (eds.) *The Marginal Revolution in Economics*, 285–304, Durham: Duke University Press.

—— (1998) "The Patrons of Economics in a Time of Transformation," in M. S. Morgan and M. Rutherford (eds.) *From Interwar Pluralism to Postwar Neoclassicism*, 53–81, Durham: Duke University Press.

Goodwin, R. M. and Punzo, L. F. (1987) *The Dynamics of a Capitalist Economy: a multi-sectoral approach*. Boulder: Westview Press.

Gordon, A. et al. (1969) "Historians Who Signed Up as Radicals at the Last AHA, and others," *Something Else!*, 2(4): 6.

Gordon, F. (1966) "Seminar on Socialist Ideology," *New Left Notes*, 1(32): 28.

—— Gordon, F. (1967) "Galbraith's Liberalism," *New Left Notes*, 2(30): 4, 8.

Gorman, R. A. (ed.) (1985) *Biographical Dictionary of Neo-Marxism*, Westport: Greenwood Press.

—— Gorman, R. A. (ed.) (1986) *Biographical Dictionary of Marxism*, Westport: Greenwood Press.

Gould, F. J. (1900) *The History of the Leicester Secular Society*, Leicester: The Leicester Secular Society.

Gowdy, J.M. (1988) "The Entropy Law and Marxian Value Theory," *Review of Radical Political Economics*, 20(2–3): 34–40.

—— Gowdy, J. M. (1994) "The Social Context of Natural Capital," *International Journal of Social Economics*, 21(8): 43–55.

Graham, J. (ed.) (1990) *"Yours for the Revolution": The Appeal to Reason, 1895–1922*, Lincoln: University of Nebraska Press.

Grahl, J. (2000) Personal communication, September.

Grant, A. (1977a) Letter to Sidney Weintraub, 29 March, S. Weintraub Papers, Box 4, folder 1.

—— (1977b) Letter to Sidney Weintraub, 13 April, S. Weintraub Papers, Box 4, folder 1.

—— (1978a) Letter to Sidney Weintraub, 23 January, S. Weintraub Papers, Box 4, folder 3.

—— (1978b) Letter to Sidney Weintraub, 23 February, S. Weintraub Papers, Box 4, folder 3.

—— (1978c) Letter to Sidney Weintraub, 14 April, S. Weintraub Papers, Box 4, folder 3.

—— (1978d) Letter to Sidney Weintraub, 15 August, S. Weintraub Papers, Box 4, folder 4.

—— (1978e) Letter to Sidney Weintraub, 20 September, S. Weintraub Papers, Box 4, folder 5.

—— (1979a) Letter to Sidney Weintraub, 21 January, S. Weintraub Papers, Box 5, folder 1.

—— (1979b) Letter to Sidney Weintraub. March 27. S. Weintraub Papers, Box 5, folder 1.

—— (1979c) Letter to Sidney Weintraub, 20 August, S. Weintraub Papers, Box 5, folder 2.

—— (1979d) "Mergers, Monopoly Power, and Relative Shares," *Journal of Post Keynesian Economics*, 2: 120–34.

—— (1982) "Reproduction Crisis," *Journal of Post Keynesian Economics*, 4: 497–515.

Green, F. (1977) "Empiricist Methodology and the Development of Economic Thought," *Thames Papers in Political Economy* (Spring).

Greer, J. (2001) "Ornaments, Tools, or Friends: literary reading at the Bryn Mawr Summer School for Women Workers, 1921–38," in A. M. Thomas and B. Ryan (eds.) *Reading Acts: U.S. readers" interactions with literature, 1800–1950*, 178–98, Knoxville: University of Tennessee Press.

Gresik, T. A. (2003) "The Economics Department Needs Reform," *Observer*, 37.91. Http://www.nd.edu/~observer/02112003/Viewpoint/3.html (accessed 20 June 2008).

Griffith, J. (1972) "Freedom and the Universities," *New Statesman* (November 17): 719–20.

Griffith, J. (1995) *Research Assessment: as strange a maze as e'er men trod*, Report No. 4, London: Council for Academic Freedom and Academic Standards.

Groenewegen, P. (1995) *A Soaring Eagle: Alfred Marshall, 1842–1924*, Aldershot: Edward Elgar.

—— (2007) "Walter Layton and the *The Relation of Capital and Labour* (1914): a Marshallian text *pur sang?*," *History of Economics Review*, 46: 19–31.

Gruber, C. S. (1975) *Mars and Minerva: World War I and the uses of the higher learning in America*, Baton Rouge: Louisiana State University Press.

Gruchy, A. G. (1947) *Modern Economic Thought: the American contribution*, New York: Prentice-Hall, Inc.

—— (1948) "The Philosophical Basis of the New Keynesian Economics," *Ethics*, 58(4): 235–44.

—— (1969) "Neoinstitutionalism and the Economics of Dissent," *Journal of Economic Issues*, 3(1): 3–17.

—— (1972) *Contemporary Economic Thought: the contribution of Neo-Institutional economics*, Clifton: Augustus M. Kelley, Publishers.

—— (1984) "Neo-Institutionalism, Neo-Marxism, and Neo-Keynesianism: an Evaluation," *Journal of Economic Issues*, 18: 547–56.

—— (1987) *The Reconstruction of Economics: an analysis of the fundamentals of Institutional economics*, Westport: Greenwood Press.

Gruenberg, G. W. (1991) "The American Jesuit Contribution to Social Action and Social Order after *Rerum Novarum*," *Review of Social Economy*, 49: 532–41.

Gurley, J. G. (1971) "The State of Political Economics," *American Economic Review*, 61: 53–62.

Gutfeld, A. (1970) "The Levine Affair: a case study in academic freedom," *Pacific Historical Review*, 39(1): 19–37.

Hader, J. J. and Lindeman, E. C. (1929) *What Do Workers Study?*, New York: The Workers Educational Bureau Press.

Halevi, J. (1995) "Letter to the Editor," *PKSG Newsletter*, Issue 2 {:} 2.

Hall, J. (1989) "Broadus Mitchell (1892–1988)," *Radical History Review*, 45: 31–38.

Hall, S. (1960) "The Supply of Demand," in E. P. Thompson et al. *Out of Apathy*, 56–97, London: Stevens and Sons.

Halsey, A. (1992) *The Decline of Donnish Dominion*, Oxford: Clarendon Press.

Hamilton, D. (2004) "Economic Heterodoxy at the University of Texas at Mid-Twentieth Century," in W. J. Samuels (ed.) *Research in the History of Economic Thought and Methodology*, vol. 22-C, *Wisconsin "Government and Business" and the History of Heterodox Economic Thought*, 261–71, Amsterdam: Elsevier.

Hamilton, W. H. (1918a) "The Place of Value Theory in Economics, I," *The Journal of Political Economy*, 26: 217–45.

—— (1918b) "The Place of Value Theory in Economics, II," *The Journal of Political Economy*, 26: 375–407.

—— (1919) "The Institutional Approach to Economic Theory," *American Economic Review*, 9: 309–18.

Hamilton, W. H. and Associates. (1938) *Price and Price Policies*, New York: McGraw-Hill Book Company, Inc.

Hamm, T. D. (1997) *Earlham College: a history, 1847–1997*, Bloomington: Indiana University Press.

Hammond, C. H. and Hammond, J. D. (2000) "The Development of Chicago Price Theory: evidence from the early Friedman-Stigler correspondence," unpublished.

Hammond, J. D. (2000) "Columbia Roots of the Chicago School: the case of Milton Friedman," unpublished.

Hansen, W. L. (1991) "The Education and Training of Economics Doctorates: major findings of the American Economic Association's Commission on graduate education on economics," *The Journal of Economic Literature*, 29(3): 1054–87.

Harcourt, G. C. (1975) "Capital Theory: much ado about something," *Thames Papers in Political Economy* (Autumn).

—— (1978) "Can Marx Survive Cambridge?" *Nation Review* (March 8–15): 15.

—— (1979) "Review of *Marx After Sraffa* by Ian Steedman," *Journal of Economic Literature*, 17(2): 534–36.

—— (1982) "Post-Keynesianism: quite wrong and/or nothing new?," *Thames Papers in Political Economy* (Summer).

—— (ed.) (1985) *Keynes and His Contemporaries*, London: Macmillan.

—— (1993–94) "Krishna Bharadwaj, August 21, 1935–March 8, 1992: a memoir," *Journal of Post Keynesian Economics,* 16(2): 299–311.

—— (2006) *The Structure of Post-Keynesian Economics: the core contributions of the pioneers*, Cambridge: Cambridge University Press.

Hardin, C. E. (1976) *Freedom in Agricultural Education*, New York City: Arno Press.

Hare, P. (1985) *Planning the British Economy*, London: Macmillan.

Hargreaves, E. L., Maud, J. P. R., and Ryle, G. (1935) *Bibliography for the Honour School of Philosophy, Politics and Economics*, Oxford: Blackwell's.

Harley, S. (2002) "The Impact of Research Selectivity on Academic Work and Identity in UK Universities," *Studies in Higher Education* 27(2): 187–205.

Harley, S. and Lee, F. S. (1997) "Research Selectivity, Managerialism, and the Academic Labor Process: the future of nonmainstream economics in U.K. universities," *Human Relations* 50(11): 1427–60.

Harmon, L. R. (1978) *A Century of Doctorates: data analyses of growth and change*, Washington, D.C.: National Academy of Sciences.

Harmon, L. R. and Soldz, H. (1963) *Doctorate Production in United States Universities, 1920–1962*, Publication No. 1142, Washington, D.C.: National Academy of Sciences—National Research Council.

Harrop, S. (ed.) (1987) *Oxford and Working-Class Education*, new edn, Nottingham: University of Nottingham.

Hartmann, H. I. (1979) "The Unhappy Marriage of Marxism and Feminism: towards a more progressive union," *Capital and Class*, 8: 1–33.

Harzing, A-W. (2005) "Journal Quality List," seventeenth edn, 4 December, http://www.harzing.com (accessed 21 June 2008).

Haskell, T. L (2000) *The Emergence of Professional Social Science*, Baltimore: The Johns Hopkins University Press.

Heal, A. J. (1973) "Marxist Education Classes in 1904," *Marx Memorial Library Quarterly Bulletin*, 66: 9–10.

Heilbroner, R. L. (1970) "On the Limited "Relevance" of Economics," *The Public Interest*, 21: 80–93.

—— (1971) "Discussion," *American Economic Review*, 61: 65–67.

Heller, R. (1984) "Blue Collars and Bluestockings: the Bryn Mawr Summer School for Women Workers, 1921–38," in J. L. Kornbluh and M. Frederickson (eds.) *Sisterhood and Solidarity: workers' education for women, 1914–1984*, 107–45, Philadelphia: Temple University Press.

—— (1986) "The Women of Summer: The Bryn Mawr Summer School for Women Workers, 1921–38," Ph.D. dissertation, Rutgers University.

Heller, W. W. (1975) "What's Right with Economics?," *American Economic Review*, 65: 1–26.

Hellman, R. (1987) *Henry George Reconsidered*, New York City: Carlton Press, Inc.

Henderson, J. P. (1988) "Political Economy and the Service of the State: The University of Wisconsin," in Barber (1988a), 318–39.

Henkel, M. (2000) *Academic Identites and Policy Change in Higher Education*, London: Jessica Kingsley Publishers.

Henrickson, G. P. (1981) "Minnesota in the McCarthy Period: 1946–54," Ph.D. dissertation, University of Minnesota.

Herman, B. (1969) "Black Economic Power," *URPE Newsletter*, 1(2): 1, 4.

Hey, J. D. (1995) "Managing Editor's Annual Report on the EJ," *Royal Economic Society Newsletter*, 88: 2–3.

—— (1996a) "Economic Journal: report of the managing editor," *Royal Economic Society Newsletter*, 92: 3–5.

—— (1996b) Letter to J. Toporowski, 22 February.

Higher Education Funding Council for England. (1993) *A Report for the Universities Funding Council on the Conduct of the 1992 Research Assessment Exercise*, June, Bristol: Higher Education Funding Councils for England, Scotland and Wales.

—— (1994) *Conduct of the 1996 Research Assessment Exercise: panel membership and units of assessment*, June, http://www.hero.ac.uk/rae/rae96/ (accessed 22 June 2008).

—— (1995a) *1996 Research Assessment Exercise: membership of assessment panels*, July, http://www.hero.ac.uk/rae/rae96/ (accessed 22 June 2008).

—— (1995b) *1996 Research Assessment Exercise: criteria for assessment*, November, http://www.hero.ac.uk/rae/rae96/ (accessed 22 June 2008).

Hill, L. E. (1978) "Social and Institutional Economics: toward a creative synthesis," *Review of Social Economy* 36(3): 311–23.

Hill, R. (ed.) (1989) *Keynes, Money and Monetarism*, Basingstoke: Macmillan.

Hinckley, B. (1969) "Personal Recollection of the URPE Conference," *URPE Newsletter* 1(3): 14.

Hirsch, A. (1988) "What is an Empiricist? Wesley Clair Mitchell in Broader Perspective," *History of Economics Society Bulletin*, 10(1): 1–12.

Hobsbawm, E. (1978) "The Historians" Group of the Communist Party," in M. Cornforth (ed.) *Rebels and their Causes: essays in honour of A. L. Morton*, 21–47, London: Lawrence and Wishart.

Hodgson, G. (1974) "The Theory of the Falling Rate of Profit," *New Left Review*, 84: 55–82.

—— (1975) "Communications," *New Left Review*, 90: 110–12.

—— (1976) "Exploitation and Embodied Labour Time," *Bulletin of the Conference of Socialist Economists*, 5: GH 1–2.

—— (1977) "Papering over the Cracks," in R. Miliband and J. Saville (eds.) *The Socialist Register, 1977*, 88–105, London: The Merlin Press.

—— (1982) *Capitalism, Value and Exploitation: a radical theory*, Oxford: Martin Robertson.

—— (1993) "The Professional Status of Heterodox Economics Journals in the UK," unpublished.

—— (1995) "In Which Journals Should We Publish?" *European Association for Evolutionary Political Economy Newsletter*, 11: 6–8.

—— (1997) "The Fate of the Cambridge Capital Controversy," in P. Arestis, G. Palma, and M. Sawyer (eds.) *Capital Controversy, Post-Keynesian Economics and the History of Economic Thought: essays in honour of Geoff Harcourt*, vol. 1, 95–110, London: Routledge.

—— (2000) Personal communication, 7 August.

—— (2001) *How Economics Forgot History: the problem of historical specificity in social science*, London: Routledge.

Hodgson, G. M., Samuels, W. J., and Tool, M. R. (eds.) (1994) *The Elgar Companion to Institutional and Evolutionary Economics*, Aldershot: Edward Elgar.

Hodgson, G. and Steedman, I. (1975) "Fixed Capital and Value Analysis," *Bulletin of the Conference of Socialist Economists*, 5 (June): 1–7.

—— (1977) "Depreciation of Machines of Changing Efficiency: a note," *Australian Economic Papers*, 16.28: 141–47.

Hodson, H. V. (1973) "Re-reading Keynes's 'General Theory': still relevant today?," *Encounter*, 40(4): 48–53.

Holland, H. S., Price, L. L., and Adams, W. G. S. (1913) *The Oxford Diploma in Economics and Political Science*, Oxford University Archives (G.A. Oxen 8 900 96).

Hollander, J. H. (1903) "The Residual Claimant Theory of Distribution," *The Quarterly Journal of Economics*, 17(2): 261–79.

Hollingsworth, P. J. (2000) "Introduction," in P. J. Hollingsworth (ed.) *Unfettered Expression: Freedom in American Intellectual Life*, 1–18, Ann Arbor: The University of Michigan Press.

Holt, R. P. F. and Pressman, S. (eds.) (1998) *Economics and its Discontents: twentieth century dissenting economists*, Edward Elgar: Cheltenham.

Horn, F. H. (1954a) Letter to E. J. McGrath, 1 March, University of Missouri-Kansas City Archives, Arts and Sciences Department of Economics, Horace Davis, KC: 3/11/4, Box 1.7.

Horn, F. H. (1954b) Letter to E. J. McGrath, 12 March, University of Missouri-Kansas City Archives, Arts and Sciences Department of Economics, Horace Davis, KC: 3/11/4, Box 1.7.

Horn, M. (1979) *The Intercollegiate Socialist Society, 1905–1921: origins of the modern American student movement*, Boulder: Westview Press.

—— (1999) *Academic Freedom in Canada: a history*, Toronto: University of Toronto Press.

—— (2000) "Canadian Universities, Academic Freedom, Labour, and the Left," *Labour/Le Travail*, 4(6): 439–67.

Horowitz, D. (1968) *Marx and Modern Economics*, New York: MacGibbon and Kee.

Horwitz, S. (1995) "Feminist Economics: an Austrian perspective," *Journal of Economic Methodology*, 2(2): 259–79.

—— (1998) "Hierarchical Metaphors in Austrian Institutionalism: a friendly subjectivist caveat," in R. Koppl and G. Mongiovi (eds.) *Subjectivism and Economic Analysis: essays in memory of Ludwig M. Lachmann*, 143–62, London: Routledge.

Howard, M. C. and King, J. E. (1989) *A History of Marxian Economics: volume I, 1883–1929*, Princeton: Princeton University Press.

—— (1992) *A History of Marxian Economics: volume II, 1929–1990*, Princeton: Princeton University Press.

—— (2004) "Ronald Meek and the Rehabilitation of Surplus Economics," in S. G. Medema and W. J. Samuels (eds.) *Historians of Economics and Economic Thought*, 185–213. London: Routledge.

Howe, I. And Coser, L. (1957) *The American Communist Party: a critical history 1919–1957*, Boston: Beacon Press.

Howells, P. (1995) "Endogenous Money," *International Papers in Political Economy*, 2(2): 1–41.

Hubback, D. (1985) *No Ordinary Press Baron*, London: Weidenfeld and Nicolson.

Hubbard, P. M. (1995) Personal communication, 11 April.

Hughes, R. M. (1925) *A Study of the Graduate Schools of America*, Oxford: Miami University.

—— (1934) "Report of the Committee on Graduate Instruction," *Educational Record*, 15(2): 192–234.

Hunt, E. K. (1972) Letter to Joan Robinson, 12 April, Joan Robinson Papers, vii/216/1.

—— (1979) "Marx as a Social Economist: the labour theory of value," *Review of Social Economy*, 37(3): 275–94.

—— (1980) "The Crisis of Authority in Capitalism," *Review of Social Economy*, 38 (3): 261–66.

Hunt, E. K. and Sievers, A. M. (2004) "Heterodox Economics at the University of Utah," in W. J. Samuels (ed.) *Research in the History of Economic Thought and Methodology*, vol. 22-C, *Wisconsin "Government and Business" and the History of Heterodox Economic Thought*, 273–80, Amsterdam: Elsevier.

Huntington, E. H. (1971) *A Career in Consumer Economics and Social Insurance*, Berkeley: University of California, Bancroft Library, Regional Oral History Office.

Hymer, S. and Roosevelt, F. (1972) "Comment," in A. Lindbeck *The Political Economy of the New Left*, 2nd edn, 119–37, New York: Harper and Row, 1977.

Ietto-Gillies, I. (1997) "Why Post Keynesians Need Fellow-Travellers (and vice versa)," *PKSG Newsletter*, Issue 6: 2–3.

Innis, N. K. (1992) "Lessons from the Controversy over the Loyalty Oath at the University of California," *Minerva*, 30(3): 337–65.

Isserman, M. (1987) *If I Had a Hammer: the death of the old left and the birth of the new left*, New York: Basic Books, Inc., Publishers.

—— (1988) "1968 and the American Left," *Socialist Review*, 18(4): 94–104.

Iversen, R. W. (1959) *The Communists and the Schools*, New York: Harcourt, Brace and Company.

Jarsulic, M. (1988) *Effective Demand and Income Distribution*, Boulder: Westview Press.

Jefferson School. (1953) *Man's Right to Knowledge: the case of the Jefferson School*, New York City: Jefferson School of Social Science.

—— (1955) *The Jefferson School of Social Science vs. The Attorney General of the United States and the Subversive Activities Control Board: excerpts from official documents*, New York City: Jefferson School of Social Science.

Jennings, A. L. (1994) "Toward a Feminist Expansion of Macroeconomics: money matters," *Journal of Economic Issues*, 28(2): 555–65.

—— (2006) Personal communication.

Jennings, B. (1977) "Revolting Students—The Ruskin College Dispute, 1908–9," *Studies in Adult Education*, 9(1): 1–16.

Jensen, H. (2001) "The Economics of Edward Everett Hale: an impressionistic fragment," in W. J. Samuels (ed.) *Research in the History of Economic Thought and Methodology*, vol. 19-B, *Edward Everett Hale: the writings of an economic maverick*, 7–26, Amsterdam: Elsevier.

Jepson, N. A. (1973) *The Beginnings of English University Adult Education—Policy and Problems*, London: Michael Joseph.

Johnson, H. G. (1968) "A Catarrh of Economists? from Keynes to Postan," *Encounter*, 30 (May): 50– 54.

—— (1971a) "Revolution and Counter-Revolution in Economics: from Lord Keynes to Milton Friedman," *Encounter*, 36 (April): 23–33.

—— (1971b) Letter to Joan Robinson, 20 August, Joan Robinson Papers, vii/225/3.

—— (1973) "National Styles in Economic Research: the United States, the United Kingdom, Canada, and various European countries," *Daedalus*, 102(2): 65–74.

—— (1974) "The Current and Prospective State of Economics," *Australian Economic Papers*, 13: 1–27.

Johnson, R. (1979) "'Really Useful Knowledge': radical education and working class culture, 1790–1848," in J. Clarke, C. Critcher, and R. Johnson *Working Class Culture*, 75–102, London: Hutchinson.

Jones, B. L. (1988) "A Quest for National Leadership: institutionalization of economics at Harvard," in Barber (1988a), 95–131.

Jones, C. V., Enros, P. C. and Tropp, H. S. (1984) "Kenneth O. May, 1915–77: his early life to 1946," *Historia Mathematica*, 11: 359–79.

Jones, D. (2002) Personal communication, 15 February.

Jones, J. (1984) "A Liverpool Socialist Education," *History Workshop*, 18: 92–101.

Kadish, A. (1982) *The Oxford Economists in the Late Nineteenth Century*, Oxford: Clarendon Press.

—— (1986) *Apostle Arnold: the life and death of Arnold Toynbee, 1852–1883*, Durham: Duke University Press.

—— (1987) "University Extension and the Working Classes: the case of the Northumberland miners," *Historical Research*, 6: 188–207.

—— (1989) *Historians, Economists and Economic History*, London: Routledge.

—— (1990) "Rewriting the *Confessions*: Hobson and the Extension Movement," in M. Freeden (ed.) *Reappraising J. A. Hobson: humanism and welfare*, 137–66, London: Unwin Hyman.

—— (1993) "The Teaching of Political Economy in the Extension Movement: Cambridge, London and Oxford," in A. Kadish and K. Tribe (eds.) *The Market for Political Economy*, 78–110, London: Routledge.

Kaldor, N. (1956) "Alternative Theories of Distribution," *Review of Economic Studies*, 23(2): 83–100.

—— (1964) *Essays on Economic Policy I*, London: Gerald Duckworth and Co., Ltd.

—— (1978) *Further Essays on Economic Theory*, London: Duckworth.

Kalecki, M. (1943) "Political Aspects of Full Employment," *Political Quarterly*, 14 (4): 322–31.

Kalaitzidakis, P., Mamuneas, T. P., and Stengos, T. (2003) "Rankings of Academic Journals and Institutions in Economics," *Journal of the European Economic Association*, 1(6): 1346–66.

Karolides, N. J (ed.) (2006) *Banned Books: literature suppressed on political grounds*, revised edn, New York: Facts on File, Inc.

Kasper, H., Woglom, G., Dixon, V., Colander, D., Kaufman, R., Saffran, B., Kupperberg, M., Bell, C. S., Yohe, G., and McPherson, M. (1991) "The Education of Economists: from undergraduate to graduate study," *The Journal of Economic Literature*, 29(3): 1054–87.

Kaufman, B. E. (2001) "On the Neoclassical Tradition in Labor Economics," unpublished.

—— (2004) "The Institutional and Neoclassical Schools in Labor Economics," in D. P. Champlin and J. T. Knoedler (eds.) *The institutionalist Tradition in Labor Economics*, 13–38, Armonk: M. E. Sharpe.

—— (2007) "The Institutional Economics of John R. Commons: complement and substitute for neoclassical economic theory," *Socio-Economic Review*, 5(1): 3–45.

Kaye, H. J. (1995) *The British Marxist Historians: an introductory analysis,*. London: Macmillan.

Keen, M. F. (1999) *Stalking the Sociological Imagination: J. Edgar Hoover's FBI surveillance of American sociology*, Westport: Greenwood Press.

Keen, S. (2001) *Debunking Economics: the naked emperor of the social sciences*, Annandale: Pluto Press Australia Limited.

Keenan, J. (1980) "Weintraub on Capitalism, Inflation and Unemployment: a review essay," *Review of Radical Political Economics*, 12(3): 64–68.

Kenny, M. (1995) *The First New Left: British intellectuals after Stalin*, London: Lawrence and Wishart.

Keniston, H. (1959) *Graduate Study and Research in the Arts and Sciences at the University of Pennsylvania*, Philadelphia: University of Pennsylvania Press.

Kern, W. S. (1997) "The Heterodox Economics of 'the Most Orthodox of Orthodox Economists': Frank H. Knight," *The American Journal of Economics and Sociology*, 56: 319–30.

Kershaw, H. (1910) "Rochdale Labour College Classes," *The Plebs Magazine*, 2(9): 219–24.

Kessler-Harris, A. (1980) "Wolfson, Theresa," in B. Sicherman et al. (eds.) *Notable American Women: the modern period, a biographical dictionary*, 742–44, Cambridge: Harvard University Press.

King, J. E. (1988) *Economic Exiles*, New York: St. Martin's Press.

—— (1995a) *Conversations with Post Keynesians*, New York City: St. Martin's Press.

—— (1995b) *Post Keynesian Economics: an annotated bibliography*, Aldershot: Edward Elgar.

—— (2000) Personal communication, 2 October.

—— (2002) *A History of Post Keynesian Economics Since 1936*, Cheltenham: Edward Elgar.

—— (ed.) (2003) *The Elgar Companion to Post Keynesian Economics*, Cheltenham: Edward Elgar.

—— (2004a) "Dickinson, Henry Douglas (1899–1969)," in D. Rutherford (ed.) *The Biographical Dictionary of British Economists*, vol. I, 324–25, Bristol: Thoemmes Continuum.

—— (2004b) "Planning for Abundance: Nicholas Kaldor and Joan Robinson on the socialist reconstruction of Britain, 1942–45," in I. Barens (ed.) *Political Events and Economic Ideas*, 306–24, Cheltenham: Edward Elgar.

—— (2005a) "Unwarping the Record: a reply to Paul Davidson," *Journal of Post Keynesian Economics*, 27(3): 377–84.

—— (2005b) "Secret Treasures of the Weintraub Archive," unpublished.

King, J. E. and Millmow, A. (2003) "Death of a Revolutionary Textbook," *History of Political Economy*, 35(1): 105–34.

Kitson, M. (2005) "Economics for the Future," *Cambridge Journal of Economics*, 29 (6): 827–35.

Klamer, A. and Colander, D. (1990) *The Making of an Economist*, Boulder: Westview Press.

Klein, L. (1947) *The Keynesian Revolution*, New York: The Macmillan Company.

—— (1980) Interview, Temple University, Conwellana-Templana Collection. Barrows Dunham/Fred Zimring Collection.

Knapp, J. (1973) "Economics or Political Economy?" *Lloyds Bank Review*, 107: 19–43.

Knoedler, J. T. (2006) Personal communication, 14 April.

Knoedler, J. T. and Underwood, D. A. (2003) "Teaching the Principles of Economics: a proposal for a multi-paradigmatic approach," *Journal of Economic Issues*, 37(3): 697–725.

Koot, G. M. (1987) *English Historical Economics, 1870–1926: the rise of economic history and neomercantilism*, Cambridge: Cambridge University Press.

Kornbluh, J. L (ed.) (1988) *Rebel Voices: an IWW anthology*, Chicago: Charles H. Kerr Publishing Company.

Kotz, D. M. 1982. "Monopoly, Inflation and Economic Crisis," *Review of Radical Political Economics*, 14(4): 1–17.

Kotz, D. M., McDonough, T., and Reich, M. (eds.) (1994) *Social Structures of Accumulation: the political economy of growth and crisis*, Cambridge: Cambridge University Press.

Kregel, J. (1971) *Rate of Profit, Distribution and Growth: two views*, Chicago: Aldine and Atherton, Inc.

—— (1972) "Post Keynesian Economic Theory and the Theory of Capitalist Crisis," *Bulletin of the Conference of Socialist Economists*, 1(4): 59–84.

—— (1973) *The Reconstruction of Political Economy: an introduction to Post-Keynesian economics*, London: The Macmillan Press Ltd.

—— (1974) "The Post-Keynesian (Radical) Approach to Monetary Theory," *Bulletin of the Conference of Socialist Economists*, 3(9): Kregel 1–12.

—— (1979) Letter to Sidney Weintraub, 21 May, S. Weintraub Papers, Box 5, folder 1.

Kriesler, P. (1996) "The Future of Post Keynesianism in Australia," *PKSG Newsletter*, Issue 4: 5–6.

Krueger, A. O., Arrow, K. J., Blanchard, O. J., Blinder, A. S., Goldin, C., Leamer, E. E., Lucas, R., Panzar, J., Penner, R. G., Schultz, T. P., Stiglitz, J. E., and Summers, L. H. (1991) "Report of the Commission on Graduate Education in Economics," *The Journal of Economic Literature* 29(3): 1035–53.

Kurz, H. D. (1990) *Capital, Distribution and Effective Demand*, Cambridge: Basil Blackwell.

Kurz, H. D. and Salvadori, N. (2005) "Representing the Production and Circulation of Commodities in Material Terms: on Sraffa's objectivism," *Review of Political Economy*, 17(3): 413–42.

Kuttner, R. (1985) "The Poverty of Economics," *The Atlantic Monthly*, (February): 74–84.

Ladd, E. C. and Lipset, S. M. (1975) *The Divided Academy: professors and politics*, New York: McGraw-Hill Book Company.

Lampman, R. J. (ed.) (1993) *Economists at Wisconsin, 1892–1992*, Madison: The Boards of Regents of the University of Wisconsin System.

Langer, E. (1989) "Notes for Next Time: A Memoir of the 1960s," in R. D. Myers (ed.) *Toward a History of the New Left: essays from within the Movement*, 63–123, Brooklyn: Carlson Publishing Inc.

Laughlin, J. L. 1892. "Appendix I: courses of study in political economy in the United States in 1876 and in 1892–93," *Journal of Political Economy*, 1(1): 143–51.

Laurent, J. (1984) "Science, Society and Politics in Late Nineteenth-Century England: a further look at Mechanics" Institutes," *Social Studies of Science*, 14(4): 585–619.

Lavoie, M. (1992) *Foundations of Post-Keynesian Economics*, Aldershot: Edward Elgar.

—— (2005) "Changing Definitions: a comment on Davidson's critique of King's history of Post Keynesianism," *Journal of Post Keynesian Economics*, 27(3): 371–76.

—— (2006) "Do Heterodox Theories Have Anything in Common? a Post-Keynesian point of view," *Intervention: Journal of Economics*, 3(1): 87–112.

"Law of Value Conference." (1973) H. Radice Personal Files.

Lawson, T. (1997) *Economics and Reality*, London: Routledge.

—— (2000) Interviewed by Steve Dunn at his office at the University of Cambridge, transcript in the possession of the author.

—— (2006) "The Nature of Heterodox Economics," *Cambridge Journal of Economics*, 30(4): 483–505.

Lawson, T. and Pesaran, H. (1985) *Keynes' Economics: methodological issues*, Armonk: M. E. Sharpe.

Lazonick, B. (1973) "The Repression of Radical Economics and the Politics of URPE," *Newsletter of the Union for Radical Political Economics*, 5(1): 3–4.

Lazonick, W. (1991) "What Happened to the Theory of Economic Development?" in P. Higonnet, D. S. Landes, and H. Rosovsky (eds.) *Favorites of Fortune*, 267–96, Cambridge: Harvard University Press.

—— (2004) Personal communication, 19 November.

Leberstein, S. (1993) "Purging the Profs: the Rapp Coudert Committee in New York, 1940–1942," in M. E. Brown et al. (eds.) *New Studies in the Politics and Culture of U.S. Communism*, 91–122, New York: Monthly Review Press.

Lebowitz, M. A. (1966) "Monopoly Capital," *Studies on the Left*, 6(5): 61–71.

—— (1973–74) "The Current Crisis of Economic Theory," *Science and Society*, 37: 385–403.

—— (2002) Personal communication, 12 March.

Lee, F. S. (1980) Memo: proposed field in political economy, 29 January 29, personal records.

—— (1981a) Memo: the economic forum, 20 January, personal records.

—— (1981b) Memo: revised schedule for the economic forum, 18 March, personal records.

—— (1981c) Memo: report of the planning committee for the Graduate Faculty, 24 April, personal records.

—— (1981d) "The Oxford Challenge to Marshallian Supply and Demand: the history of the Oxford Economists" Research Group," *Oxford Economic Papers*, 33(3): 339–51.

—— (1984) "The Marginalist Controversy and the Demise of Full Cost Pricing," *Journal of Economic Issues*, 17(4): 1107–32.

—— (1990) "*The Modern Corporation* and Gardiner Means's Critique of Neoclassical Economics," *Journal of Economic Issues*, 24(3): 673–93.

—— (1993) "Introduction: Philip Walter Sawford Andrews, 1914–71," in F. S. Lee and P. E. Earl (eds.) *The Economics of Competitive Enterprise: selected essays of P. W. S. Andrews*, 1–34, Aldershot: Edward Elgar.

—— (1995) "The Death of Post Keynesian Economics?" *PKSG Newsletter*, Issue 1: 1–2.

—— (1996) "The Future of Post Keynesian Economics: a response," *PKSG Newsletter*, Issue 5: 4–5.

—— (1997) "Philanthropic Foundations and the Rehabilitation of Big Business, 1934–1977: a case study of directed economic research," *Research in the History of Economic Thought and Methodology*, 15: 51–90.

—— (1998) *Post Keynesian Price Theory*, Cambridge: Cambridge University Press.

—— (1999a) "Administered Price Hypothesis and the Dominance of Neoclassical Price Theory: the case of the *Industrial Prices* dispute," *Research in the History of Economic Thought and Methodology*, 17: 23–42.

—— (1999b) "Report on the Fringe Conference," 8 April, personal records.

—— (2000a) "On the Genesis of Post Keynesian Economics: Alfred S. Eichner, Joan Robinson and the founding of Post Keynesian economics," in W. J. Samuels (ed.) *Research in the History of Economic Thought and Methodology*, vol. 18-C, *Twentieth-Century Economics*, 1–258, Amsterdam: JAI/Elsevier.

—— (2000b). "Report on the Other Economics Conference," 5 July, personal records.

—— (2002) "The Association for Heterodox Economics: past, present, and future," *Journal of Australian Political Economy*, 50: 29–43.

—— (2006) "The Ranking Game, Class and Scholarship in American Mainstream Economics," *Australasian Journal of Economics Education*, 3(1–2): 1–41.

—— (2008) "A Comment on "The Citation Impact of Feminist Economics," *Feminist Economics*, 14(1): 137–42.

—— (2009) "Appendix to *Challenging the Mainstream: essays on the history of heterodox economics in the twentieth century*," http://www.heterodoxnews.com/APPENDIX–formatted.pdf (accessed 15 July 2008).

Lee, F. S., Cohn, S., Schneider, G., and Quick, P. (2005) *Informational Directory for Heterodox Economists: journals, book series, websites, and graduate and undergraduate programs*, 2nd edition, http://www.heterodoxnews.com (accessed 1 July 2008).

Lee, F. S. and Harley, S. (1998) "Peer Review, the Research Assessment Exercise and the Demise of Non-Mainstream Economics," *Capital and Class*, 66: 23–51.

Lee, F. S. and Irving-Lessmann, J. (1992) "The Fate of an Errant Hypothesis: the doctrine of normal-cost prices," *History of Political Economy*, 24(2): 273–09.

Lee, F. S. and Keen, S. (2004) "The Incoherent Emperor: a heterodox critique of neoclassical microeconomic theory," *Review of Social Economy*, 62(2): 169–99.

Lee, F. S. and Samuels, W. J. (eds.) (1992) *The Heterodox Economics of Gardiner C. Means: a Collection*, Armonk: M. E. Sharpe, Inc.

Lees-Smith, H. B. (1905) "The Unemployment Workmen Bill," *Economic Journal*, 15: 248–54.

—— (1906) "The London Unemployment Fund, 1904–5: report of the Central Executive Committee," *Economic Journal*, 16: 156–58.

—— (1907) "Economic Theory and Proposals for a Legal Minimum Wage," *Economic Journal*, 17: 504–12.

Leijonhufvud, A. (1981) "Life Among the Econ," in A. Leijonhufvd *Information and Coordination: essays in macroeconomic theory*, 347–59, New York: Oxford University Press.

Lemisch, J. (1989) "Radicals, Marxists and Gentlemen: a memoir of twenty years ago," *Radical Historians Newsletter*, 59: 1, 7–8.

Leonard, T. C. (2000) "The Very Idea of Applying Economics: the modern minimum-wage controversy and its antecedents," *History of Political Economy Annual Supplement*, 32: 117–44.

Leontief, W. (1971) "Theoretical Assumptions and Nonobserved Facts," *The American EconomicReview*, 61(1): 1–7.

—— (1982) "Academic Economics," *Science*, 217 (July 9): 106–7.

Lesile, C. (1990) "Scientific Racism: reflections on peer review, science and ideology," *Social Science and Medicine*, 31(8): 891–91 2.

Levey, D. (2004) Personal communication, 22–24 September.

Levin, L. (1995) "Toward a Feminist, Post-Keynesian Theory of Investments," in E. Kuiper and J. Sap with S. Finer, N. Ott, and S. Tzannatos (eds.) *Out of the Margins: feminist perspectives on economics*, 100–119, London: Routledge.

Levine, A. (1969) "A Reading of Marx," *Radical America*, 3(5): 3–17

—— (1970) "Reply: a reading of Marx, II," *Radical America*, 4(6): 54–69.

Levine, D. P. (1975) "The Theory of the Growth of the Capitalist Economy," *Economic Development and Cultural Change*, 23: 47–75.

Levy, L. W. (1993) *Blasphemy: verbal offense against the sacred from Moses to Salman Rushie*, New York: Alfred A. Knopf.

Levy, T. (2002) "The Theory of Conventions and a New Theory of the Firm," in E. Fullbrook (ed.) *Intersubjectivity in Economics: agents and structures*, 254–72. London: Routledge.

Lewis, J. (1950) "The Modern Quarterly and Academic Freedom," *The Modern Quarterly*, 5(4): 358–60.

Lewis, L. S. (1988) *Cold War on Campus: a study of the politics of organizational control*, New Brunswick: Transaction Books.

Lewis, R. (1976) "The South Wales Miners and the Ruskin College Strike of 1909," *Llafur* 2(1): 57–72.

—— (1984) "The Central Labour College: its decline and fall, 1919–29," *The Welsh History Review*, 12(2): 225–45.

—— (1993) *Leaders and Teachers: adult education and the challenge of labour in south Wales, 1906–1940*, Cardiff: University of Wales Press.

Lichtenstein, P. M. (1986) "Post-Keynesian Economics: future prospects," *Review of Institutional Thought*, 3: 87–88.

Lifschultz, L. S. (1974) "Could Karl Marx Teach Economics in America?" *Ramparts*, 12 (April): 27-30, 52–59.

Lindbeck, A. (1977) *The Political Economy of the New Left: an outsider's view*, 2nd edn, New York: Harper and Row.

Liner, G. H. and Amin, M. (2004) "Methods of Ranking Economic Journals," *Atlantic Economic Journal*, 32(2): 140–49.

Lipset, S. M. (1975) "Harvard's Economics Department: the storm over ideology," *Change: The Magazine of Higher Learning*, 7(3): 22–24, 64.

Lipset, S. M. and Riesman, D. (1975) *Education and Politics at Harvard*, New York: McGraw-Hill Book Company.

Livingston, J. (1987) "The Social Analysis of Economic History and Theory: conjectures on late nineteenth-century American development," *American Historical Review*, 92: 69–95.

Llewellyn, G. E. J. and Tarling, R. J. (1974) "Cycles, Lags, and Causality," *Australian Economic Papers*, 13(23): 287–92.

Lloyd, C. (1993) *The Structures of History*, Oxford: Basil Blackwell Ltd.

Lock, S. (1985) *A Difficult Balance: editorial peer review in medicine*, London: The Nuffield Provincial Hospitals Trust.

Loube, B. (2003) Personal communication, 6 January.

Lovell, M. C. (1973) "The Production of Economic Literature: an interpretation," *Journal of Economic Literature*, 11(1): 27–55.

Lowen, R. S. (1997) *Creating the Cold War University: the transformation of Stanford*, Berkeley: University of California Press.

Lower, M. (2004) Personal communication, 1 November.

Lund, R. D. (ed.) (1995a) *The Margins of Orthodoxy: heterodox writings and cultural response, 1660–1750*, Cambridge: Cambridge University Press.

—— (1995b) "Irony as Subversion: Thomas Woolston and the crime of wit," in R. D. Lund (ed.) *The Margins of Orthodoxy: heterodox writings and cultural response, 1660–1750*, 170–94, Cambridge: Cambridge University Press.

Lydenberg, J. (ed.) (1977) *A Symposium on Political Activism and the Academic Conscience: the Harvard experience, 1936–1941*, Hobart and William Smith Colleges.

Macintyre, S. (1980) *A Proletarian Science: Marxism in Britain, 1917–1933*, Cambridge: Cambridge University Press.

MacGregor, D. H. (1942) "Marshall and his Book," *Economica*, 9: 313–24.

Maclean, J. (1916) *A Plea for a Labour College for Scotland*, Glasgow.

—— (n.d.) "Notes of Lectures on Economics," Glasgow: Scottish Labour College, in the Gallacher Memorial Library, Special Collections, Glasgow Caledonian University, Glasgow, United Kingdom.

MacLennan, B. (1969a) Letter to M. Dobb, 11 June, Maurice Dobb Papers, DD216.29.

—— (1969b) Letter to M. Dobb, 19 September, Maurice Dobb Papers, DD216.26.

Macmillan, D. (1942) "The *Principles of Economics*—A Bibliographical Note," *The Economic Journal*, 52(4): 290–93.

Magdoff, H. (1969) *The Age of Imperialism*, New York: Monthly Review Press.

Mainwaring, L. (1976) "Heterogeneous Capital Goods Model," *Australian Economic Papers*, 15(26): 109–18.

Malizia, E. (1975) A Review of *The Reconstruction of Political Economy: an introduction to Post-Keynesian economics* by J. A. Kregel. *Review of Radical Political Economics*, 7(4): 90–94.

Mallach, S. (1970) "Red Kate O'Hare Comes to Madison: the politics of free speech," *Wisconsin Magazine of History*, 53: 204–22.

Mansbridge, A. (1913) *University Tutorial Classes*, London: Longmans, Green and Co.

Marcuzzo, M. C. (1996) "Alternative Microeconomic Foundations for Macroeconomics: the controversy over the L-shaped cost curve," *Review of Political Economy*, 8(1): 7–22.

—— (2001) "Sraffa and Cambridge Economics, 1928–1931," in T. Cozzi and R. Marchionatti (eds.) *Piero Sraffa's Political Economy*, 81–99, London: Routledge.

—— (2005) "Robinson and Sraffa," in B. Gibson (ed.) *Joan Robinson's Economics*, 29–42, Cheltenham: Edward Elgar.

MARHO. (1978) "Political Firings in the Universities: the case of Bertell Ollman," *Radical History Review*, 18: 105–7.

Marsh, C. S. (1936) *American Universities and Colleges*, 3rd edn, Washington, D.C.: American Council on Education.

Marshall, A. and Marshall, M. P. (1890) *Economics of Industry*, 2nd edn, London: Macmillan and Co.

Marshall, J. N. (1992) *William J. Fellner: a bio-bibliography*, Westport: Greenwood Press.

Martinez-Alier, J. (2003) *The Environmentalism of the Poor: a study of ecological conflicts and Valuation*, Cheltenham: Edward Elgar.

Mason, E. S. (1939) "Price and Production Policies of Large-Scale Enterprise," *The American Economic Review Supplement*, 29: 61–74.

—— (1982) "The Harvard Department of Economics from the Beginning to World War II," *The Quarterly Journal of Economics*, 97: 383–433.

Mason, J. W. (1980) "Political Economy and the Response to Socialism in Britain, 1870–1914," *The Historical Journal*, 23(3): 565–87.

Mata, T. J. F. (2005) "Dissent in Economics: making radical political economics and Post Keynesian economics, 1960–80," D. Phil. dissertation, London School of Economics and Political Science.

—— (2006) "The Importance of Being Cambridge: old school, new school, and Cambridge Journal in the 1970s," unpublished.

—— (2007) "Migrations and Boundary Work: Harvard, radical economists, and the Committee on Political Discrimination," unpublished.

Mata, T. and Lee, F. S. (2007) "The Role of Oral History in the Historiography of Heterodox Economics," in E. R. Weintraub and E. L. Forget (eds.) *Economists' Lives: biography and autobiography in the history of economics*, 154–71, Durham: Duke University Press.

Mathews, M. E. (1973) "On the Hither Edge of Free Land: Lindley Miller Keasbey and the evolution of the frontier thesis," M.A. thesis, Southwest Texas State University.

Matthews, J. B. (1953) "Communism and the Colleges," *The American Mercury*, 76 (May): 111–44.

Matthaei, J. (1984) "Rethinking Scarcity: neoclassicism, neoMalthusianism, and neoMarxism," *Review of Radical Political Economics*, 16(2/3): 81–94.

—— (1996) "Why Feminist, Marxist, and Anti-Racist Economists Should be Feminist-Marxist-Anti-Racist Economists," *Feminist Economics*, 2(1): 22–42.

—— (2004) Personal communication, 21 September.

Mattick, P. (1969) "Some Comments on Mandel's Marxist Economic Theory," *Radical America*, 3(4): 12–19.

Mattson, K. (2003) "Between Despair and Hope: revisiting *Studies on the Left*," in J. McMillian and P. Buhle (eds.) *The New Left Revisited*, 28–47, Philadelphia: Temple University Press.

Mayhew, A. (1987) "The Beginnings of Institutionalism," *Journal of Economic Issues*, 21(3): 971–8.

—— (2002) Personal communication, 16 February.

McCaughey, R. A. (1976) "American University Teachers and Opposition to the Vietnam War: a reconsideration," *Minerva*, 14(1): 307–29.

McCormick, K. (2002) "Veblen and the New Growth Theory: community as the source of capital's productivity," *Review of Social Economy*, 60(2): 263–77.

McCumber, J. (2001) *Time in the Ditch: American philosophy and the McCarthy era*, Evanston: Northwestern University Press.

McCutchen, C. W. (1991) "Peer Review: treacherous servant, disastrous master", *Technology Review*, 94(7): 29–40.

McDowell, G. (2002) Personal communication, 12 February.

McGrath, E. J. (1954a). "Statement Regarding the Case of Dr. Horace B. Davis," University of Missouri-Kansas City Archives, Arts and Sciences Department of Economics, Horace Davis. KC: 3/11/4, Box 1.15.

—— (1954b) Letter to F. H. Horn, 8 March, University of Missouri-Kansas City Archives, Arts and Sciences Department of Economics, Horace Davis. KC: 3/11/4, Box 1.7.

McIlroy, J. (1990a) "The Demise of the National Council of Labour Colleges," in Simon (1990a), 173–207.

—— (1990b) "The Triumph of Technical Training?" in Simon (1990a), 208–43.

—— (1990c). "Trade Union Education for a Change," in Simon (1990a), 244–75.

—— (1996) "Independent Working Class Education and Trade Union Education and Training," in Fieldhouse and Associates (1996), 264–89.

McKelvey, D. (1969) "Too Academic," *URPE Newsletter*, 1(2): 5–6.

McLaine, W. (1923) *An Outline of Economics*. London: Plebs League.

McMahon, T. (1989) "My Story," in G. J. Clifford (ed.) *Lone Voyagers: academic women in coeducational universities, 1870–1937*, 238–80, New York: The Feminist Press.

McMillan, J. (2000) "Love Letters to the Future: REP, *Radical America*, and New Left history," *Radical History Review*, 77: 20–59.

McVey, F. L. and Hughes, R. M. (1952) *Problems of College and University Administration*, Ames: The Iowa State College Press.

Medio, A. (1972) "Profits and Surplus-Value: appearance and reality in capitalist production," in E. K. Hunt and J. G. Schwartz (eds.) *A Critique of Economic Theory*, 312–46, Harmondsworth: Penguin Books Ltd.

—— (1977) "Neoclassicals, Neo-Ricardians, and Marx," in J. Schwartz (ed.) *The Subtle Anatomy of Capitalism*, 381–411, Santa Monica, California: Goodyear Publishing Company, Inc.

Meek, R. L. (1950–51) "The Place of Keynes in the History of Economic Thought," *The Modern Quarterly*, 6(1): 34–51.

—— (1955) "Lecture Notes on Theories of Value, Distribution and Welfare," originals in the possession of Mrs. Meek, Leicester, United Kingdom.

—— (1959a) "Economics for the Age of Oligopoly: Mr Strachey's Economics," *The New Reasoner*, 8: 41–57.

—— (1959b) "Economics for the Age of Oligopoly – 2: Professor Blyumin's economics," *The New Reasoner*, 9: 50–67.

—— (1959c) "Economics for the Age of Oligopoly – 3: Karl Marx's economics," *The New Reasoner*, 10: 14–31.

—— (1961) "Piero Sraffa's Rehabilitation of Classical Economics," *Science and Society*, 25(2): 139–56.

—— (1977) "Maurice Herbert Dobb, 1900–1976," *The Proceedings of the British Academy*, 63: 333–44.

—— (1978) "Surplus, Price, and Profit: an introduction to the history of value and distribution theory," original in the possession of Mrs. Meek, Leicester, United Kingdom.

Melman, S. (1962) "Economics of Armament and Disarmament," *New University Thought*, 2(3): 79–91.

Menashe, L. and Radosh, R. (eds.) (1967) *Teach-ins: U.S.A., reports, opinions, documents*, New York: Frederick A. Praeger, Publishers.

Meranto, P. J., Meranto, O. J., and Lippman, M. R. (1985) *Guarding the Ivory Tower: repression and rebellion in higher education*, Denver: Lucha Publications.

Merrett, S. (1997) *Introduction to the Economics of Water Resources: an international perspective*, Lanham: Rowman and Littlefield.

Michaels, M. I. 1937–38. "Revolt in Economics," *The Highway*, 30: 115–16.

Michelson, S. (1969a) "Chicago, Chicago," *URPE Newsletter*, 1(1): 1, 5–6.

—— (1969b) "Report of URPE National Conference," *URPE Newsletter*, 1(3): 15–16.

Michl, T. 1982. "Review of *Capital Accumulation and Income Distribution* by D. Harris," *Review of Radical Political Economics*, 14(2): 106–7.

Middleton, R. (1998) *Charlatans or Saviours? Economists and the British economy from Marshall to Meade*, Cheltenham: Edward Elgar.

Miles, A. (1984) "Workers' Education: the Communist Party and the Plebs League in the 1920s," *History Workshop*, 18: 102–14.

Milgate, M. (1982) *Capital and Employment: a study of Keynes's economics*, London: Academic Press.

Millar, J. P. M. and Lowe, J. (1979) *The Labour College Movement*, London: N.C.L.C. Publishing Society Ltd.

Millmow, A. (2003) "Joan Robinson's Disillusion with Economics," *Review of Political Economy*, 15(4): 561–74.

Milton, N. (1973) *John Maclean*, London: Pluto Press.

Minkler, A. (2004) Personal communication, 21 September.

Minsky, H. (1974) Letter to Sidney Weintraub, 29 November, S. Weintraub Papers, Box 3, folder 3.

Mirowski, P. (2007) "The Mirage of an Economics of Knowledge," unpublished.

Mirowski, P. and Hands, W. D. (1998) "A Paradox of Budgets: the postwar stabilization of American neoclassical demand theory," in M. S. Morgan and M. Rutherford (eds.) *From Interwar Pluralism to Postwar Neoclassicism*, 260–92, Durham: Duke University Press.

Mitchell, W. F. (1996) "Post Keynesian Thought Archive," unpublished.

Mitgang, H. (1988) *Dangerous Dossiers*, New York: Donald I. Fine, Inc.

Modigliani, M. (2001) *Adventures of an Economist*, New York: Texere LLC.

Mohr, J. C. (1970) "Academic Turmoil and Public Opinion: the Ross case at Stanford," *Pacific Historical Review*, 39(1): 39–61.

Mohun, S. and Fine, B. (1975) "Discussion Document on the C.S.E," CSE Records.

Mongiovi, G. (1994) "Capital, Expectations, and Economic Equilibrium: some notes on Lachmann and the so-called Cambridge School," *Advances in Austrian Economics*, 1: 257–77.

—— (2001) "The Cambridge Tradition in Economics: an interview with G. C. Harcourt," *Review of Political Economy*, 13(4): 503–21.

Monhollon, R. L. (2002) *"This is America?" the sixties in Lawrence, Kansas*, New York: Palgrave.

Moore, B. (1984) "Unpacking the Post-Keynesian Black Box: wages, bank lending and the money supply," *Thames Papers in Political Economy*, (Spring).

Moore, H. L. (2002) "The Business of Funding: science, social science and wealth in the United Kingdom," *Anthropological Quarterly*, 75(3): 537–35.

Moore, W. J. (1972) "The Relative Quality of Economics Journals: a suggested rating system," *Western Economic Journal*, 10(2): 156–69.

—— (1973) "The Relative Quality of Graduate Programs in Economics, 1958–72: who published and who perished," *Western Economic Journal*, 11(1): 1–23.

Morgan, K. J. (2004) "The Research Assessment Exercise in English Universities, 2001," *Higher Education,* 48: 461–82.

Morgan, M. S. and Rutherford, M. (1998) "American Economics: the character of the transformation," in M. S. Morgan and M. Rutherford (eds.) *From Interwar Pluralism to Postwar Neoclassicism,* 1–26, Durham: Duke University Press.

Morris, D. J. (1968) "Caucus for a New Political Science," *Radicals in the Professions Newsletter,* 1(7): 13–14.

Moseley, F. (ed.) (1995) *Heterodox Economic Theories: true or false?* Aldershot: Edward Elgar.

—— (2006) Personal communication, 2 February.

Mouhammed, A. H. (2000) "Veblen's Economic Theory: a radical analysis," *Review of Radical Political Economics,* 32(2): 197–221.

Mount, E. (1936) "The Equilibrists and Mr. Keynes," *New Masses,* (September 1 and 8): 18–19, 17–18.

M.R. (1936–37) "An Adventure in Economics," *The Highway,* 29: 13–15.

Mumy, G. E. (1979) Review of *Marx After Sraffa* by I. Steedman, *Review of Radical Political Economics,* 11(3): 71–74.

Munk, M. (1992) "Reversing the Verdicts: the case of Reed College," *Monthly Review,* 43(10): 38–49.

Murphy, J. (2007) "Learning from the Past: a small quibble with Fred Lee's history of American radical economics," *Review of Radical Political Economics,* 39(1): 108–15.

Murray, R. K. (1955) *Red Scare: a study in national hysteria, 1919–1920,* Minneapolis: University of Minnesota Press.

Mutari, E. (2001) ""… As Broad as our Life Experience": visions of feminist political economy, 1972–91," *Review of Radical Political Economics,* 33(4): 379–99.

Myrdal, G. (1972) "Response to Introduction," *American Economic Review,* 62: 456–62.

Nader, L. (1997) "The Phantom Factor: impact of the Cold War on anthropology," in A. Schiffrin (ed.) *The Cold War and the University: toward an intellectual history of the postwar years,* 107–46, New York: The New Press.

Nash, D. (1992) *Secularism, Art and Freedom,* Leicester: Leicester University Press.

—— (1999) *Blasphemy in Modern Britain, 1789 to the Present,* Aldershot: Ashgate Publishing Limited.

Nearing, S. (2000) *The Making of a Radical: a political biography,* White River Junction: Chelsea Green Publishing Company.

Nell, E. J. (1967a) "Automation and the Abolition of the Market," *New Left Notes,* 2 (28): 3–6.

—— (1967b) "Theories of Growth and Theories of Value," *Economic Development and Cultural Change,* 16: 15–26.

—— (1972) "Property and the Means of Production: a primer on the Cambridge controversy," *The Review of Radical Political Economics,* 4(2): 1–27.

—— (ed.) (1980) *Growth, Profits and Property: essays in the revival of political economy,* Cambridge: Cambridge University Press.

Nelson, J. A. (1993) "Gender and Economic Ideologies," *Review of Social Economy,* 51(3): 287–301.

Newman, M. (2002) *Ralph Miliband and the Politics of the New Left,* London: The Merlin Press.

Nickerman, J. (1967) "Radical Scholars Group Proposed," *Radicals in the Profession Newsletter,* 1(1): 5–6.

Nicolaus, M. (1973) "The Professional Organization of Sociology: a view from below," in R. Blackburn (ed.) *Ideology in Social Science*, 45–60, New York City: Vintage Books.

Nielsen, P. (2002) "Reflections on Critical Realism in Political Economy," *Cambridge Journal of Economics*, 26(6): 727–38.

Niggle, C. J. (2003) "Globalization, Neoliberalism and the Attack on Social Security," *Review of Social Economy*, 61(1): 51–71.

Nilsson, E. (1995) "Heterodox Journal Information," Http://web.archive.org/web/19970617215216/http://csf.colorado.edu/pkt/het.html (accessed 1 July 2008).

—— (2006) Personal communication, 9 February.

Nisonoff, L. (2004) Personal communication, 20 September.

Nore, P. (1976) "Six Myths of British Oil Policies," *Thames Papers in Political Economy*, (Summer).

Novick, P. (1988) *That Noble Dream: the "objectivity question" and the American historical Profession*, Cambridge: Cambridge University Press.

Nuti, D. M. (1970a) "Comments on M.H. Dobb, "Some Reflections on the Sraffa System and the Critique of the so-called Neo-Classical Theory of Value and Distribution," 10 January, Maurice Dobb Papers, DD210.48–50.

—— (1970b) ""Vulgar Economy" in the Theory of Income Distribution," *De Economist* 118: 363–69.

O'Connor, J. (1960) "Concentration, Centralization, and Control," *Dissent*, 7(4): 355–61.

—— (1964a) "Towards a Theory of Community Unions," *Studies on the Left*, 4(2): 143–49.

—— (1964b) "Towards a Theory of Community Unions II," *Studies on the Left*, 4(3): 99–102.

O'Driscoll, G. P. and Rizzo, M. J. (1985) *The Economics of Time and Ignorance*, Oxford: Basil Blackwell.

Ogata, T. (1981) "The Movements of Post-Keynesian Economic Studies in USA" (in Japanese), *The Annual of the Institute of Economic Research, Chuo University*, 12: 227–52.

O'Hara, P. A. (1995) "The Association for Evolutionary Economics and the Union for Radical Political Economics: general issues of continuity and integration," *Journal of Economic Issues*, 29(1): 137–59.

—— (ed.) (1999a) *Encyclopedia of Political Economy*, London: Routledge.

—— (1999b) "Association for Evolutionary Economics and Association for Institutional Thought," in P. A. O'Hara (ed.) *Encyclopedia of Political Economy*, 20–23, London: Routledge.

—— (2000) *Marx, Veblen, and Contemporary Institutional Political Economy: principles and unstable dynamics of capitalism*, Cheltenham: Edward Elgar.

—— (2002a) "The Contemporary Relevance of Thorstein Veblen's Institutional-Evolutionary Political Economy," *History of Economics Review*, 35: 78–103.

—— (2002b) "The Role of Institutions and the Current Crises of Capitalism: a reply to Howard Sherman and John Henry," *Review of Social Economy*, 60(4): 609–18.

—— (2005) "Major Principles of Political and Social Economy for Unifying the Schools of Heterodoxy," unpublished.

—— (2007a) "Principles of Institutional-Evolutionary Political Economy – Converging Themes from the Schools of Heterodoxy," *Journal of Economic Issues*, 51(1): 1–42.

—— (2007b) "Heterodox Political Economy Specialization and Interconnection – Concepts of Contradiction, Heterogeneous Agents, and Uneven Development," *Intervention: Journal of Economics*, 4(1): 99–120.

Ohmann, R. (1997) "English and the Cold War," in A. Schiffrin (ed.) *The Cold War and the University: toward an intellectual history of the postwar years*, 73–105, New York: The New Press.

Olson, M. and Clague, C. K. (1971) "Dissent in Economics: the convergence of extremes," *Social Research*, 38: 751–76.

O'Neill, W. L. (2001) *The New Left: a history*, Wheeling: Harlan Davidson, Inc.

Oswald, A. J. (1995) "Understanding Economic Behaviour: a report for the ESRC," unpublished.

Owen, W. F. (1979) *Guide to Graduate Study in Economics, Agricultural Economics, and Related Fields*, 5th edn, Boulder: Economics Institute.

Owen, W. F. and Antoine, G. H. (1977) *Guide to Graduate Study in Economics and Agricultural Economics*, 4th edn, Boulder: Economics Institute.

Owen, W. F. and Cross, L. R. (1982) *Guide to Graduate Study in Economics and Agricultural Economics in the United States of America and Canada*, 6th edn, Boulder: Economics Institute.

Owen, W. F. and Glahe, F. R. (1974) *Guide to Graduate Study in Economics and Agricultural Economics*, 3rd edn, Boulder: Economics Institute.

Palacio-Vera, A. (2005) "The 'Modern' View of Macroeconomics: some critical reflections," *Cambridge Journal of Economics*, 29(5): 747–67.

Palermo, G. (2005) "Are We All Post-Keynesians?" *History of Economic Ideas*, 13(1): 145–62.

Panico, C. (1988) *Interest and Profit in the Theories of Value and Distribution*, London: Macmillan Press Ltd.

—— (1991) "Some Notes on Marshallian Supply Functions," *Economic Journal*, 101: 557–69.

Parenti, P. (1995) *Against Empire*, San Francisco: City Light Books.

Parker, C. S. (1919) *An American Idyll: the life of Carleton H. Parker*, Boston: The Atlantic Monthly Press.

Parker, R. (2005) *John Kenneth Galbraith: his life, his politics, his economics*, New York: Farrar, Straus and Giroux.

Parrish, J. B. (1967) "Rise of Economics as an Academic Discipline: the formative years to 1900," *The Southern Economic Journal*, 34(1): 1–16.

Parry, T. W., et al. (1986) "The First Half Century: reminiscences and reflections," *Science and Society*, 50(3): 321–41.

Pasour, E. C. (1988) "Financial Support and Freedom of Inquiry in Agricultural Economics," *Minerva*, 26(1): 31–52.

Pasinetti, L. L. (1974) *Growth and Income Distribution: essays in economic theory*, Cambridge: Cambridge University Press.

—— (1992) "At the Source of Alfred Eichner's Post-Keynesian Economics: a personal note," in W. Milberg (ed.) *The Megacorp and Macrodynamics: essays in memory of Alfred Eichner*, 307–13, Armonk, New York: M. E. Sharpe, Inc.

—— (1993) *Structural Economic Dynamics*, Cambridge: Cambridge University Press.

—— (2005) "The Cambridge School of Keynesian Economics," *Cambridge Journal of Economics*, 29(6): 837–48.

—— (2007) *Keynes and the Cambridge Keynesians: a "revolution in economics" to be accomplished*, Cambridge: University Press.

Peach, W. N. (1966) Interview, Oral History Collection, University of North Texas.

Pentland, H. C. (1977) *The University of Manitoba, Department of Economics: a brief history*, Manitoba: The University of Manitoba.

Peters, D. P. and Ceci, S. J. (1982) "Peer-Review Practices of Psychological Journals: the fate of published articles, submitted again," *The Behavioural and Brain Sciences*, 5 (2): 187–95.

Peterson, J. and Brown, D. (eds.) (1994) *The Economic Status of Women under Capitalism: Institutional economics and feminist theory*, Aldershot: Edward Elgar.

Peterson, J. and Lewis, M. (eds.) (1999) *The Elgar Companion to Feminist Economics*, Cheltenham: Edward Elgar.

Peterson, W. (1998) Personal communication, 15 February.

Petr, J. L. (1984) "An Assault on the Citadel: is a constructive synthesis feasible?" *Journal of Economic Issues,* 38(2): 589–98.

Petri, F. (2004) *General Equilibrium, Capital and Macroeconomics: a key to recent controversies in equilibrium theory*, Cheltenham: Edward Elgar.

Pheby, J. (ed.) (1989) *New Directions in Post-Keynesian Economics*, Aldershot: Edward Elgar.

—— (1999) Personal communication, 5 July.

Phelps, C. (1999) "Introduction: a socialist magazine in the American Century," *Monthly Review*, 51(1): 1–30.

Phelps Brown, E. H. (1972) "The Underdevelopment of Economics," *Economic Journal*, 82(1): 1–10.

Phillimore, A. J. (1989) "University Research Performance indicators in Practice: the University Grants Committee's evaluation of British universities, 1985–86," *Research Policy*, 18: 255–71.

Phillips, A. and Putnam, T. (1980) "Education and Emancipation: the movement for Independent Working Class Education 1908–28," *Capital and Class*, 10: 18–42.

Phillips, R. (1989) "Radical Institutionalism and the Texas School of Economics," in W. M. Dugger (ed.) *Radical Institutionalism: contemporary voices*, 21–37, New York City: Greenwood Press.

—— (1994) "Texas School of Institutional Economics," in G. M. Hodgson, W. J. Samuels, and M. R. Tool (eds.) *The Elgar Companion to Institutional and Evolutionary Economics*, 383–86, Aldershot: Edward Elgar.

—— (1995) *Economic Mavericks: the Texas Institutionalists*, Greenwich: JAI Press Inc.

Picciotto, S. (1986) "The Years of Capital and Class," *Capital and Class*, 30: 7–15.

Pickering, A. (1995) *The Mangle of Practice: time, agency, and science*, Chicago: The University of Chicago Press.

Pivetti, M. (1991) *An Essay on Money and Distribution*, London: Macmillan.

Plehn, C. C. (1924) "The Progress of Economics During the Last Thirty-Five Years," in *Faculty Research Lecture*, 253–76. Berkeley: University of California, Berkeley.

Plotnick, A. 1983–84. "Memorial Note: Arthur I. Grant," *Journal of Post Keynesian Economics*, 6: 324–25.

Podsakoff, P. M., Mackenzie, S. B., Bachrach, D. G., and Podsakoff, N. P. (2005) "The Influence of Management Journals in the 1980s and 1990s," *Strategic Management Journal*, 26: 473–88.

Poirot, C. (2002) Personal communication, 11 February.

Pollins, H. (1984) *The History of Ruskin College*, Oxford: Ruskin College.

Pollitt, B. H. (1988) "The Collaboration of Maurice Dobb in Sraffa's Edition of Ricardo," *Cambridge Journal of Economics*, 12(1): 55–66.

Postan, M. M. (1968) "A Plague of Economists? on some current myths, errors, and fallacies," *Encounter*, 30: 42–47.

Pressman, S. (1996) "Political Economy at Malvern," in S. Pressman (ed.) *Interactions in Political Economy: Malvern after ten years*, 1–9, London: Routledge.

Price, D. H. (2004) *Threatening Anthropology: McCarthyism and the FBI's surveillance of activist anthropologists*, Durham: Duke University Press.

—— (2004–5) "Theoretical Dangers: the FBI investigations of *Science and Society*," *Science and Society*, 68(4): 475–82.

Prychitko, D. L. (1993) "After Davidson, Who Needs the Austrians? reply to Davidson," *Critical Review*, 7(2–3): 371–80.

—— (1998) *Why Economists Disagree: an introduction to the alternative schools of Thought*, Albany: State University of New York Press.

—— (2002) *Markets, Planning and Democracy: essays after the collapse of communism*, Cheltenham: Edward Elgar.

—— (2006) Personal communication, 13 February.

Quick, P. (2002) Personal communication, 2 March.

Radice, H. (1969) "Economics or Political Economy?" H. Radice Personal Files.

—— (1970) Conference on "the Economic Role of the State in Modern Capitalism," CSE Records.

—— (1971a) "Conference of Socialist Economists," CSE Records.

—— (1971b) "Socialist Economists Group," February, H. Radice Personal Files.

—— (1972a) "Notes on the Seminar on Capital Theory and Marxist Political Economy," H. Radice Personal Files.

—— (1972b) "Report on the Year's Activities (Dec. 1971–Nov. 1972)," 8 December, H. Radice Personal Files.

—— (1973a) "Notes on the 1973 CSE Conference on Money and Inflation," H. Radice Personal Files.

—— (1973b) "CSE Conference on Money and Inflation," *Bulletin of the Conference of Socialist Economists*, 2(7): 35h.

—— (1973c) "The Conference of Socialist Economists (CSE)," *Working Papers on the Kapitalistate*, 2: 84–88.

—— (1980) "A Short History of the CSE," *Capital and Class*, 10: 43–9.

Radice, H. and Picciotto, S. (1971) "European integration: capital and the state," *Bulletin of the Conference of Socialist Economists*, 1: 32–54.

RAE. (2006) *RAE 2008: panel criteria and working methods*, http://www.rae.ac.uk/pubs/2006/01/ (accessed 1 July 2008).

Ramstad, Y. (1995) "John R. Commons's Puzzling Inconsequentiality as an Economic Theorist," *Journal of Economic Issues*, 29(4): 991–1012.

Reder, M. W. (1982) "Chicago Economics: permanence and change," *The Journal of Economic Literature*, 20(1): 1–38.

Reich, M. (1995) "Radical Economics: successes and failures," in F. Mosely (ed.) *Heterodox Economic Theories: true or false?*, 45–70, Aldershot: Edward Elgar.

Resnick, S. (2003) Personal communication, 21 June.

Reynolds, P. J. (1980) "Kalecki and the Post-Keynesians: a reinterpretation," North Staffordshire Polytechnic, Department of Economics, Discussion Paper Series, Working Paper 4, January.

—— (1987) *Political Economy: a synthesis of Kaleckian and Post Keynesian economics*, New York: St. Martin's Press.

Riach, P. (1995) "Additional Letter to the Editor," *PKSG Newsletter*, Issue 2: 4.

Richardson, D. B. 1982. "Marxism in U.S. Classrooms," *U.S. News and World Report*, 92(3): 42–45.

Rizvi, S. A. T. (1994) "Game Theory to the Rescue?" *Contributions to Political Economy*, 13 1–28.

Robinson, A. (1990) "Prologue: Cambridge economics in the post-Marshallian period," in R. Tullberg (ed.) *Alfred Marshall in Retrospect*, 1–7, Aldershot: Edward Elgar.

Robinson, J. (1942,1991) *An Essay on Marxian Economics*, 2nd edn, Philadelphia: Orion Editions.

—— (1956) *The Accumulation of Capital*, London: Macmillan.

—— (1965) "Piero Sraffa and the Rate of Exploitation," *New Left Review*, 31: 28–34.

—— (1969a) Letter to Paul Davidson, 22 September, Joan Robinson Papers, vii/114/72.

—— (1969b) Letter to Paul Davidson, 20 November, Joan Robinson Papers, vii/114/81.

—— (1972) "The Second Crisis of Economic Theory," *American Economic Review*, 62(2): 1–9.

—— (1974) "History versus Equilibrium," *Thames Papers in Political Economy*, (Autumn).

—— (1979) Letter to Paul Davidson, 27 April, Joan Robinson Papers, vii/114/8.

Robinson, J. and Eatwell, J. (1973) *An Introduction to Modern Economics*, London: McGraw-Hill Book Company Ltd.

Rock, C. (2002) Personal communication, 11 February.

Roets, P. J. (1991) "Bernard W. Dempsey, S.J," *Review of Social Economy*, 49: 546–58.

Roose, K. D. and Andersen, C. J. (1970) *A Rating of Graduate Programs*, Washington, D. C.: American Council on Education.

Roosevelt, F. (1975) "Cambridge Economics as Commodity Fetishism," *The Review of Radical Political Economics*, 7(4): 1–32.

Root, E. M. (1956) *Collectivism on the Campus: the battle for the mind in American colleges*, New York: The Devin-Adair Company.

Ropke, I. (2004) "The Early History of Modern Ecological Economics," *Ecological Economics*, 50: 293–314.

—— (2005) "Trends in the Development of Ecological Economics from the Late 1980s to the Early 2000s," *Ecological Economics*, 55: 262–90.

Rose, J. (2002) *The Intellectual Life of the British Working Classes*, New Haven: Yale University Press.

Rosenof, T. (1997) *Economics in the Long Run: New Deal theorists and their legacies, 1933–1993*, Chapel Hill: The University of North Carolina Press.

Ross, D. (1991) *The Origins of American Social Science*, Cambridge: Cambridge University Press.

Rosser, J. B. (2002) Personal communication, 11 February.

Rossinow, D. (1998) *The Politics of Authenticity: liberalism, christianity, and the New Left in America*. New York: Columbia University Press.

Rowthorn, B. (1967) "They"re Our Enemies, That's the Key Point," in D. Widgery (ed.) *The Left in Britain, 1956–1968*, 227–30, Harmondsworth: Penguin Books.

—— (1972) "Marxism and the Capital Theory Controversy," *Bulletin of the Conference of Socialist Economists*, 1 (Autumn): 22–35.

—— (1973) "Vulgar Economy (Part 2)," *Bulletin of the Conference of Socialist Economists*, 2 (Spring): 1–11.

—— (1974) "Neo-Classicism, Neo-Ricardianism and Marxism," *New Left Review*, 86: 63–87.

—— (1980) "Introduction," in B. Rowthorn *Capitalism, Conflict and Inflation: essays in political economy*, 7–13, London: Lawrence and Wishart.

Rowthorn, B., Radice, H., Aaronovitch, S., and Murray, R. (1969) General Letter, 26 August, CSE Records.

Roy, R. 1982. "Peer Review of Proposals—Rationale, Practice and Performance," *Bulletin of Science and Technology in Society, 2:* 505–22.

—— (1984) "Alternatives to Review by Peers: a contribution to the theory of scientific choice," *Minerva, 22:* 316–28.

Royal Economic Society. (n.d.) "Joint Funding Bodies" Review of Research Assessment: submission from the Royal Economic Society," http://www.ra-review.ac.uk/invite/responses/subj/101.pdf (accessed 1 July 2008).

Royle, E. (1980) *Radicals, Secularists and Republicans: popular freethought in Britain, 1866–1915*, Manchester: Manchester University Press.

Rozwadowski, F. (1988) "From Recitation Room to Research Seminar: political economy at Columbia University," in Barber (1988a), 169–202.

Rudy, W. (1996) *The Campus and a Nation in Crisis: from the American Revolution to Vietnam*, Madison: Fairleigh Dickinson University Press.

Ruggles, N. D. (ed.) (1970a) *Economics*, Englewood Cliffs: Prentice-Hall, Inc.

—— (1970b) "The Goals and Achievements of Economics," in N. Ruggles (ed.) *Economics*, 3–11, Englewood Cliffs: Prentice-Hall, Inc.

Runde, J. (1993) "Paul Davidson and the Austrians: reply to Davidson," *Critical Review*, 7(2–3): 381–97.

Rustin, M. (1980) "The New Left and the Present Crisis," *New Left Review*, 121: 63–89.

Rutherford, M. (1997) "American Institutionalism and the History of Economics," *Journal of the History of Economic Thought*, 19: 178–95.

—— (2000a) "Understanding Institutional Economics: 1918–29," *Journal of the History of Economic Thought*, 22: 277–308.

—— (2000b) "Institutionalism Between the Wars," *Journal of Economic Issues*, 34(2): 291–303.

—— (2001) "Institutional Economics: then and now," *Journal of Economic Perspectives*, 15(3): 173–94.

—— (2002) "Morris A. Copeland: a case study in the history of Institutional economics," *Journal of the History of Economic Thought*, 24(3): 261–90.

—— (2003a) "On the Economic Frontier: Walton Hamilton, Institutional economics and education," *History of Political Economy*, 35(4): 611–53.

—— (2003b) "Chicago Economics and Institutionalism," unpublished.

—— (2004) "Institutional Economics at Columbia University," *History of Political Economy*, 36(1): 31–78.

—— (2006) "Wisconsin Institutionalism: John R. Commons and his students," *Labor History*, 47(2): 161–88.

Rutherford, M. and C. T. DesRoches. (2008) "The Institutionalist Reaction to Keynesian Economics," *Journal of the History of Economic Thought* 30(1): 29–48.

Rutkoff, P. M. and Scott, W. B. (1986) *New School: a history of the New School for Social Research*. New York: The Free Press.

Sabine, G. H. and Wittke, C. (1929) "Academic Freedom at the University of Pittsburgh," *Bulletin of the American Association of University Professors*, 15(8): 578–91.

Sachs, K. (1967) "At the AAA Meeting," *Radicals in the Profession Newsletter*, 1(2): 12.

Sale, F. (1974) *SDS*, New York: Vintage Books.

Salmans S. (1970) "Boat Gets Rocked in Economics," *New York Times* (December 27, Section F): 2.

Saltmarsh, J. A. (1991) *Scott Nearing: the making of a homesteader*, White River Junction: Chelsea Green Publishing Company.

Samuel, R. (1960) ""Bastard" Capitalism," in E. P. Thompson et al. *Out of Apathy*, 19–55, London: Stevens and Sons.

Samuels, W. J. (1992) *Essays in the History of Heterodox Political Economy*, New York: New York University Press.

—— (2002) Personal communication, 14 February.

—— (2003) "The *Journal of Economic Issues* and the Present State of Heterodox Economics," in W. J. Samuels (ed.) *Research in the History of Economic Thought and Methodology*, vol. 21-C, *Documents on Modern History of Economic Thought*, 159–89, Amsterdam: Elsevier.

—— (2004) "Papers from a Conference on the History of Heterodox Economics in the 20th Century: introduction," in W. J. Samuels (ed.) *Research in the History of Economic Thought and Methodology*, vol. 22-C, *Wisconsin "Government and Business" and the History of Heterodox Economic Thought*, 161–66, Amsterdam: Elsevier.

Samuelson, P. A. (1998) "Requiem for the Classic Tarshis Textbook that First Brought Keynes to Introductory Economics," in O. F. Hamouda and B. B. Price (eds.) *Keynesianism and the Keynesian Revolution in America: a memorial volume in honour of Lorie Tarshis*, 53–58, Cheltenham: Edward Elgar.

Sandilands, R. (2001) "The New Deal and "Domesticated Keynesianism" in America," in M. Keaney (ed.) *Economist with a Public Purpose: essays in honour of John Kenneth Galbraith*, 219–46, London: Routledge.

Sass, S. A. (1982) *The Pragmatic Imagination: a history of the Wharton School, 1881–1981*, Philadelphia: University of Pennsylvania Press.

—— (1988) "An Uneasy Relationship: the business community and academic economists at the University of Pennsylvania," in Barber (1988a), 225–40.

Sawers, L. and Weaver, J. (1970) "Report on Washington URPE Conference," *URPE Newsletter*, 2(1): 12–16.

Sawyer, M. C. (1982) *Macroeconomics in Question*, Armonk: M. E. Sharpe, Inc.

—— (1985) *The Economics of Michal Kalecki*, London: Macmillan.

—— (1988) *Post-Keynesian Economics*, Aldershot: Edward Elgar.

—— (2007) Personal communication, 29 March.

Schaniel, W. C. (1992) Letter to Dean C. Warren Neel, 24 August, Paul Davidson Papers, Box 8, Folder: University of Tennessee.

Schiffrin, A. (1968) "The Student Movement in the 1950's: a reminiscence," *Radical America*, 2(3): 26–41.

Schlabach, T. F. (1963–64) "An Aristocrat on Trial: the case of Richard T. Ely," *Wisconsin Magazine of History*, 47: 146–59.

Schmid, A. A. (2004) "The Spartan School of Institutional Economics at Michigan State University," in W. J. Samuels (ed.) *Research in the History of Economic Thought and Methodology*, vol. 22-C, *Wisconsin "Government and Business" and the History of Heterodox Economic Thought*, 207–43, Amsterdam: Elsevier.

Schrecker, E. W. (1979) "The House Marxists," *The Nation*, 228(3): 81–84.

—— (1986) *No Ivory Tower: McCarthyism and the universities*, Oxford: Oxford University Press.

—— (1998) *Many are the Crimes: McCarthyism in America*, Princeton: Princeton University Press.

Schultze, C. L. (1971) "The Reviewers Reviewed," *American Economic Review*, 61(2): 45–52.

Schultz, B. and Schultz, R. (2001) *Price of Dissent*, Berkeley: University of California Press.

Schwartz, R. C. (1984) "The Rand School of Social Science, 1906–24: a study of worker education in the socialist era," Ph.D. dissertation, SUNY at Buffalo.

Schwarz, B. (1982) "'The People' in History: the Communist Party Historians" Group, 1946–56," in R. Johnson, G. McLennan, B. Schwarz, and D. Sutton (eds.) *Making Histories: studies in history-writing and politics*, 44–95, London: Hutchinson.

Schweitzer, A. (1969) "Goals in Social Economics," *Journal of Economic Issues*, 3(2): 147–65.

Sclar, E. (1969) "Advocacy Economics: how a radical economist can work with Liberals and still sleep at night," *URPE Newsletter*, 1(1): 8–10.

Seed, W. H. (1910) "The Case Against Ruskin College," *The Plebs Magazine*, 1(12): 271–72.

Selcraig, J. T. 1982. *The Red Scare in the Midwest, 1945–1955: a state and local study*, Ann Arbor: UMI Research Press.

Seligman, B. B. (1955) "Merger and Monopoly in the US," *Dissent*, 2: 144–51.

—— (1956) "Keynesian Economics," *Dissent*, 3: 51–67.

—— (1958) "Marxian Economics Revisited," *Dissent*, 5(4): 342–52.

—— (1959) "Socialism without Marx," *Dissent*, 6(3): 258–74.

—— (1964) "The American Corporation: ideology and reality," *Dissent*, 11(3): 316–27.

—— (1965) "Automation and the Unions," *Dissent*, 12(1): 33–53.

—— (1966) "On Theories of Automation," *Dissent*, 13(3): 243–64.

Seligman, E. R. A. (1909) *Principles of Economics*, 4th edn, New York: Longmans, Green, and Co.

Seminars on Marxism (1969–70). Maurice Dobb Papers, Lectures DD 220.

"Seminars on Capital Theory and Marxist Political Economy." (1972) H. Radice Personal Files.

Semmler, W. (1981) "Competition, Monopoly and Differentials of Profit Rates: theoretical considerations and empirical evidence," *Review of Radical Political Economics*, 13(4): 39–52.

Seretan, L. G. (1979) *Daniel De Leon: the odyssey of an American Marxist*, Cambridge: Cambridge University Press.

Shackelford, J. (2002) "A Short History of IAFFE and *Feminist Economics*," unpublished.

Shaffer, E. H. (1998a) Letter to Martin Gold, 6 May.

—— (1998b) Letter to Martin Gold, 12 May.

—— (2002) Personal communication, 10 May.

—— (2004) "Repression at the University of Michigan," in W. J. Samuels (ed.) *Research in the History of Economic Thought and Methodology*, vol. 22-C, *Wisconsin "Government and Business" and the History of Heterodox Economic Thought*, 195–205, Amsterdam: Elsevier.

Shaikh, A. (1973) Letter to Joan Robinson, 6 August, Joan Robinson Papers, vii/409/3–7.

—— (1974) "Laws of Production and Laws of Algebra: the humbug production function," *The Review of Economics and Statistics*, 56: 115–20.

Shannon, D. A. (1959) *The Decline of American Communism: a history of the Communist Party of the United States since 1945*, Chatham: The Chatham Bookseller.

Shapin, S. and Barnes, B. (1977) "Science, Nature and Control: interpreting Mechanics' Institutes," *Social Studies of Science*, 7(1): 31–74.

Shapiro, J. (2005) Personal communication, 2 June.

Shapiro, N. (1976) "The Neoclassical Theory of the Firm," *Review of Radical Political Economics*, 8(4): 17–29.

—— (1977) "The Revolutionary Character of Post-Keynesian Economics," *Journal of Economic Issues*, 11(3): 541–60.

Sharpe, M. E. (2002) Interview with Frederic Lee, 21 April.

Sharpe, M. E. et al. (1966) "Marxism and Monopoly Capital: a symposium," *Science and Society*, 30(4): 461–96.

Shepherd, G. B. (ed.) (1995) *Rejected: leading economists ponder the publication process*, Sun Lakes, Arizona: Thomas Horton and Daughters.

Sherman, H. J. (1970) "The Marxist Theory of Value Revisited," *Science and Society*, 34(3): 257–92.

—— (1975) "The Sad State of Orthodox Economics," *Journal of Economic Issues*, 9(2): 243–50.

—— (1976) *Stagflation: a radical theory of unemployment and inflation*, New York: Harper and Row, Publishers.

—— (1994) Personal communication, 11 March.

—— (2006) "The Making of Radical Economists," *Review of Radical Political Economics*, 38(4): 519–38.

Shute, L. (2002) Personal communication, 28 March.

Siegfried, J. J. et al. (1991) "The Status and Prospects of the Economics Major," *Journal of Economic Education*, 22: 197–224.

Signorino, R. (2005) "Piero Sraffa's Lectures on the Advanced Theory of Value 1928–31 and the Rediscovery of the Classical Approach," *Review of Political Economy*, 17(3): 359–80.

Simon, B. (1965) *Education and the Labour Movement, 1870–1920*, London: Lawrence and Wishart.

—— (ed.) (1990a) *The Search for Enlightenment*, London: Lawrence and Wishart.

—— (1990b) "The Struggle for Hegemony, 1920–26," in Simon (1990a), 15–70.

Simonetti, R. (2007) "The Impact of the Economics Benchmarking Statement on Pluralism in Economics Teaching in the UK," in J. Groenewegen (ed.) *Teaching Pluralism in Economics*, 104–22, Cheltenham: Edward Elgar.

Sinclair, U. (1923) *The Goose-step: a study of American education*, Pasadena, California.

Singh, A. (1995) "Competitive Markets and Economic Development: a commentary on World Bank analysis," *International Papers in Political Economy*, 2(1): 1–40.

Singh, V. B. (ed.) (1956) *Keynesian Economics: a symposium*, Delhi: People's Publishing House Ltd.

Skotnes, A. (ed.) (2001) "A Conversation about the *Radical History Review*: former and current collective members reminisce," *Radical History Review*, 79: 15–47.

Skouras, T. (1999) Personal communication, 2 September.

Smelser, N. J. and Swedberg, R. (eds.) (2005) *The Handbook of Economic Sociology*, 2nd edn,. Princeton: Princeton University Press.

Smith, H. (1937) "Marx and the Trade Cycle," *The Review of Economic Studies*, 4(3): 192–204.

—— (1939) "Marx as a Pure Economist," *Economic History*, 3(14): 245–58.

—— (1993) *The Impersonal Autobiography of an Economist*, Stroud: Alan Sutton Publishing Ltd.

Smith, R. (1988a) "Peering into the Bowels of the MRC—II: review systems," *British Medical Journal*, 296: 556–60.

—— (1988b) "Problems with Peer Review and Alternatives," *British Medical Journal*, 296: 774–77.

Smithin, J. (1996) "The Crisis in Academic Economics," *PKSG Newsletter*, Issue 4: 2–4.

Snavely, T. R. (1967) *The Department of Economics at the University of Virginia, 1825–1956*, Charlottesville: The University Press of Virginia.

Soderbaum, P. (2000) *Ecological Economics*, London: Earthscan Publications Ltd.

Solberg, W. U. and Tomilson, R. W. (1997) "Academic McCarthyism and Keynesian Economics: the Bowen controversy at the University of Illinois," *History of Political Economy*, 29(1): 55–81.

Solomon, B. M. (1980) "Balch, Emily Greene," in B. Sicherman et al. (eds.) *Notable American Women: the modern period, a biographical dictionary*, 41–45, Cambridge: Harvard University Press.

Solow, R. M. (1970a) "Microeconomic Theory," in N. Ruggles (ed.) *Economics*, 31–43, Englewood Cliffs: Prentice-Hall, inc.

—— (1970b) "Science and Ideology in Economics," *The Public Interest*, 21: 94–107.

—— (1971) "Discussion," *American Economic Review*, 61(2): 63–65.

Solterer, J. (1991) "The Economics of Justice," *Review of Social Economy*, 49: 559–65.

Sorenson, D. R. (1980) "The Anticommunist Consensus in Indiana, 1945–58," Ph.D. dissertation, Indiana University.

Sowell, T. (1993) "A Student's Eye View of George Stigler," *Journal of Political Economy*, 101(5): 784–92.

Sraffa, P. (1925) "Sulla Relazioni tra costo e quantita prodotta," *Annali of Economia*, 2: 277–328; trans. J. Eatwell and A. Roncaglia, "On the Relation Between Cost and Quantity Produced," in L. L. Pasinetti (ed.) (1998) *Italian Economic Papers*, vol. 3, 323–63, Oxford: Oxford University Press.

—— (1926) "The Laws of Returns Under Competitive Conditions," *Economic Journal*, 36(4): 535–50.

—— (1960) *Production of Commodities by Means of Commodities*, Cambridge: Cambridge University Press.

Standing Committee. (1988–94) Conference of Heads of University Departments of Economics, Minutes, Royal Economic Society.

Stanfield, J. R. (1978) "On Social Economics," *Review of Social Economy*, 35: 349–61.

—— (1979) "Marx's Social Economics: the theory of alienation," *Review of Social Economy*, 36: 295–312.

—— (1994) "Learning From Japan About the Nurturance Gap in America," *Review of Social Economy*, 52(1): 2–19.

—— (1995) *Economics, Power and Culture*, London: Macmillan Press, Ltd.

—— (1998) Personal communication, 7 May.

—— (2002) Personal communication, 11 February.

Steedman, I. (1971) "Marx on the Falling Rate of Profit," *Australian Economic Papers*, 10(16): 61–66.

—— (1972a) "An Expository Note on the Switching of Techniques," *Bulletin of the Conference of Socialist Economists*, 1 (Autumn): 5–21.

—— (1972b) "Marx on the Rate of Profit," *Bulletin of the Conference of Socialist Economists*, 1 (Winter): 104–9.

—— (1973) "The Transformation Problem Again," *Bulletin of the Conference of Socialist Economists*, 2 (Autumn): 37–41.

—— (1975) "Value, Price and Profit," *New Left Review*, 90: 71–80.

—— (1976) Letter to Mrs. Dobb, 20 August. Maurice Dobb Papers, AG35.

—— (1977) *Marx after Sraffa*, London: NLB.

—— (1979) "Thinking Again About Profits," *New Statesman* (January 5): 10–12.

—— (1989a) *From Exploitation to Altruism*, Boulder: Westview Press.

—— (1989b) "P.H. Wicksteed's Jevonian Critique of Marx," in I. Steedman *From Exploitation to Altruism*, 117–44, Boulder: Westview Press.

—— (ed.) (1995) *Socialism and Marginalism in Economics, 1870–1930*, London: Routledge.

—— (2004) "British Economists and Philosophers on Marx's Value Theory, 1920–25," *Journal of the History of Economic Thought*, 26(1): 45–68.

Steedman, I. and Metcalfe, J. S. (1973) "The Non-Substitution Theorem and International Trade Theory," *Australian Economic Papers*, 12(21): 267–69.

Steedman, I. et al. (1981) *The Value Controversy*, London: New Left Books-Verso.

Steele, T. and Taylor, R. (2004) "Marxism and Adult Education in Britain," *Policy Futures in Education*, 2(3–4): 578–92.

Stein, P. (1973) "Institutional Repression in Higher Education," *The Insurgent Sociologist* 3(4): 75–81.

Steinberg, B. (1981) "Review of *Sraffa and the Theory of Prices* by A. Roncaglia," *Review of Radical Political Economics*, 13(2): 48–51.

Stern, R. (1963) Letter to Edward H. Shaffer, 27 May.

Stewart, W. A. C. (1989) *Higher Education in Postwar Britain*, London: Macmillan.

Stigler, G. J. (1959) "The Politics of Political Economists," *The Quarterly Journal of Economics*, 73: 522–32.

—— (1969) "Alfred Marshall's Lectures on Progress and Poverty," *The Journal of Law and Economics*, 12(1): 181–226.

Stigler, G. J. and Kindahl, J. (1973) "Industrial Prices, as Administered by Dr. Means," *American Economic Review*, 63: 717–21.

Stigler, G. J., Stigler, S. M., and Friedland, C. (1995) "The Journals of Economics," *Journal of Political Economy*, 103(2): 331–59.

Stigler, S. M. (1994) "Citation Patterns in the Journals of Statistics and Probability," *Statistical Science*, 9(1): 94–108.

Stimpson, C. R. (2000) "Dirty Minds, Dirty Bodies, Clean Speech," in P. J. Hollingsworth (ed.) *Unfettered Expression: freedom in American intellectual life*, 51–71, Ann Arbor: The University of Michigan Press.

Storrs, L. (2003) "Red Scare Politics and the Suppression of Popular Front Feminism: the loyalty investigation of Mary Dublin Keyserling," *Journal of American History*, 90(2): 491–524.

—— (2006) "Left-Feminism, the Consumer Movement, and Red Scare Politics in the United States, 1935–60," *Journal of Women's History*, 18(3): 40–67.

Street, J. H. (1983) "The Reality of Power and the Poverty of Economic Doctrine," *Journal of Economic Issues*, 17(2): 295–313.

Street, J. H., Arestis, P., and Tool, M. R. (1988) "In Memoriam: Alfred S. Eichner, 1937–88," *Journal of Economic Issues*, 22(4): 1239–42.

Struik, D. (1993) "The Struik Case of 1951," *Monthly Review*, 44(8): 31–47.

Sturgeon, J. I. (1981) "The History of the Association for Institutional Thought," *The Review of Institutional Thought*, 1: 40–53.

—— (1986) "In Memoriam: W. Nelson Peach," *Review of Institutional Thought*, 3: 9–12.

—— (2002) Personal communication, 12 February.

Sutter, M. and Kocher, M. G. (2001) "Tools for Evaluating Research Output: are citation-based rankings of economics journals stable?," *Evaluation Review*, 25(5): 555–66.

Swaney, J. (2002) Personal communication, 11 February.

Sweezy, P. M. (1958) "Veblen's Critique of the American Economy," *American Economic Review*, 48(2): 21–29.

—— (1965) "Paul Alexander Baran: a personal memoir," *Monthly Review*, 16(11): 28–62.

Tabb, W. (2004) Personal communication, 22–23 September.

Tap, B. (1992) "Suppression of Dissent: academic freedom at the University of Illinois during the World War I era," *Illinois Historical Journal*, 85(1): 2–22.

Tarascio, V. J. (1999) "An Intellectual Autobiography," *Journal of the History of Economic Thought*, 21(1): 53–63.

Teitelbaum, K. (1993) *Schooling for 'Good Rebels': socialist education for children in the United States, 1900–1920*, Philadelphia: Temple University Press.

Terzi, A. (1986) "Finance, Investment, and Saving: a comment on Asimakopulos," *Cambridge Journal of Economics*, 10(1): 77–80.

—— (1998) Personal communication, 1 November.

Thanawala, K. (1996) "Solidarity and Community in the World Economy," in E. J. O'Boyle (ed.) *Social Economics: premises, findings and policies*, 75–89, London: Routledge.

Tharp, L. (1970) "Columbia Radicals Fight for their Academic Freedom," *URPE Newsletter*, 2(4): 1–3.

Thirlwall, A. P. (ed.) 1982. *Keynes as a Policy Advisor*, London: Macmillan.

—— (ed.) (1987) *Keynes and Economic Development*, Basingstoke: Macmillan.

Thomas, J. (1922) "The Economic Doctrines of Karl Marx and their Influence on the Industrial Areas of South Wales Particularly Among Miners," Essay submitted to the 1922 National Eisteddfod at Ammanford, South Wales Miners" Library, University of Wales Swansea.

Thompson, E. P. (1980) *Writing by Candlelight*, London: Merlin.

Tobin, J. (1973) "Cambridge (U.K.) vs. Cambridge (Mass.)," *The Public Interest*, 31: 102–09.

Tomasson, G. (2001) Personal communication, 4 April.

Tonak, E. A. and Savran, S. (1987) "Interview with Paul M. Sweezy," *Monthly Review*, 38(11): 1–28.

Tool, M. R. (1989) "An Institutionalist Legacy," *Journal of Economic Issues* 23(2): 327–36.

Tool, M. R. (1998) Personal communication, 28 August.

Toporowski, J. (1996) "Making Post Keynesianism Safe for its Fellow-Travellers," *PKSG Newsletter*, Issue 5: 3–4.

—— (2007) Personal communication, 24 November.

Torr, C. (1988) *Equilibrium, Expectations and Information*, Boulder: Westview Press.

Toruno, M. (2006) Personal communication, 6 February.

Tower, E. (1995) *Microeconomics Reading Lists*, Chapel Hill: Eno River Press.

Trachtenberg, A. (ed.) (1920) *The American Labor Year Book, 1919–1920*, New York: The Rand School of Social Science.

Tribe, K. (1990) "Political Economy to Economics via Commerce: the evolution of British academic economics, 1860–1920," in P. Wagner, B. Wittrock, and R. Whitley (eds.) *Discourses on Society: the shaping of the social science disciplines*, 273–302, Dordrecht: Kluwer Academic Publishers.

—— (2000) "The Cambridge Economics Tripos 1903–55 and the Training of Economists," *The Manchester School*, 68(2): 222–48.

Trigg, A. (2001) "Report: Association for Heterodox Economics 3rd Annual Conference," July 27.

Tsuzuki, C. (1983) "Anglo-Marxism and Working-Class Education," in J. Winter (ed.) *The Working Class in Modern British History*, 187–99, Cambridge: Cambridge University Press.

Turner, M. S. (1989) *Joan Robinson and the Americans*, Armonk: M. E. Sharpe, Inc.

Tymoigne, E. and Lee, F. S. (2003–4) "Post Keynesian Economics Since 1936: a history of a promise that bounced?" *Journal of Post Keynesian Economics*, 26(2): 273–87.

Tyrrell, A. (1969) "Political Economy, Whiggism and the Education of Working-Class Adults in Scotland, 1817–40," *Scottish Historical Review*, 48(2): 151–65.

Ulmer, M. J. (1970) "More than Marxist," *The New Republic*, 163 (December 26): 13–14.

Unger, I. (1974) *The Movement: a history of the American New Left, 1959–1972*, New York: Dodd, Mead and Company.

URPE. (1969) "Report on URPE," *Something Else!*, 2(1): 12.

—— (1970) "Political Economy for the University of Michigan," *Newsletter of the Union for Radical Political Economics*, 2(4): 12–16.

—— (1971) "Political Economy at the New School," *Newsletter of the Union for Radical Political Economics*, 3(2): 14–16.

—— (1972) "Way Out West," *Newsletter of the Union for Radical Political Economics*, 4(1): 4–7.

—— (1973a) "URPER Jailed," *Newsletter of the Union for Radical Political Economics*, 5(2): 1, 20–23.

—— (1973b) "Repression: we win one," *Newsletter of the Union for Radical Political Economics*, 5(3): 17.

—— (1973c) "Successful Struggle at Michigan," *Newsletter of the Union for Radical Political Economics*, 5(4): 11.

—— (1973d) "UCR: a small victory," *Newsletter of the Union for Radical Political Economics*, 5(6): 24.

—— (1974a) "Could Karl Marx Teach Economics in America?" *Newsletter of the Union for Radical Political Economics*, 6(3): 32–33.

—— (1974b) "Political Firings!," *Newsletter of the Union for Radical Political Economics*, 6(6): 5–8.

—— (1974c) "URPE Program for the ASSA Meetings," *Newsletter of the Union for Radical Political Economics*, 6(6): 20–23.

—— (1975a) "Economics at Stanford," *Newsletter of the Union for Radical Political Economics*, 7(6): 34.

—— (1975b) "URPE at Dallas," *Newsletter of the Union for Radical Political Economics*, 7(6): 4–7.

—— (1976) "Political Economy at UNH," *Newsletter of the Union for Radical Economics*, 8(1): 21–22.

—— (1977a). "1976 URPE Program at the ASSA," *Newsletter of the Union for Radical Economics*, 9(1): 9–10.

—— (1977b) "URPE at ASSA," *Newsletter of the Union for Radical Economics*, 9(6): 3–8.

—— (1978a) "New Ph.D. Field in Political Economy at Berkeley," *Newsletter of the Union for Radical Political Economics*, 10(2): 14.

—— (1978b) "Political Economy Programs," *Newsletter of the Union for Radical Economics*, 10(3-4): 27-33.

—— (1979) "URPE ASSA Program: the political economy of gender and race," *Newsletter of the Union for Radical Economics*, 11(6): 16-20.

—— (1980a) "Update on Pol Econ Programs," *Newsletter of the Union for Radical Economics*, 12(1): 23.

—— (1980b) "Program," *Newsletter of the Union for Radical Economics*, 12(4): 2-5.

—— (1981) "Program Schedule URPE Meetings at the Allied Social Sciences Associations," *Newsletter of the Union for Radical Economics*, 13(5): 1-3.

Universities Funding Council. (1989) *Report on the 1989 Research Assessment Exercise,* December.

—— (1992) *Research Assessment Exercise 1992 Membership of Assessment Panels,* 24/92.

Van Horn, R. and Mirowski, P. (2005) "The Road to a World Made Safe for Corporations: the rise of the Chicago School of Economics," unpublished.

Van Staveren, I. (2006) "Post Keynesianism Meets Feminism," unpublished.

Vatn, A. (2005) *Institutions and the Environment*, Cheltenham: Edward Elgar

Vatter, H. G. (1999) Interview, Sound Recording Collection, Oregon Historical Society.

Veblen, T. (1919) *The Place of Science in Modern Civilization*, New York: B. W. Huebsch.

Villarejo, D. (1961) "Stock Ownership and the Control of Corporations," *New University Thought* 2(1): 33-77.

—— (1962) "Stock Ownership and the Control of Corporations, Part III," *New University Thought,* 2(2): 47-65.

Wachtel, H. (1968) "The Union for Radical Political Economics: a prospectus," *Radicals in the Professions Newsletter,* 1(10): 17-19.

—— (1973) Letter to Al Eichner, 20 November, Joan Robinson Papers, vii/130/6.

—— (2004) Personal communication, 23 September.

Wachtel, H. and Bluestone, B. (eds.) (1969) *The Conference Papers of the Union for Radical Political Economics: Philadelphia, December 1968*, Ann Arbor: The Union for Radical Political Economics.

Wachtel, H. and Vanderslice, L. (1973) "Notes on URPE History," *Newsletter of the Union for Radical Political Economics*m, 5(3): 14-16.

Waller, W. (2005) "Accidental Veblenian, Intentional Institutionalist, and Inevitable Feminist," *Journal of Economic Issues,* 39(2): 327-34.

Walsh, J. (1978) "Radicals and the Universities: "Critical Mass" at U. Mass," *Science,* 199 (January 6): 34-38.

Ward, D. (1977) *Toward a Critical Political Economics: a critique of liberal and radical economic thought*. Santa Monica: Goodyear Publishing Company, Inc.

Warne, C. E. (1993) *The Consumer Movement*, Manhattan: Family Economics Trust Press.

Waters, W. R. (1988) "Social Economics: a solidarist," *Review of Social Economy*, 46: 113-43.

—— (1993) "A Review of the Troops: social economics in the twentieth century," *Review of Social Economy*, 51: 262-86.

Weaver, J. H. (1969) "Middle Atlantic Conference," *Newsletter of the Union for Radical Economics*, 1(1): 1, 3-4.

—— (1970) "Toward a Radical Political Economics," *The American Economist*, 14: 57-61.

—— (2004) Personal communication, 23 September.

Weeks, J. (1969) "Political Economy and the Politics of Economists," *Review of Radical Political Economics*, 1(1): 1–10.

Weintraub, E. R. (2002) *How Economics Became a Mathematical Science,* Durham: Duke University Press.

Weintraub, S. (1974) Letter to Hyman Minsky, 19 November, S. Weintraub Papers, Box 3, folder 3.

—— (1977a) Letter to Alfred Eichner, 23 January, S. Weintraub Papers, Box 4, folder 1.

—— (1977b) Letter to J. K. Galbraith, 4 May, S. Weintraub Papers, Box 9, folder 1.

—— (1977c) Letter to J. K. Galbraith, 27 May, S. Weintraub Papers, Box 9, folder 1.

—— (1977d) Letter to J. K. Galbraith, 25 August, S. Weintraub Papers, Box 9, folder 2.

Weisbrot, M. (2004) Personal communication, 21 September.

Weisskopf, T. (2002) Personal communication, 11 February.

Welch, E. (1973) *The Peripatetic University: Cambridge local lectures, 1873–1973*, Cambridge: Cambridge University Press.

Wellman, B. and Berkowitz, S. D. (eds.) (1997) *Social Structures: a network approach*, Greenwich: JAI Press.

Whalen, C. J. (1996) "Beyond Neoclassical Thought: political economy for the twenty-first century," in C. J. Whalen (ed.) *Political Economy for the 21st Century*, 3–28, Armonk: M. E. Sharpe.

Whitaker, J. K. (ed.) (1975) *The Early Economic Writings of Alfred Marshall, 1867–1890*, vol. I, London: The Macmillan Press Ltd.

White, G. (2004) "Capital, Distribution and Macroeconomics: 'core' beliefs and theoretical foundations," *Cambridge Journal of Economics*, 28(4): 527–47.

Whitley, R. (1986) "The Structure and Context of Economics as a Scientific Field," *Research in the History of Economic Thought and Methodology*, 4: 179–209.

—— (1991) "The Organization and Role of Journals in Economics and Other Scientific Fields," *Economic Notes*, 20(1) 6–32.

—— (2000) *The Intellectual and Social Organization of the Sciences*, 2nd edn, Oxford: Clarendon Press.

Widgery, D. (1976) *The Left in Britain, 1956–1968*, Harmondsworth: Penguin Books.

Wiegand, S. A. and Wiegand, W. A. (2007) *Books on Trial: red scare in the heartland*, Norman: University of Oklahoma Press.

Wiener, J. M. (1989) "Radical Historians and the Crisis in American History, 1959–80," *The Journal of American History*, 76(2): 399–434.

Wilber, C. (2004) Personal communication, 23 September.

Wilber, C. K. and Jameson, K. P. (1983) *An Inquiry into the Poverty of Economics*, Notre Dame: University of Notre Dame Press.

Will, T. E. 1901. "A Menace to Freedom: the College Trust," *Arena*, 26: 244–57.

Williams, R. (ed.) (1968) *May Day Manifesto 1968*, Harmondsworth: Penguin Books Ltd.

—— (1970) "An Experimental Tendency," *The Listener*, 84: 785–86.

—— 1976–77. "Notes on Marxism in Britain Since 1945," *New Left Review*, 100: 233–51.

—— (1979) *Politics and Letters: interviews with New Left Review*, London: Verso.

Williamson, H. F. (ed.) (1970) "1969 Handbook of the American Economic Association," *American Economic Review*, 59(6): 213.

Willis, K. (1977) "The Introduction and Critical Reception of Marxist Thought in Britain, 1850–1900," *The Historical Journal*, 20(2): 417–59.

Winnett, A. (1973) Letter to Hugo Radice, 2 October, H. Radice Personal Files.

Woirol, G. R. (1999) "The Contributions of Frederick C. Mills," *Journal of the History of Economic Thought*, 21: 163–85.

Wolfe, A. (1971) "Unthinking about the Thinkable: reflections on the failure of the Caucus for a New Political Science," *Politics and Society*, 1: 393–406.

Wolff, R. (2002) Personal communication, 19 February.

Wolfram, B. (1976) *Political Economy: Marxist study courses*, Chicago: Banner Press.

Wood, A. (1968) "The Distribution of Income in the United Kingdom 1870–1965: a study in the application of Post-Keynesian theory," Fellowship Dissertation, King's College, Cambridge.

Wood, N. (1959) *Communism and British Intellectuals*, New York: Columbia University Press.

Worland, S. T. (1972) "Radical Political Economy as a 'Scientific Revolution,'" *Southern Economic Journal*, 39: 274–84.

—— (1998) Personal communication, 30 January.

Worswick, G. D. N. (1972) "Is Progress in Economic Science Possible?" *Economic Journal*, 82(1): 73–86.

Wrenn, M. V. (2004) "What is Heterodox Economics?" Ph.D. dissertation, Colorado State University.

Wright, D. (1948) Review of *The Keynesian Revolution* by Lawrence R. Klein. *American Economic Review*, 38(1): 145–52.

Wynkoop, M. A. (2002) *Dissent in the Heartland: the sixties at Indiana University*, Bloomington: Indiana University Press.

Yaffe, D. (1994) "Value, Price and the Neo-Ricardians: an introductory note," in S. Mohun (ed.) *Debate in Value Theory*, 82–88, London: The Macmillan Press Ltd.

Yonay, Y. P. (1998) *The Struggle over the Soul of Economics: Institutionalist and neoclassical economists in America between the wars*, Princeton: Princeton University Press.

Yorke, P. (1977) *Ruskin College, 1899–1909*, Oxford: Ruskin College.

Young, A. A. (1925) "The Trend of Economics, as seen by Some American Economists," *Quarterly Journal of Economics*, 39: 155–83.

Young, J. D. (1992) *John Maclean: Clydside socialist*, Glasgow: Clydeside Press.

Young, W. and Lee, F. S. (1993) *Oxford Economics and Oxford Economists*, London: The Macmillan Press Ltd.

Zinn, H. (1969) "Marxism and the New Left," in P. Land (ed.) *The New Left: a collection of eassys*, 56–71, Boston: Extending Horizons Books.

—— (1997) "The Politics of History in the Era of the Cold War: repression and resistance," in A. Schiffrin (ed.) *The Cold War and the University: toward an intellectual history of the postwar years*, 35–72, New York: The New Press.

Zis, G. (1973) "Inflation as an International Phenomenon," CSE Records.

Zweig, M. (1968) "Teaching at a Newly Established Public University," *Radicals in the Profession Newsletter*, 1(4): 16–17.

—— (1969) "New Left Critique of Economics," in H. Watchel and B. Bluestone (eds.) *The Conference Papers of the Union for Radical Political Economics*, 46–52, Ann Arbor: The Union for Radical Political Economics.

—— (1971) "On Economics and the Politics of Economists (a response to John Weeks)," *Review of Radical Political Economics*, 3(2): 84–88.

Zwerdling, D. (1978) *Workplace Democracy: a guide to workplace ownership, participation, and self-management experiments in the United States and Europe*, New York: Harper and Row, Publishers.

Archives

CSE Records, Conference of Socialist Economists, London, United Kingdom

Paul Davidson Papers, Special Collections Library, Duke University, Durham, North Carolina, United States

Maurice Dobb Papers, Trinity College, Cambridge, United Kingdom

Hugh Radice Personal Files, University of Leeds, Leeds, United Kingdom

Joan V. Robinson Papers, Modern Archives, King's College, Cambridge, United Kingdom

Oxford University Archives, Bodlian Library, University of Oxford, Oxford, United Kingdom

Royal Economic Society, United Kingdom

University of Missouri-Kansas City Archives, Kansas City, Missouri, United States

Sidney Weintraub Papers, Special Collections Library, Duke University, Durham, North Carolina, United States

Index

80025 75540

Printed in the USA/Agawam, MA
December 8, 2011

562817.006